Volume Six
by Choi Kyung-ah

English Adaptation
by Sarah Dyer

HAMBURG // LONDON // LOS ANGELES // TOKYO

Snow Drop Vol. 6

created by Choi Kyung-ah

Translation - Jennifer Hahm
English Adaptation - Sarah Dyer
Associate Editor - Suzanne Waldman
Retouch and Lettering - Riho Sakai
Production Artist - Vicente Rivera, Jr.
Cover Artist - Anna Kernbaum

Editor - Julie Taylor
Digital Imaging Manager - Chris Buford
Pre-Press Manager - Antonio DePietro
Production Managers - Jennifer Miller and Mutsumi Miyazaki
Art Director - Matt Alford
Managing Editor - Jill Freshney
VP of Production - Ron Klamert
President and C.O.O. - John Parker
Publisher and C.E.O. - Stuart Levy

A  Manga

TOKYOPOP Inc.
5900 Wilshire Blvd. Suite 2000
Los Angeles, CA 90036

E-mail: info@TOKYOPOP.com
Come visit us online at www.TOKYOPOP.com

ISBN: 1-59182-689-6

First TOKYOPOP printing: November 2004

10 9 8 7 6 5 4 3 2 1

Printed in the USA

Previously in

Snow Drop

As Hae-Gi and So-Na's love continues
to bloom, another ray of hope shines on
Hae-Gi's life when his mother returns
from her recent operation. However, not
everything is coming up roses: Hae-Gi is
blacklisted in the modeling industry and
So-Na tries to fight off an arranged
engagement! Meanwhile, Charles and
ever-jealous Sun-Mi team up to crush the
flowers of romance and get what they're
both after -- Hae-Gi!

C·O·N·T·E·N·T·S

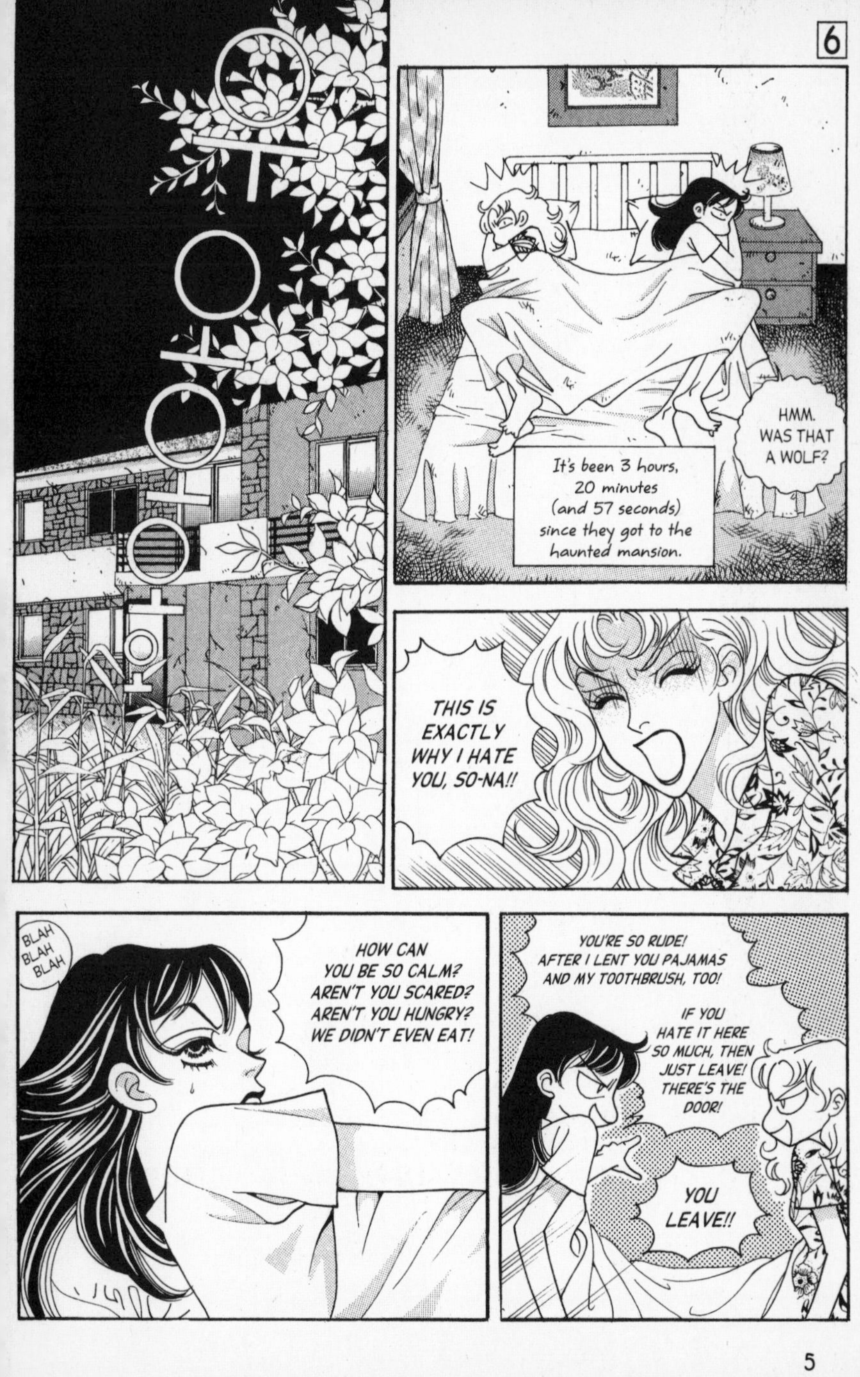
6
It's been 3 hours, 20 minutes (and 57 seconds) since they got to the haunted mansion.
HMM. WAS THAT A WOLF?
THIS IS EXACTLY WHY I HATE YOU, SO-NA!!
BLAH BLAH BLAH
HOW CAN YOU BE SO CALM? AREN'T YOU SCARED? AREN'T YOU HUNGRY? WE DIDN'T EVEN EAT!
YOU'RE SO RUDE! AFTER I LENT YOU PAJAMAS AND MY TOOTHBRUSH, TOO!
IF YOU HATE IT HERE SO MUCH, THEN JUST LEAVE! THERE'S THE DOOR!
YOU LEAVE!!

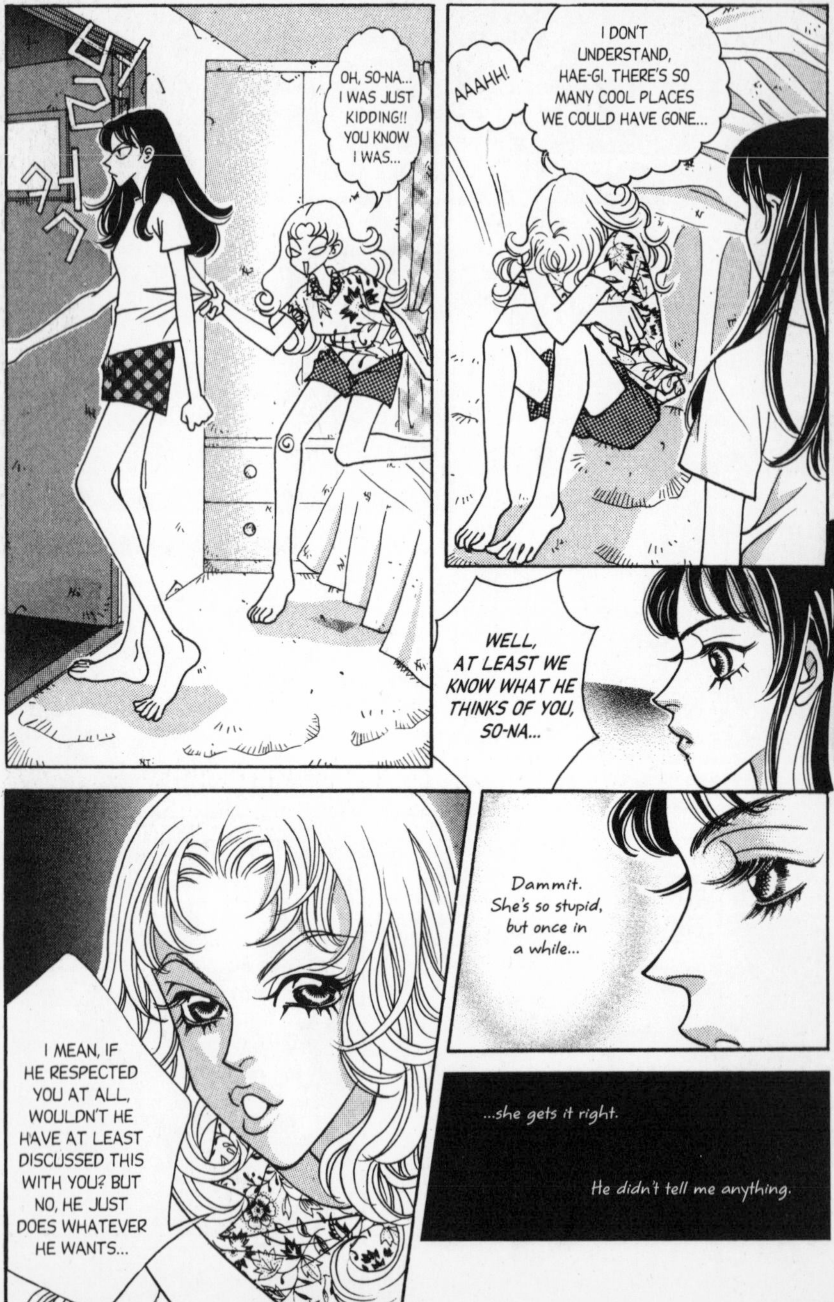
OH, SO-NA... I WAS JUST KIDDING!! YOU KNOW I WAS...
AAAHH!
I DON'T UNDERSTAND, HAE-GI. THERE'S SO MANY COOL PLACES WE COULD HAVE GONE...
WELL, AT LEAST WE KNOW WHAT HE THINKS OF YOU, SO-NA...
I MEAN, IF HE RESPECTED YOU AT ALL, WOULDN'T HE HAVE AT LEAST DISCUSSED THIS WITH YOU? BUT NO, HE JUST DOES WHATEVER HE WANTS...
Dammit. She's so stupid, but once in a while...
...she gets it right.
He didn't tell me anything.

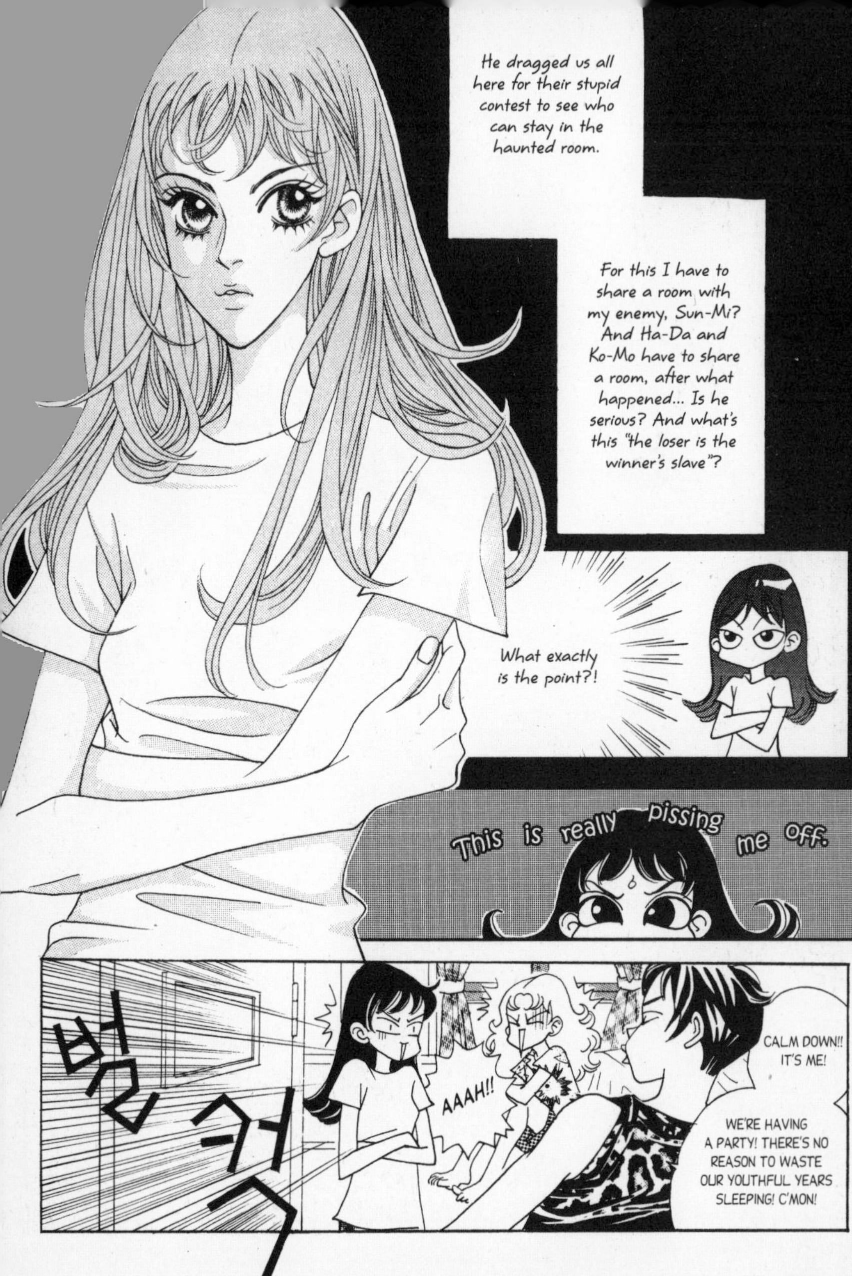
He dragged us all here for their stupid contest to see who can stay in the haunted room.
For this I have to share a room with my enemy, Sun-Mi? And Ha-Da and Ko-Mo have to share a room, after what happened... Is he serious? And what's this "the loser is the winner's slave"?
What exactly is the point?!
This is really pissing me off.
AAAH!!
CALM DOWN!! IT'S ME!
WE'RE HAVING A PARTY! THERE'S NO REASON TO WASTE OUR YOUTHFUL YEARS SLEEPING! C'MON!

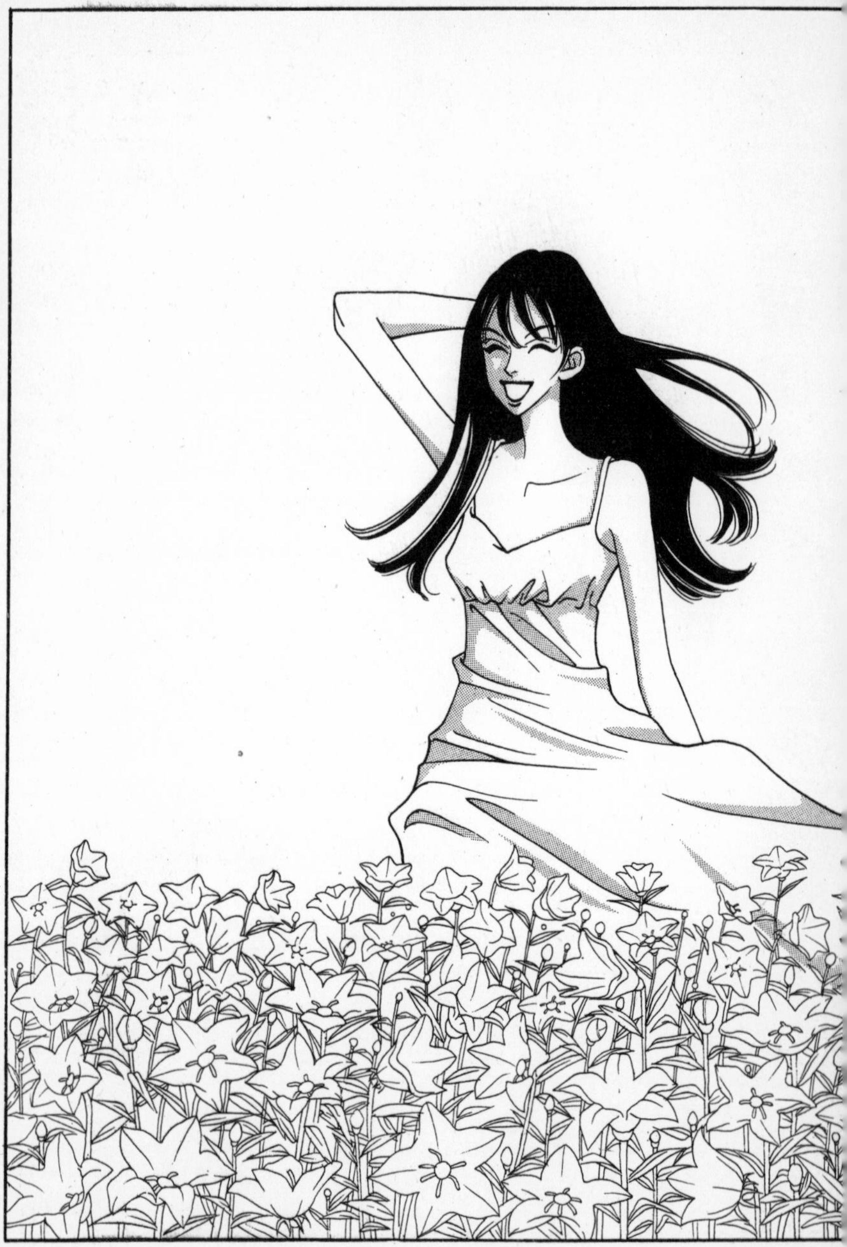

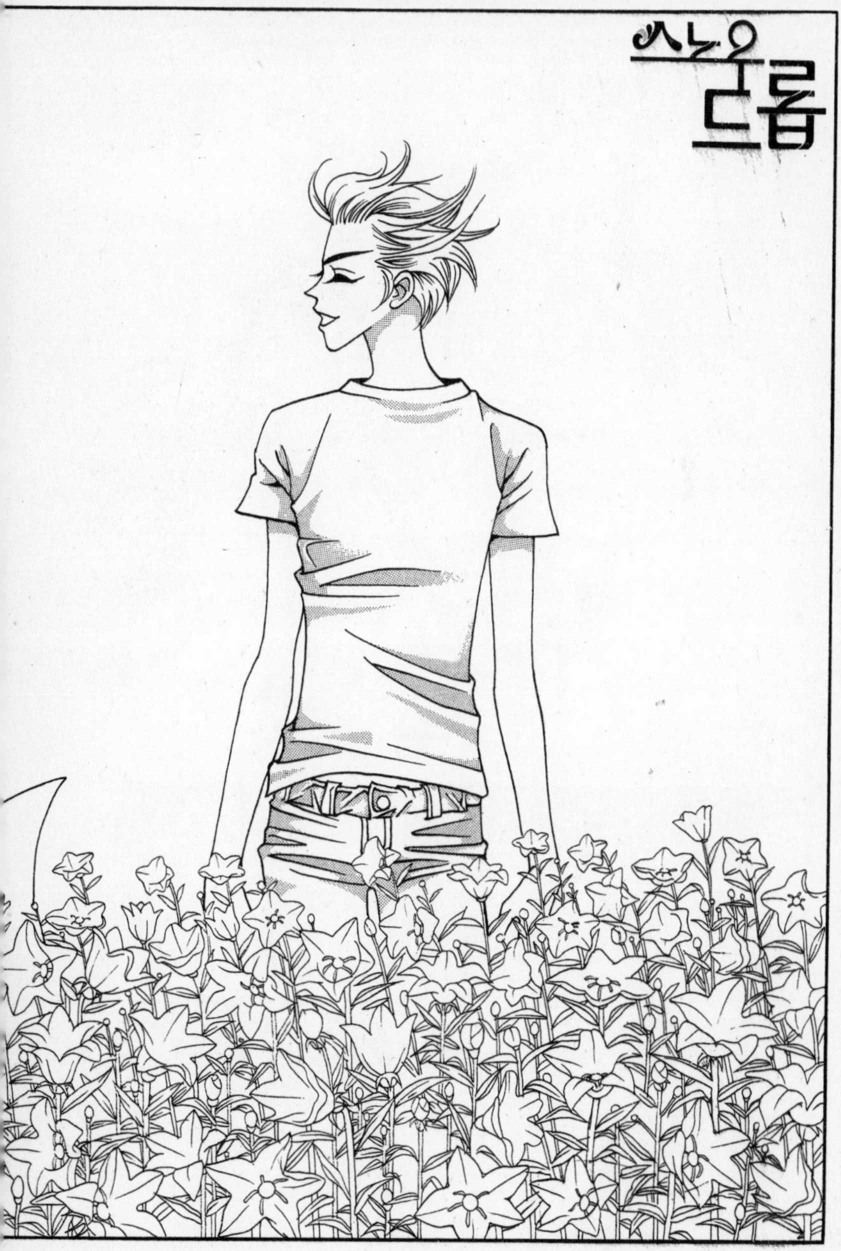
스노우 드롭

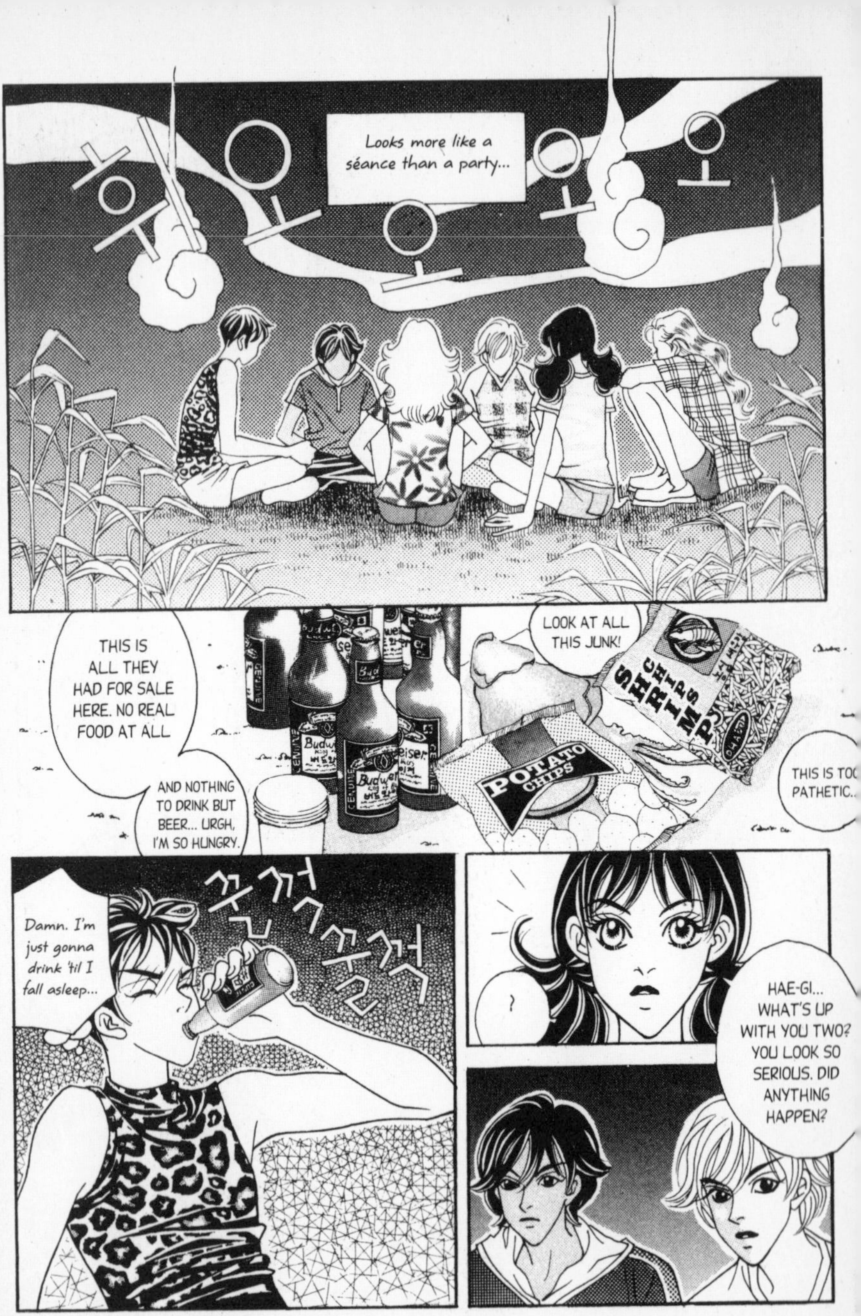
Looks more like a séance than a party...
THIS IS ALL THEY HAD FOR SALE HERE. NO REAL FOOD AT ALL
AND NOTHING TO DRINK BUT BEER... URGH, I'M SO HUNGRY.
LOOK AT ALL THIS JUNK!
POTATO CHIPS
THIS IS TOO PATHETIC...
Damn. I'm just gonna drink 'til I fall asleep...
HAE-GI... WHAT'S UP WITH YOU TWO? YOU LOOK SO SERIOUS. DID ANYTHING HAPPEN?

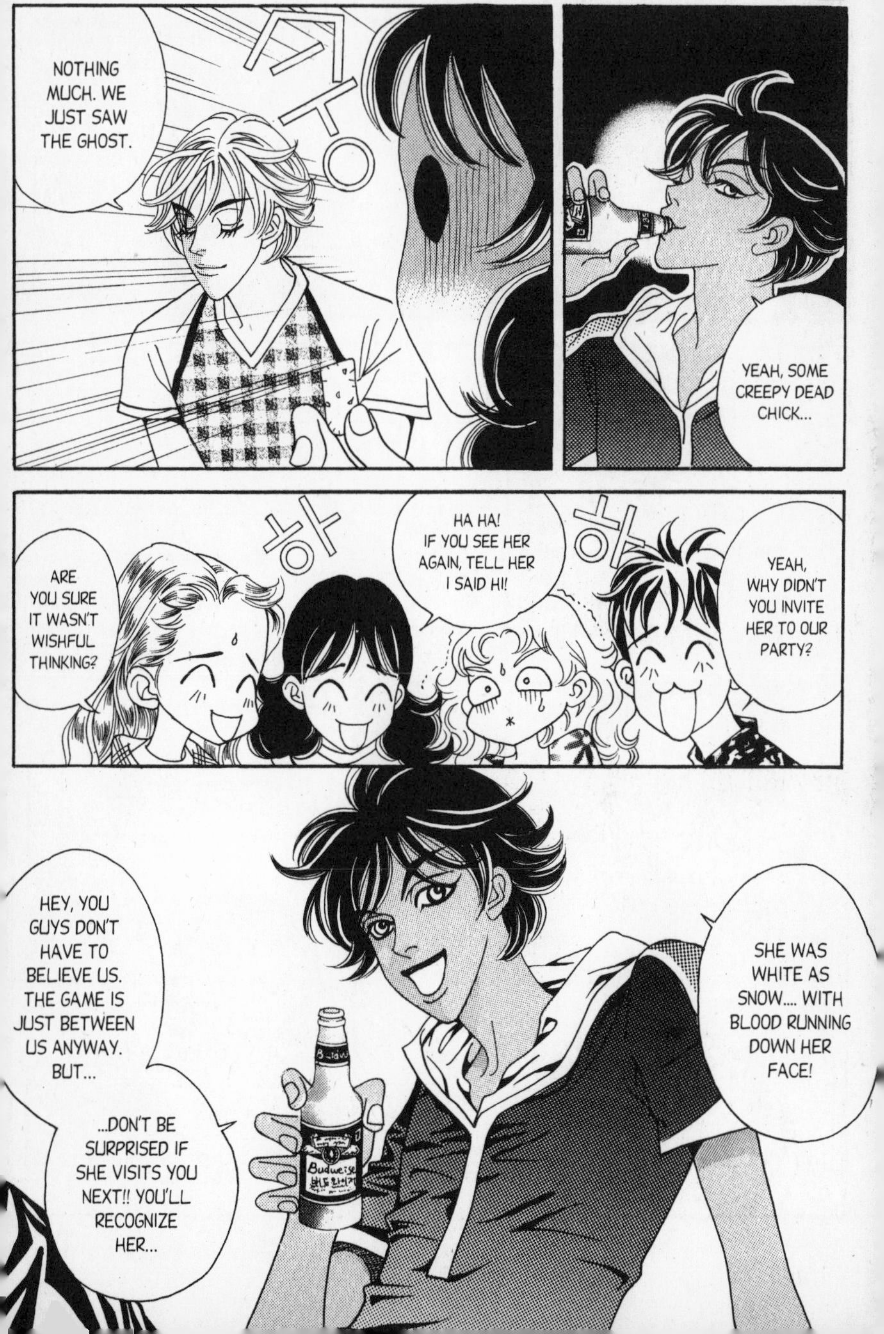
NOTHING MUCH. WE JUST SAW THE GHOST.
YEAH, SOME CREEPY DEAD CHICK...
ARE YOU SURE IT WASN'T WISHFUL THINKING?
하
HA HA! IF YOU SEE HER AGAIN, TELL HER I SAID HI!
하
YEAH, WHY DIDN'T YOU INVITE HER TO OUR PARTY?
HEY, YOU GUYS DON'T HAVE TO BELIEVE US. THE GAME IS JUST BETWEEN US ANYWAY. BUT...
...DON'T BE SURPRISED IF SHE VISITS YOU NEXT!! YOU'LL RECOGNIZE HER...
SHE WAS WHITE AS SNOW.... WITH BLOOD RUNNING DOWN HER FACE!

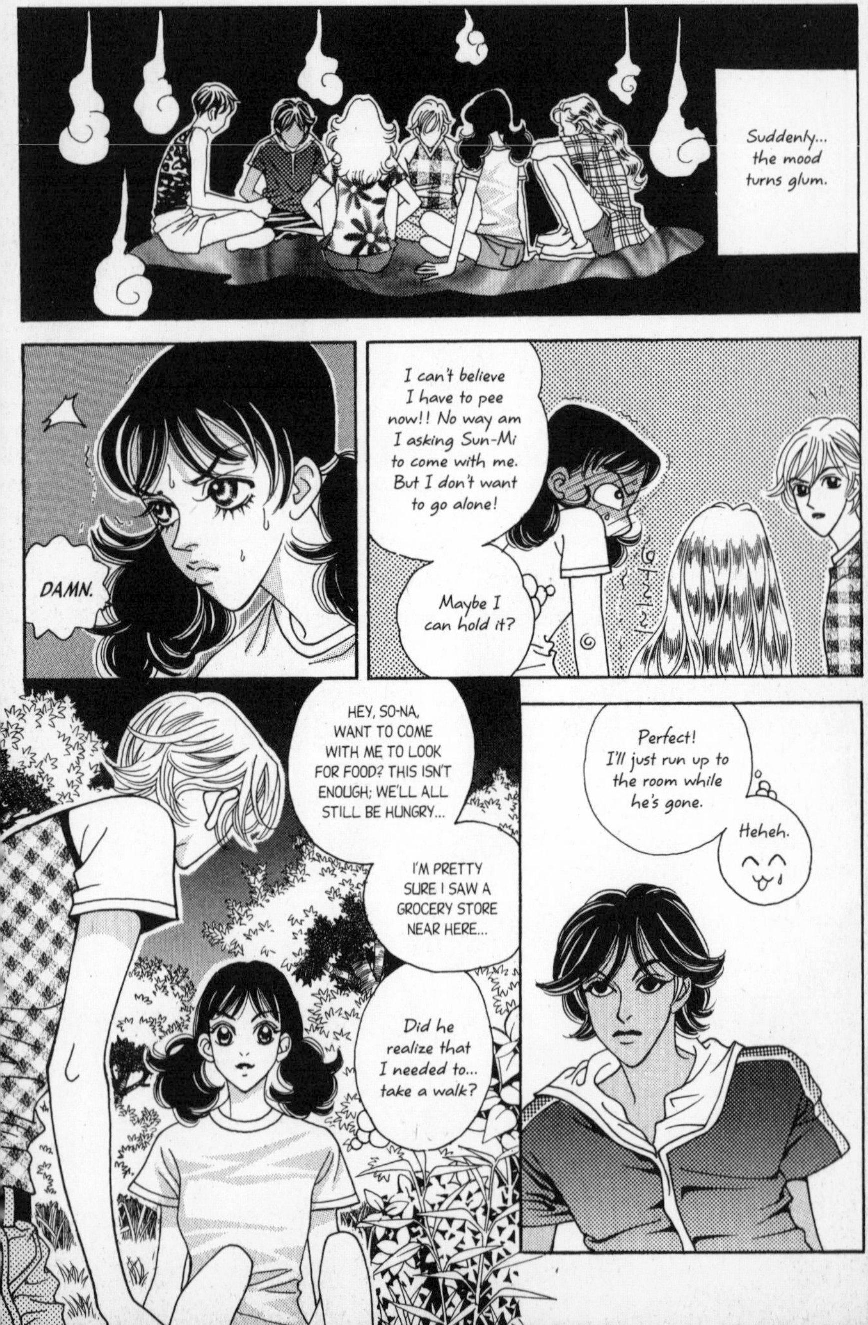
Suddenly... the mood turns glum.
DAMN.
I can't believe I have to pee now!! No way am I asking Sun-Mi to come with me. But I don't want to go alone!
Maybe I can hold it?
HEY, SO-NA, WANT TO COME WITH ME TO LOOK FOR FOOD? THIS ISN'T ENOUGH; WE'LL ALL STILL BE HUNGRY...
I'M PRETTY SURE I SAW A GROCERY STORE NEAR HERE...
Did he realize that I needed to... take a walk?
Perfect! I'll just run up to the room while he's gone.
Heheh.

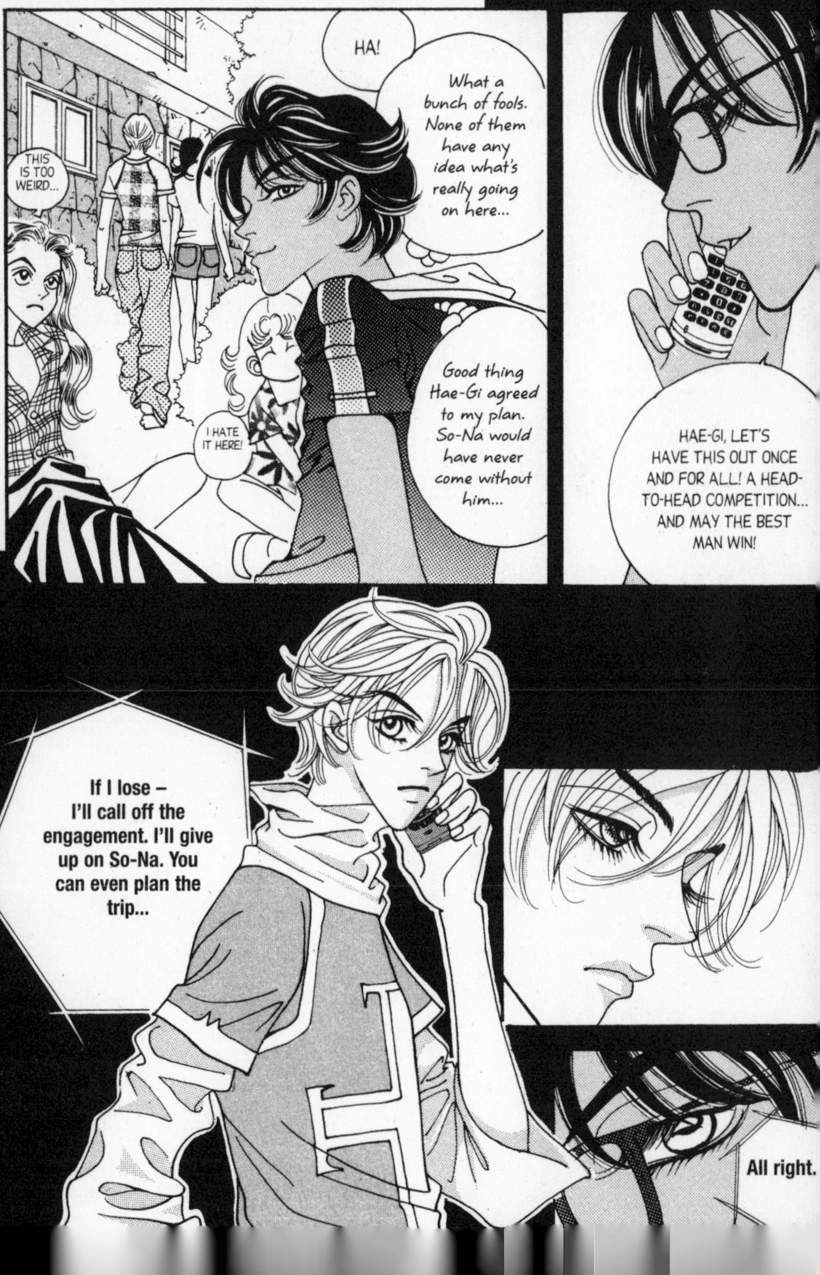
THIS IS TOO WEIRD...
HA!
What a bunch of fools. None of them have any idea what's really going on here...
I HATE IT HERE!
Good thing Hae-Gi agreed to my plan. So-Na would have never come without him...
HAE-GI, LET'S HAVE THIS OUT ONCE AND FOR ALL! A HEAD-TO-HEAD COMPETITION... AND MAY THE BEST MAN WIN!
If I lose – I'll call off the engagement. I'll give up on So-Na. You can even plan the trip...
All right.

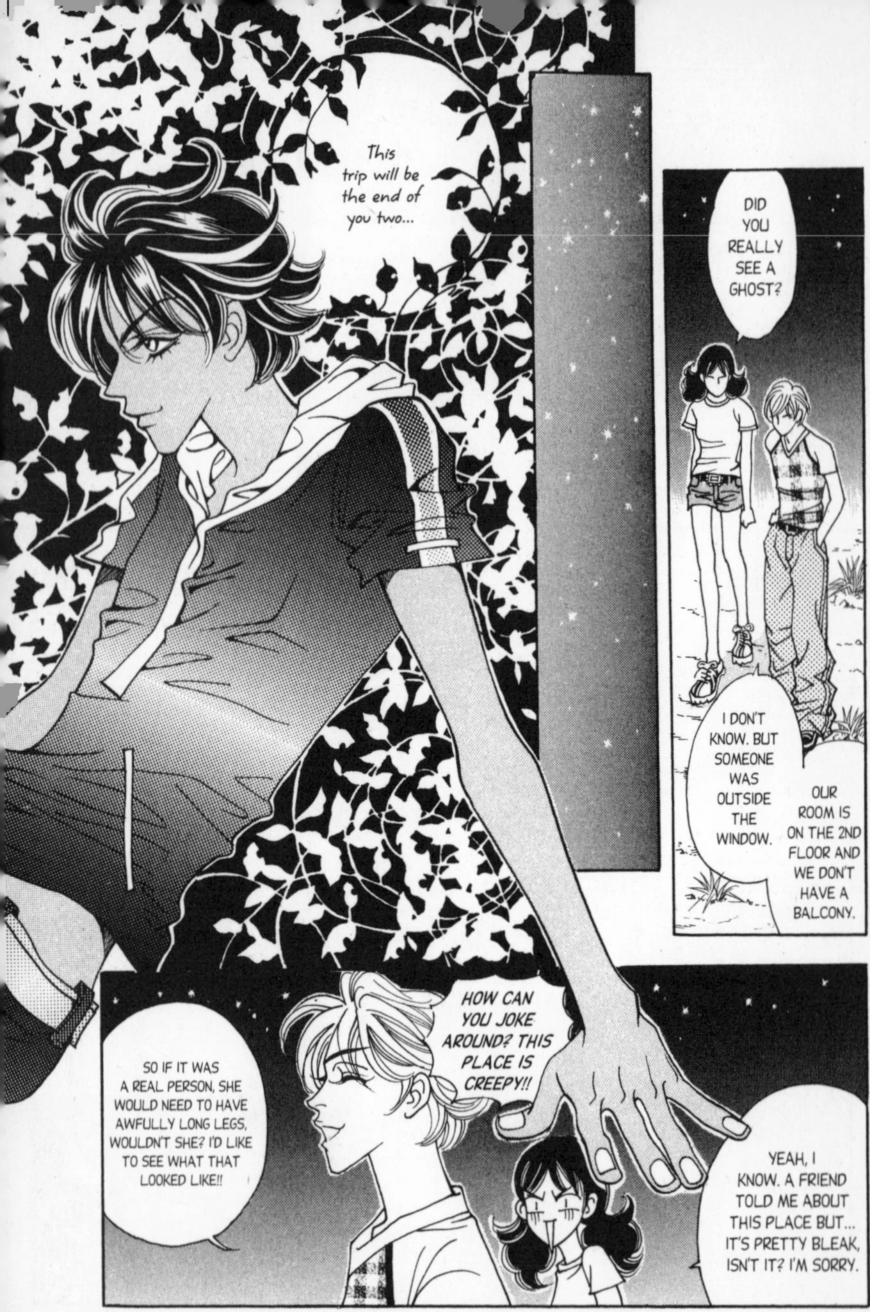
DID YOU REALLY SEE A GHOST?
I DON'T KNOW. BUT SOMEONE WAS OUTSIDE THE WINDOW.
OUR ROOM IS ON THE 2ND FLOOR AND WE DON'T HAVE A BALCONY.
SO IF IT WAS A REAL PERSON, SHE WOULD NEED TO HAVE AWFULLY LONG LEGS, WOULDN'T SHE? I'D LIKE TO SEE WHAT THAT LOOKED LIKE!!
HOW CAN YOU JOKE AROUND? THIS PLACE IS CREEPY!!
YEAH, I KNOW. A FRIEND TOLD ME ABOUT THIS PLACE BUT... IT'S PRETTY BLEAK, ISN'T IT? I'M SORRY.
This trip will be the end of you two...

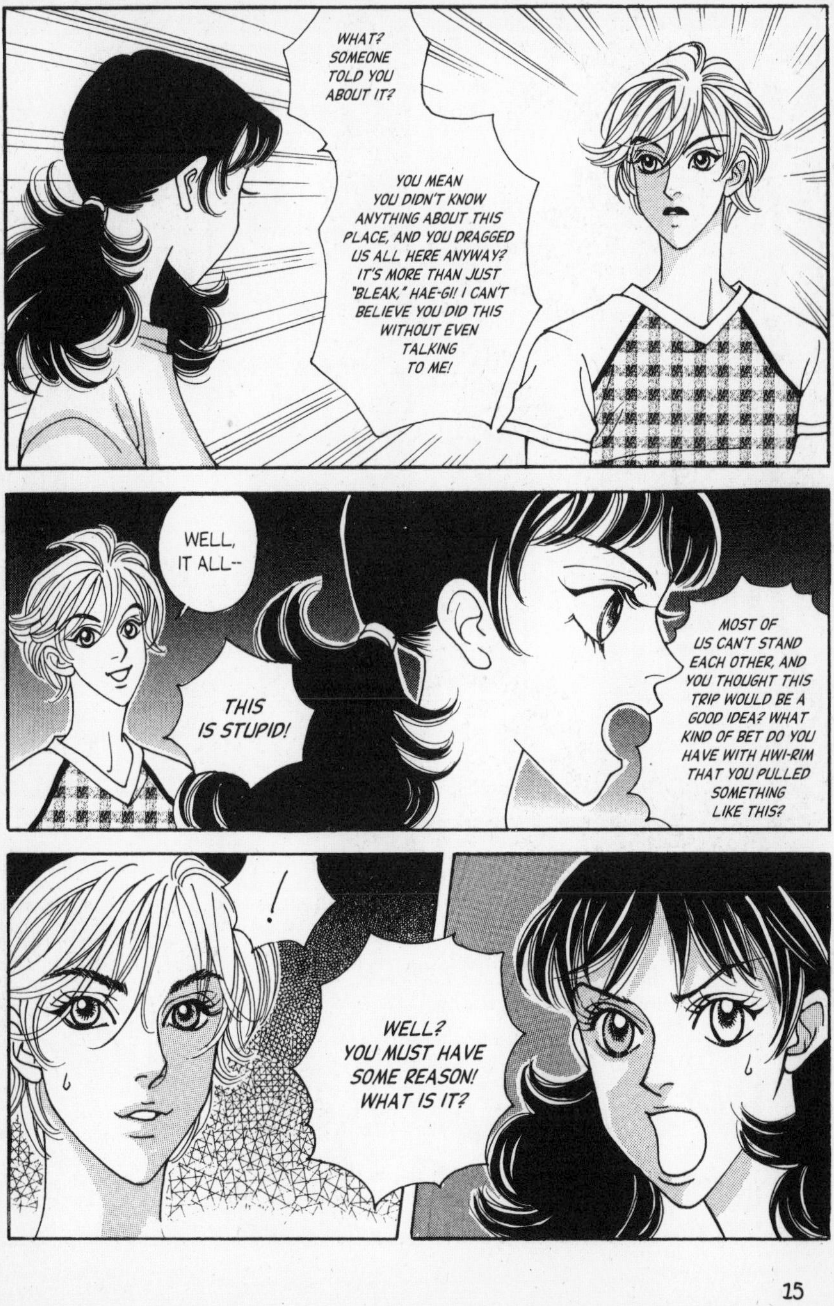
WHAT? SOMEONE TOLD YOU ABOUT IT?
YOU MEAN YOU DIDN'T KNOW ANYTHING ABOUT THIS PLACE, AND YOU DRAGGED US ALL HERE ANYWAY? IT'S MORE THAN JUST "BLEAK," HAE-GI! I CAN'T BELIEVE YOU DID THIS WITHOUT EVEN TALKING TO ME!
WELL, IT ALL--
THIS IS STUPID!
MOST OF US CAN'T STAND EACH OTHER, AND YOU THOUGHT THIS TRIP WOULD BE A GOOD IDEA? WHAT KIND OF BET DO YOU HAVE WITH HWI-RIM THAT YOU PULLED SOMETHING LIKE THIS?
!
WELL? YOU MUST HAVE SOME REASON! WHAT IS IT?

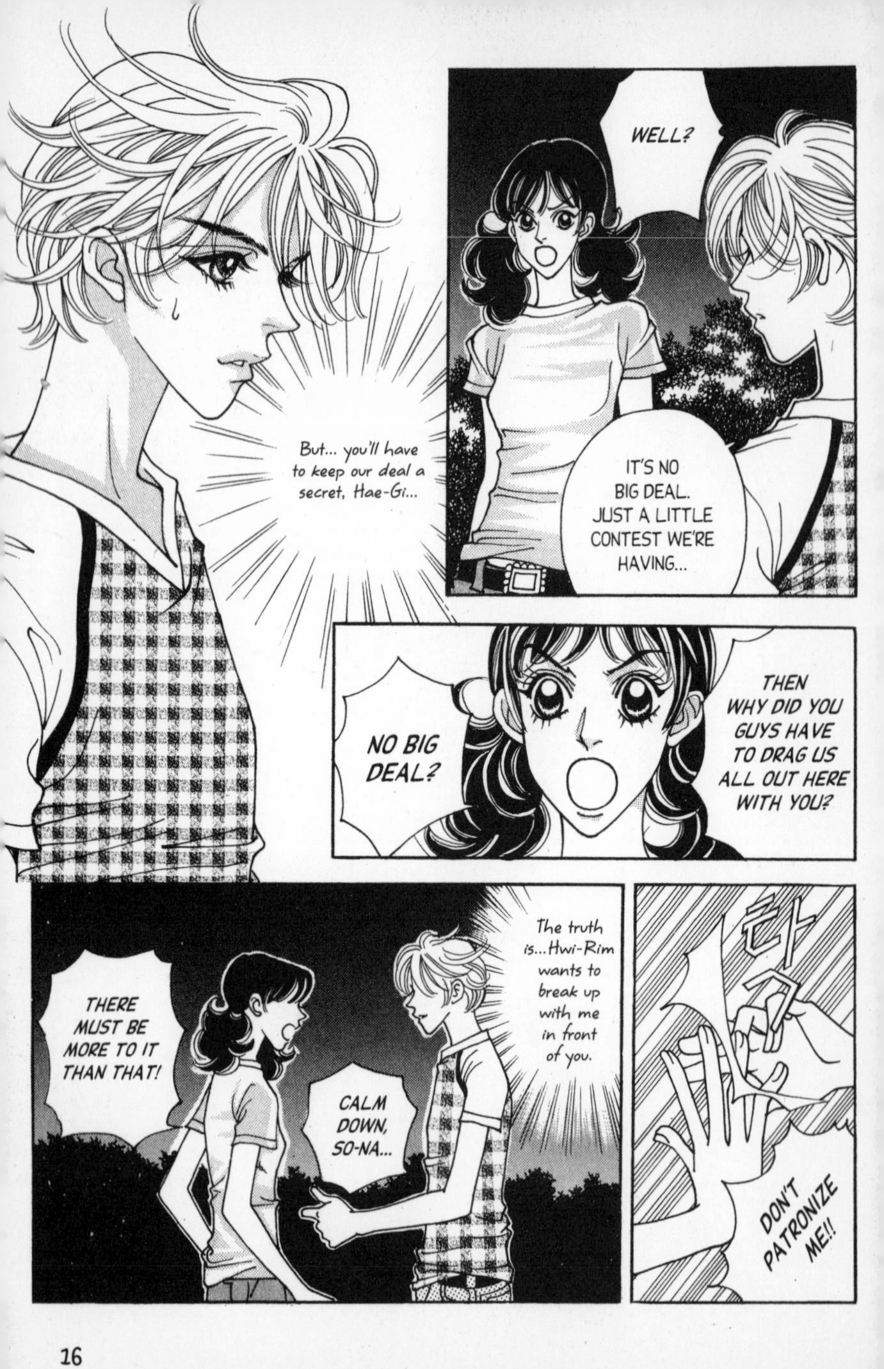
But... you'll have to keep our deal a secret, Hae-Gi...
WELL?
IT'S NO BIG DEAL. JUST A LITTLE CONTEST WE'RE HAVING...
NO BIG DEAL?
THEN WHY DID YOU GUYS HAVE TO DRAG US ALL OUT HERE WITH YOU?
THERE MUST BE MORE TO IT THAN THAT!
CALM DOWN, SO-NA...
The truth is...Hwi-Rim wants to break up with me in front of you.
DON'T PATRONIZE ME!!

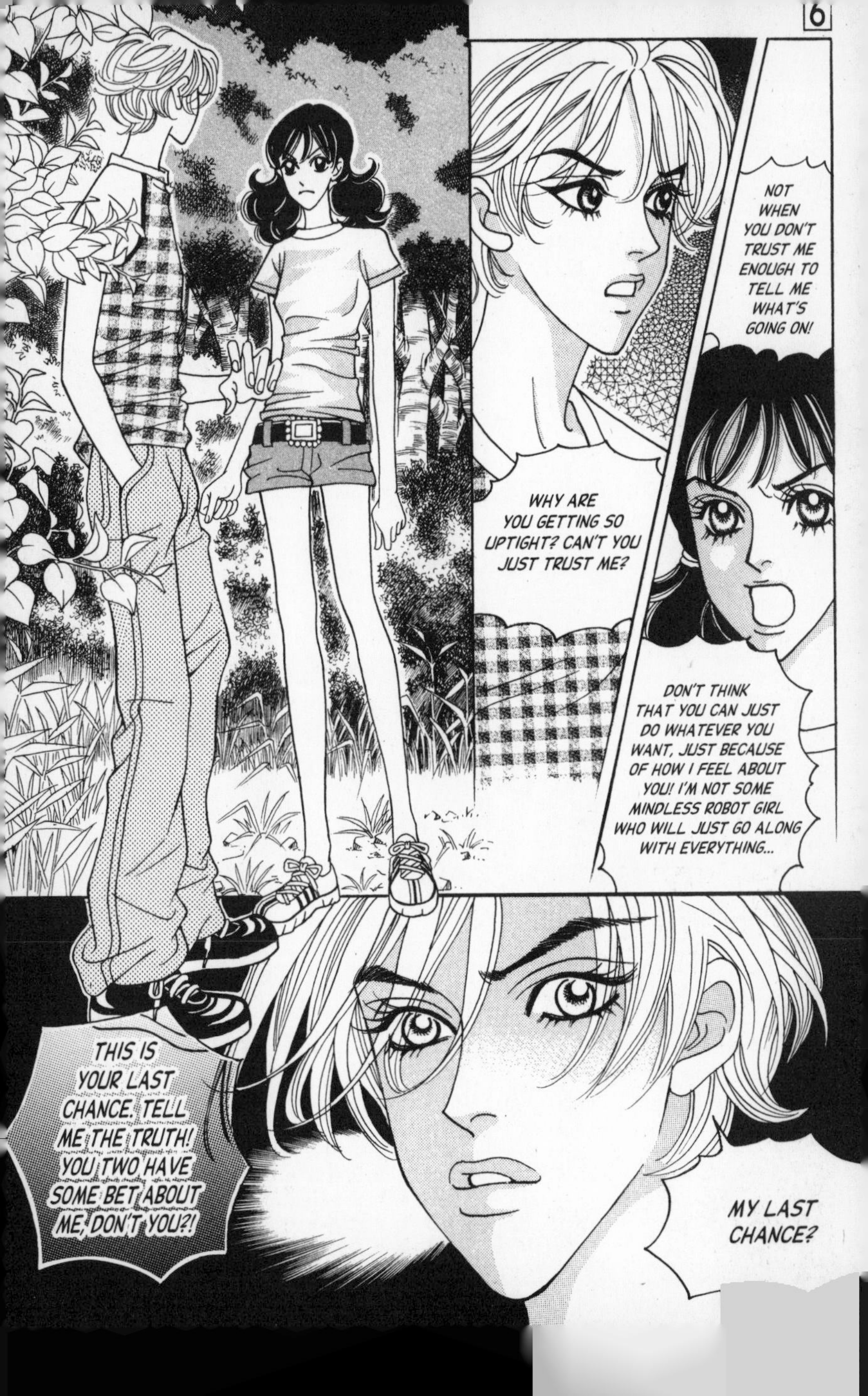
WHY ARE YOU GETTING SO UPTIGHT? CAN'T YOU JUST TRUST ME?
NOT WHEN YOU DON'T TRUST ME ENOUGH TO TELL ME WHAT'S GOING ON!
DON'T THINK THAT YOU CAN JUST DO WHATEVER YOU WANT, JUST BECAUSE OF HOW I FEEL ABOUT YOU! I'M NOT SOME MINDLESS ROBOT GIRL WHO WILL JUST GO ALONG WITH EVERYTHING...
THIS IS YOUR LAST CHANCE. TELL ME THE TRUTH! YOU TWO HAVE SOME BET ABOUT ME, DON'T YOU?!
MY LAST CHANCE?

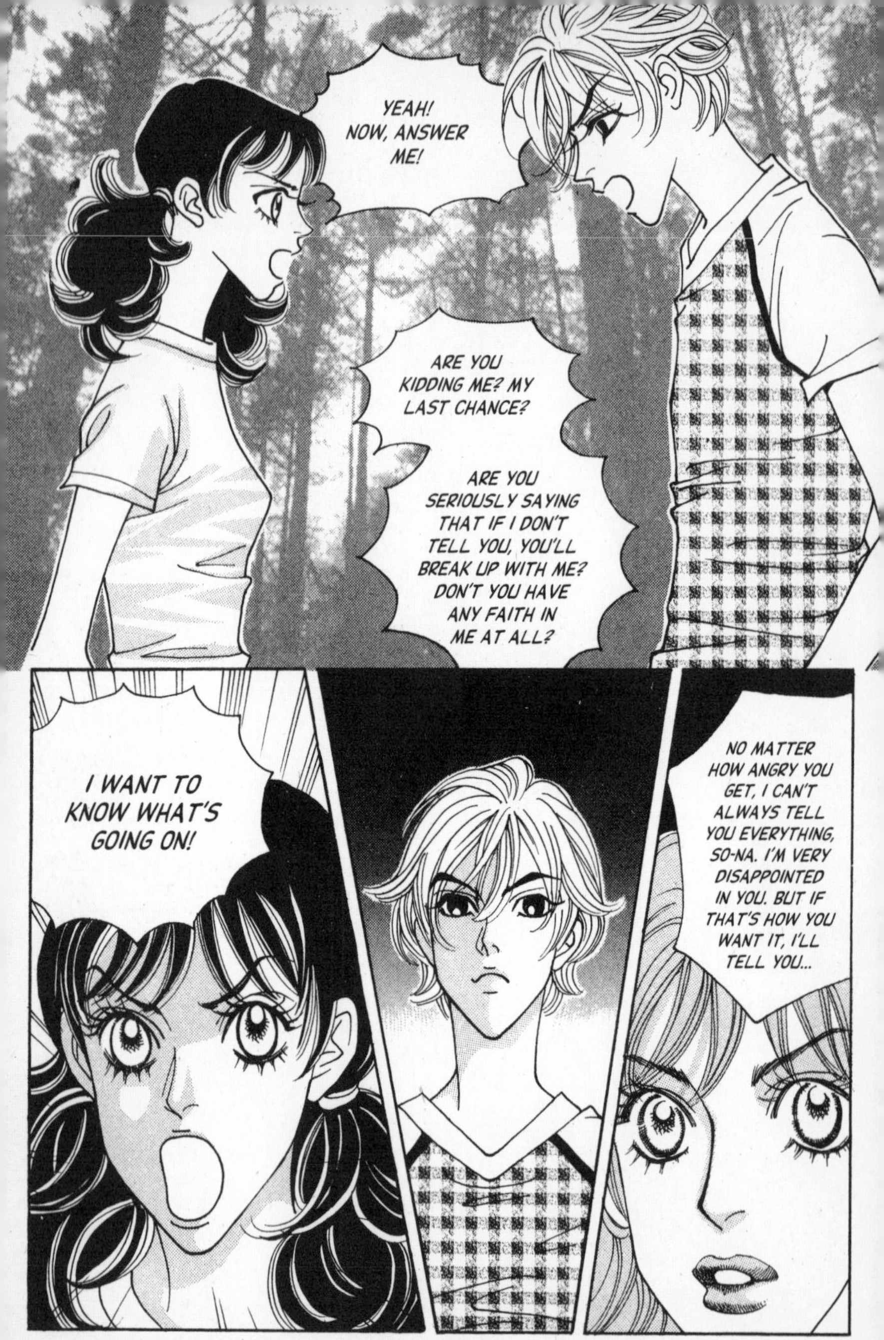
YEAH! NOW, ANSWER ME!
ARE YOU KIDDING ME? MY LAST CHANCE?
ARE YOU SERIOUSLY SAYING THAT IF I DON'T TELL YOU, YOU'LL BREAK UP WITH ME? DON'T YOU HAVE ANY FAITH IN ME AT ALL?
NO MATTER HOW ANGRY YOU GET, I CAN'T ALWAYS TELL YOU EVERYTHING, SO-NA. I'M VERY DISAPPOINTED IN YOU. BUT IF THAT'S HOW YOU WANT IT, I'LL TELL YOU...
I WANT TO KNOW WHAT'S GOING ON!

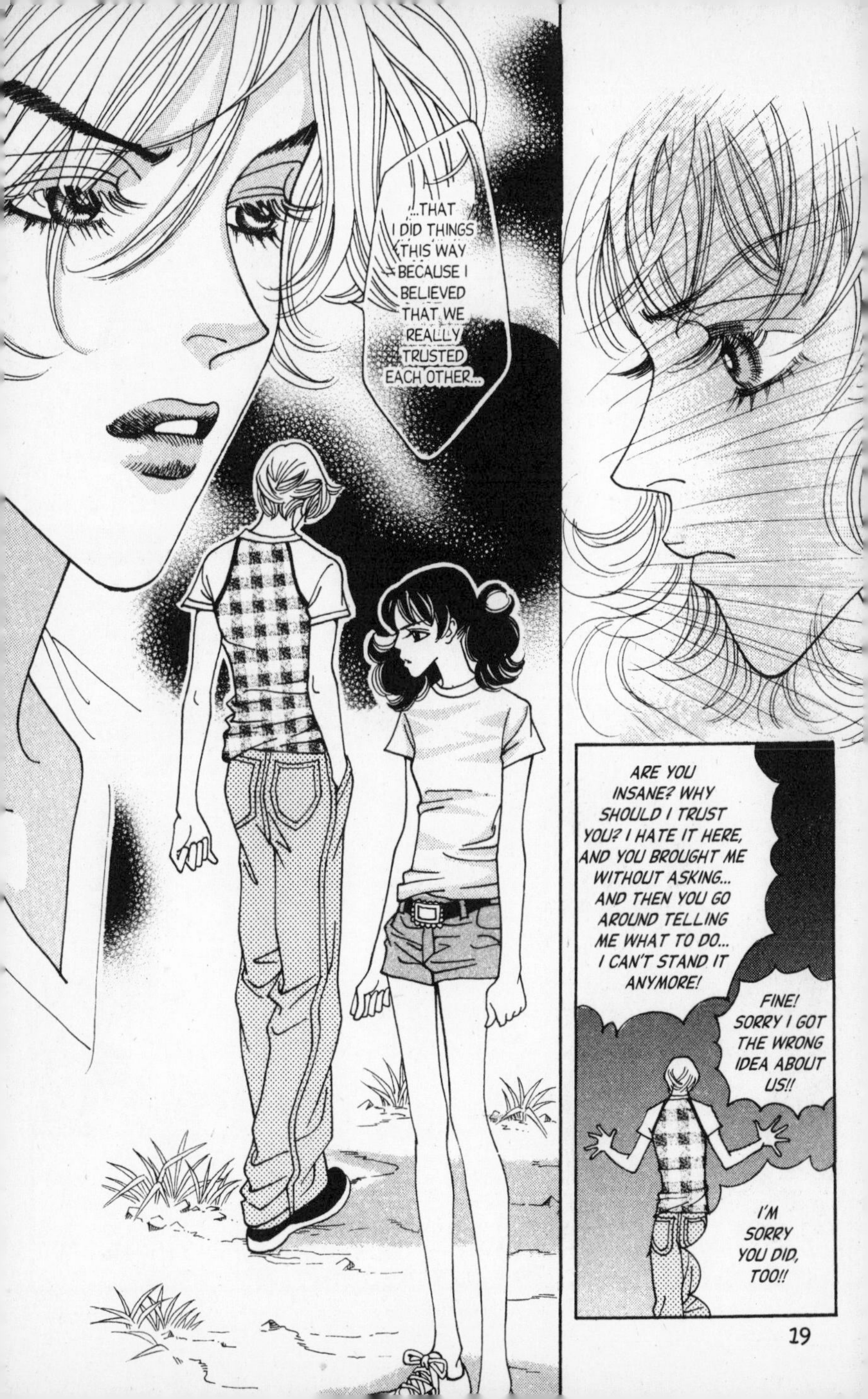
ARE YOU INSANE? WHY SHOULD I TRUST YOU? I HATE IT HERE, AND YOU BROUGHT ME WITHOUT ASKING... AND THEN YOU GO AROUND TELLING ME WHAT TO DO... I CAN'T STAND IT ANYMORE!
FINE! SORRY I GOT THE WRONG IDEA ABOUT US!!
I'M SORRY YOU DID, TOO!!
...THAT I DID THINGS THIS WAY BECAUSE I BELIEVED THAT WE REALLY TRUSTED EACH OTHER...

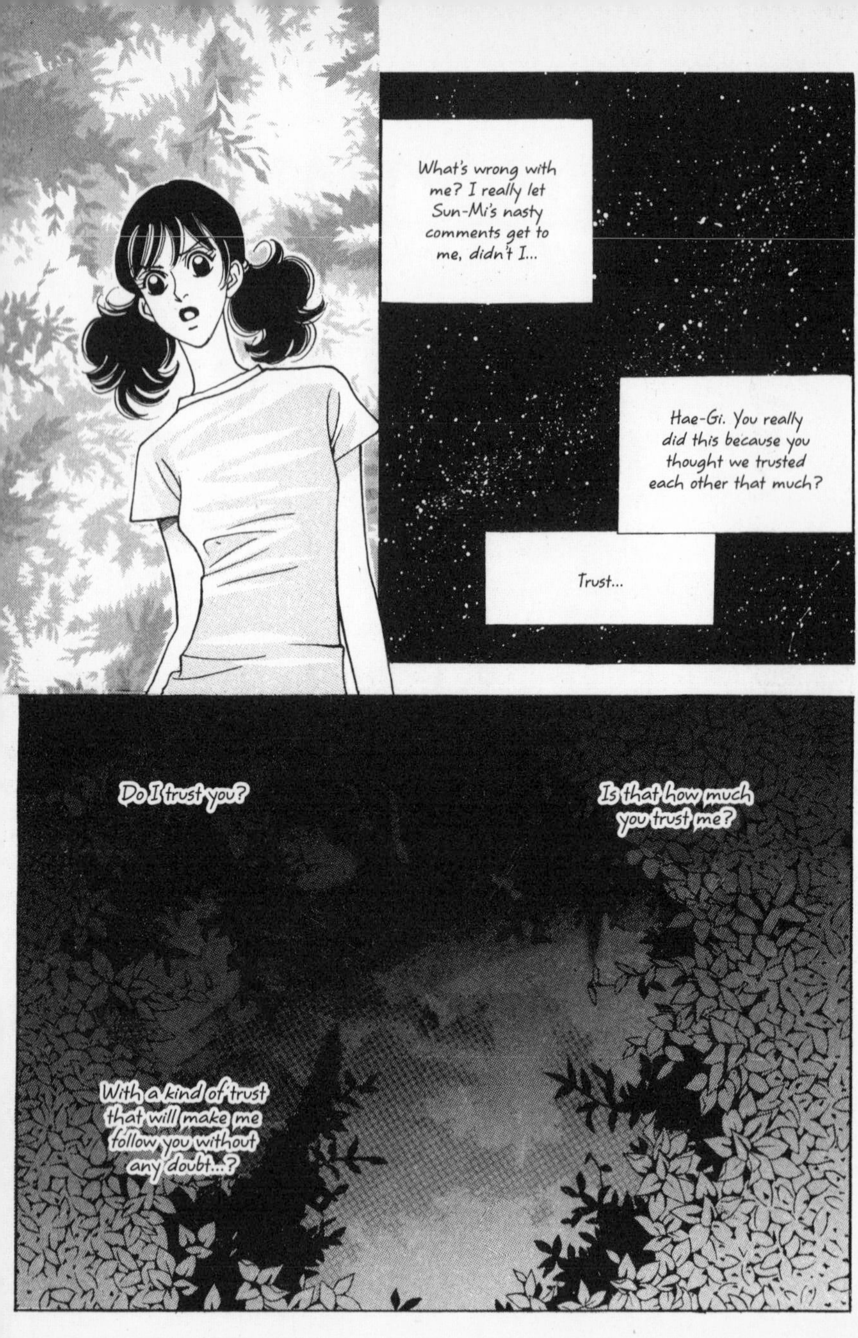
What's wrong with me? I really let Sun-Mi's nasty comments get to me, didn't I...
Hae-Gi. You really did this because you thought we trusted each other that much?
Trust...
Is that how much you trust me?
Do I trust you?
With a kind of trust that will make me follow you without any doubt...?

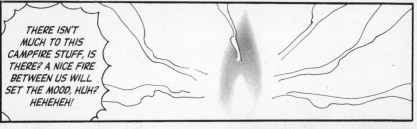

THERE ISN'T MUCH TO THIS CAMPFIRE STUFF, IS THERE? A NICE FIRE BETWEEN US WILL SET THE MOOD, HUH? HEHEHEH!

WOULD YOU QUIT IT ALREADY? THE SMOKE IS KILLING ME!

I HOPE YOU SET YOUR OWN HAIR ON FIRE, YOU MORON!

NOW, NOW, LET'S NOT BE NASTY. MAYBE YOU NEED SOME CAMPFIRE SONGS TO CHEER YOURSELVES UP...

ARE YOU KIDDING ME? WHAT ARE WE, GIRL SCOUTS?

SCOFF AWAY! I'M JANG HA-DA, THE MOOD MAKER! I'LL LIFT YOUR SPIRITS WHETHER YOU LIKE IT OR NOT!

DON'T UNDER-ESTIMATE ME!

HA-DA!! WHERE DID YOU GET THAT SNAKE?

EEEEE!!

JEEZ... I CAN'T BELIEVE HOW FAST HE GOT DRUNK!

TO HELL WITH THIS! I'VE HAD IT. I'M GOING TO SLEEP.

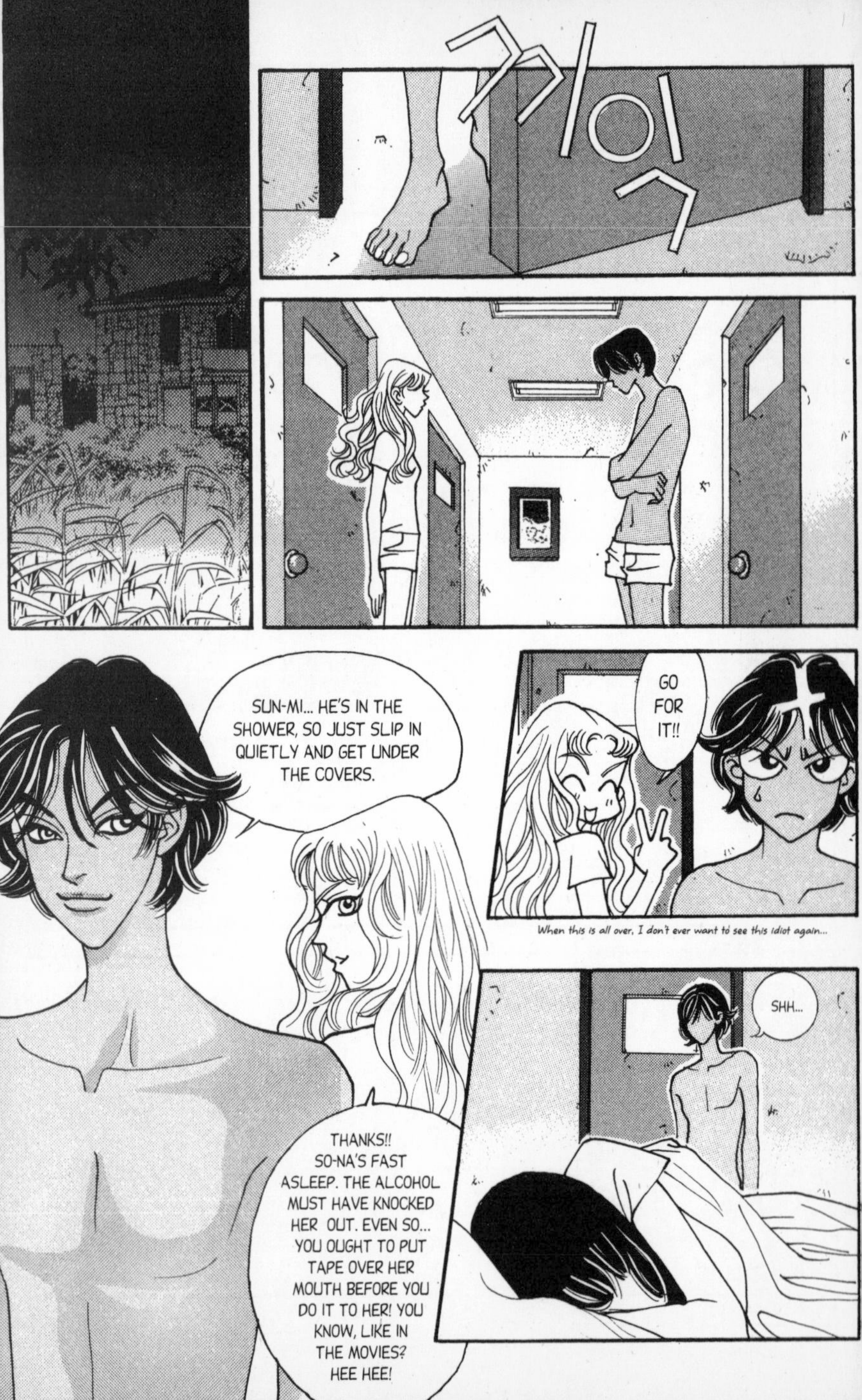
끼익
SUN-MI... HE'S IN THE SHOWER, SO JUST SLIP IN QUIETLY AND GET UNDER THE COVERS.
THANKS!! SO-NA'S FAST ASLEEP. THE ALCOHOL MUST HAVE KNOCKED HER OUT. EVEN SO... YOU OUGHT TO PUT TAPE OVER HER MOUTH BEFORE YOU DO IT TO HER! YOU KNOW, LIKE IN THE MOVIES? HEE HEE!
GO FOR IT!!
When this is all over, I don't ever want to see this idiot again...
SHH...

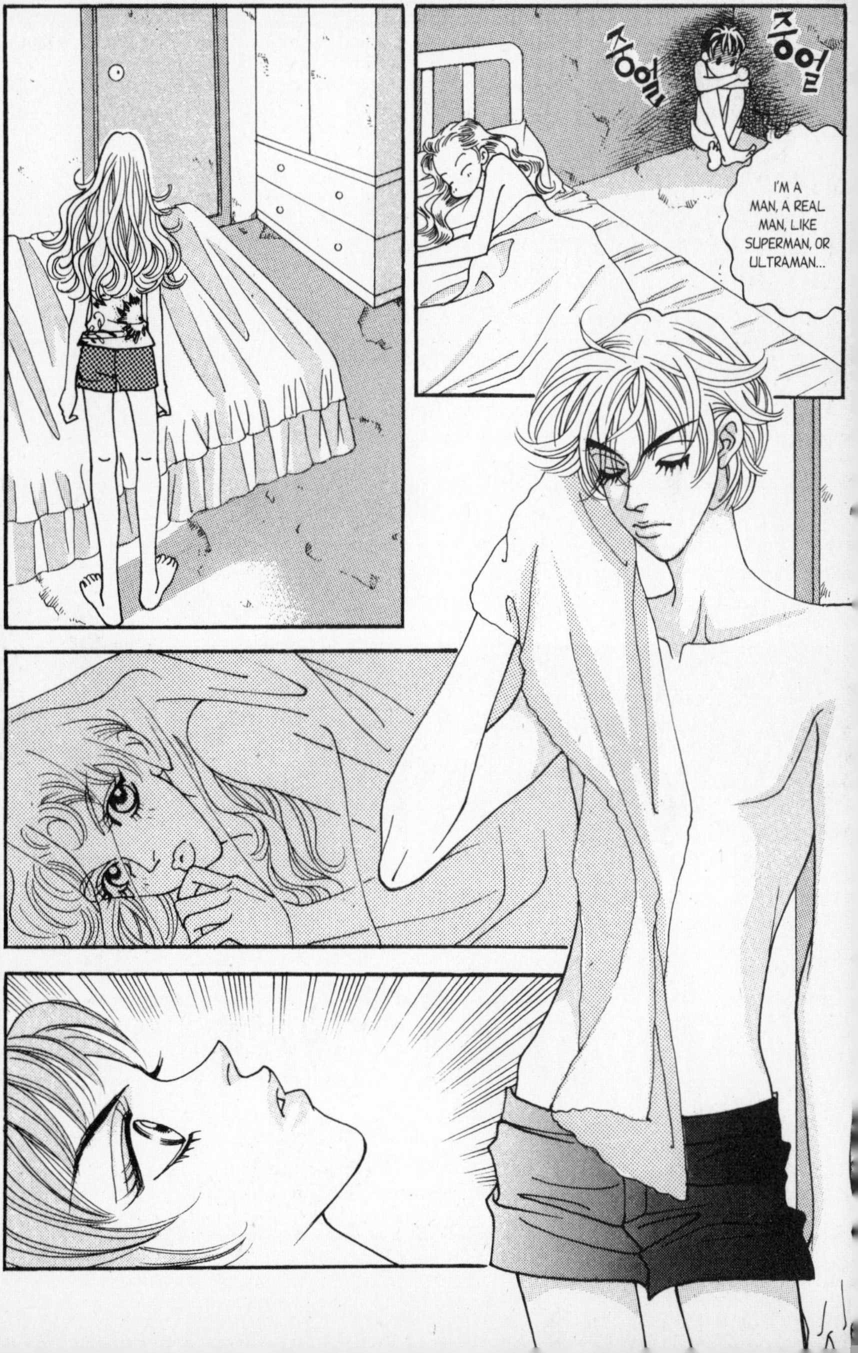
중얼
중얼
I'M A MAN, A REAL MAN, LIKE SUPERMAN, OR ULTRAMAN...

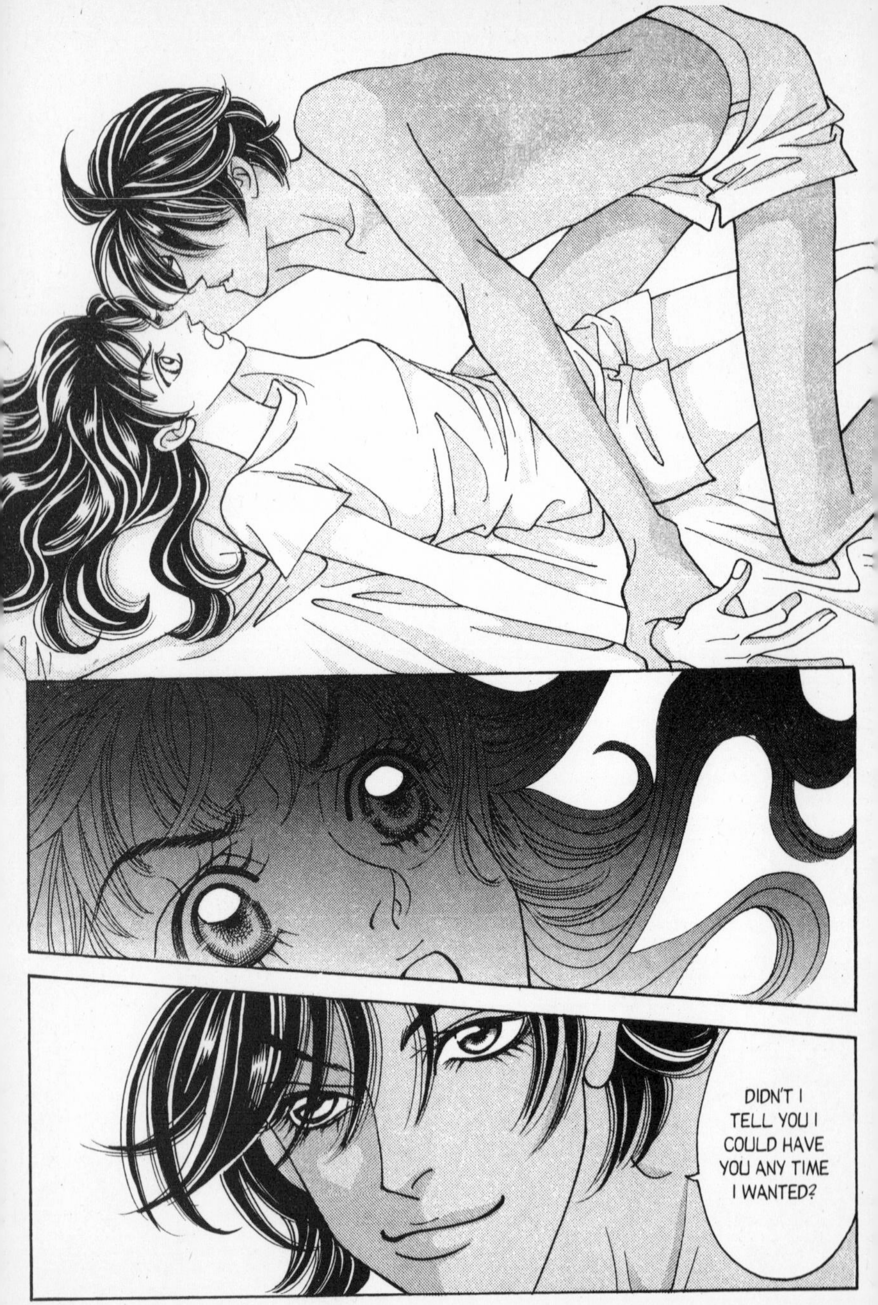
DIDN'T I TELL YOU I COULD HAVE YOU ANY TIME I WANTED?

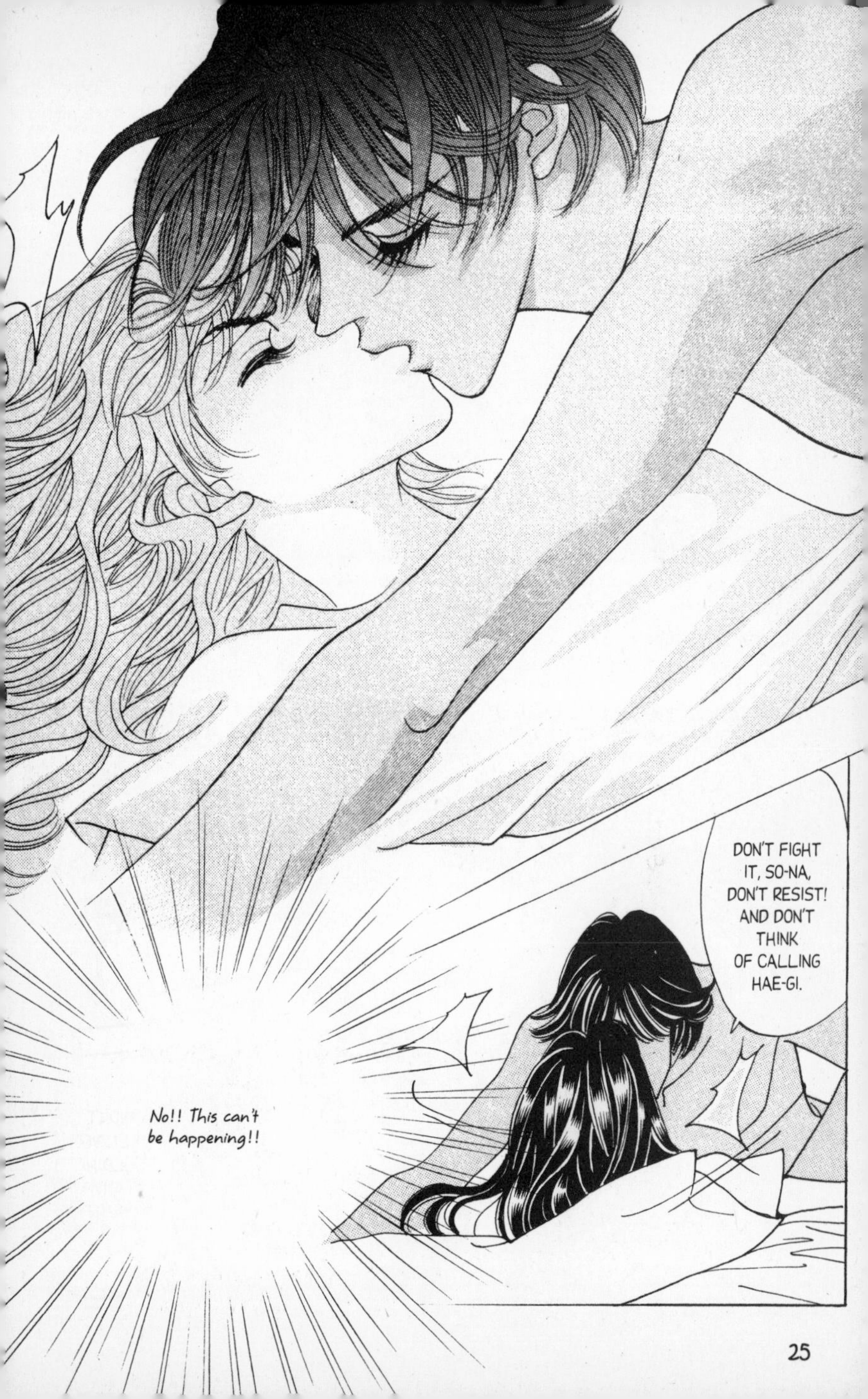
DON'T FIGHT IT, SO-NA, DON'T RESIST! AND DON'T THINK OF CALLING HAE-GI.
No!! This can't be happening!!

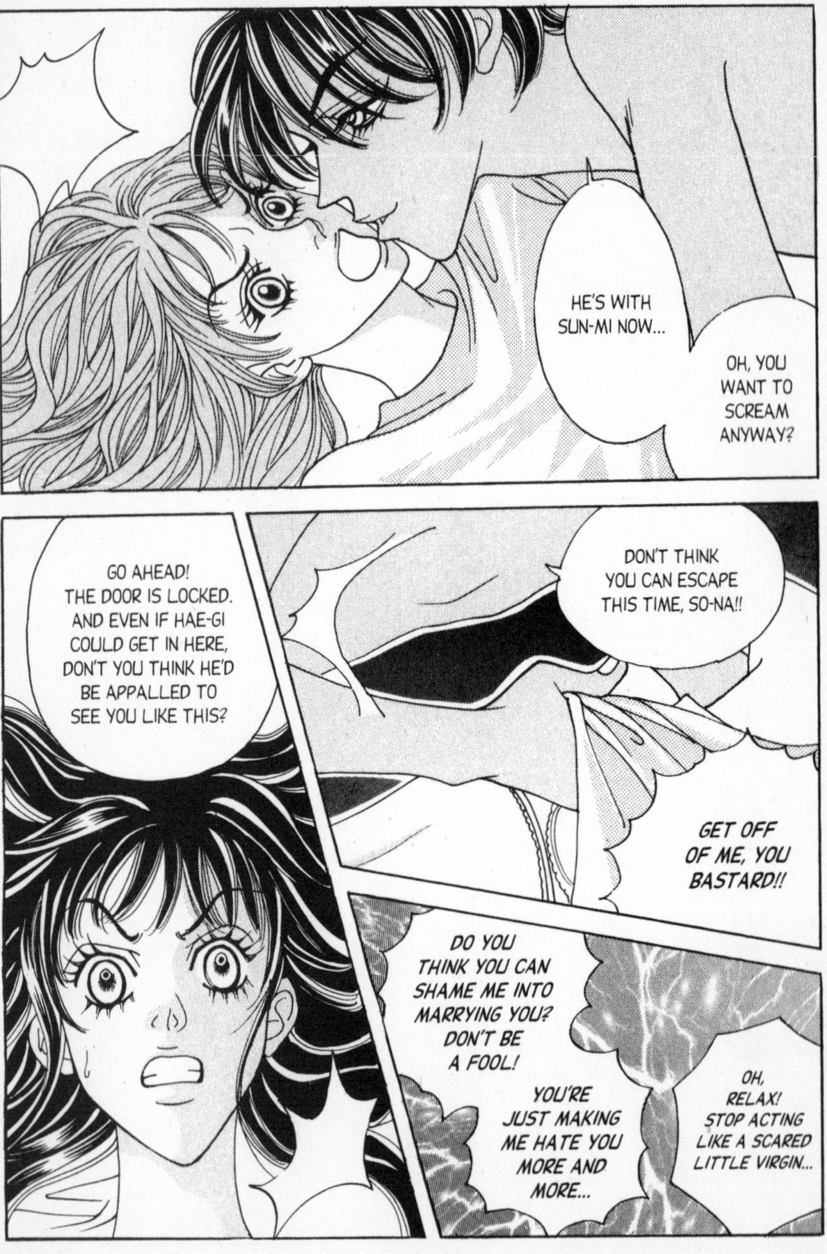
HE'S WITH SUN-MI NOW...
OH, YOU WANT TO SCREAM ANYWAY?
GO AHEAD! THE DOOR IS LOCKED. AND EVEN IF HAE-GI COULD GET IN HERE, DON'T YOU THINK HE'D BE APPALLED TO SEE YOU LIKE THIS?
DON'T THINK YOU CAN ESCAPE THIS TIME, SO-NA!!
GET OFF OF ME, YOU BASTARD!!
DO YOU THINK YOU CAN SHAME ME INTO MARRYING YOU? DON'T BE A FOOL!
YOU'RE JUST MAKING ME HATE YOU MORE AND MORE...
OH, RELAX! STOP ACTING LIKE A SCARED LITTLE VIRGIN...

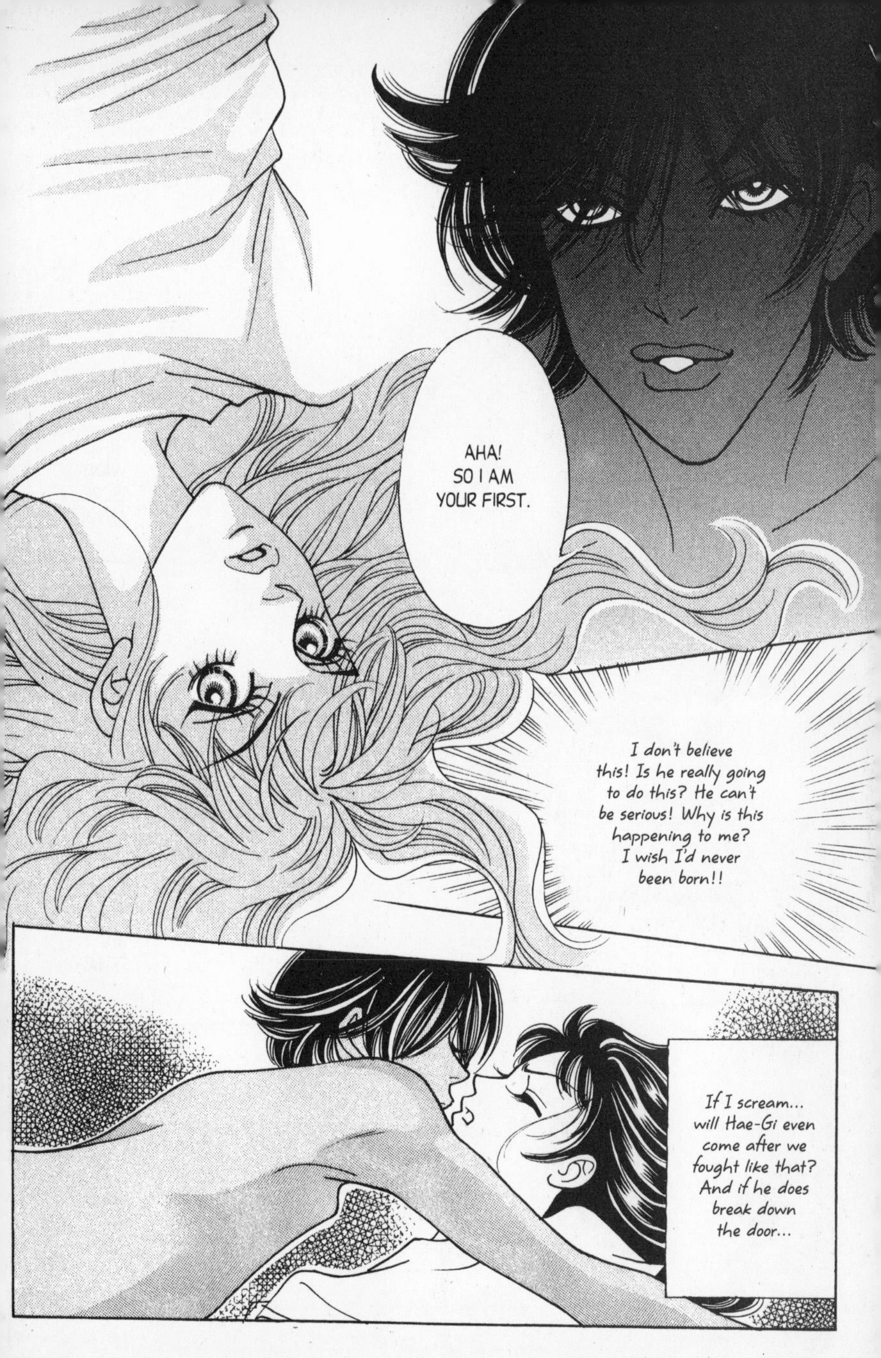
AHA! SO I AM YOUR FIRST.
I don't believe this! Is he really going to do this? He can't be serious! Why is this happening to me? I wish I'd never been born!!
If I scream... will Hae-Gi even come after we fought like that? And if he does break down the door...

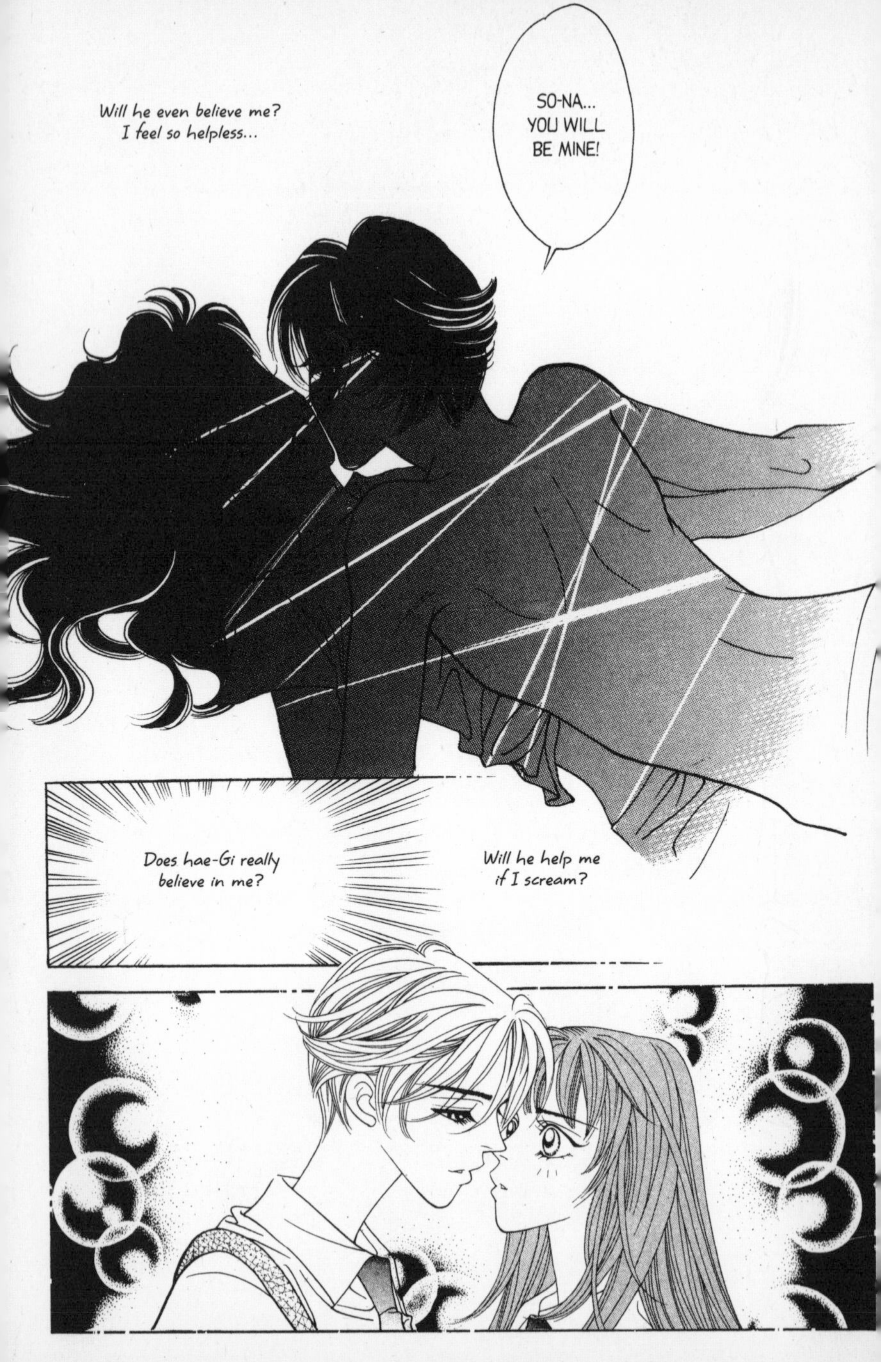
SO-NA... YOU WILL BE MINE!
Will he even believe me? I feel so helpless...
Will he help me if I scream?
Does hae-Gi really believe in me?

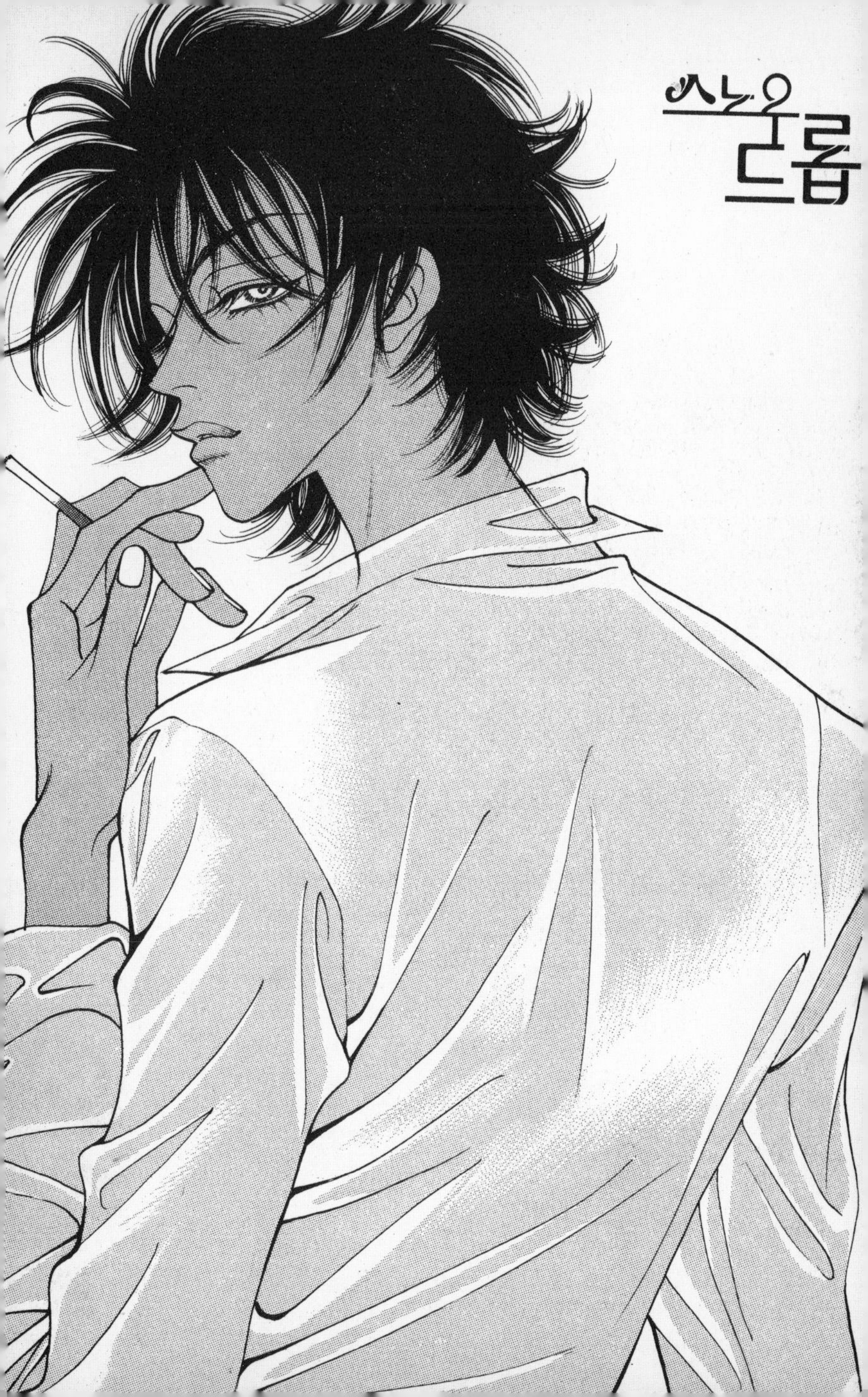
스노우 드롭

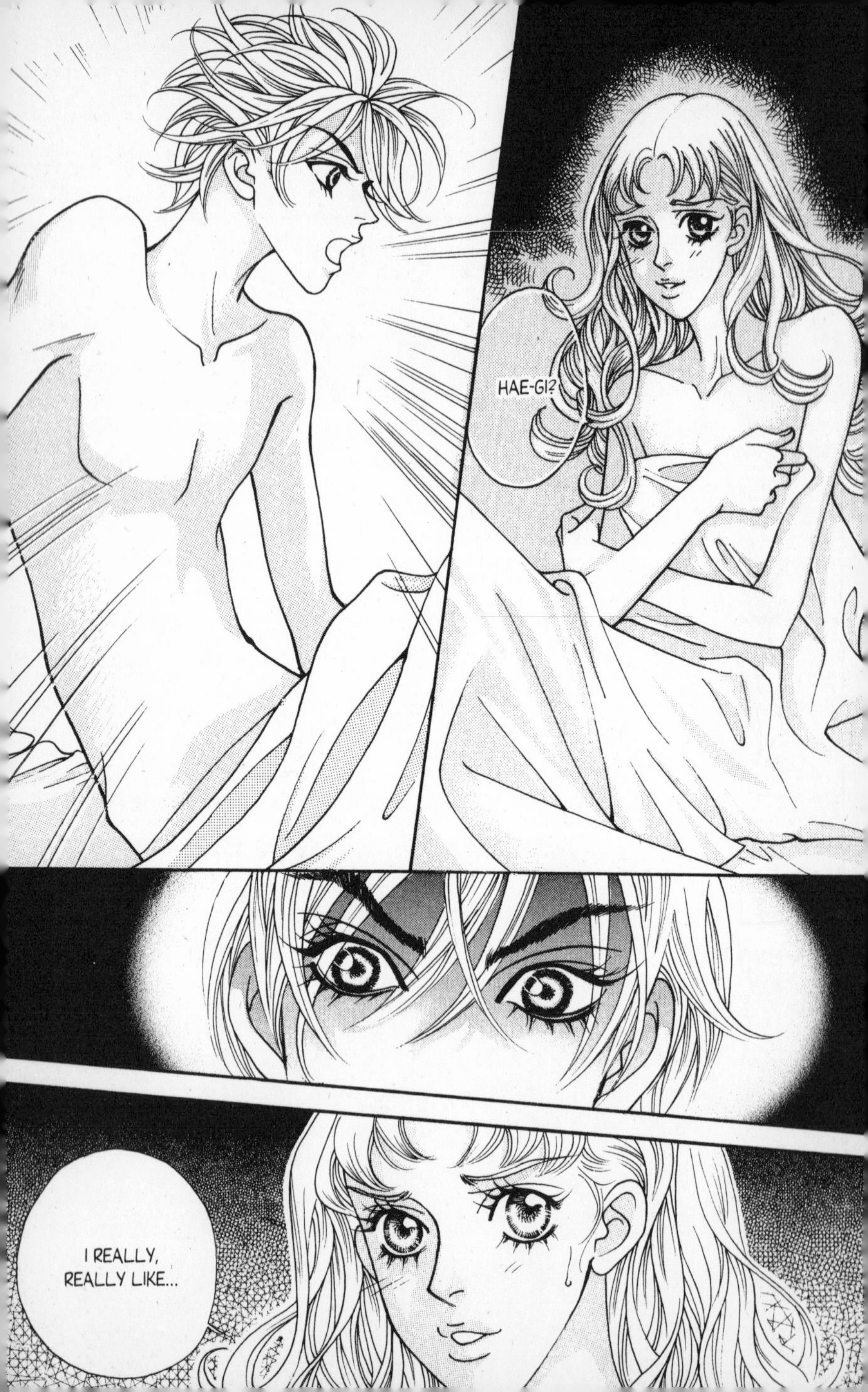
HAE-GI?
I REALLY, REALLY LIKE...

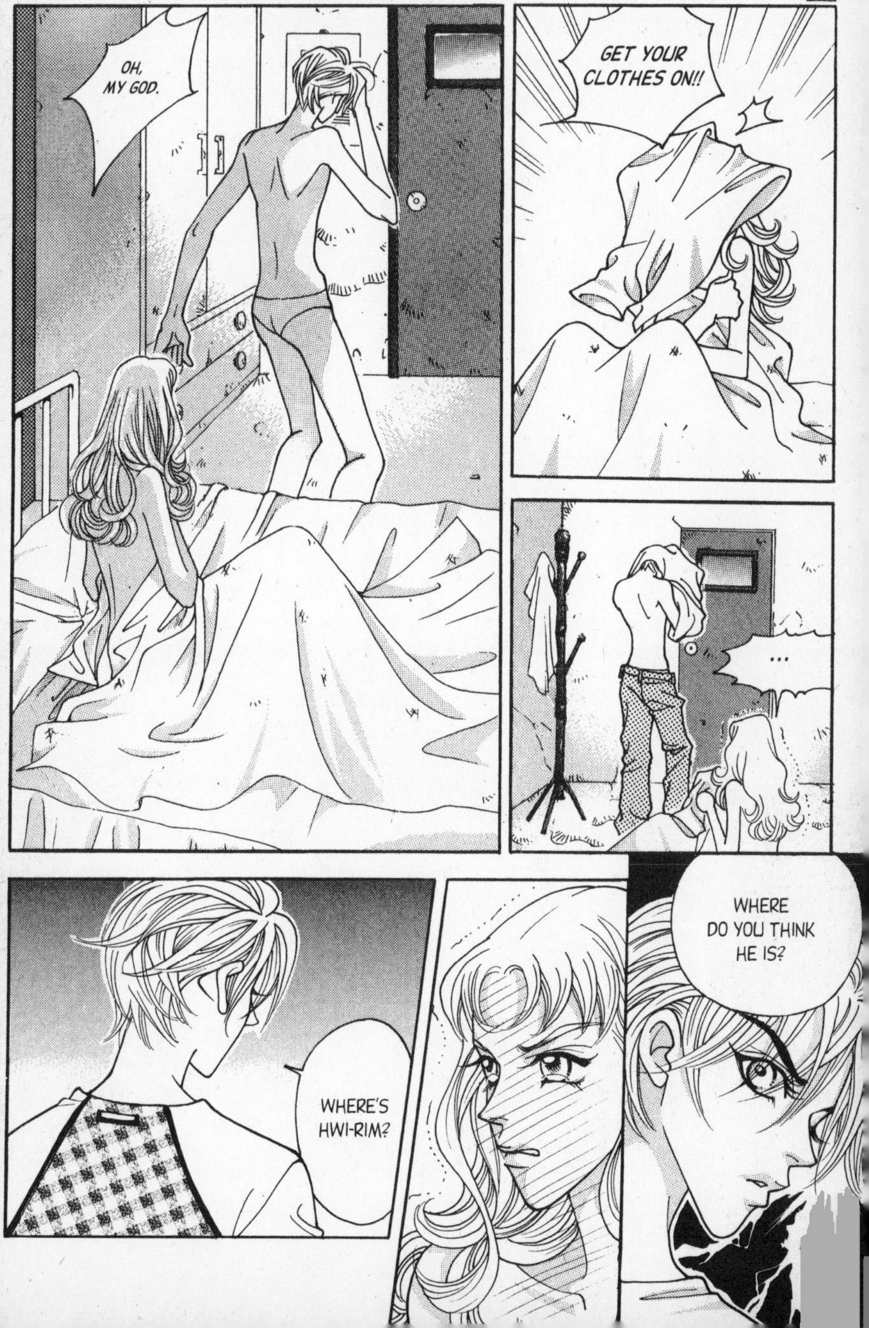
OH, MY GOD.
GET YOUR CLOTHES ON!!
...
WHERE'S HWI-RIM?
WHERE DO YOU THINK HE IS?

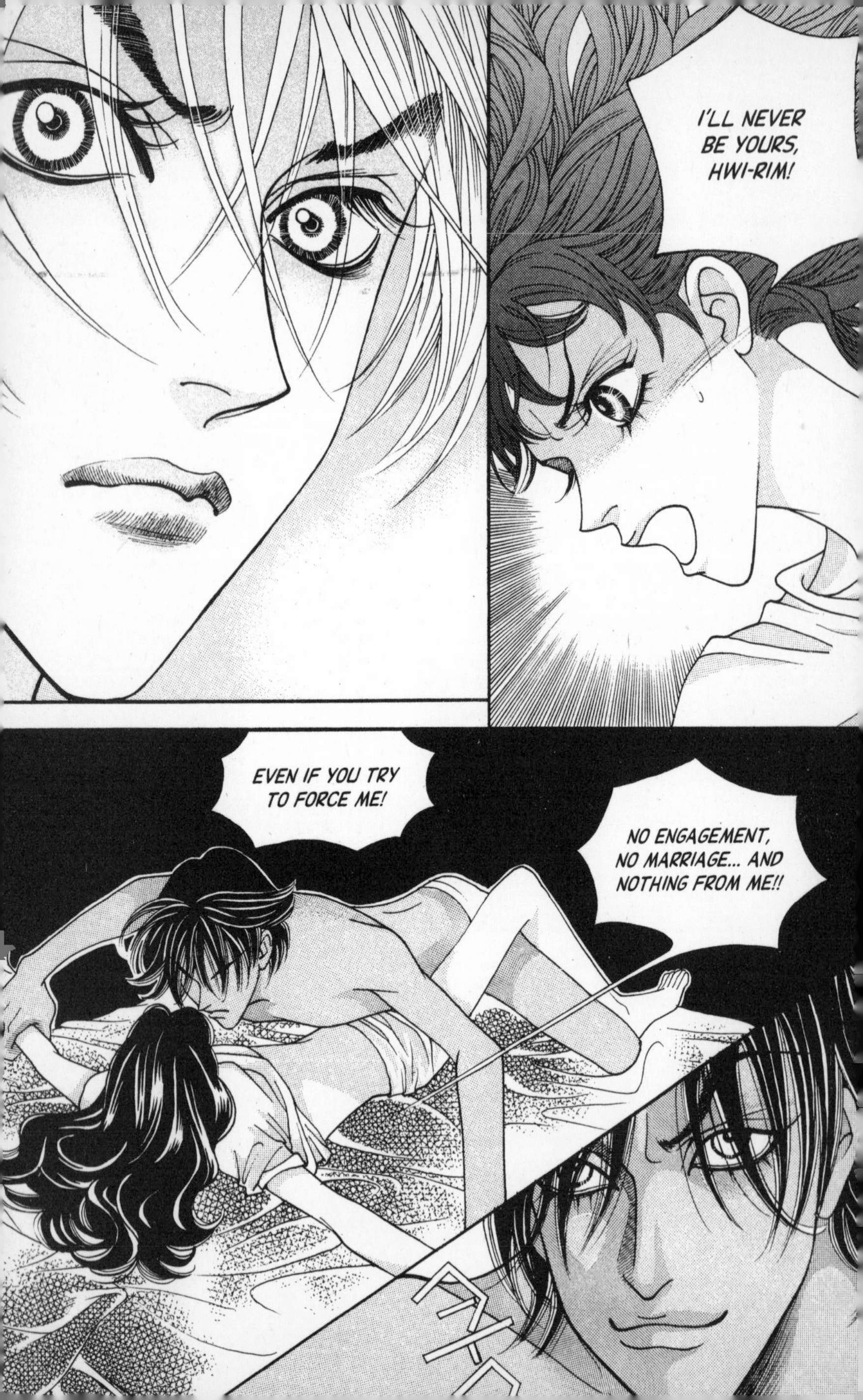
I'LL NEVER BE YOURS, HWI-RIM!
EVEN IF YOU TRY TO FORCE ME!
NO ENGAGEMENT, NO MARRIAGE... AND NOTHING FROM ME!!

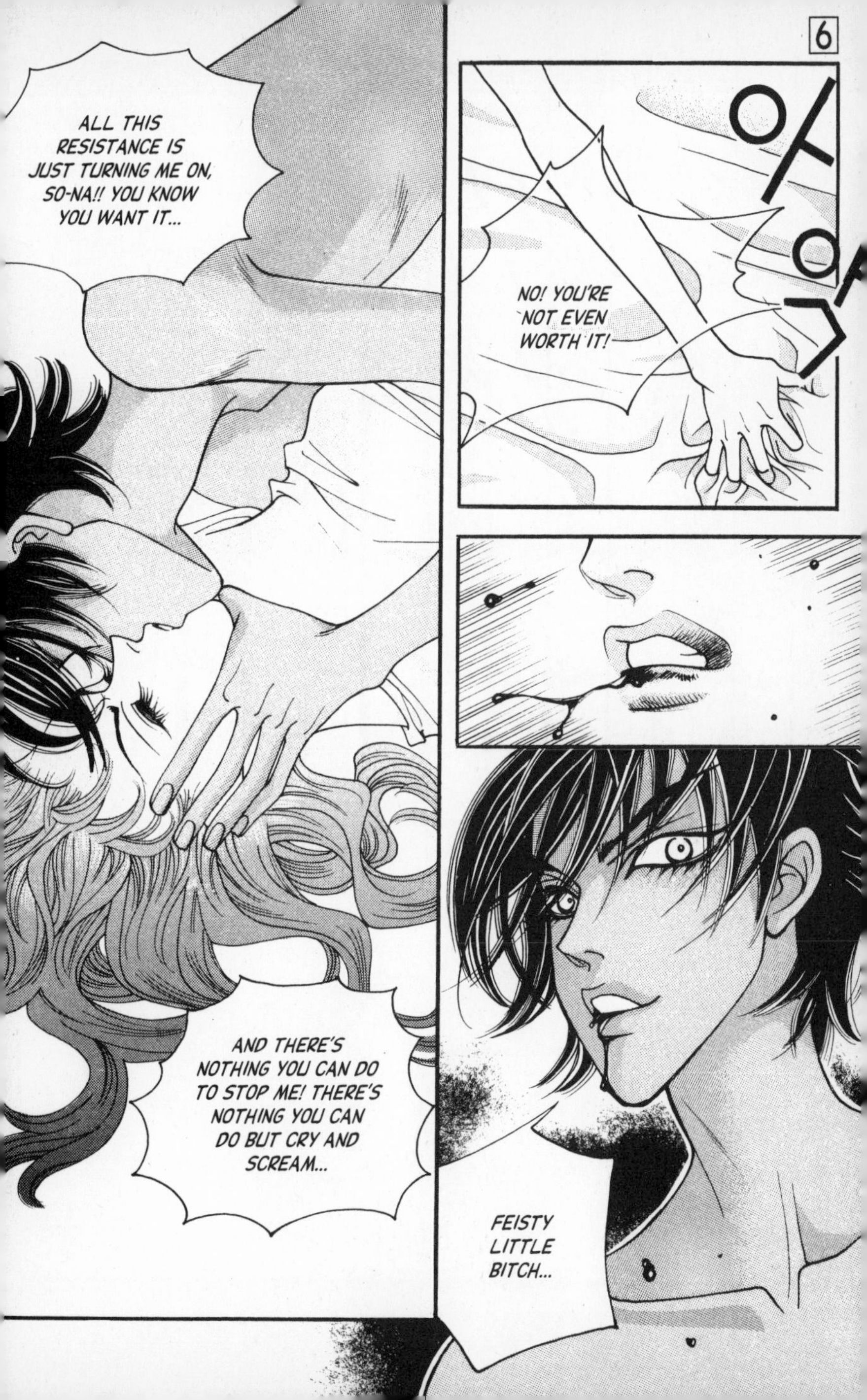
6
ALL THIS RESISTANCE IS JUST TURNING ME ON, SO-NA!! YOU KNOW YOU WANT IT...
AND THERE'S NOTHING YOU CAN DO TO STOP ME! THERE'S NOTHING YOU CAN DO BUT CRY AND SCREAM...
아악
NO! YOU'RE NOT EVEN WORTH IT!
FEISTY LITTLE BITCH...

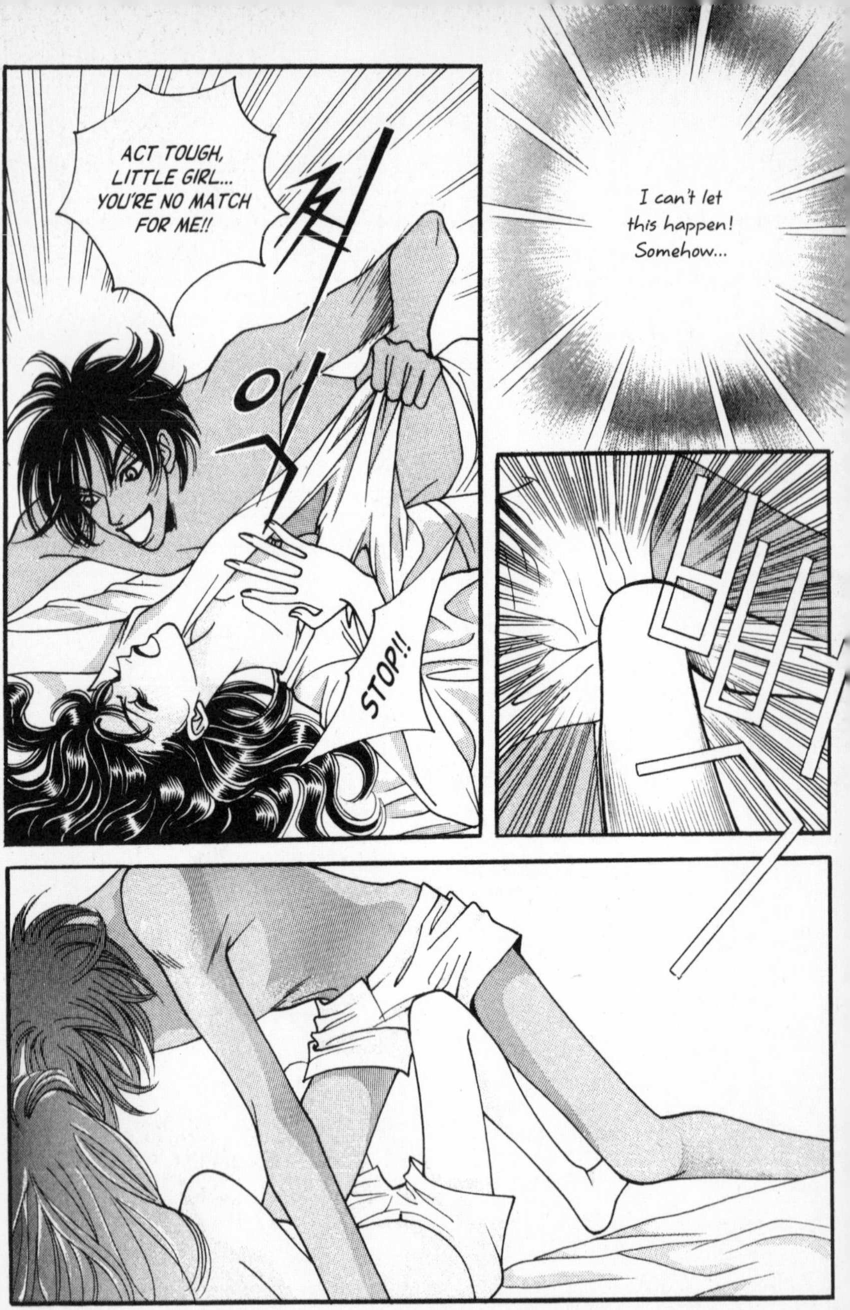
I can't let this happen! Somehow...
ACT TOUGH, LITTLE GIRL... YOU'RE NO MATCH FOR ME!!
STOP!!

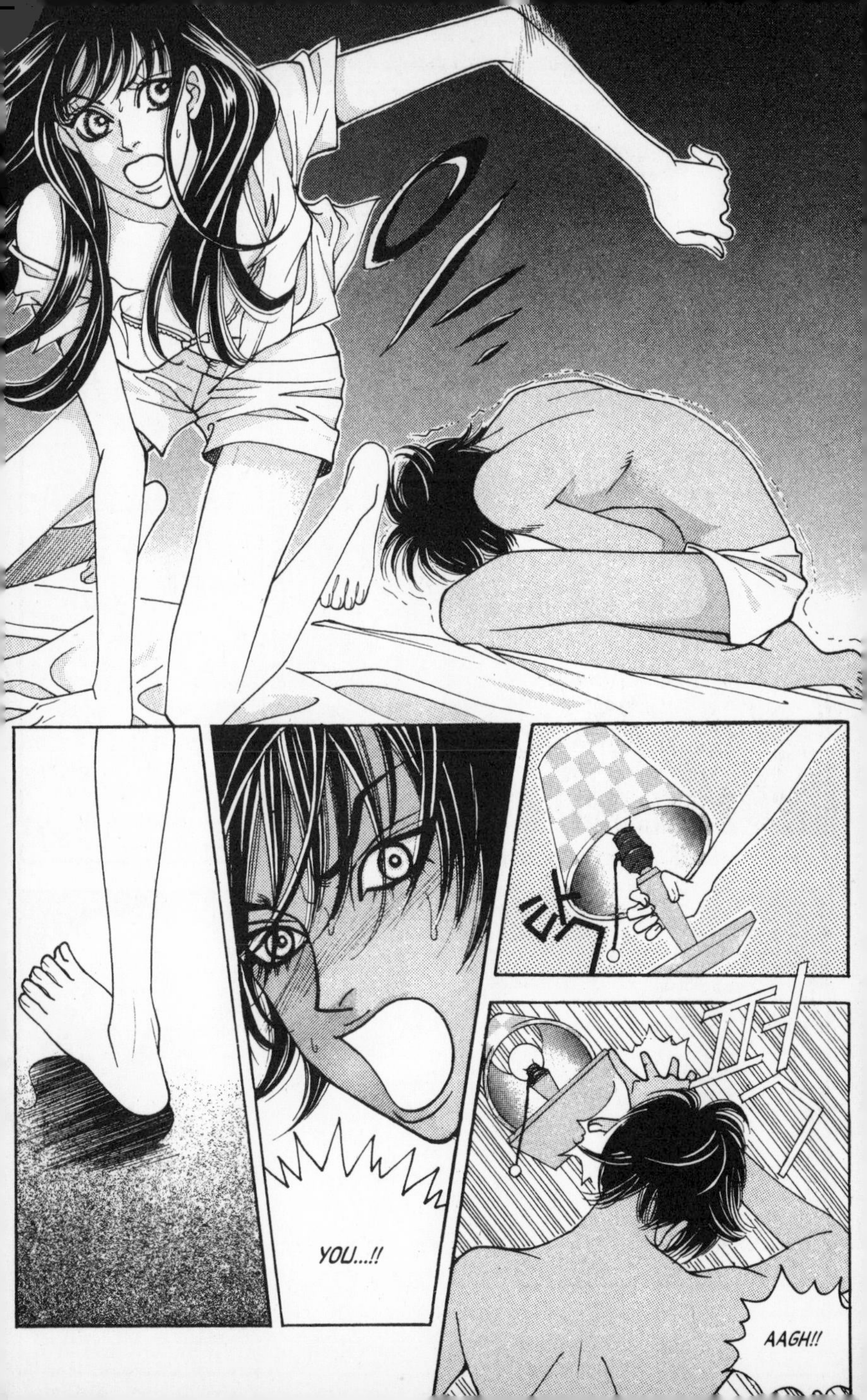
YOU...!!
AAGH!!

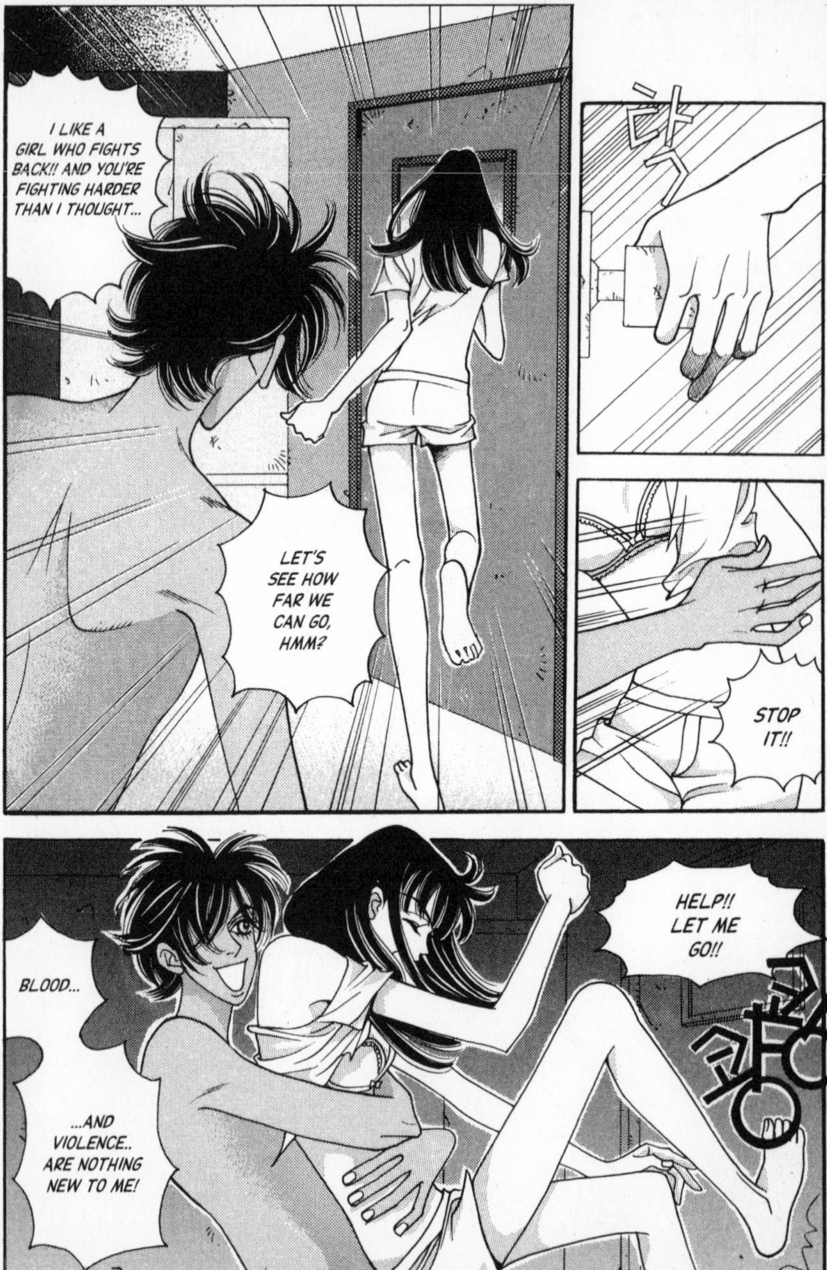
STOP IT!!
I LIKE A GIRL WHO FIGHTS BACK!! AND YOU'RE FIGHTING HARDER THAN I THOUGHT...
LET'S SEE HOW FAR WE CAN GO, HMM?
HELP!! LET ME GO!!
BLOOD...
...AND VIOLENCE.. ARE NOTHING NEW TO ME!

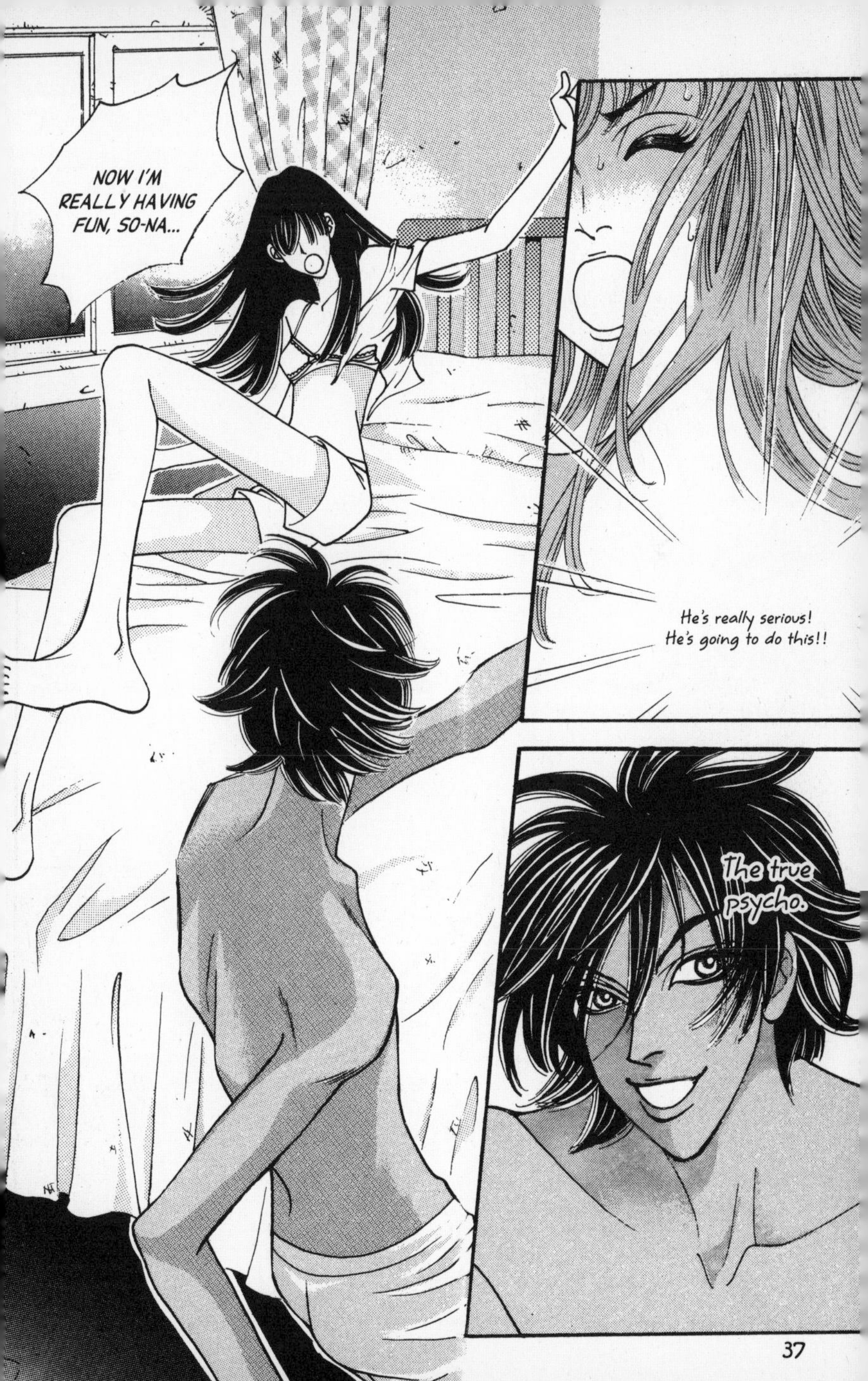
He's really serious!
He's going to do this!!
NOW I'M REALLY HAVING FUN, SO-NA...
The true psycho.

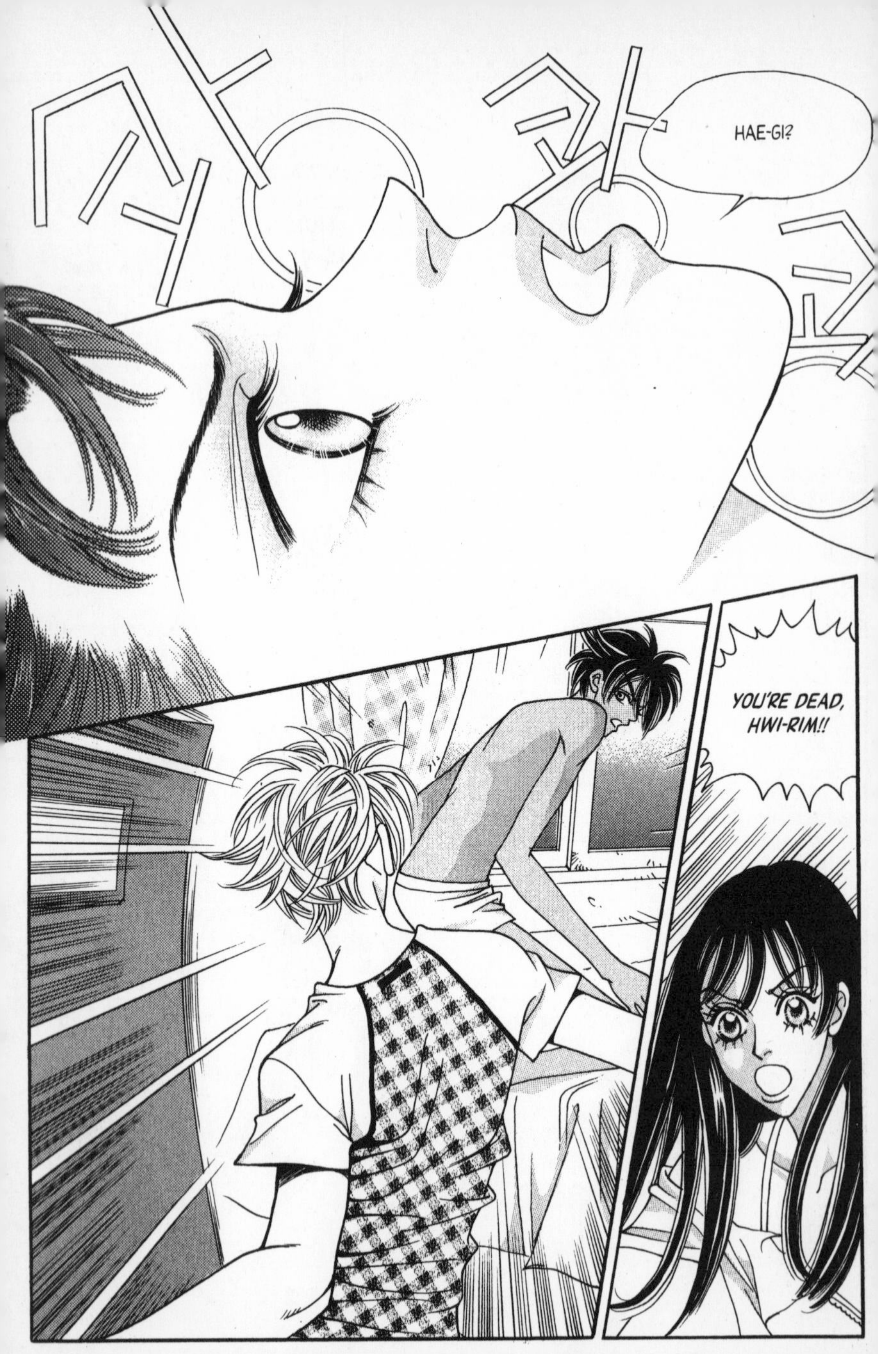
HAE-GI?
YOU'RE DEAD, HWI-RIM!!

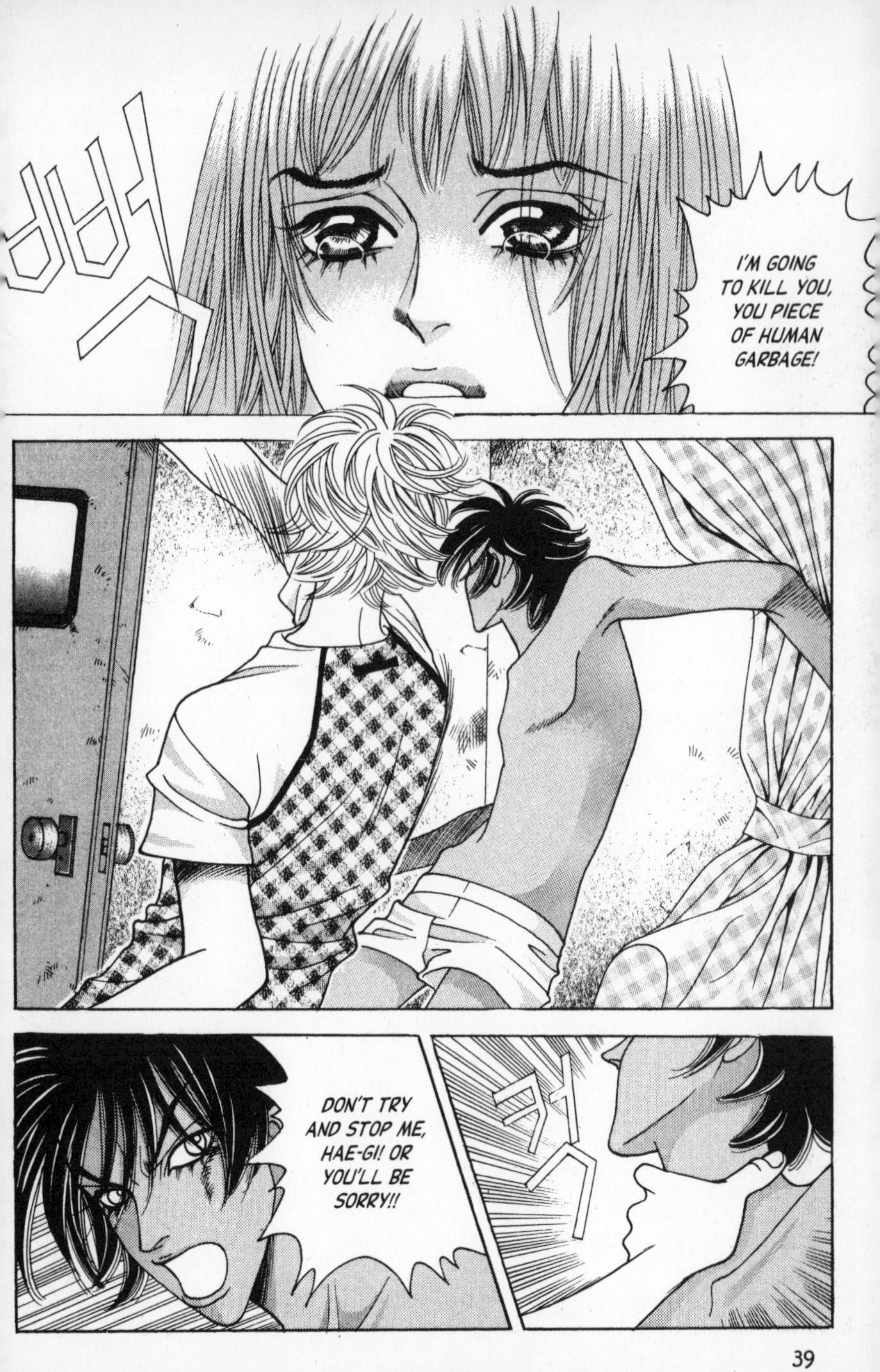
I'M GOING TO KILL YOU, YOU PIECE OF HUMAN GARBAGE!
DON'T TRY AND STOP ME, HAE-GI! OR YOU'LL BE SORRY!!

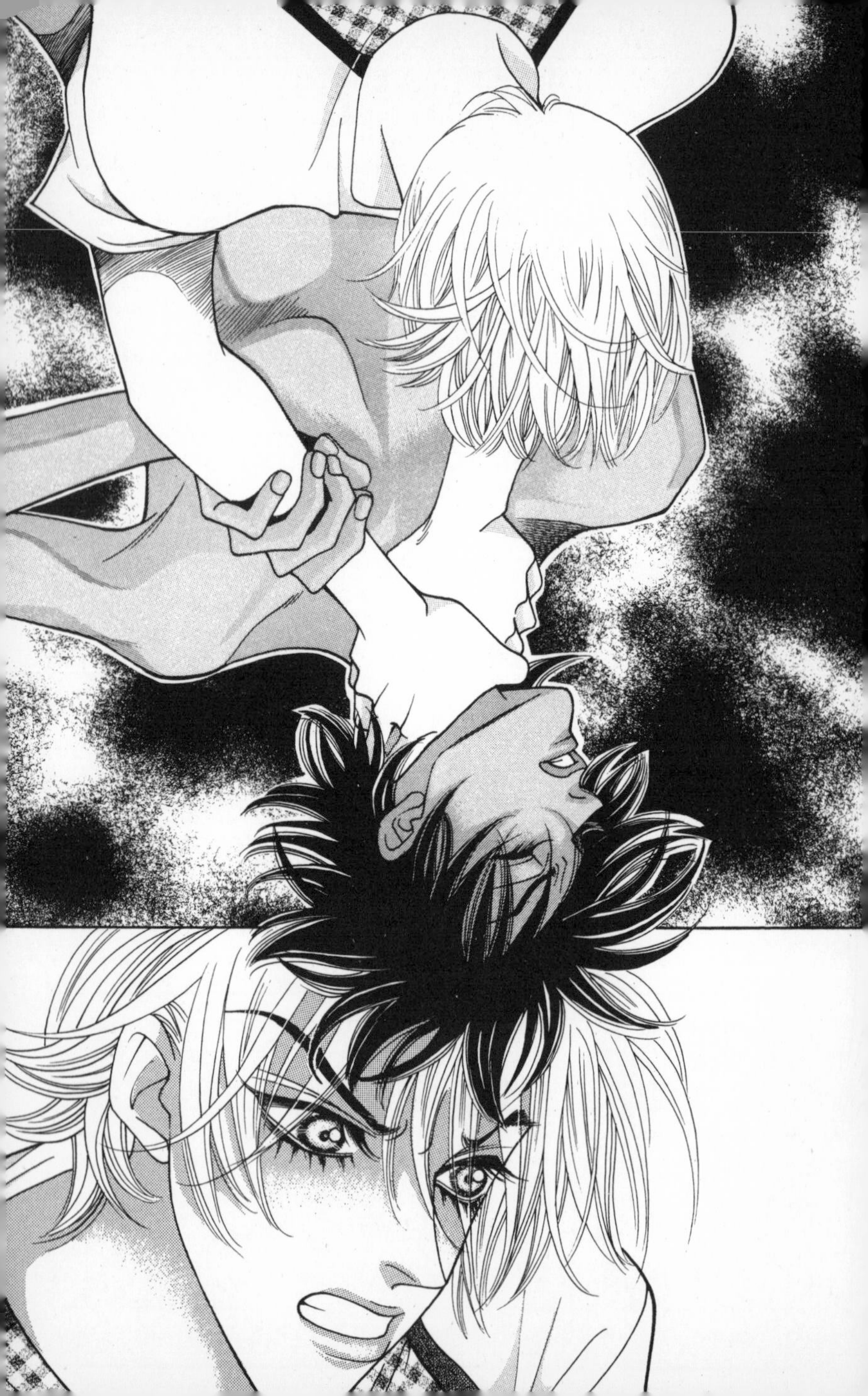

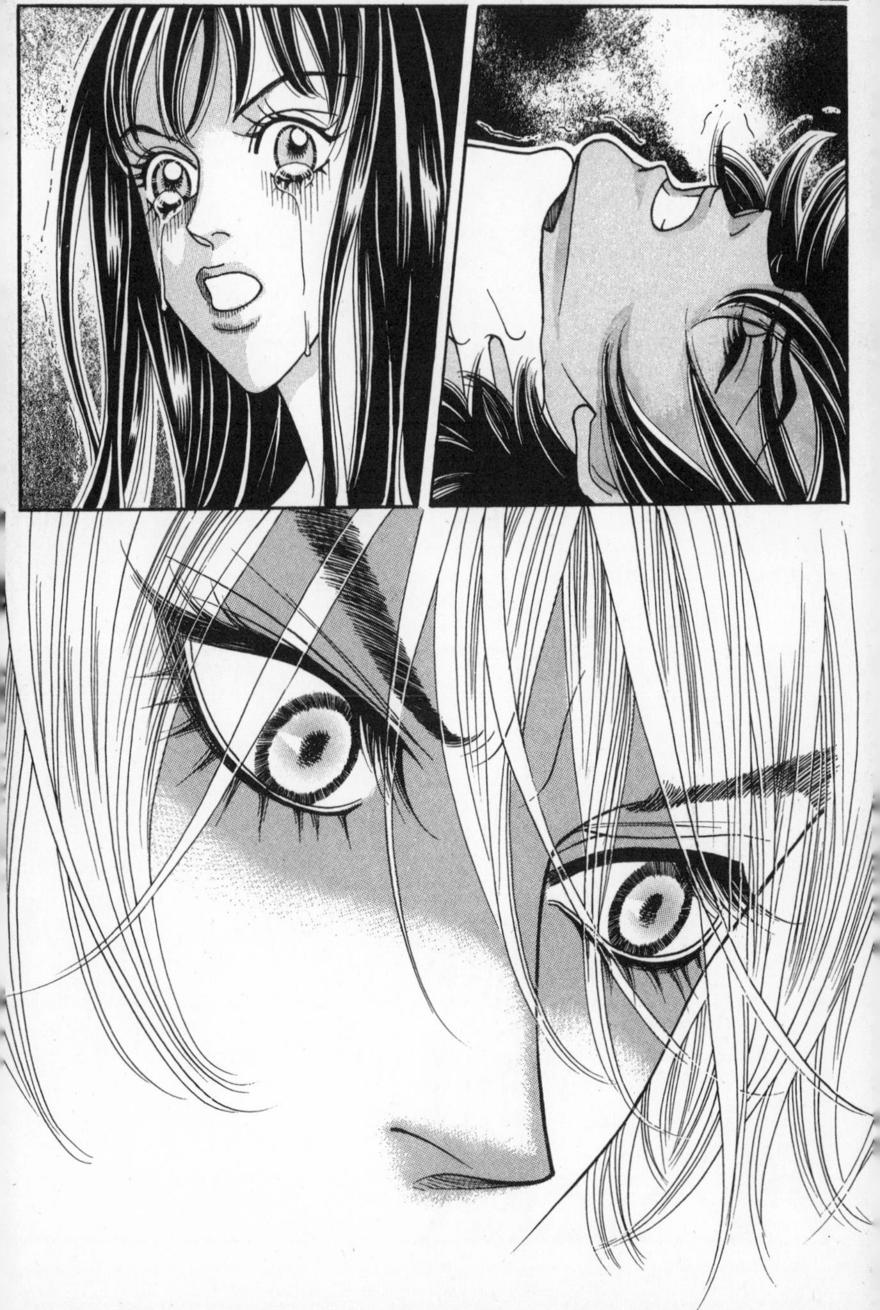

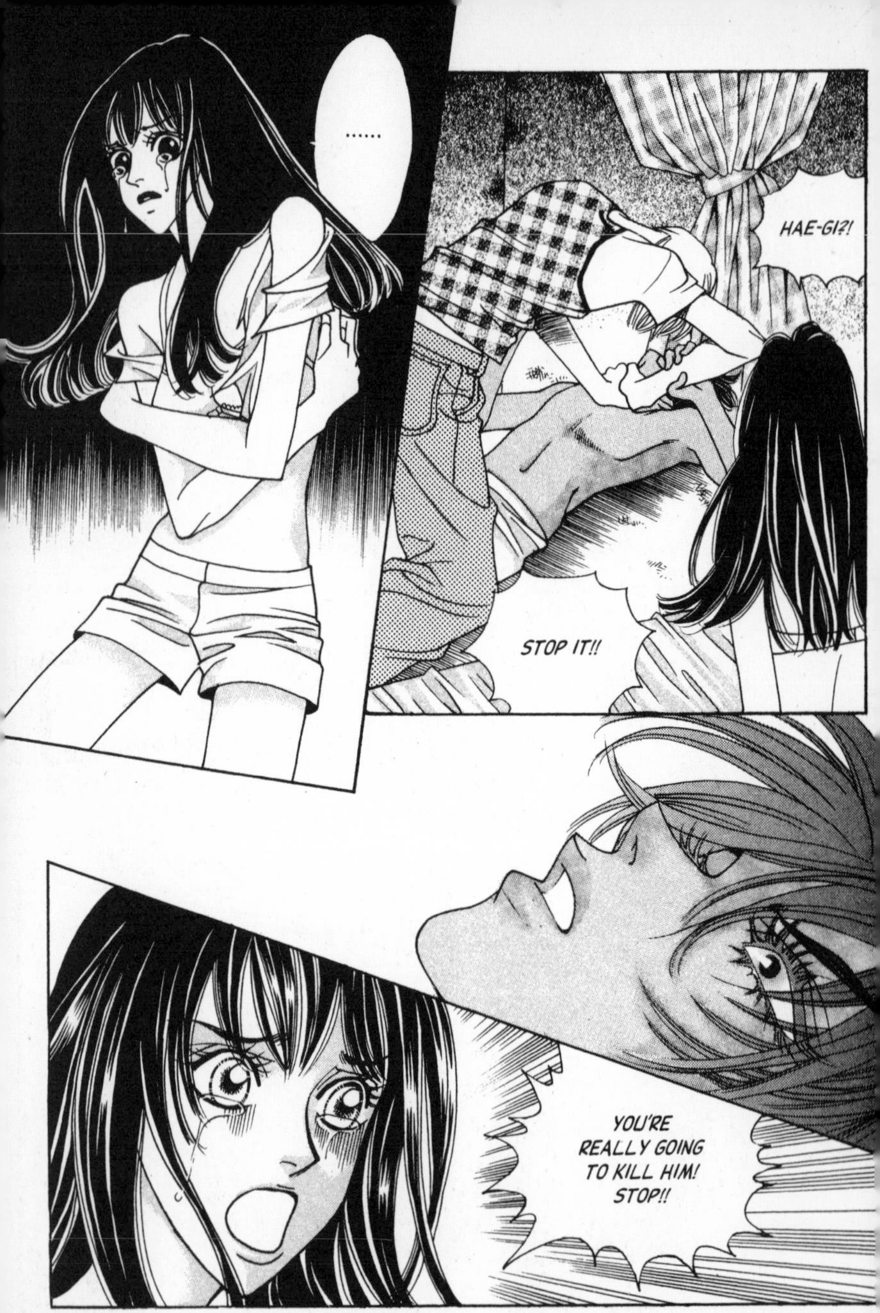
HAE-GI?!
STOP IT!!
......
YOU'RE REALLY GOING TO KILL HIM! STOP!!

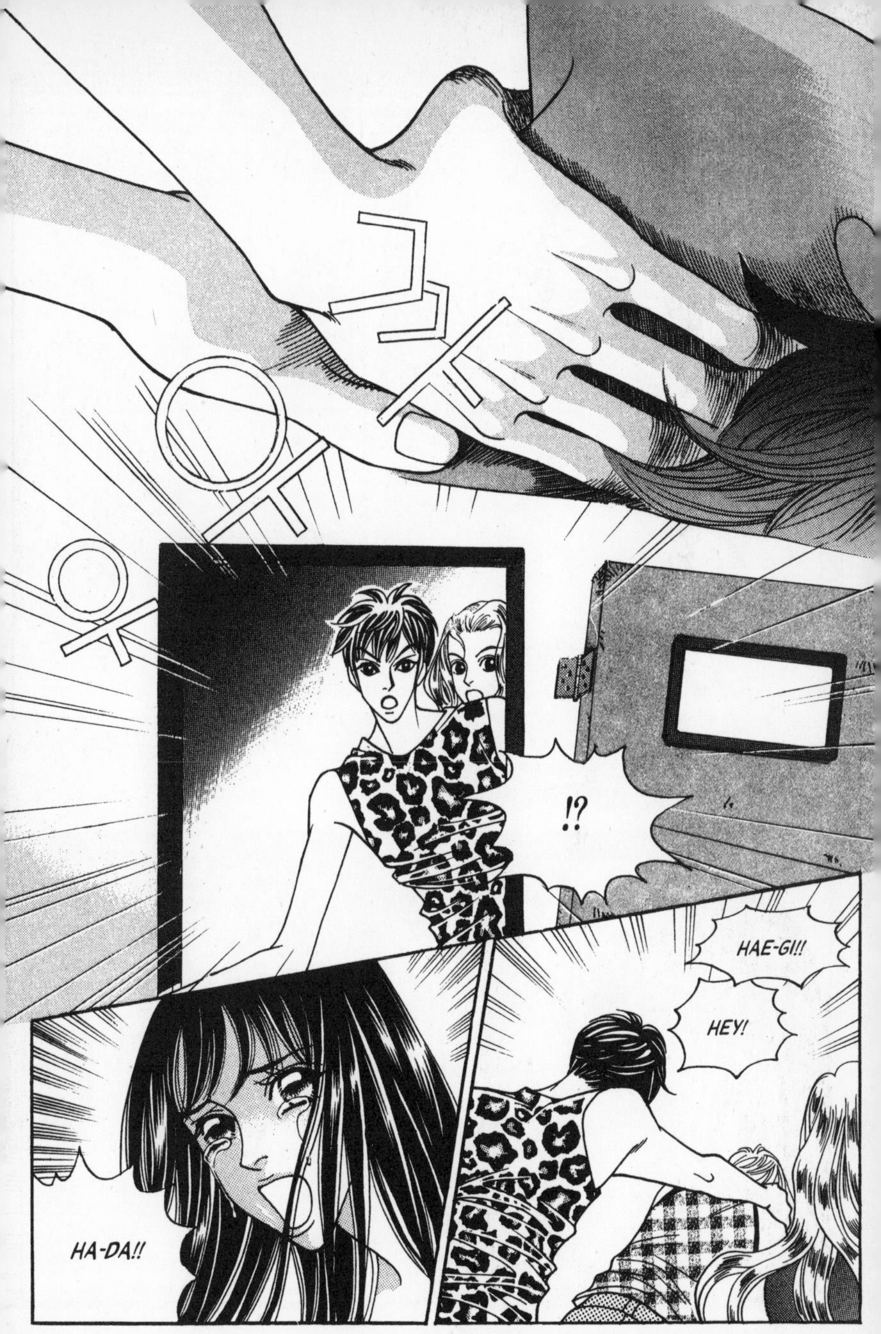
!?
HA-DA!!
HAE-GI!!
HEY!

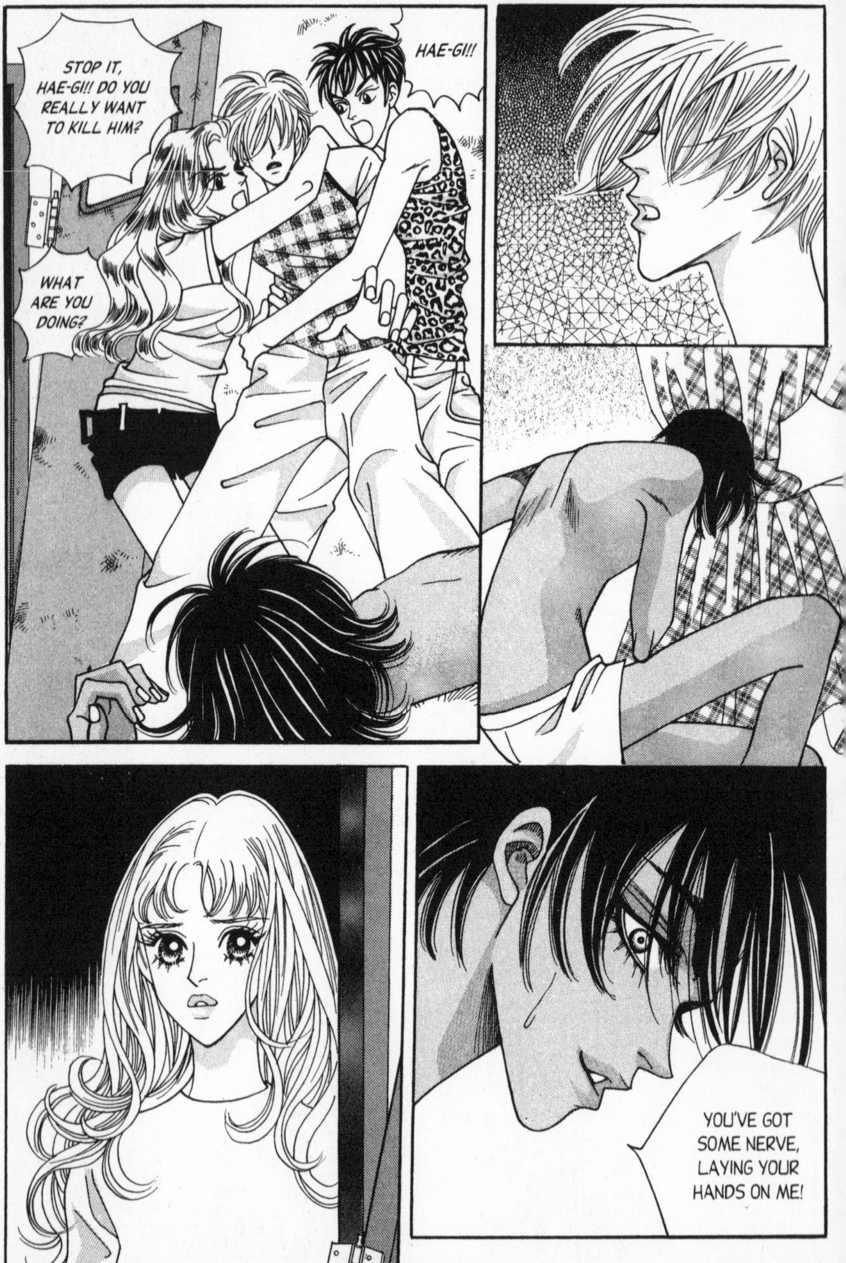
STOP IT, HAE-GI!! DO YOU REALLY WANT TO KILL HIM?
HAE-GI!!
WHAT ARE YOU DOING?
YOU'VE GOT SOME NERVE, LAYING YOUR HANDS ON ME!

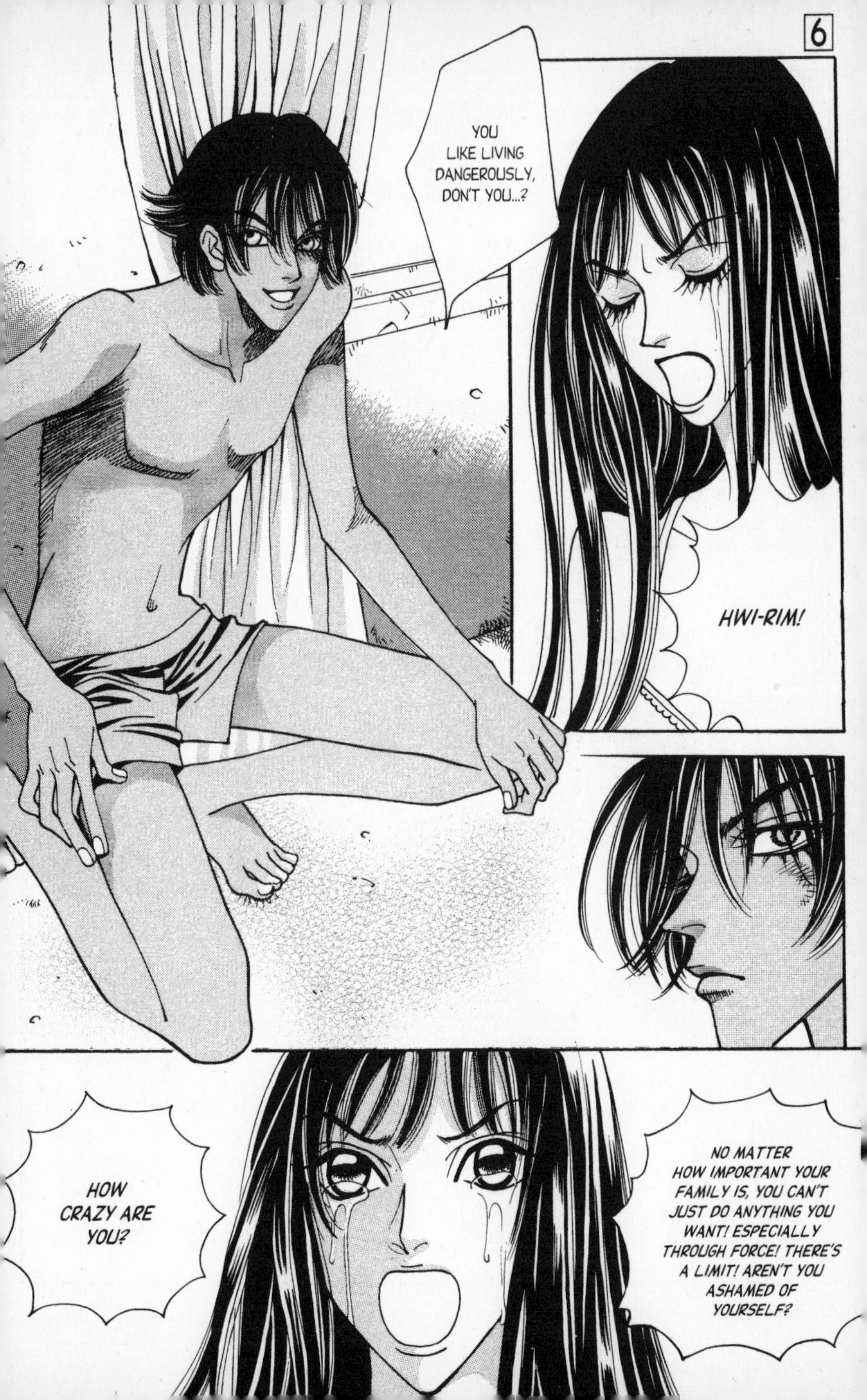
YOU LIKE LIVING DANGEROUSLY, DON'T YOU...?
HWI-RIM!
HOW CRAZY ARE YOU?
NO MATTER HOW IMPORTANT YOUR FAMILY IS, YOU CAN'T JUST DO ANYTHING YOU WANT! ESPECIALLY THROUGH FORCE! THERE'S A LIMIT! AREN'T YOU ASHAMED OF YOURSELF?

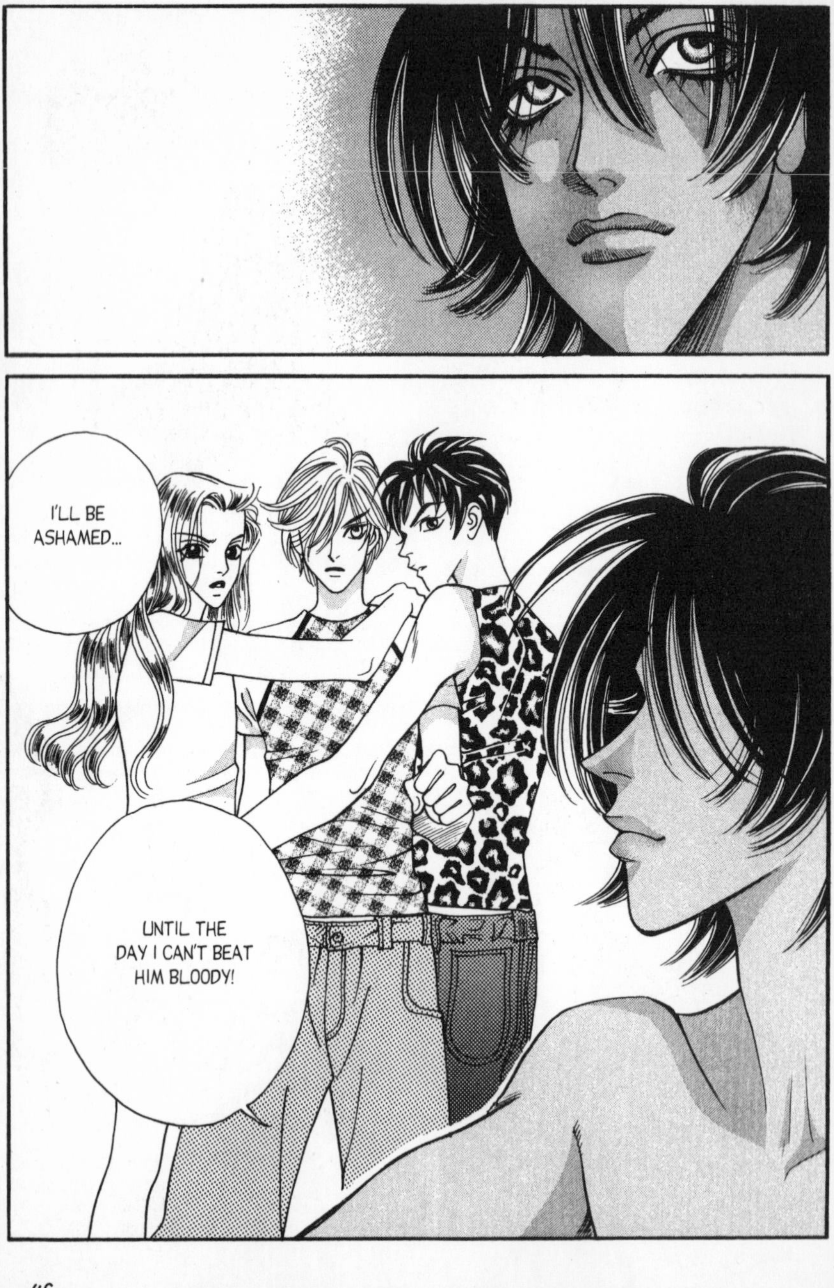
I'LL BE ASHAMED...
UNTIL THE DAY I CAN'T BEAT HIM BLOODY!

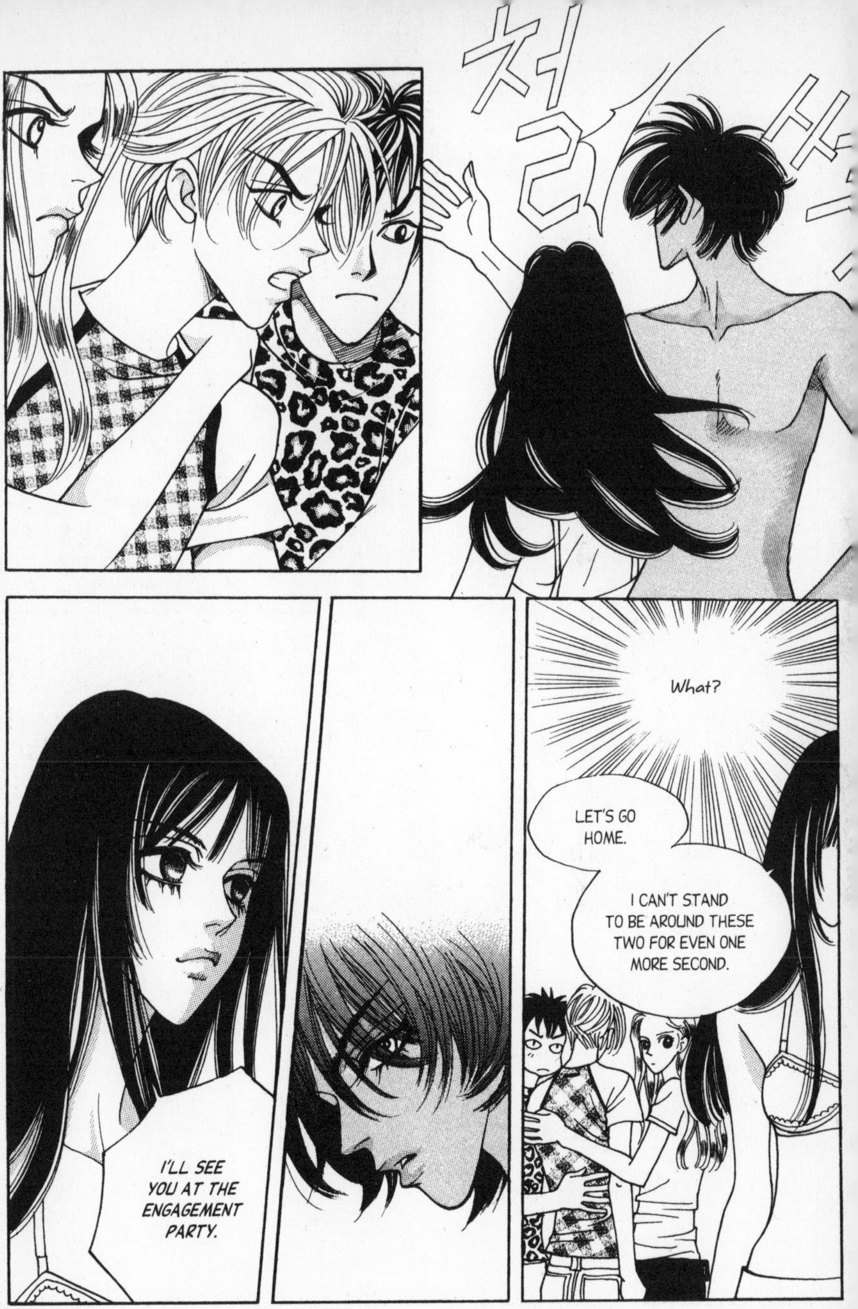
I'LL SEE YOU AT THE ENGAGEMENT PARTY.
What?
LET'S GO HOME.
I CAN'T STAND TO BE AROUND THESE TWO FOR EVEN ONE MORE SECOND.

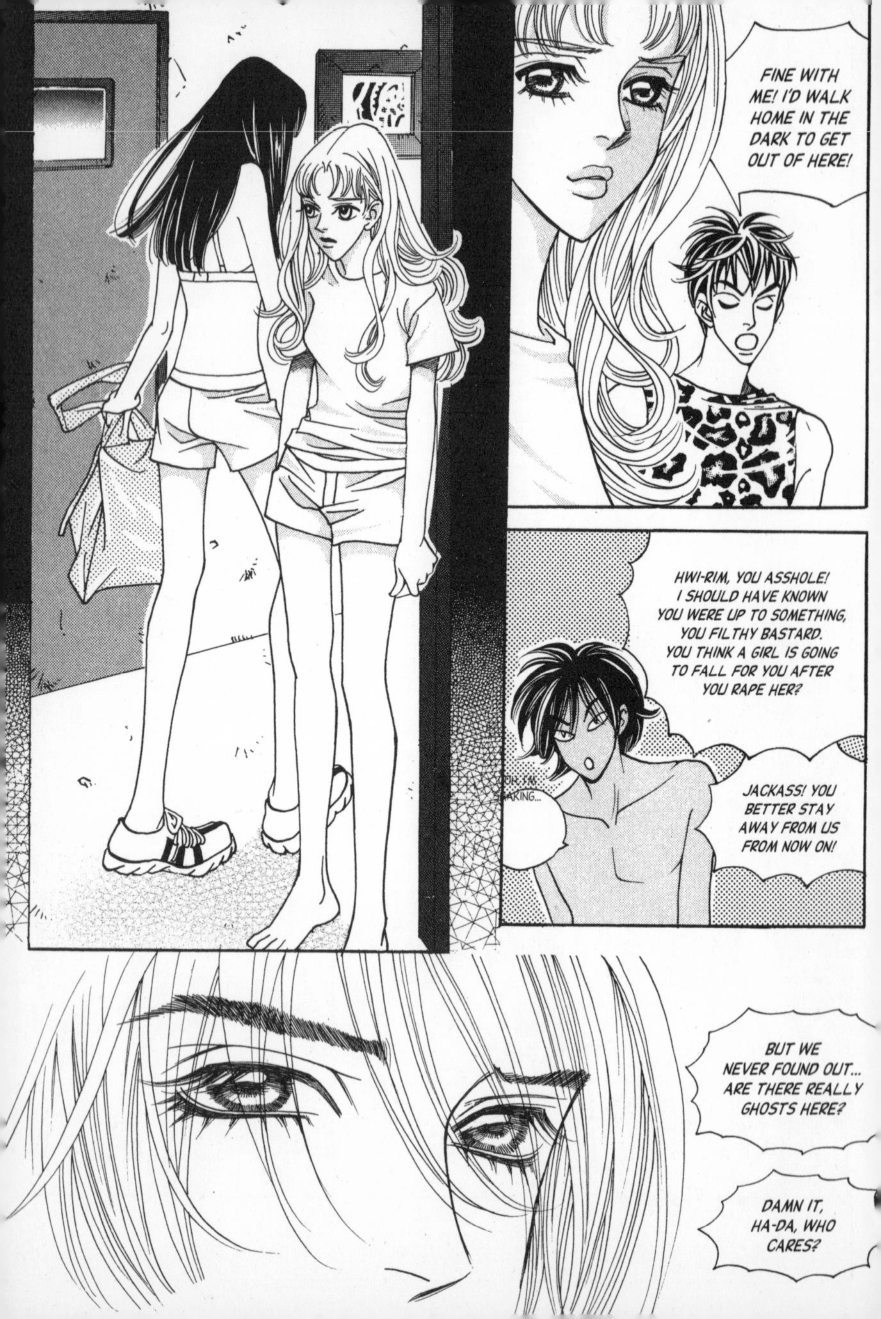
FINE WITH ME! I'D WALK HOME IN THE DARK TO GET OUT OF HERE!
HWI-RIM, YOU ASSHOLE! I SHOULD HAVE KNOWN YOU WERE UP TO SOMETHING, YOU FILTHY BASTARD. YOU THINK A GIRL IS GOING TO FALL FOR YOU AFTER YOU RAPE HER?
JACKASS! YOU BETTER STAY AWAY FROM US FROM NOW ON!
BUT WE NEVER FOUND OUT... ARE THERE REALLY GHOSTS HERE?
DAMN IT, HA-DA, WHO CARES?

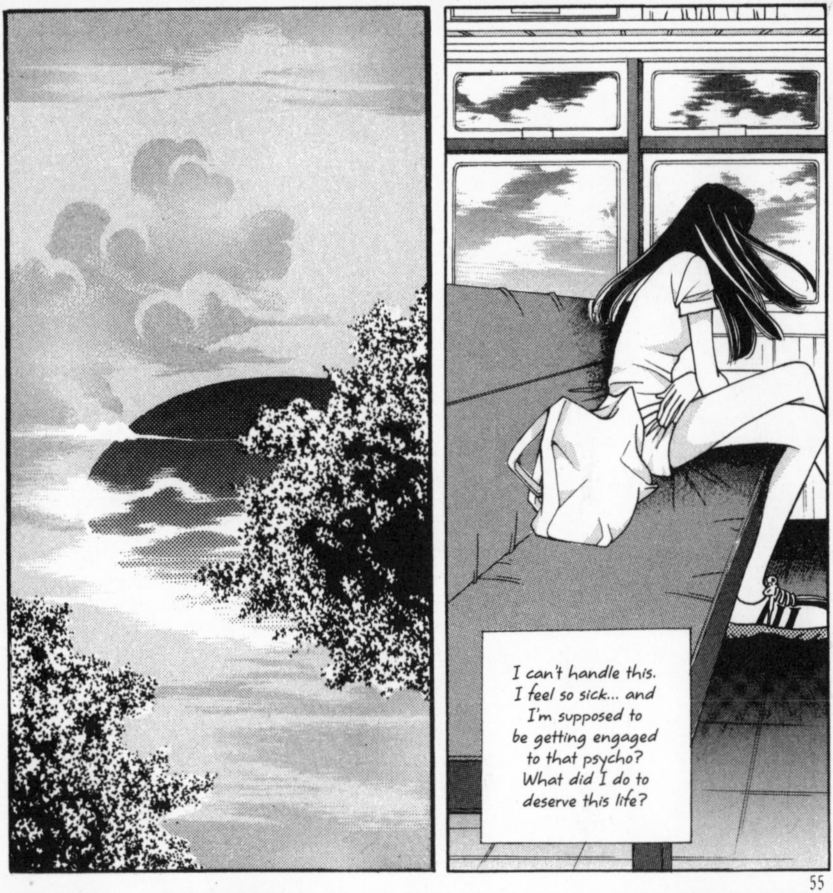
I can't handle this. I feel so sick... and I'm supposed to be getting engaged to that psycho? What did I do to deserve this life?

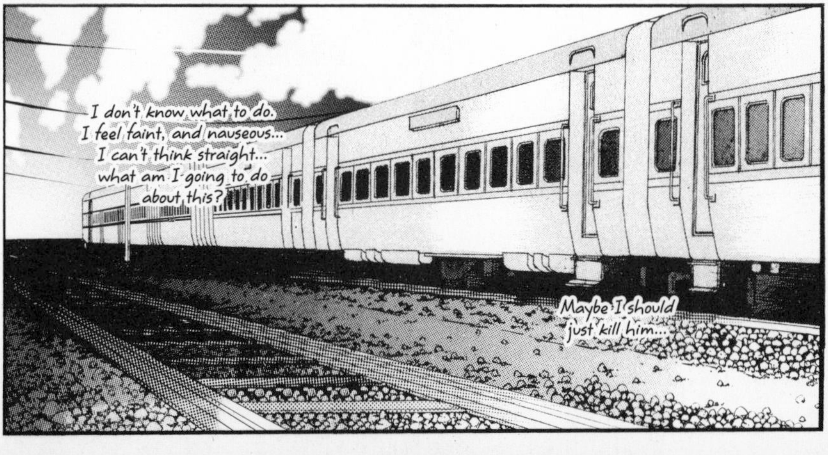
I don't know what to do. I feel faint, and nauseous... I can't think straight... what am I going to do about this?
Maybe I should just kill him...

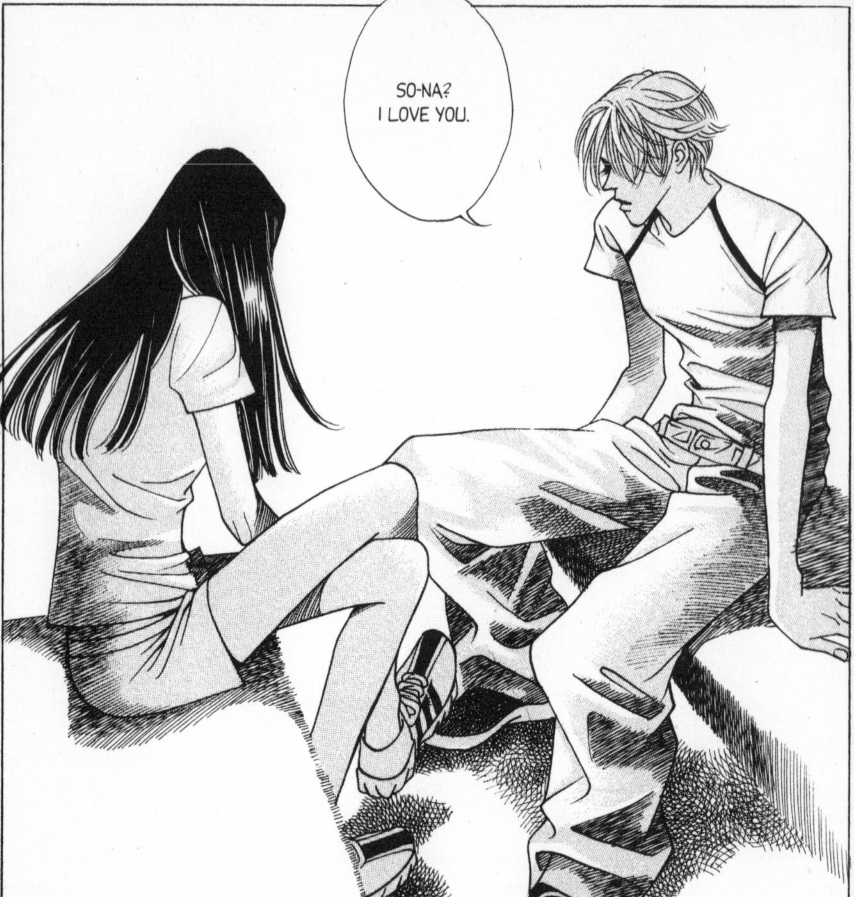
SO-NA? I LOVE YOU.
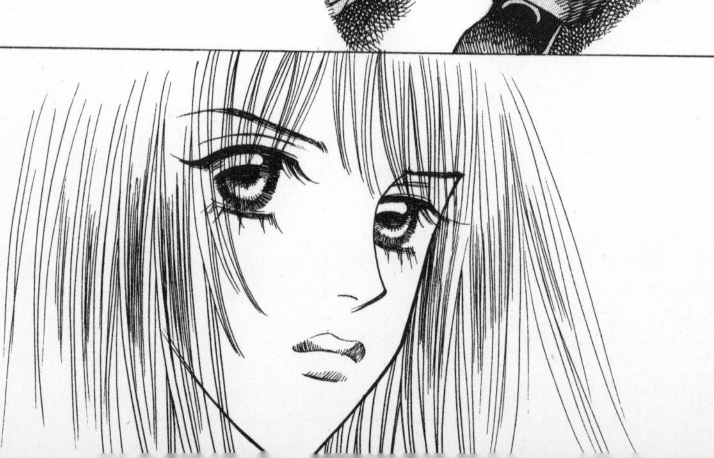

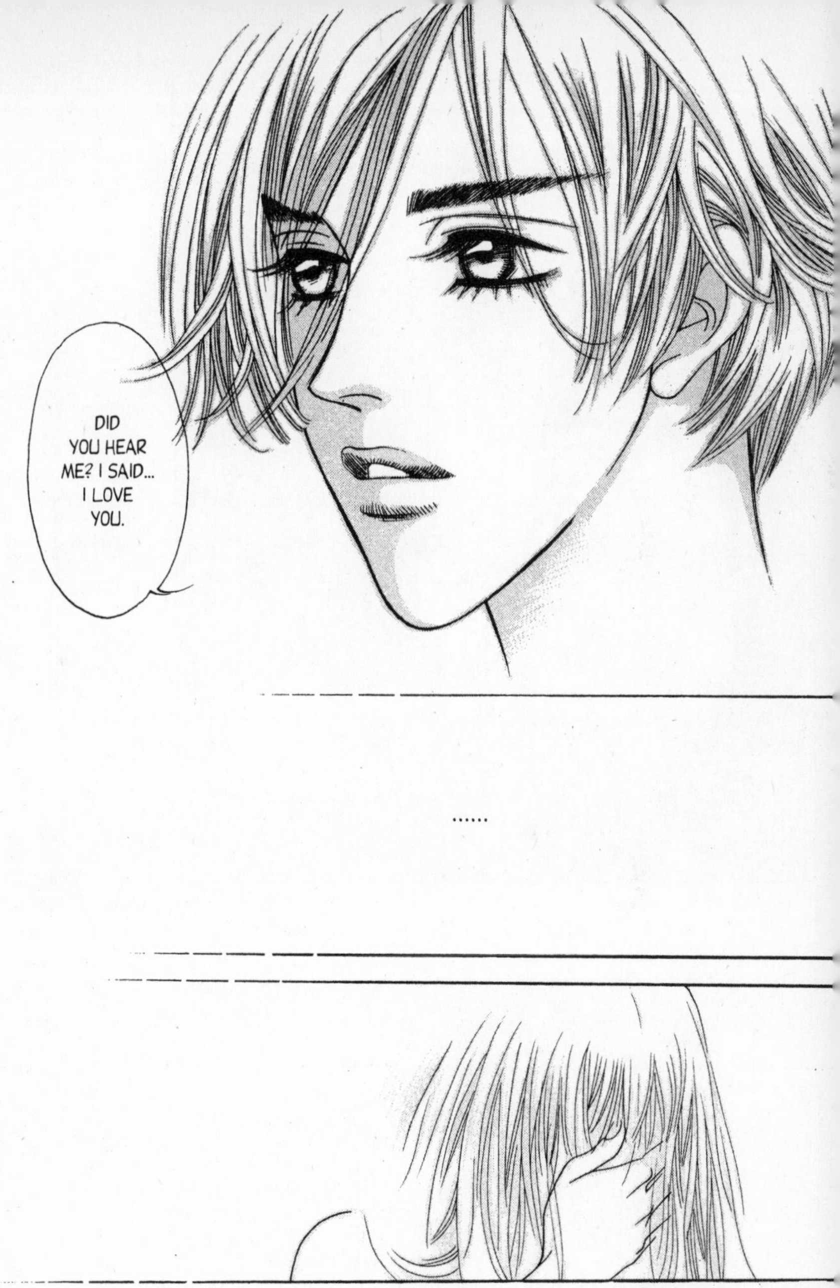
DID YOU HEAR ME? I SAID... I LOVE YOU.
......

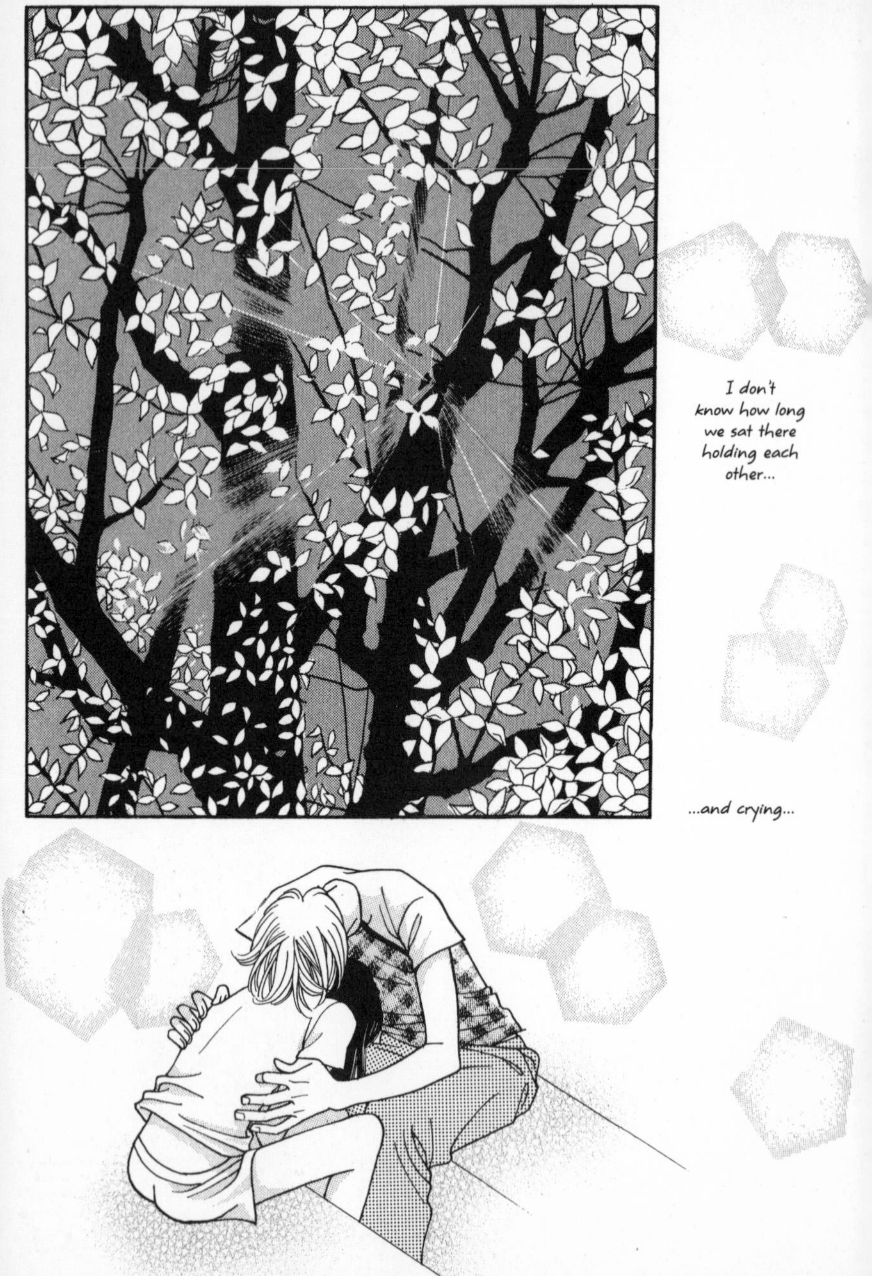
I don't know how long we sat there holding each other...
...and crying...

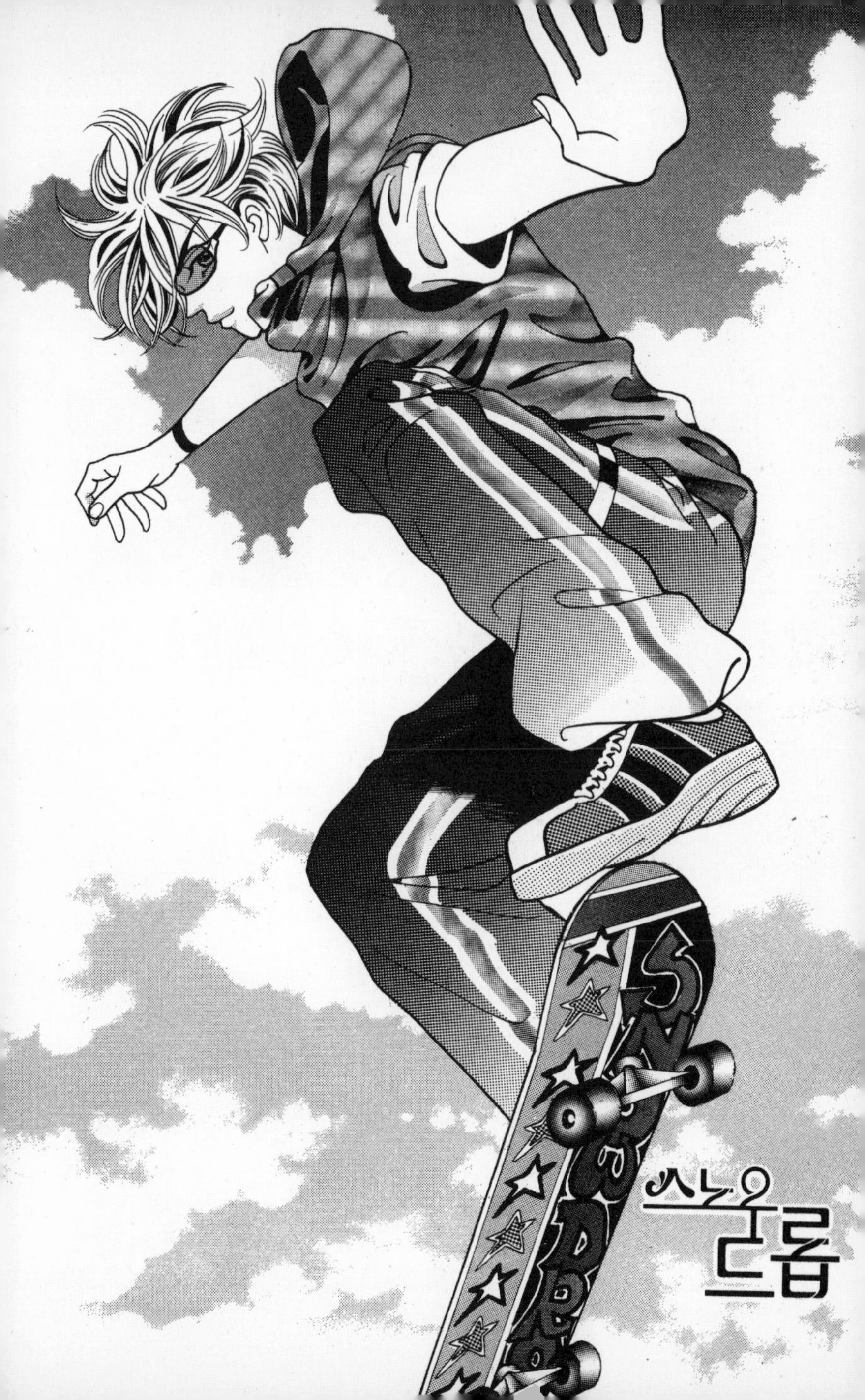
스노우 드롭

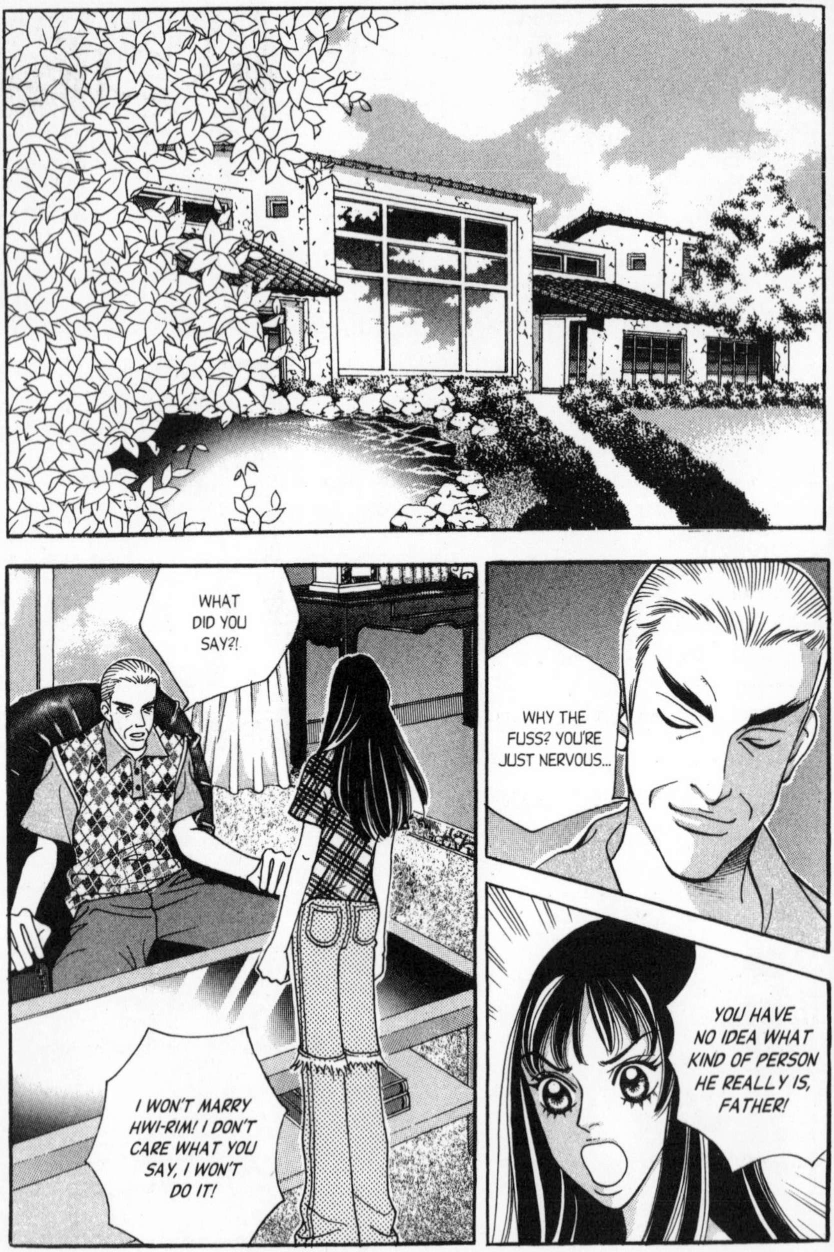
I WON'T MARRY HWI-RIM! I DON'T CARE WHAT YOU SAY, I WON'T DO IT!
WHAT DID YOU SAY?!
WHY THE FUSS? YOU'RE JUST NERVOUS...
YOU HAVE NO IDEA WHAT KIND OF PERSON HE REALLY IS, FATHER!

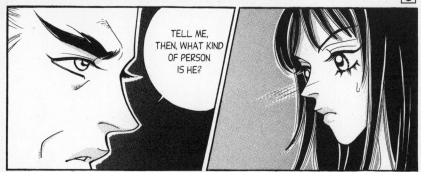

TELL ME, THEN, WHAT KIND OF PERSON IS HE?

HE'S COMPLETELY SCHIZO! HE ACTS LIKE SOME MODEL STUDENT IN FRONT OF YOU AND OTHER GROWN-UPS, BUT THE REST OF THE TIME HE'S A DISGUSTING, PERVERTED CREEP! I'VE NEVER MET ANYONE AS HORRIBLE AS HIM!

THE THINGS HE DOES -- I CAN'T EVEN TELL YOU! HE'S A TOTALLY UNBALANCED PSYCHO!!

REALLY, SO-NA. COULD AN "UNBALANCED PSYCHO" BE NUMBER ONE IN HIS CLASS?

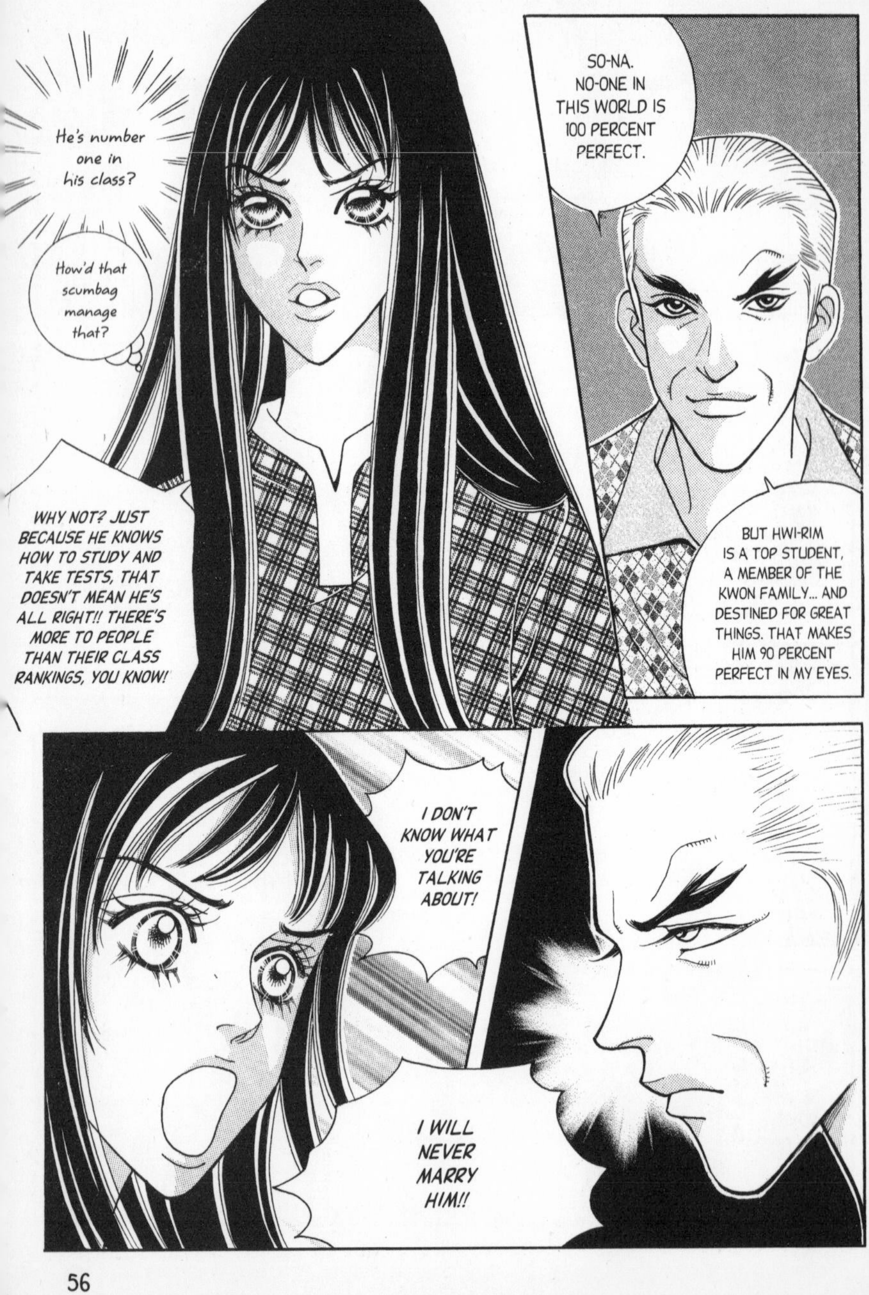
He's number one in his class?
How'd that scumbag manage that?
WHY NOT? JUST BECAUSE HE KNOWS HOW TO STUDY AND TAKE TESTS, THAT DOESN'T MEAN HE'S ALL RIGHT!! THERE'S MORE TO PEOPLE THAN THEIR CLASS RANKINGS, YOU KNOW!
SO-NA. NO-ONE IN THIS WORLD IS 100 PERCENT PERFECT.
BUT HWI-RIM IS A TOP STUDENT, A MEMBER OF THE KWON FAMILY... AND DESTINED FOR GREAT THINGS. THAT MAKES HIM 90 PERCENT PERFECT IN MY EYES.
I DON'T KNOW WHAT YOU'RE TALKING ABOUT!
I WILL NEVER MARRY HIM!!

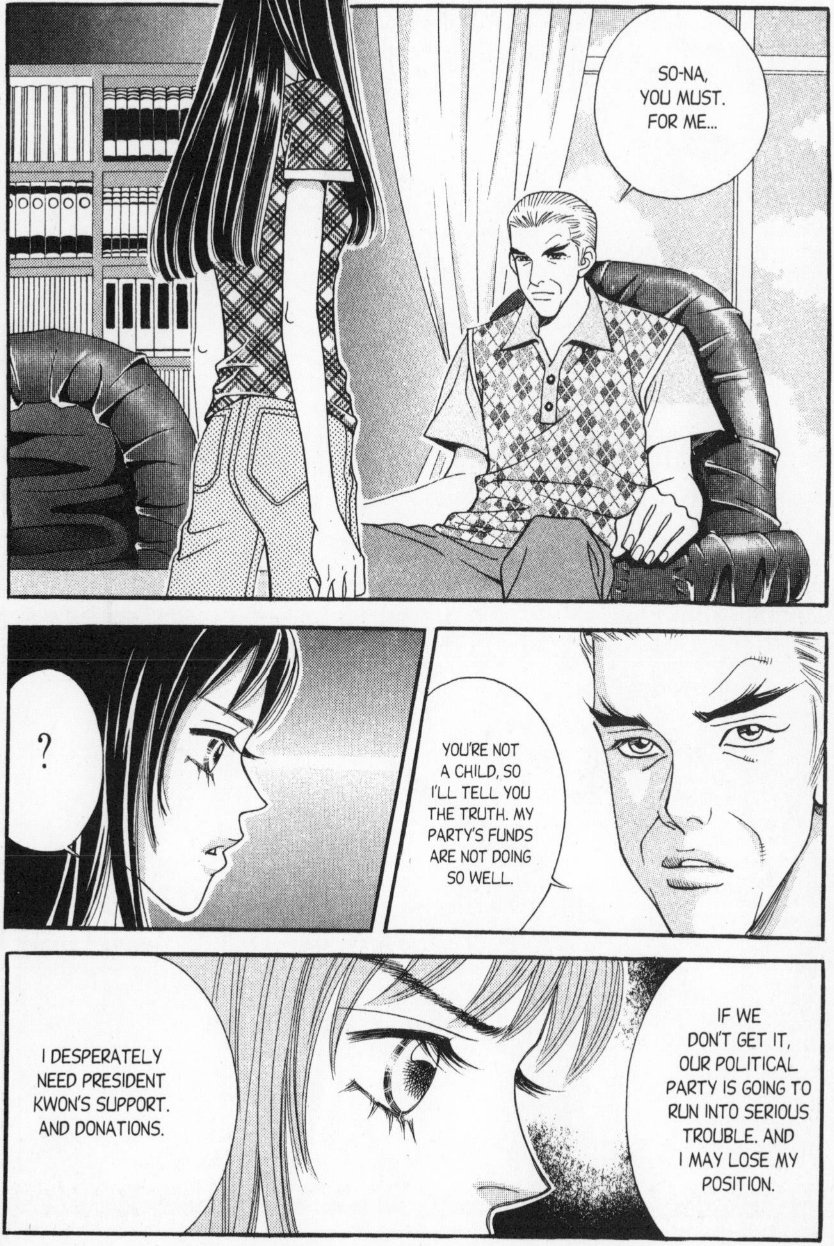
SO-NA, YOU MUST. FOR ME...
?
YOU'RE NOT A CHILD, SO I'LL TELL YOU THE TRUTH. MY PARTY'S FUNDS ARE NOT DOING SO WELL.
I DESPERATELY NEED PRESIDENT KWON'S SUPPORT. AND DONATIONS.
IF WE DON'T GET IT, OUR POLITICAL PARTY IS GOING TO RUN INTO SERIOUS TROUBLE. AND I MAY LOSE MY POSITION.

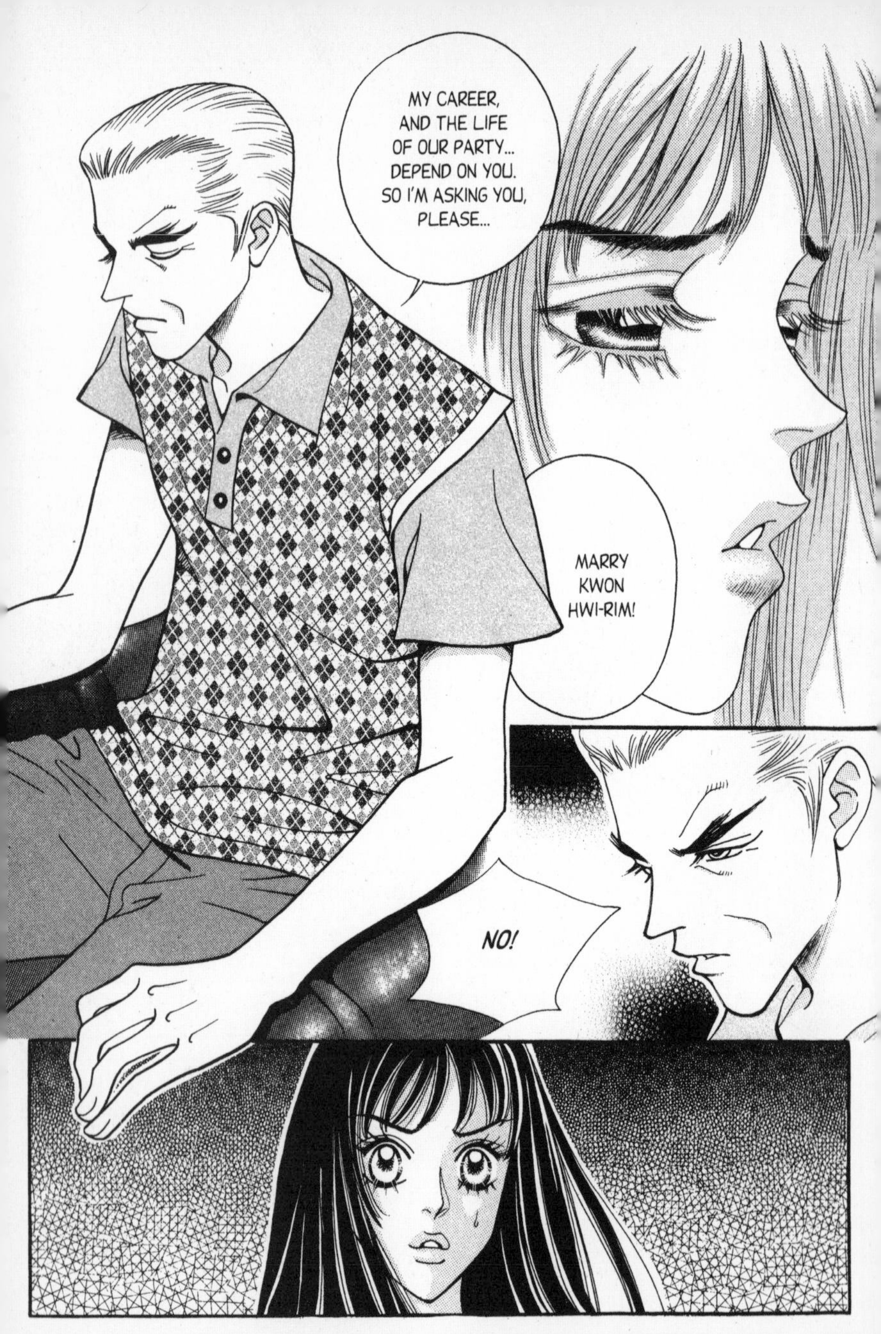
MY CAREER, AND THE LIFE OF OUR PARTY... DEPEND ON YOU. SO I'M ASKING YOU, PLEASE...
MARRY KWON HWI-RIM!
NO!

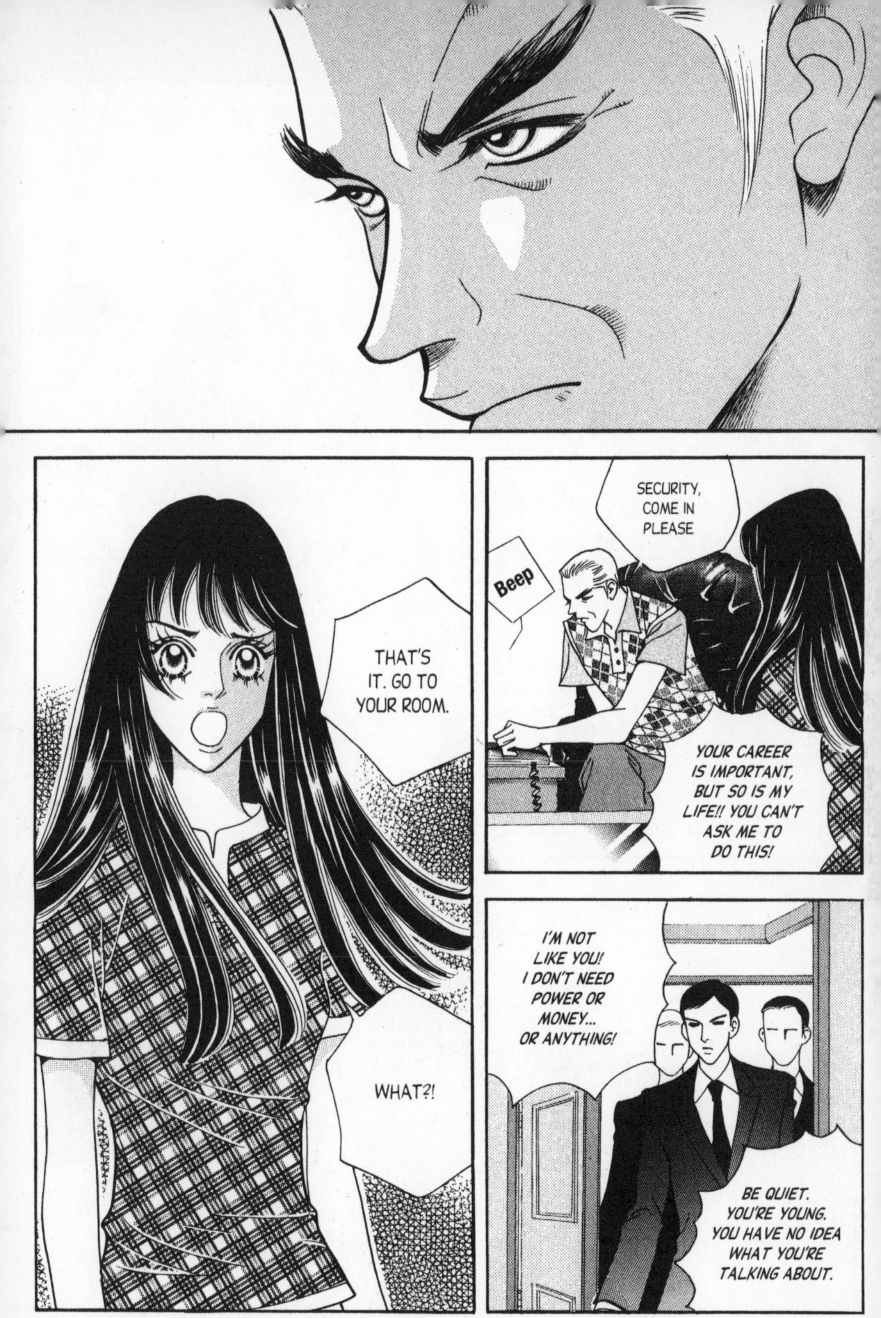
SECURITY, COME IN PLEASE
Beep
YOUR CAREER IS IMPORTANT, BUT SO IS MY LIFE!! YOU CAN'T ASK ME TO DO THIS!
I'M NOT LIKE YOU! I DON'T NEED POWER OR MONEY... OR ANYTHING!
BE QUIET. YOU'RE YOUNG. YOU HAVE NO IDEA WHAT YOU'RE TALKING ABOUT.
THAT'S IT. GO TO YOUR ROOM.
WHAT?!

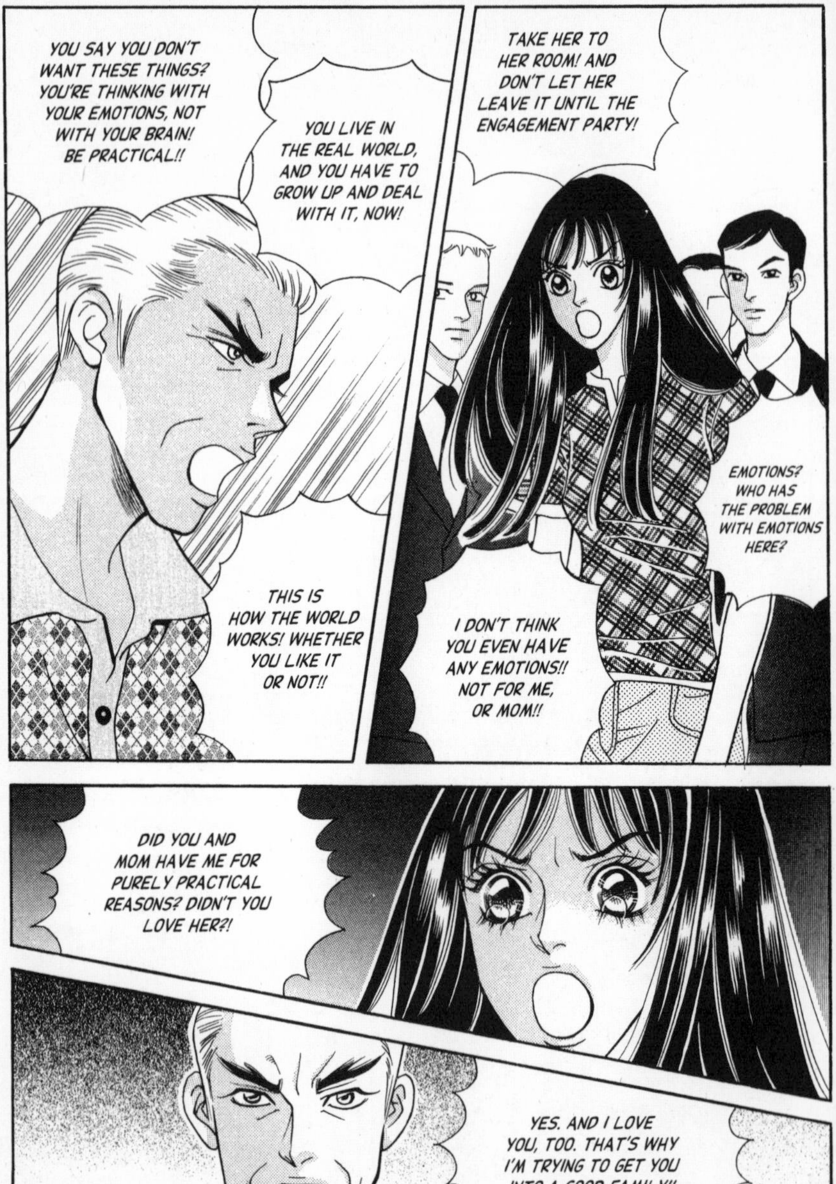

YOU SAY YOU DON'T WANT THESE THINGS? YOU'RE THINKING WITH YOUR EMOTIONS, NOT WITH YOUR BRAIN! BE PRACTICAL!!
YOU LIVE IN THE REAL WORLD, AND YOU HAVE TO GROW UP AND DEAL WITH IT, NOW!
THIS IS HOW THE WORLD WORKS! WHETHER YOU LIKE IT OR NOT!!
TAKE HER TO HER ROOM! AND DON'T LET HER LEAVE IT UNTIL THE ENGAGEMENT PARTY!
EMOTIONS? WHO HAS THE PROBLEM WITH EMOTIONS HERE?
I DON'T THINK YOU EVEN HAVE ANY EMOTIONS!! NOT FOR ME, OR MOM!!
DID YOU AND MOM HAVE ME FOR PURELY PRACTICAL REASONS? DIDN'T YOU LOVE HER?!
YES. AND I LOVE YOU, TOO. THAT'S WHY I'M TRYING TO GET YOU INTO A GOOD FAMILY!!

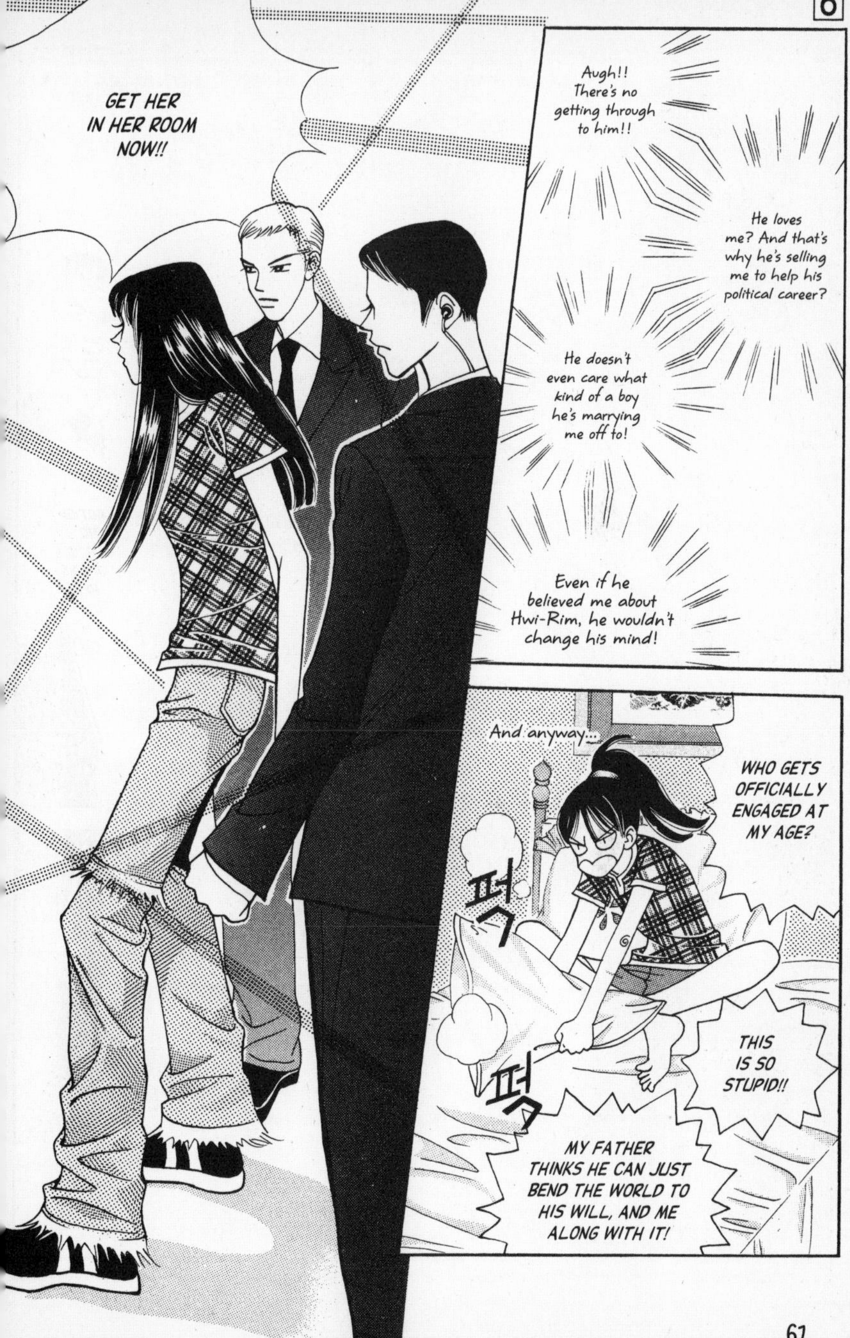
GET HER IN HER ROOM NOW!!
Augh!! There's no getting through to him!!
He loves me? And that's why he's selling me to help his political career?
He doesn't even care what kind of a boy he's marrying me off to!
Even if he believed me about Hwi-Rim, he wouldn't change his mind!
And anyway...
WHO GETS OFFICIALLY ENGAGED AT MY AGE?
퍽
퍽
THIS IS SO STUPID!!
MY FATHER THINKS HE CAN JUST BEND THE WORLD TO HIS WILL, AND ME ALONG WITH IT!

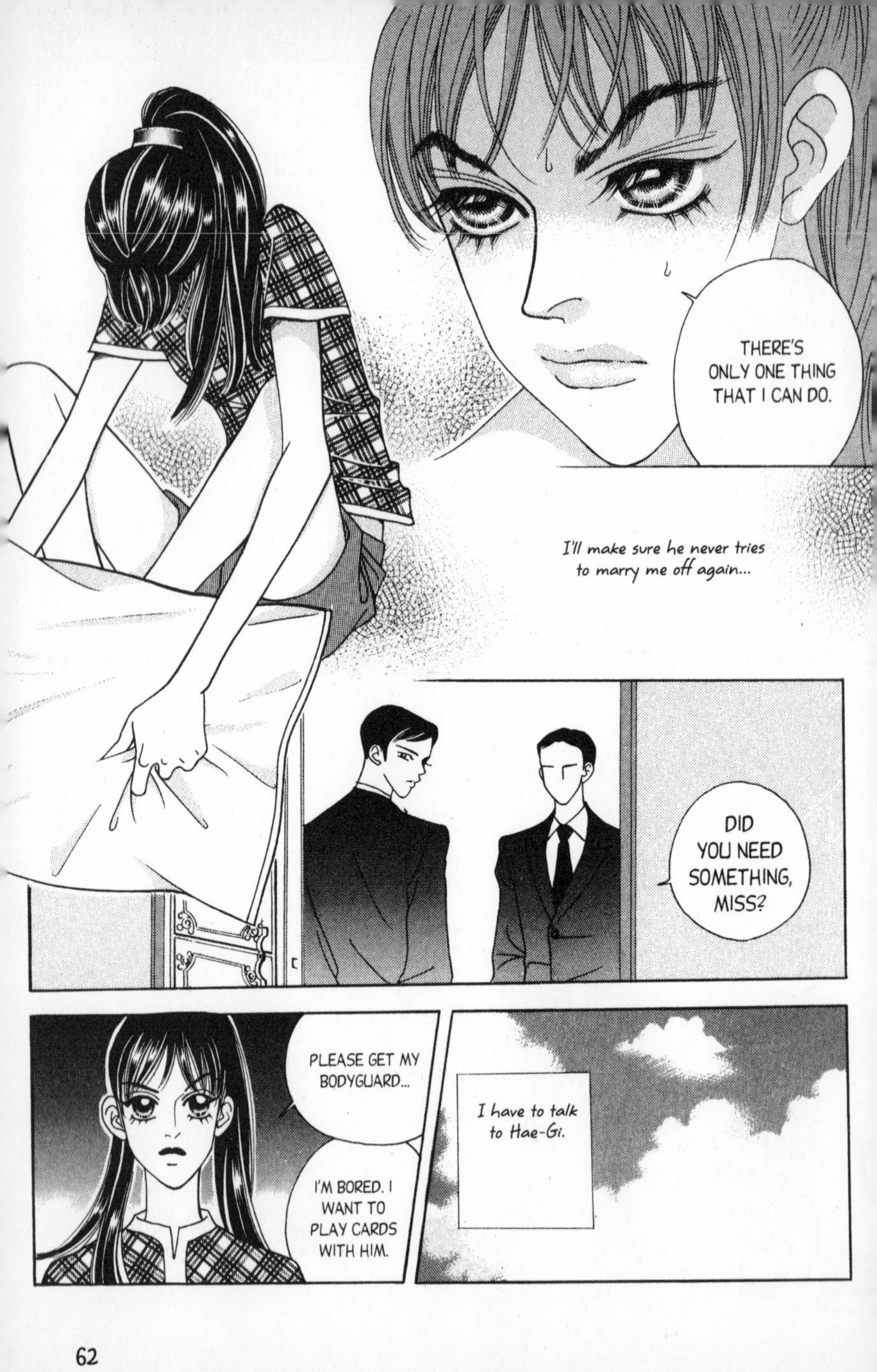
THERE'S ONLY ONE THING THAT I CAN DO.
I'll make sure he never tries to marry me off again...
DID YOU NEED SOMETHING, MISS?
I have to talk to Hae-Gi.
PLEASE GET MY BODYGUARD...
I'M BORED. I WANT TO PLAY CARDS WITH HIM.

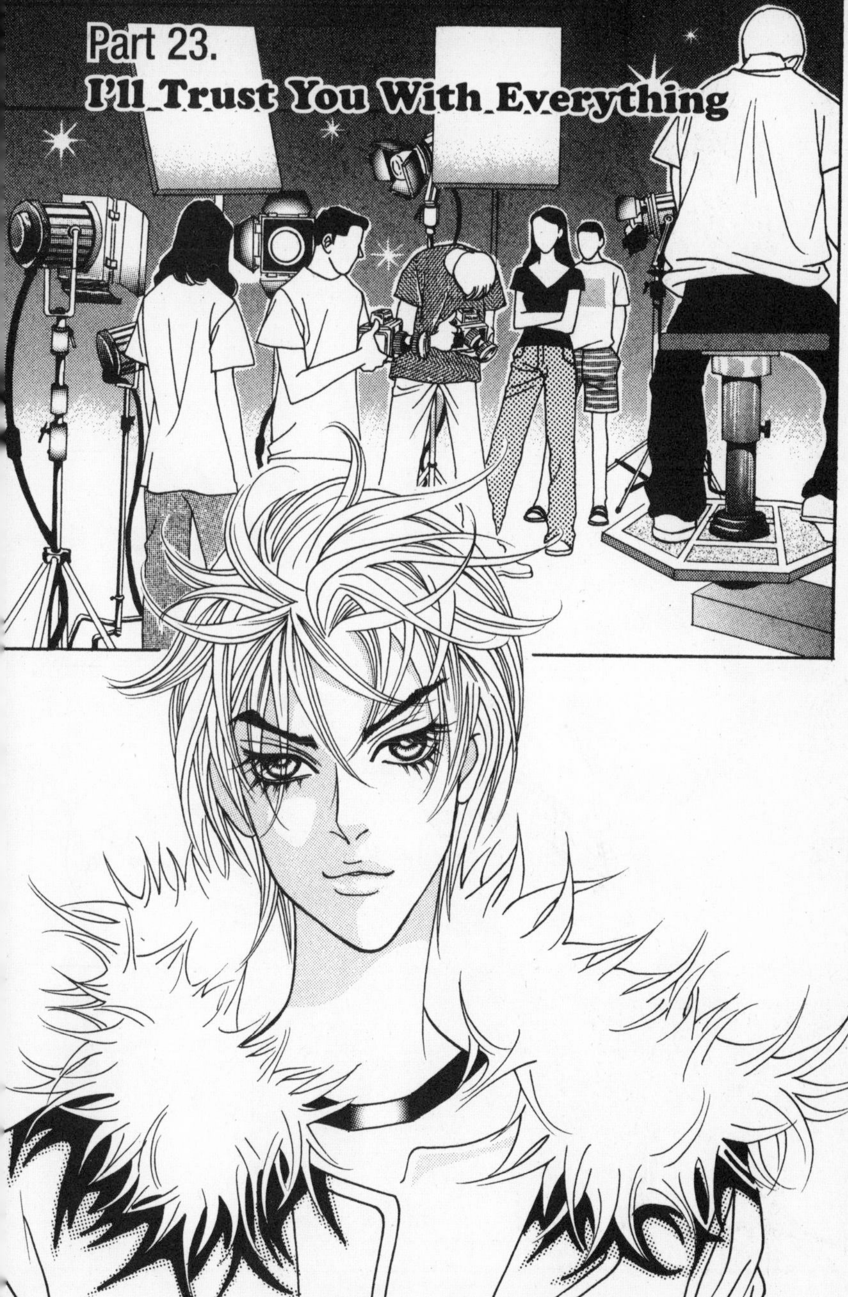
Part 23.
I'll Trust You With Everything

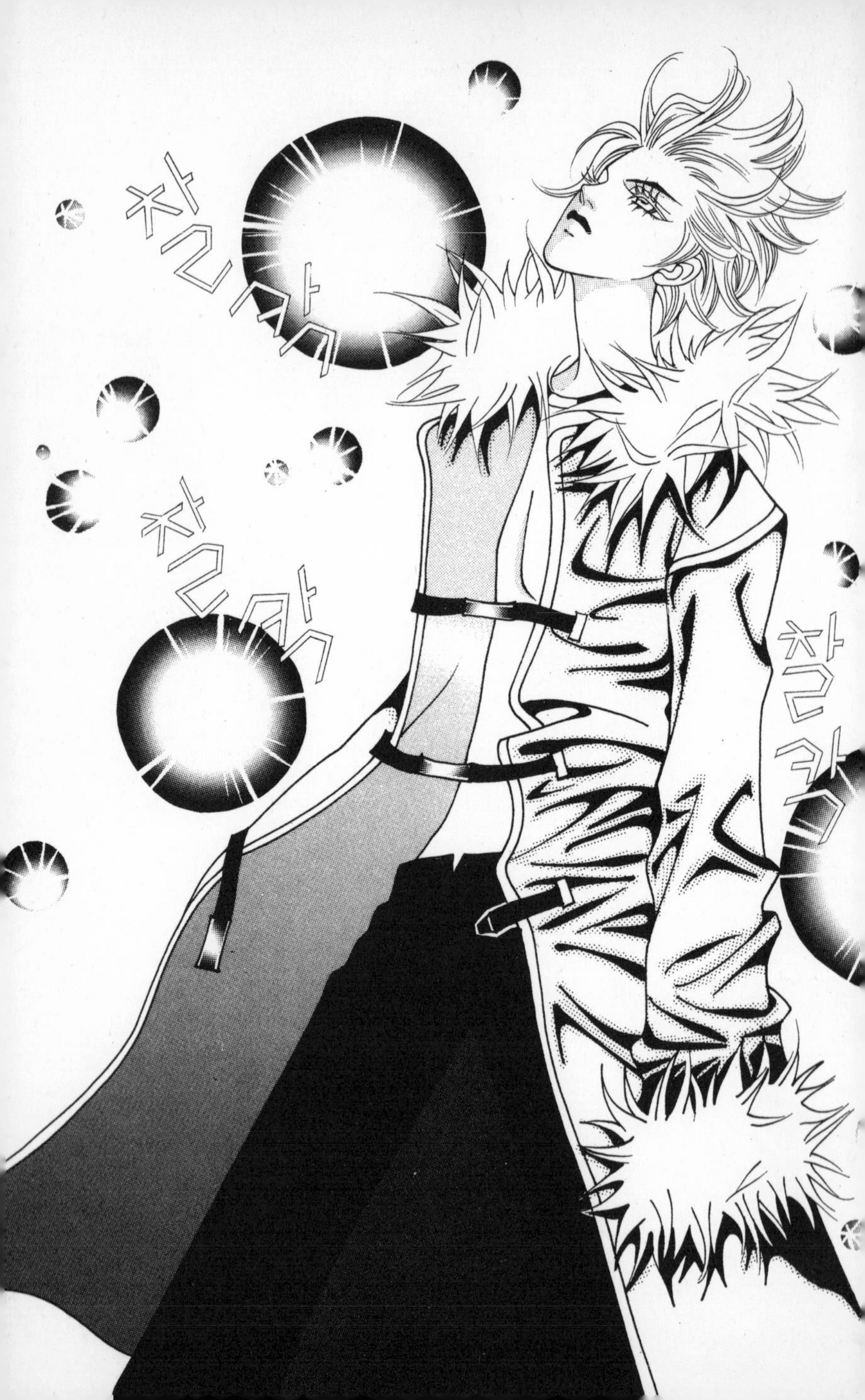
찰랑
찰랑
찰랑

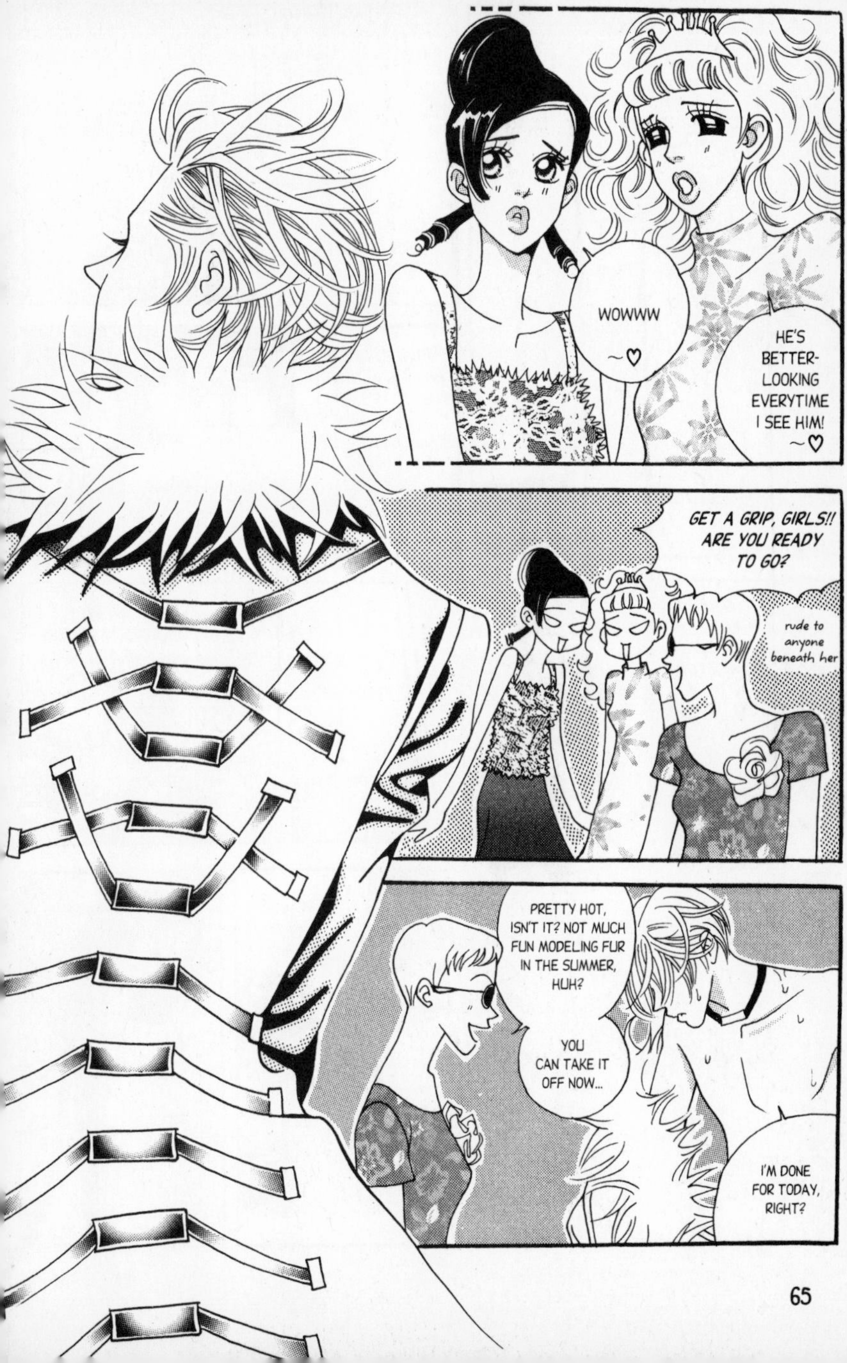
HE'S BETTER-LOOKING EVERYTIME I SEE HIM! ~♡
WOWWW ~♡
GET A GRIP, GIRLS!! ARE YOU READY TO GO?
rude to anyone beneath her
PRETTY HOT, ISN'T IT? NOT MUCH FUN MODELING FUR IN THE SUMMER, HUH?
YOU CAN TAKE IT OFF NOW...
I'M DONE FOR TODAY, RIGHT?

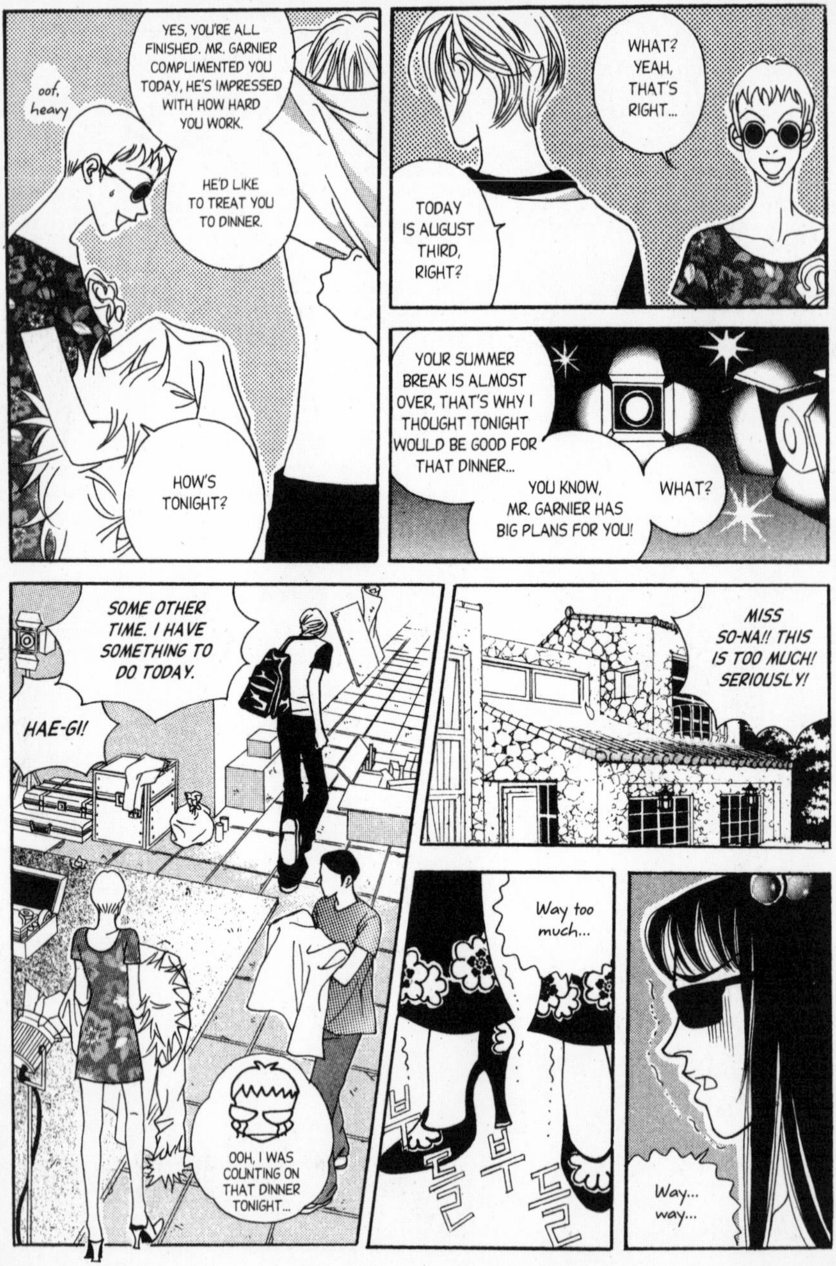
YES, YOU'RE ALL FINISHED. MR. GARNIER COMPLIMENTED YOU TODAY, HE'S IMPRESSED WITH HOW HARD YOU WORK.
oof, heavy
HE'D LIKE TO TREAT YOU TO DINNER.
HOW'S TONIGHT?
TODAY IS AUGUST THIRD, RIGHT?
WHAT? YEAH, THAT'S RIGHT...
YOUR SUMMER BREAK IS ALMOST OVER, THAT'S WHY I THOUGHT TONIGHT WOULD BE GOOD FOR THAT DINNER...
WHAT?
YOU KNOW, MR. GARNIER HAS BIG PLANS FOR YOU!
SOME OTHER TIME. I HAVE SOMETHING TO DO TODAY.
HAE-GI!
OOH, I WAS COUNTING ON THAT DINNER TONIGHT...
MISS SO-NA!! THIS IS TOO MUCH! SERIOUSLY!
Way too much...
부들 부들
Way... way...

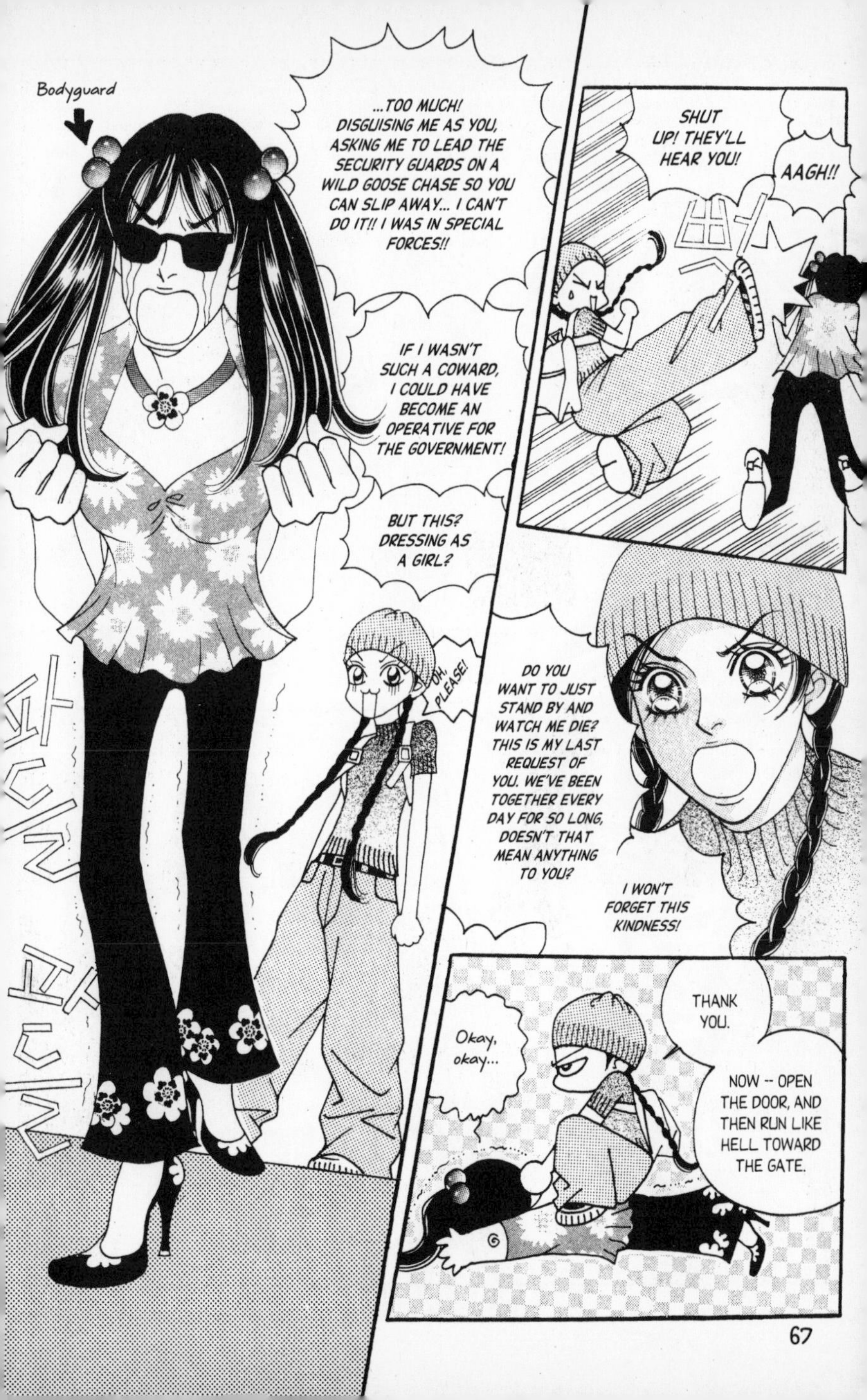
Bodyguard
...TOO MUCH! DISGUISING ME AS YOU, ASKING ME TO LEAD THE SECURITY GUARDS ON A WILD GOOSE CHASE SO YOU CAN SLIP AWAY... I CAN'T DO IT!! I WAS IN SPECIAL FORCES!!
IF I WASN'T SUCH A COWARD, I COULD HAVE BECOME AN OPERATIVE FOR THE GOVERNMENT!
BUT THIS? DRESSING AS A GIRL?
OH, PLEASE!
SHUT UP! THEY'LL HEAR YOU!
AAGH!!
DO YOU WANT TO JUST STAND BY AND WATCH ME DIE? THIS IS MY LAST REQUEST OF YOU. WE'VE BEEN TOGETHER EVERY DAY FOR SO LONG, DOESN'T THAT MEAN ANYTHING TO YOU?
I WON'T FORGET THIS KINDNESS!
Okay, okay...
THANK YOU.
NOW -- OPEN THE DOOR, AND THEN RUN LIKE HELL TOWARD THE GATE.

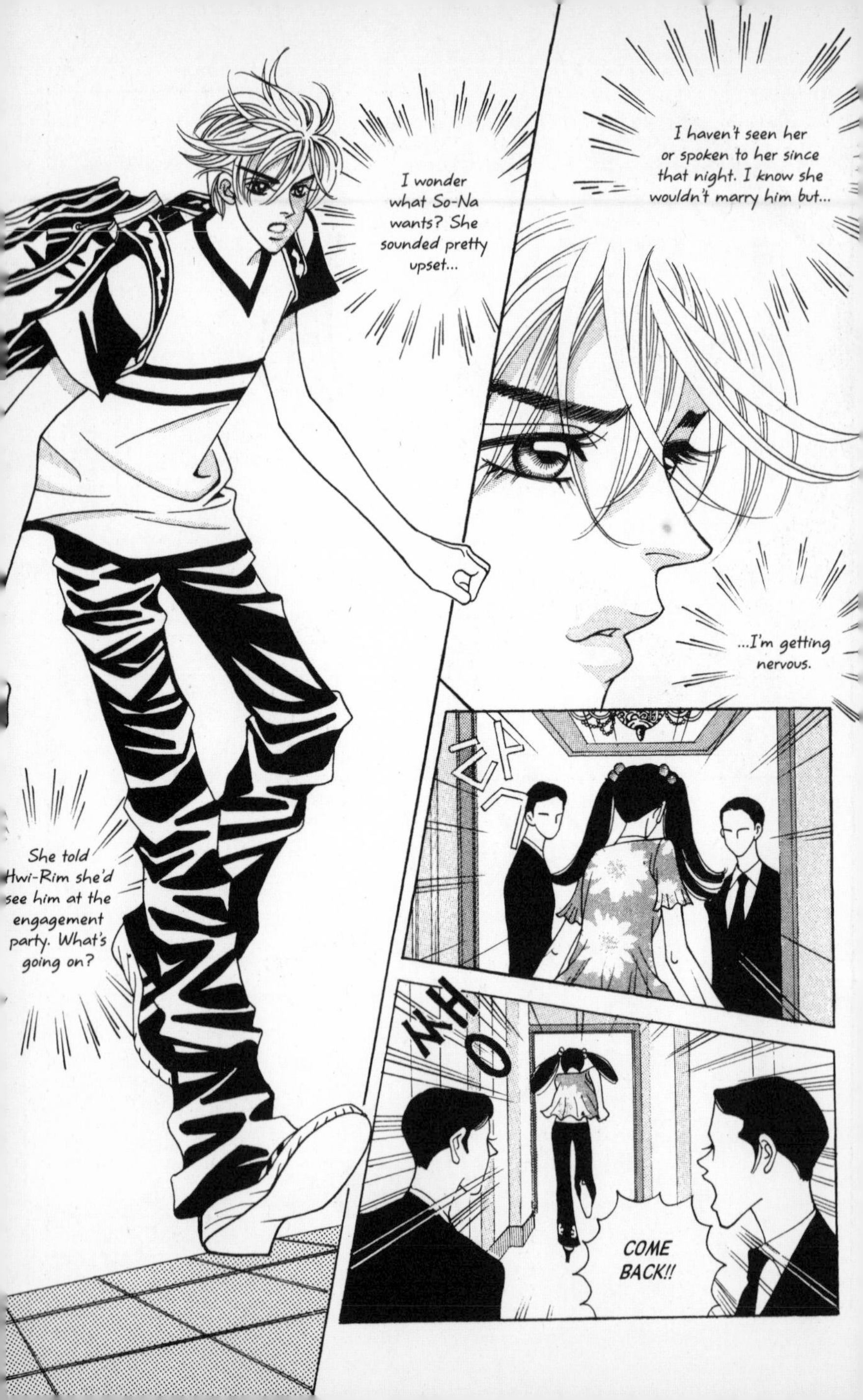
I wonder what So-Na wants? She sounded pretty upset...
She told Hwi-Rim she'd see him at the engagement party. What's going on?
I haven't seen her or spoken to her since that night. I know she wouldn't marry him but...
...I'm getting nervous.
COME BACK!!

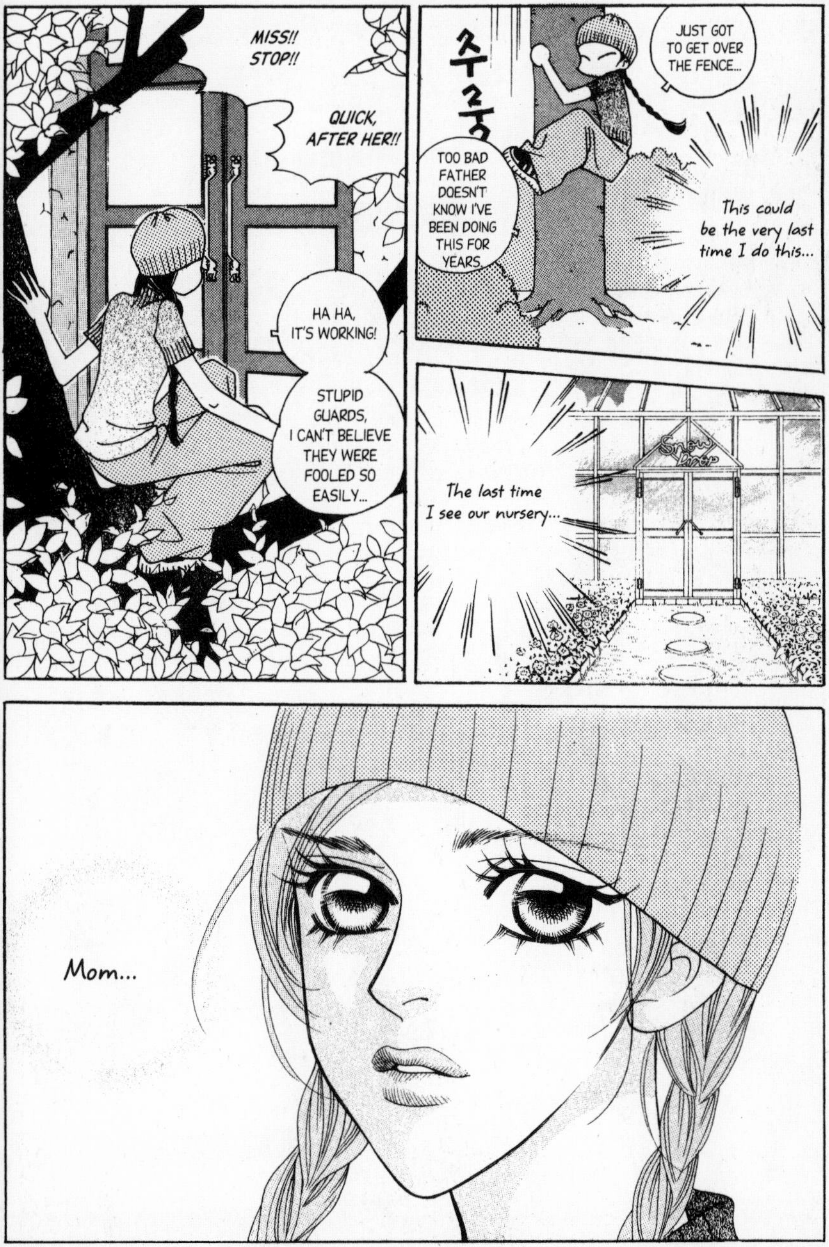
MISS!! STOP!!
QUICK, AFTER HER!!
HA HA, IT'S WORKING!
STUPID GUARDS, I CAN'T BELIEVE THEY WERE FOOLED SO EASILY...
JUST GOT TO GET OVER THE FENCE...
TOO BAD FATHER DOESN'T KNOW I'VE BEEN DOING THIS FOR YEARS.
This could be the very last time I do this...
The last time I see our nursery...
Mom...

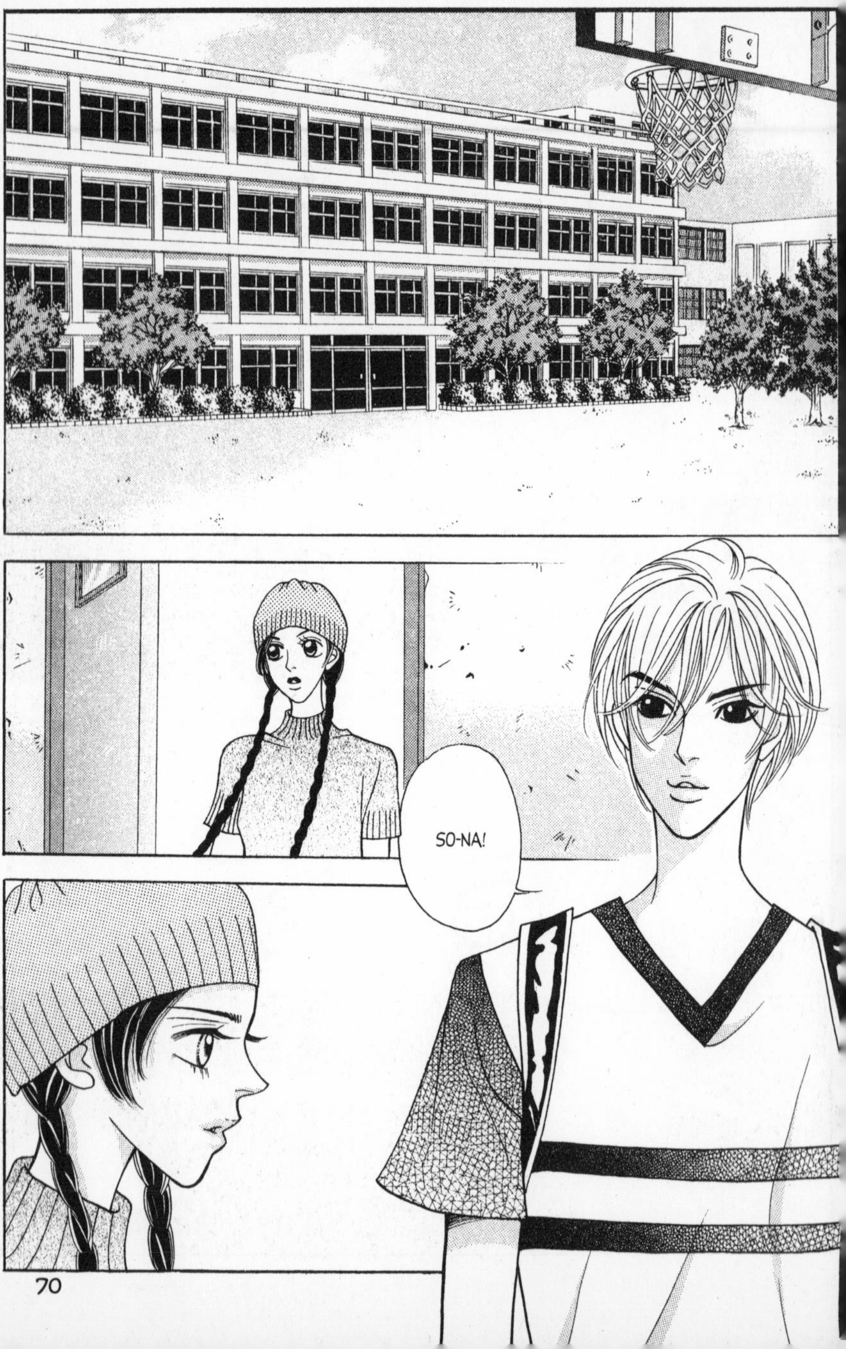
SO-NA!

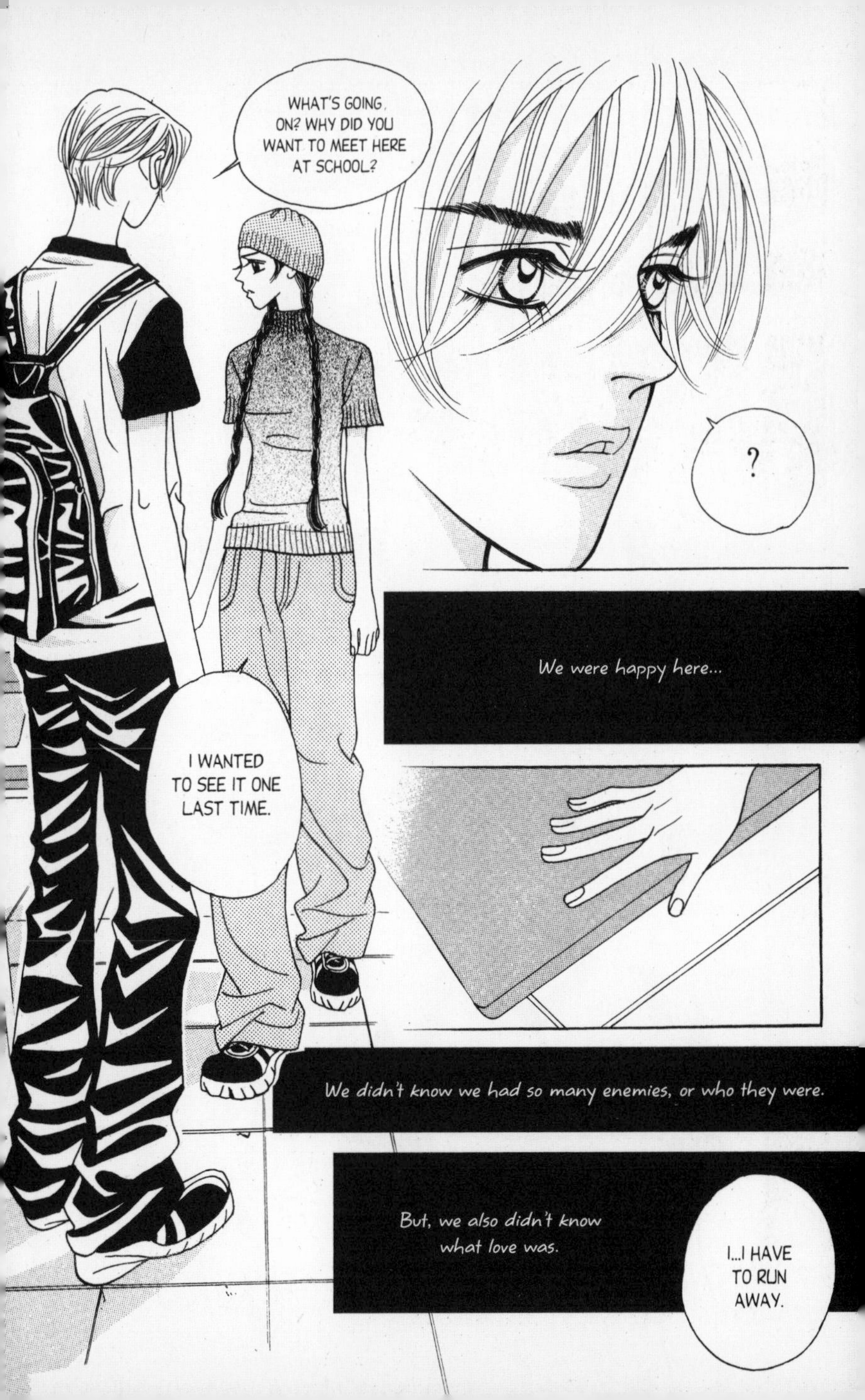
WHAT'S GOING ON? WHY DID YOU WANT TO MEET HERE AT SCHOOL?
I WANTED TO SEE IT ONE LAST TIME.
?
We were happy here...
We didn't know we had so many enemies, or who they were.
But, we also didn't know what love was.
I...I HAVE TO RUN AWAY.

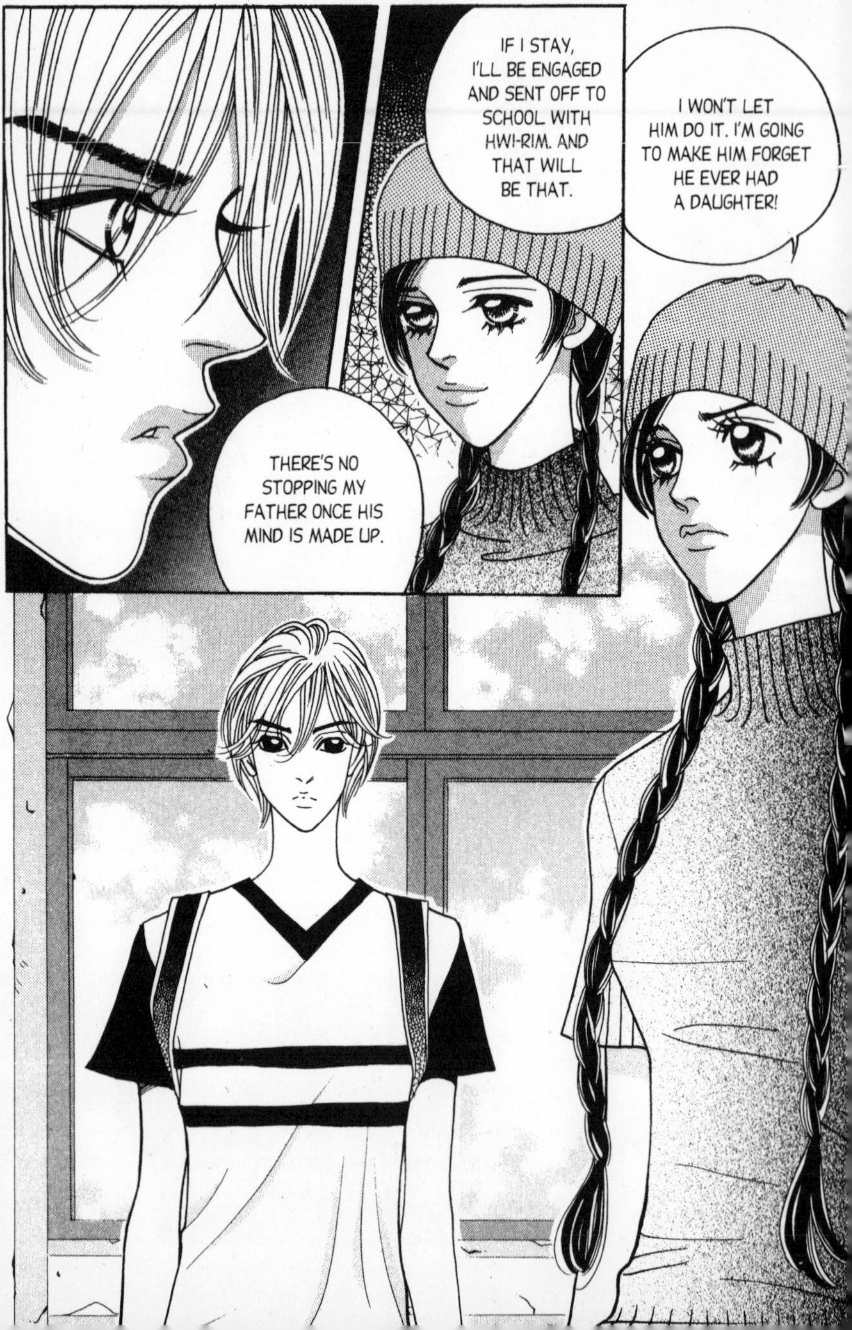
IF I STAY, I'LL BE ENGAGED AND SENT OFF TO SCHOOL WITH HWI-RIM. AND THAT WILL BE THAT.
THERE'S NO STOPPING MY FATHER ONCE HIS MIND IS MADE UP.
I WON'T LET HIM DO IT. I'M GOING TO MAKE HIM FORGET HE EVER HAD A DAUGHTER!

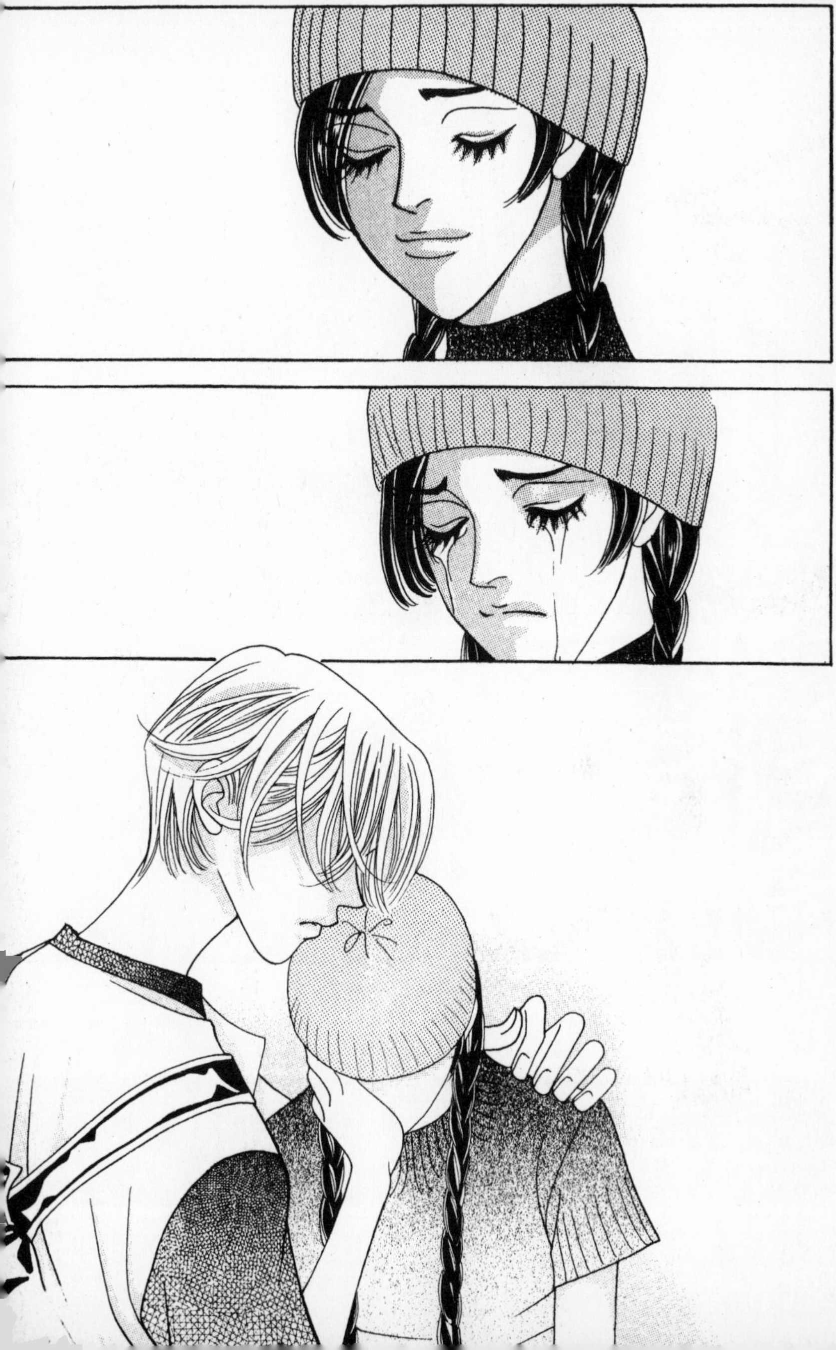

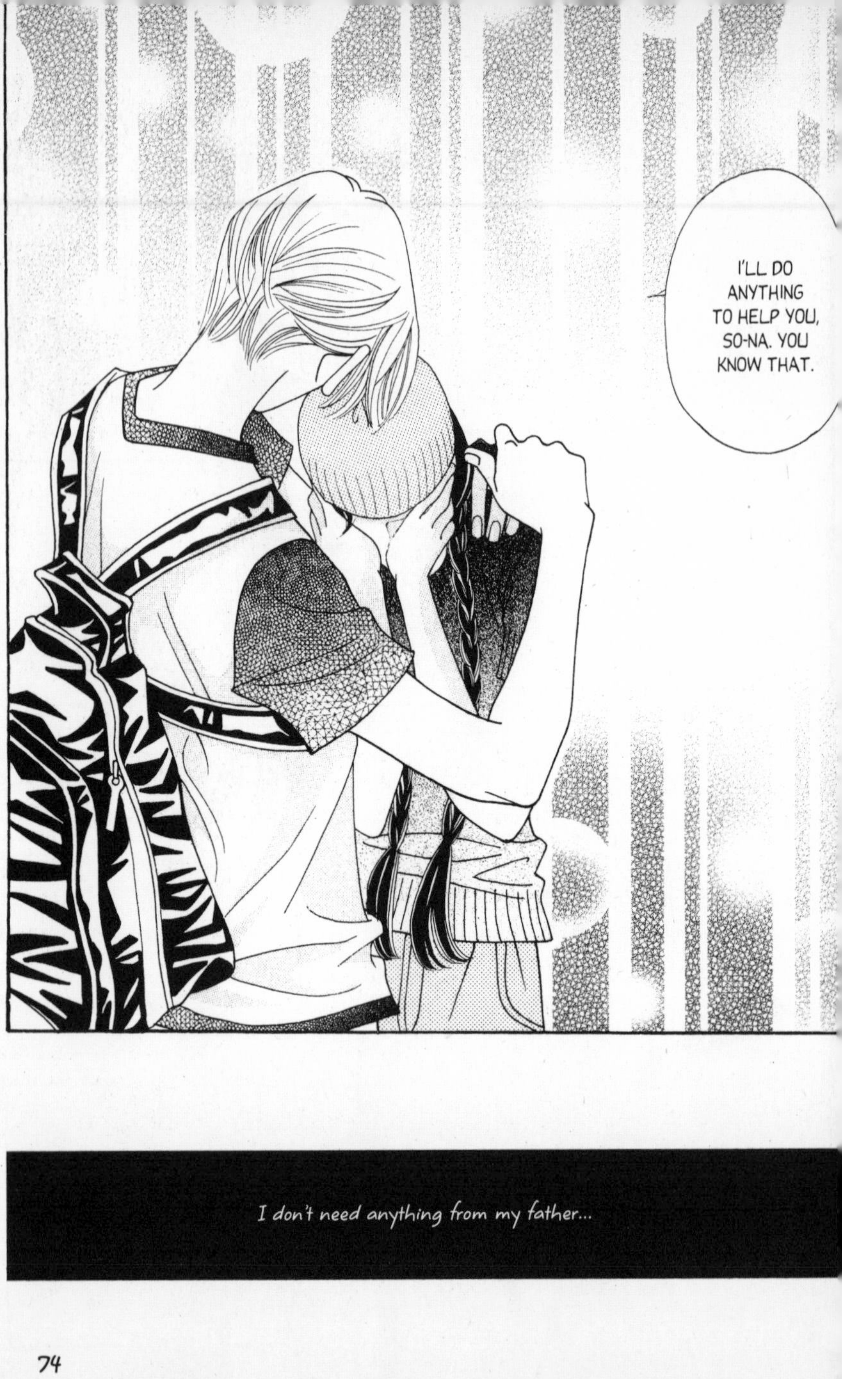
I'LL DO ANYTHING TO HELP YOU, SO-NA. YOU KNOW THAT.

I don't need anything from my father...

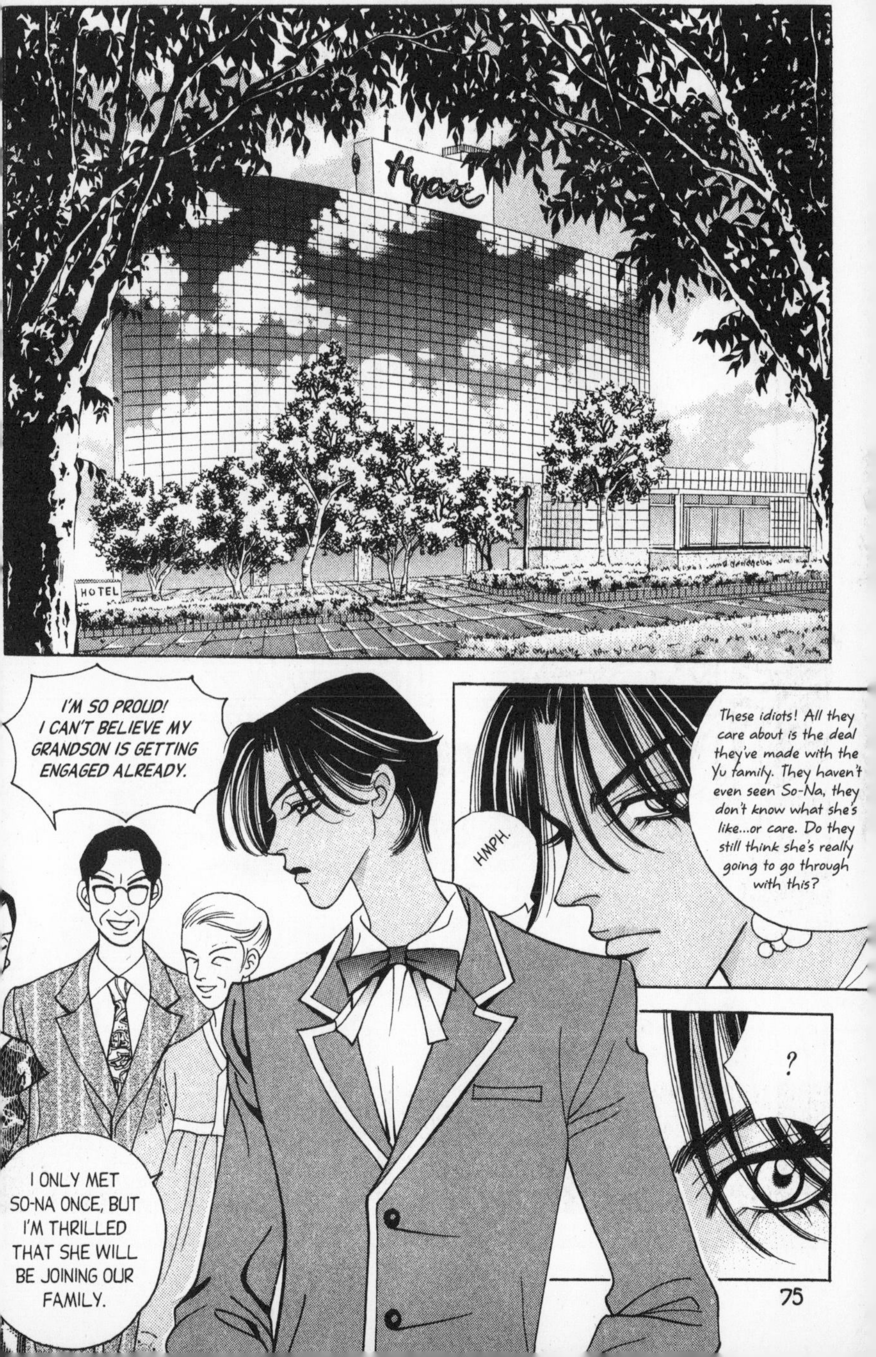
Hyatt
HOTEL
I'M SO PROUD! I CAN'T BELIEVE MY GRANDSON IS GETTING ENGAGED ALREADY.
I ONLY MET SO-NA ONCE, BUT I'M THRILLED THAT SHE WILL BE JOINING OUR FAMILY.
HMPH.
These idiots! All they care about is the deal they've made with the Yu family. They haven't even seen So-Na, they don't know what she's like...or care. Do they still think she's really going to go through with this?
?

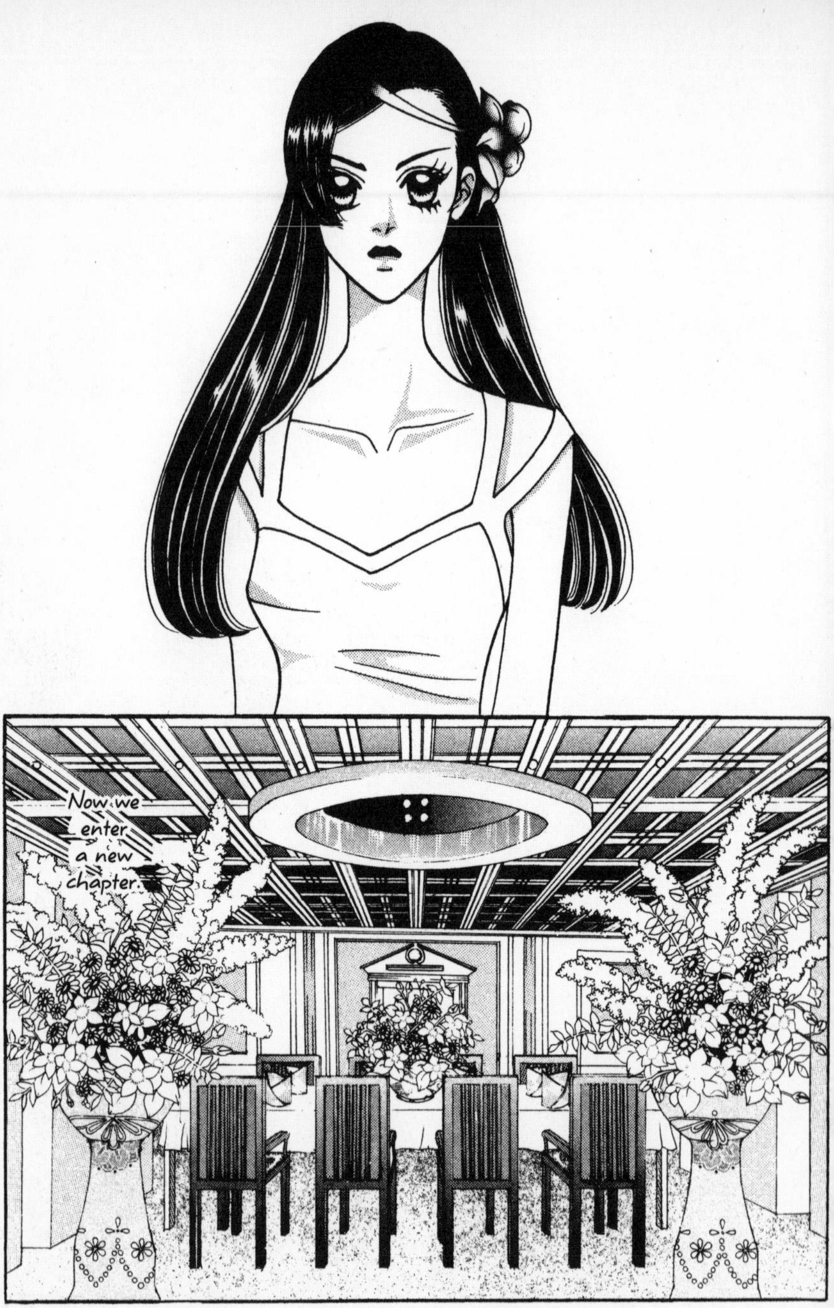
Now we enter a new chapter.

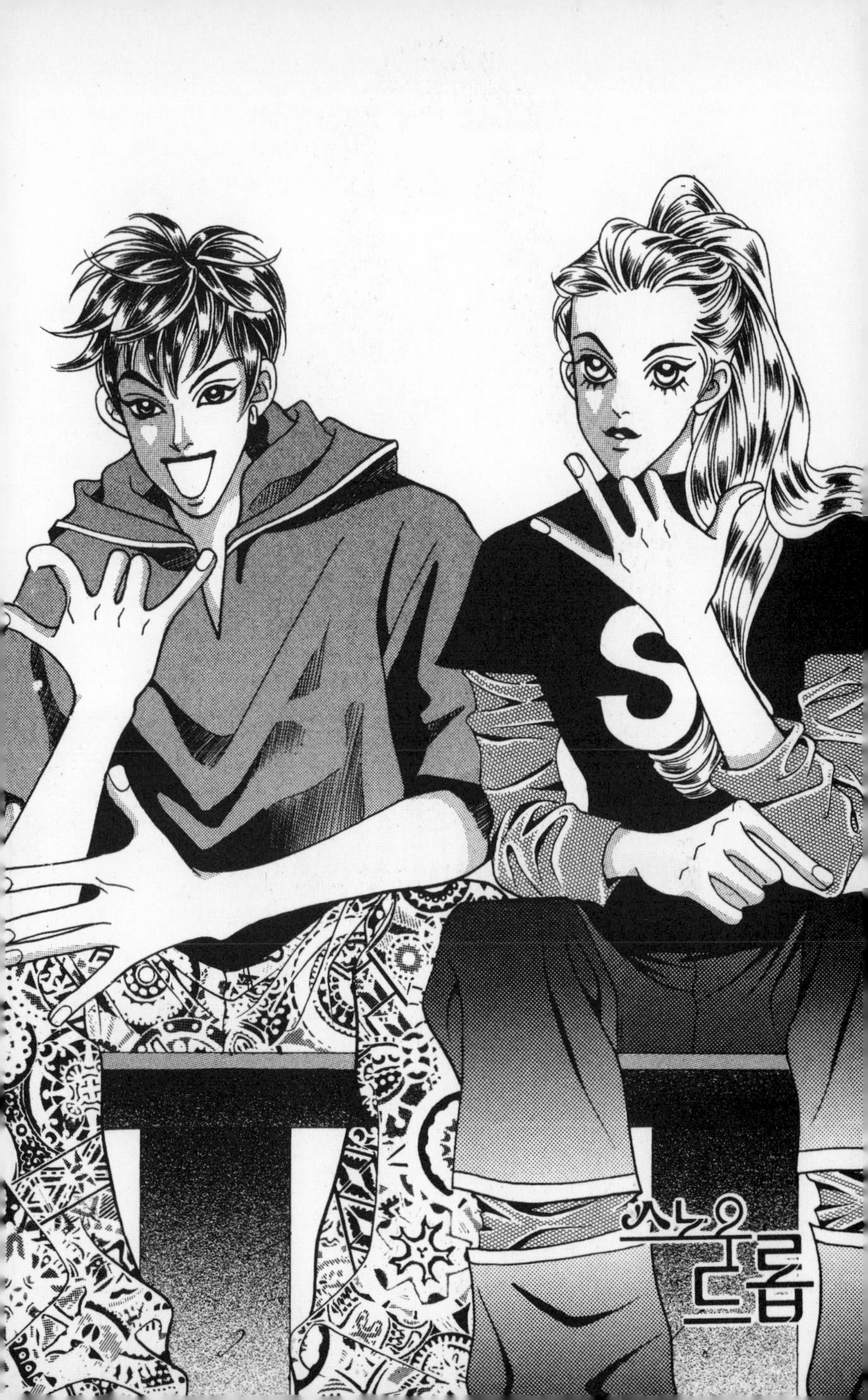
스노우
드롭

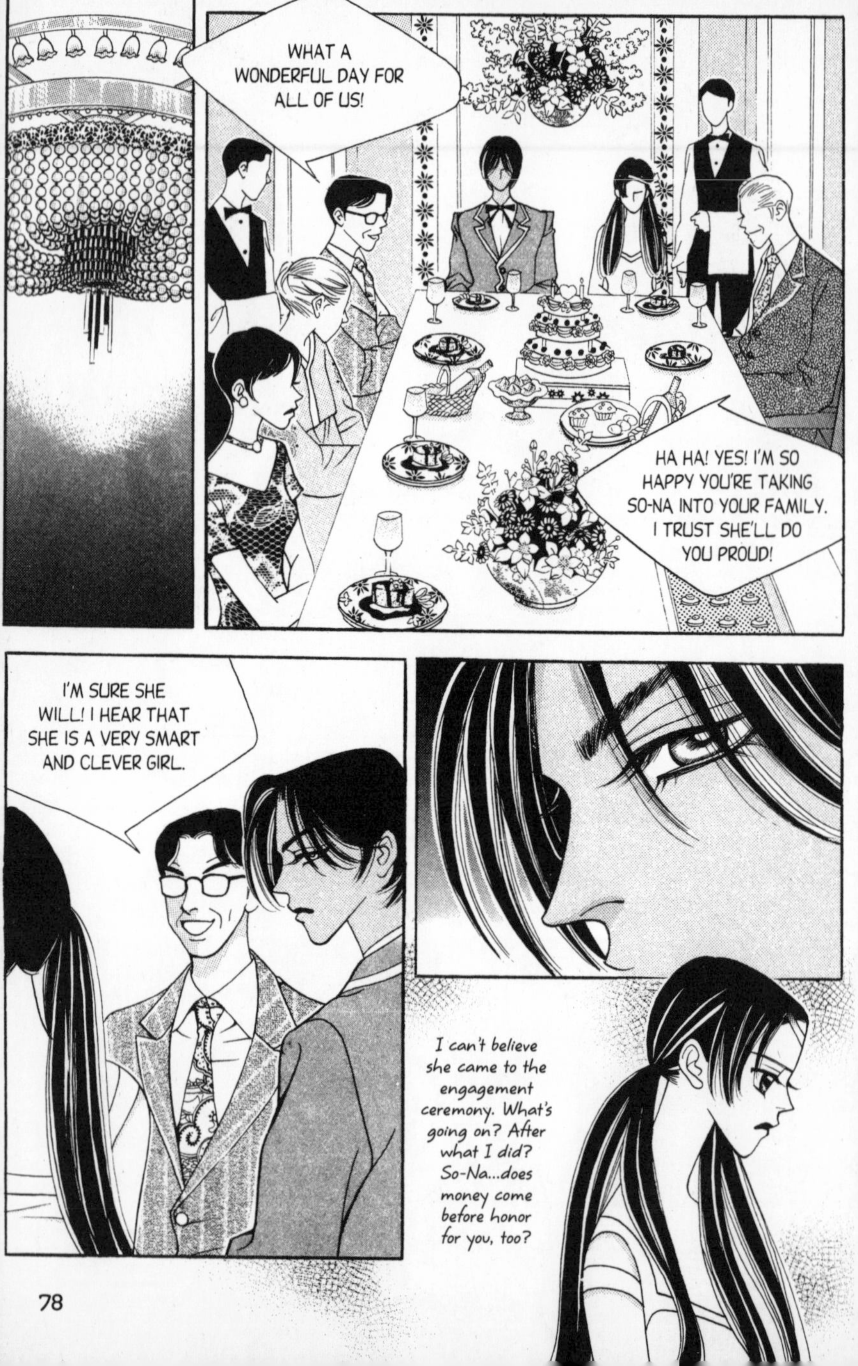
WHAT A WONDERFUL DAY FOR ALL OF US!
HA HA! YES! I'M SO HAPPY YOU'RE TAKING SO-NA INTO YOUR FAMILY. I TRUST SHE'LL DO YOU PROUD!
I'M SURE SHE WILL! I HEAR THAT SHE IS A VERY SMART AND CLEVER GIRL.
I can't believe she came to the engagement ceremony. What's going on? After what I did? So-Na...does money come before honor for you, too?

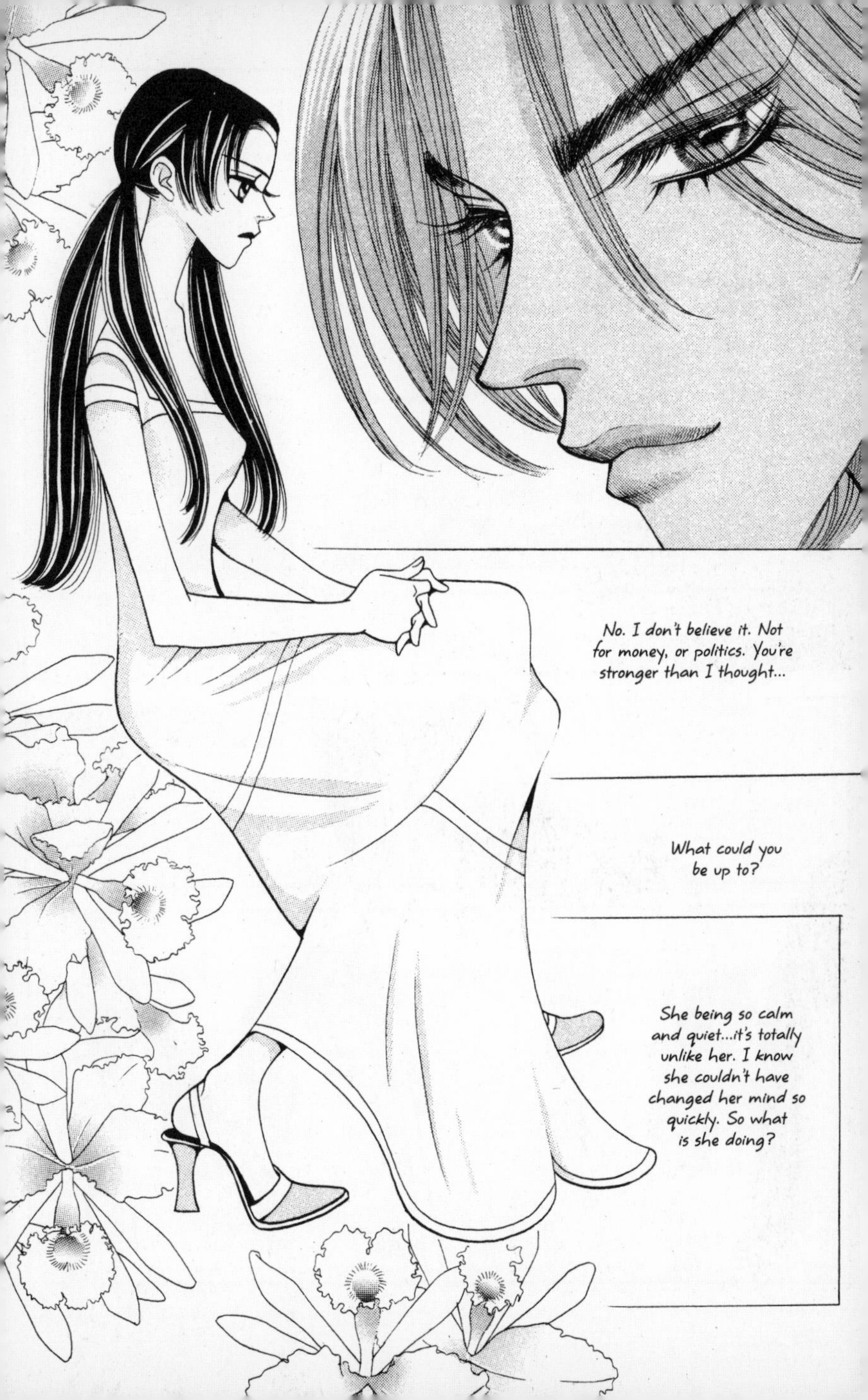
No. I don't believe it. Not for money, or politics. You're stronger than I thought...
What could you be up to?
She being so calm and quiet...it's totally unlike her. I know she couldn't have changed her mind so quickly. So what is she doing?

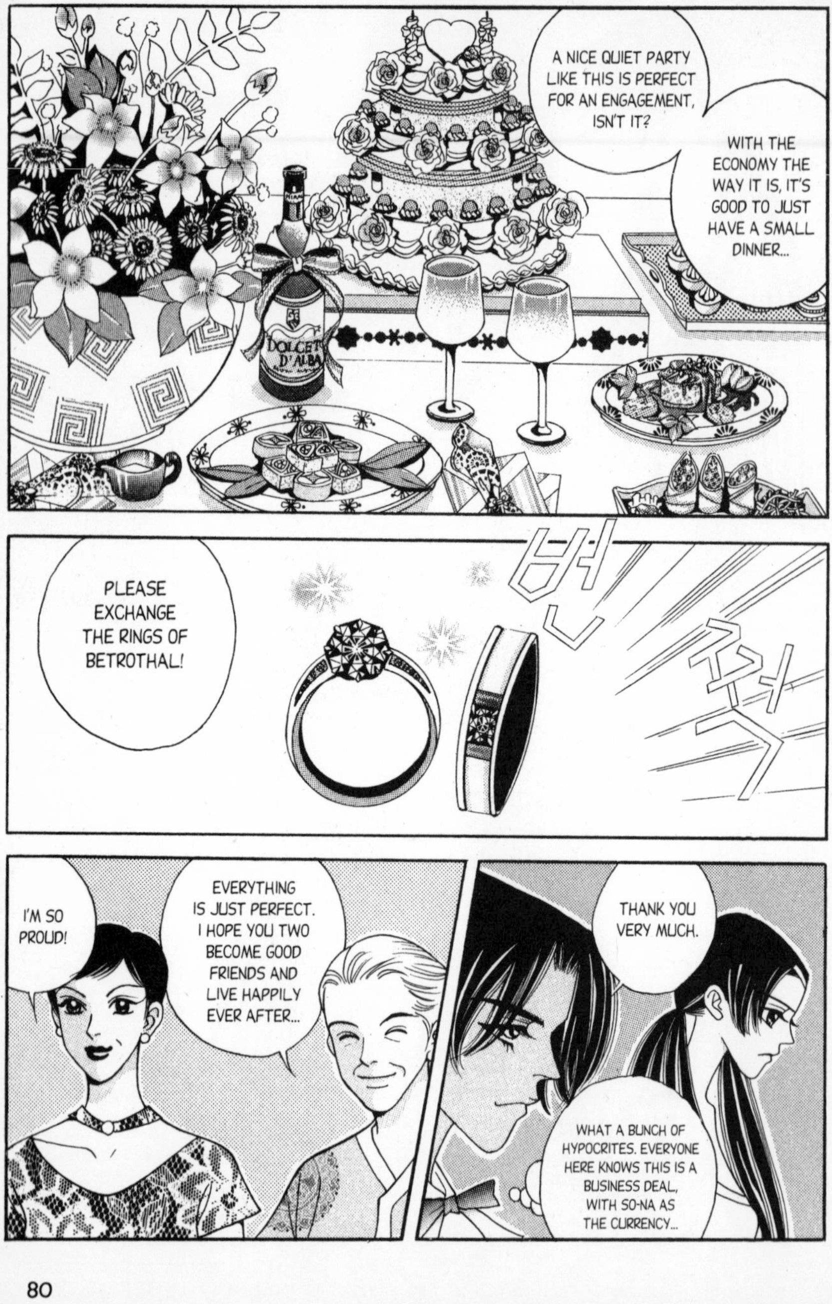
A NICE QUIET PARTY LIKE THIS IS PERFECT FOR AN ENGAGEMENT, ISN'T IT?
WITH THE ECONOMY THE WAY IT IS, IT'S GOOD TO JUST HAVE A SMALL DINNER...
DOLCETTO D'ALBA
PLEASE EXCHANGE THE RINGS OF BETROTHAL!
번쩍
I'M SO PROUD!
EVERYTHING IS JUST PERFECT. I HOPE YOU TWO BECOME GOOD FRIENDS AND LIVE HAPPILY EVER AFTER...
THANK YOU VERY MUCH.
WHAT A BUNCH OF HYPOCRITES. EVERYONE HERE KNOWS THIS IS A BUSINESS DEAL, WITH SO-NA AS THE CURRENCY...

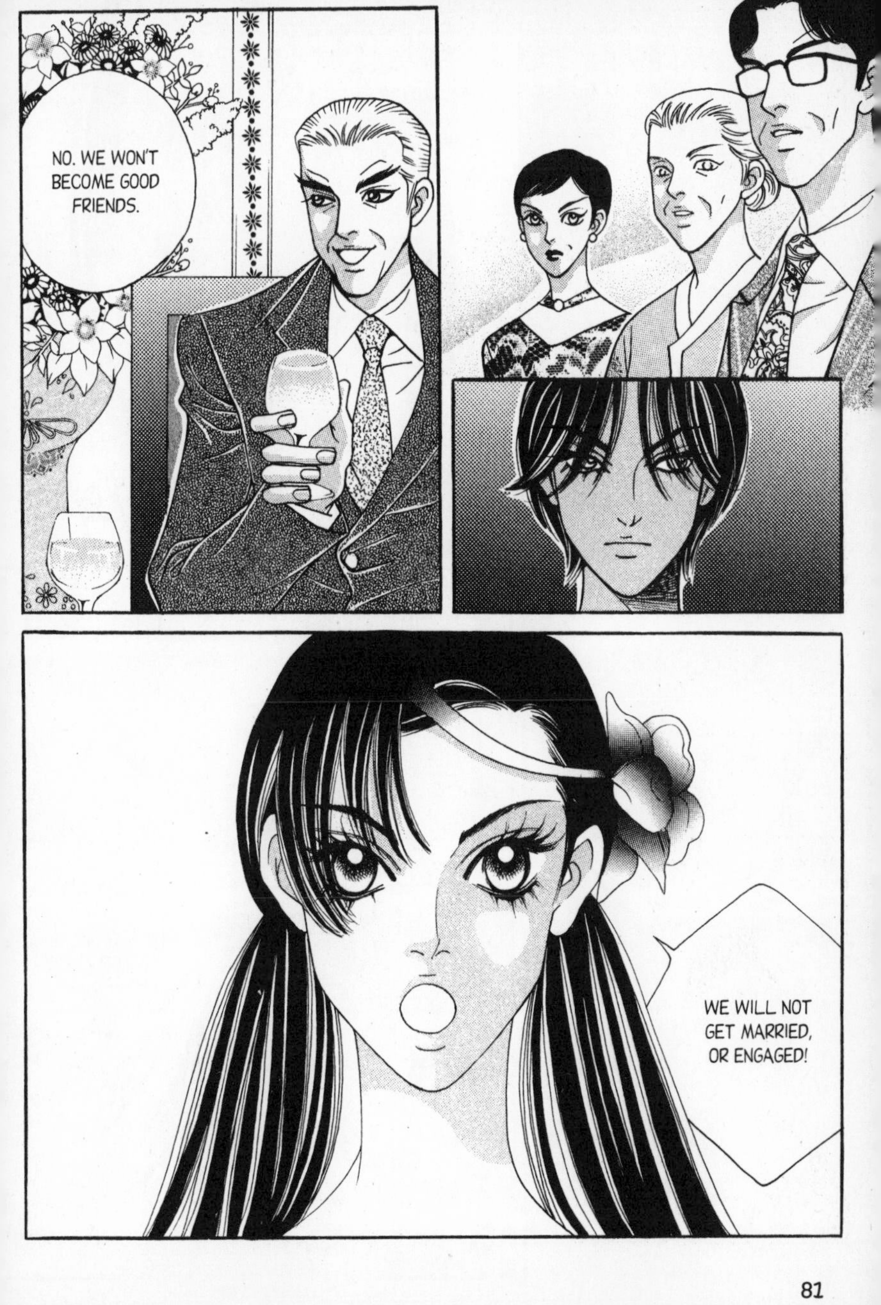
NO. WE WON'T BECOME GOOD FRIENDS.
WE WILL NOT GET MARRIED, OR ENGAGED!

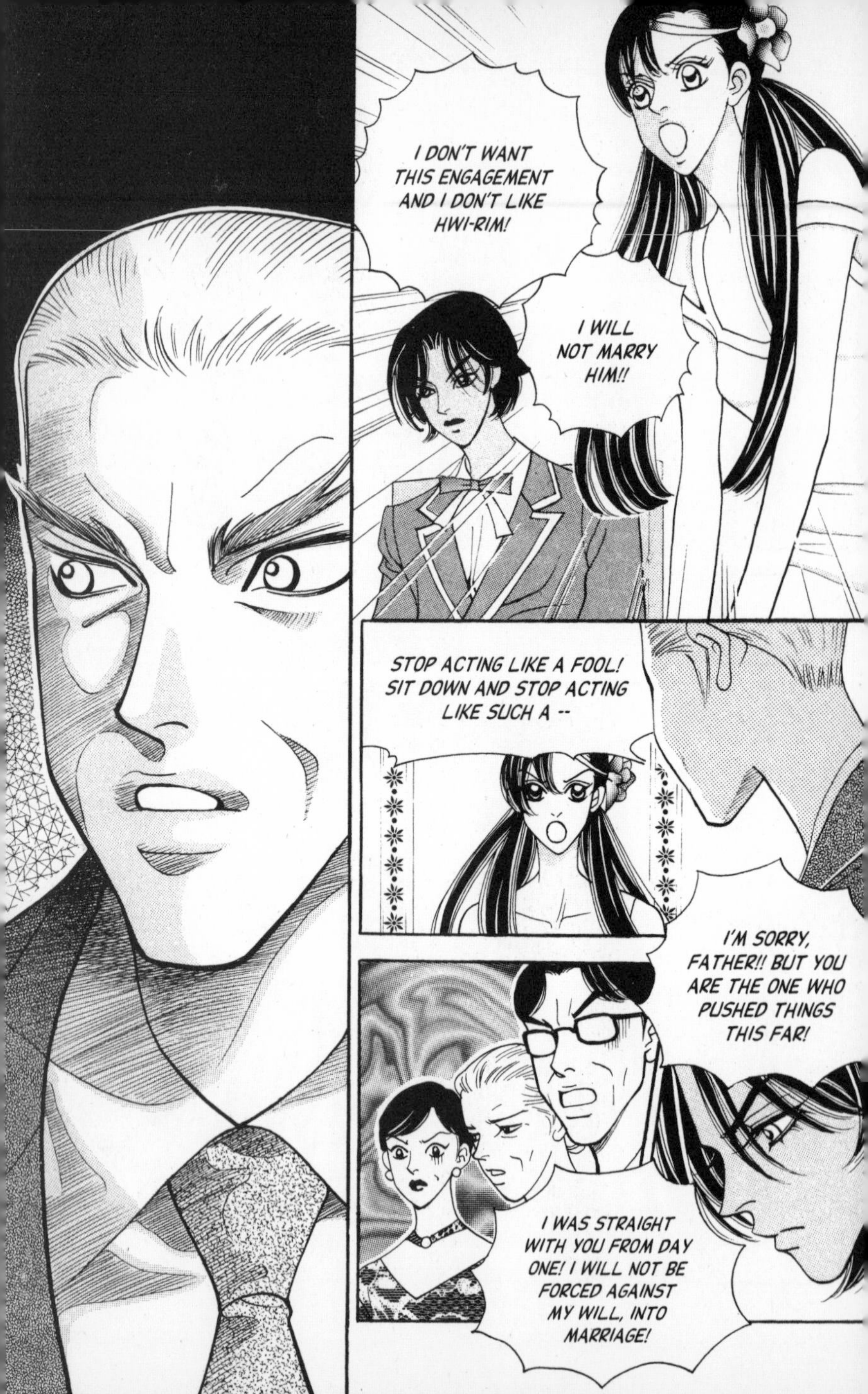
I DON'T WANT THIS ENGAGEMENT AND I DON'T LIKE HWI-RIM!
I WILL NOT MARRY HIM!!
STOP ACTING LIKE A FOOL! SIT DOWN AND STOP ACTING LIKE SUCH A --
I'M SORRY, FATHER!! BUT YOU ARE THE ONE WHO PUSHED THINGS THIS FAR!
I WAS STRAIGHT WITH YOU FROM DAY ONE! I WILL NOT BE FORCED AGAINST MY WILL, INTO MARRIAGE!

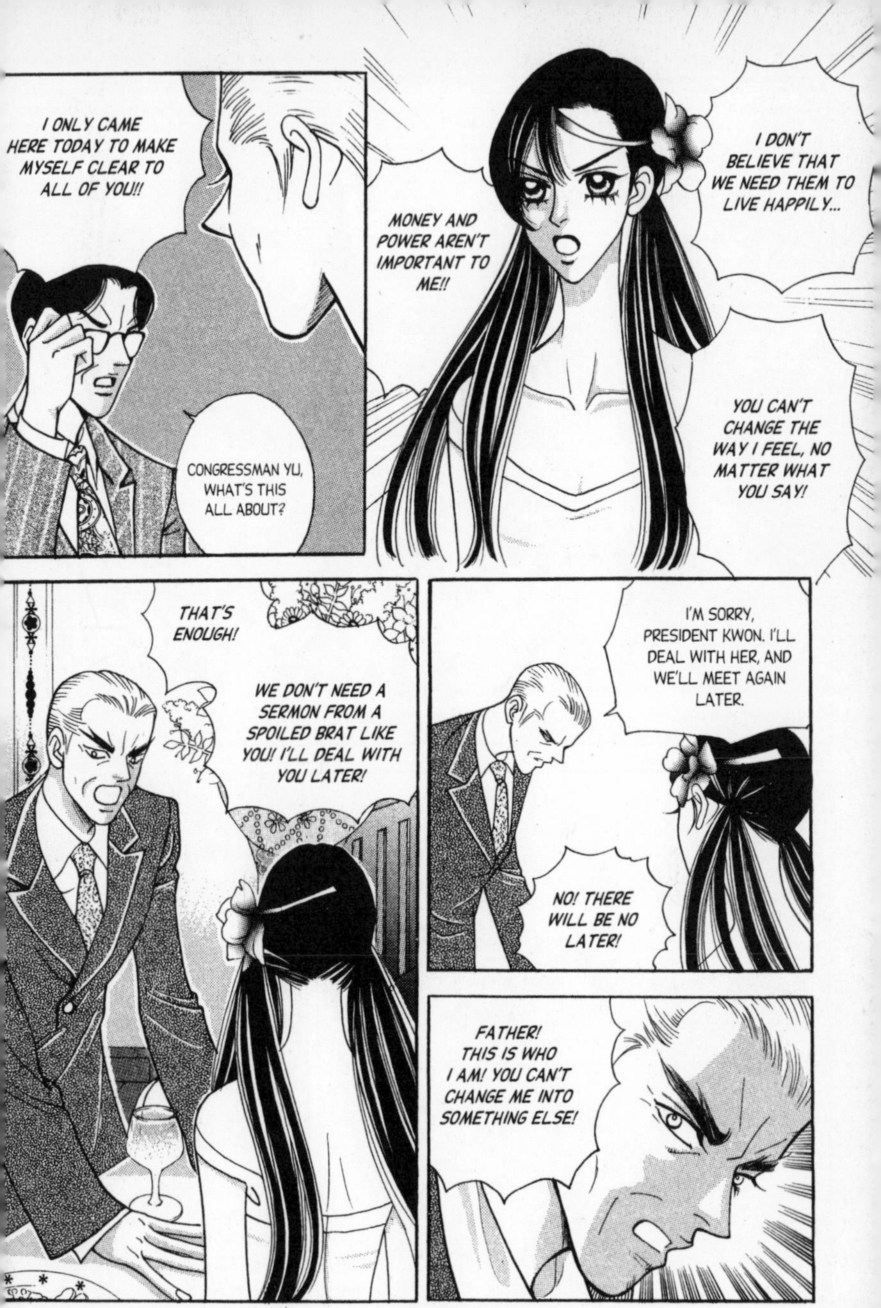
CONGRESSMAN YU, WHAT'S THIS ALL ABOUT?
I ONLY CAME HERE TODAY TO MAKE MYSELF CLEAR TO ALL OF YOU!!
MONEY AND POWER AREN'T IMPORTANT TO ME!!
I DON'T BELIEVE THAT WE NEED THEM TO LIVE HAPPILY...
YOU CAN'T CHANGE THE WAY I FEEL, NO MATTER WHAT YOU SAY!
THAT'S ENOUGH!
WE DON'T NEED A SERMON FROM A SPOILED BRAT LIKE YOU! I'LL DEAL WITH YOU LATER!
I'M SORRY, PRESIDENT KWON. I'LL DEAL WITH HER, AND WE'LL MEET AGAIN LATER.
NO! THERE WILL BE NO LATER!
FATHER! THIS IS WHO I AM! YOU CAN'T CHANGE ME INTO SOMETHING ELSE!

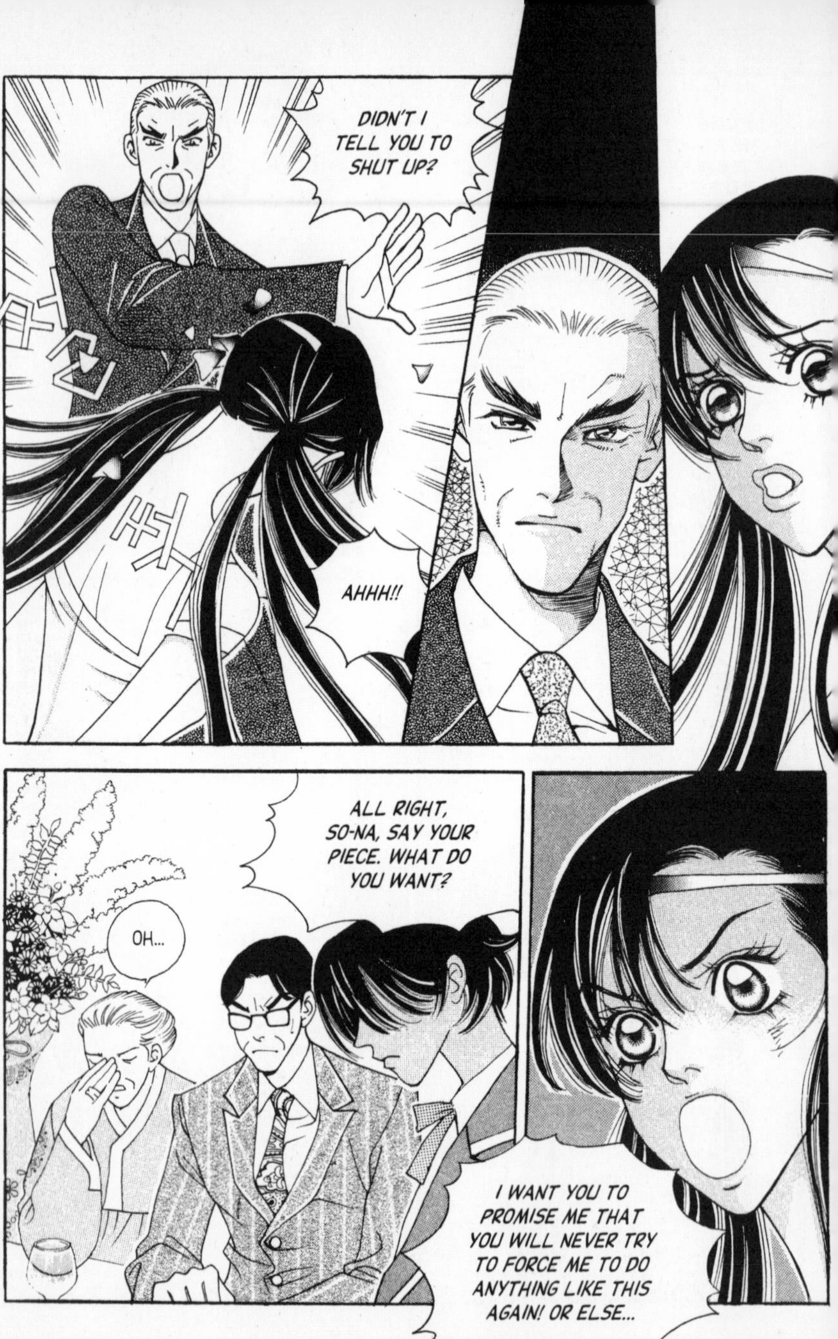
DIDN'T I TELL YOU TO SHUT UP?
AHHH!!
ALL RIGHT, SO-NA, SAY YOUR PIECE. WHAT DO YOU WANT?
OH...
I WANT YOU TO PROMISE ME THAT YOU WILL NEVER TRY TO FORCE ME TO DO ANYTHING LIKE THIS AGAIN! OR ELSE...

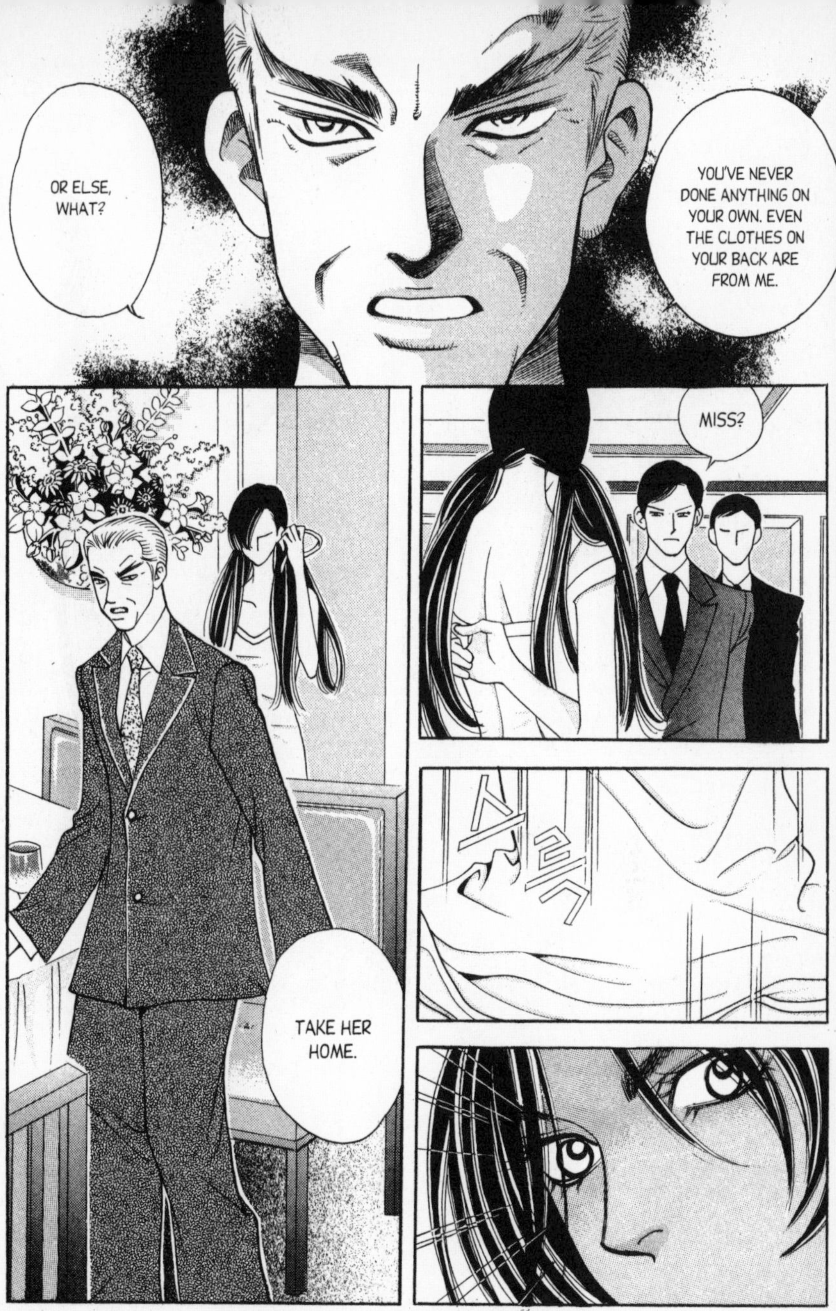
OR ELSE, WHAT?
YOU'VE NEVER DONE ANYTHING ON YOUR OWN. EVEN THE CLOTHES ON YOUR BACK ARE FROM ME.
TAKE HER HOME.
MISS?

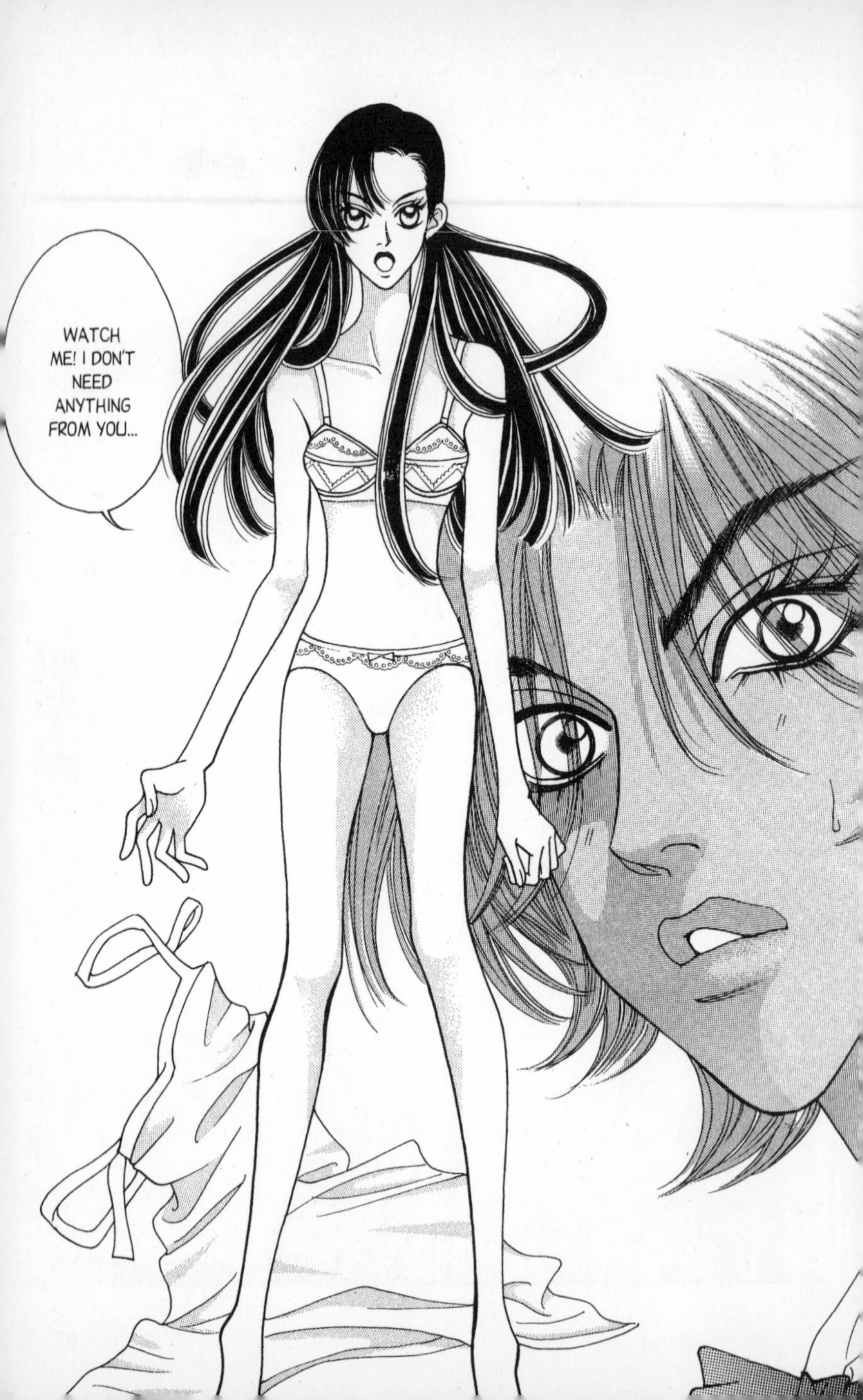
WATCH ME! I DON'T NEED ANYTHING FROM YOU...

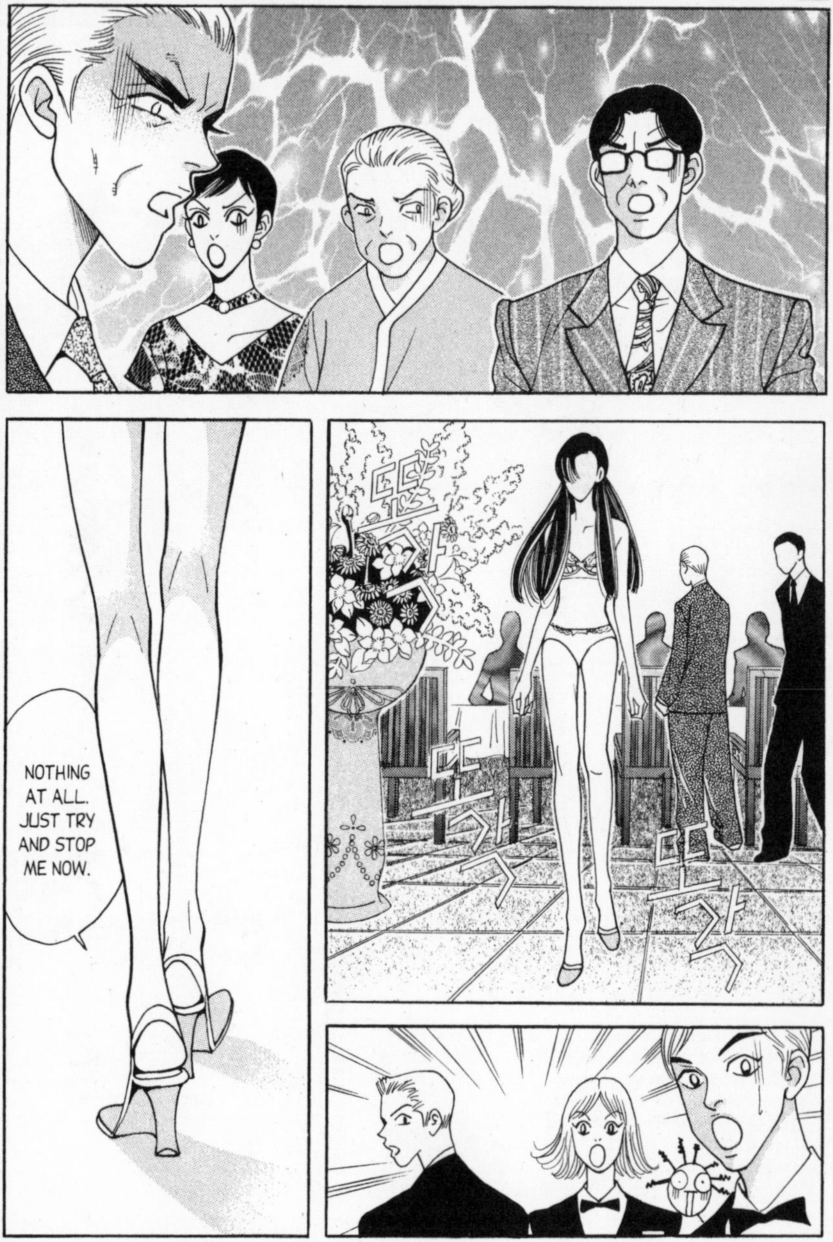
NOTHING AT ALL. JUST TRY AND STOP ME NOW.

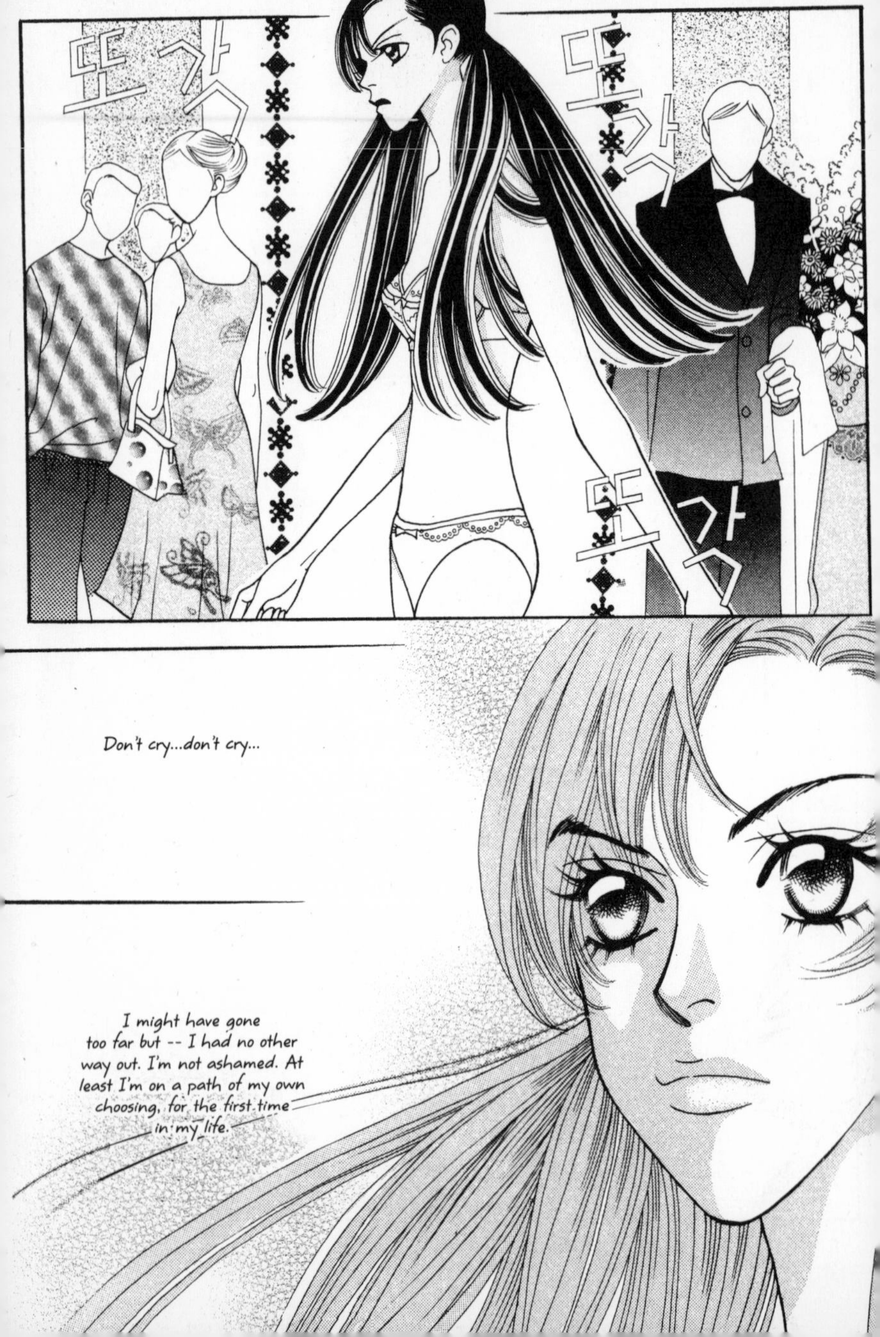
또각
또각
또각
Don't cry...don't cry...
I might have gone too far but -- I had no other way out. I'm not ashamed. At least I'm on a path of my own choosing, for the first time in my life.

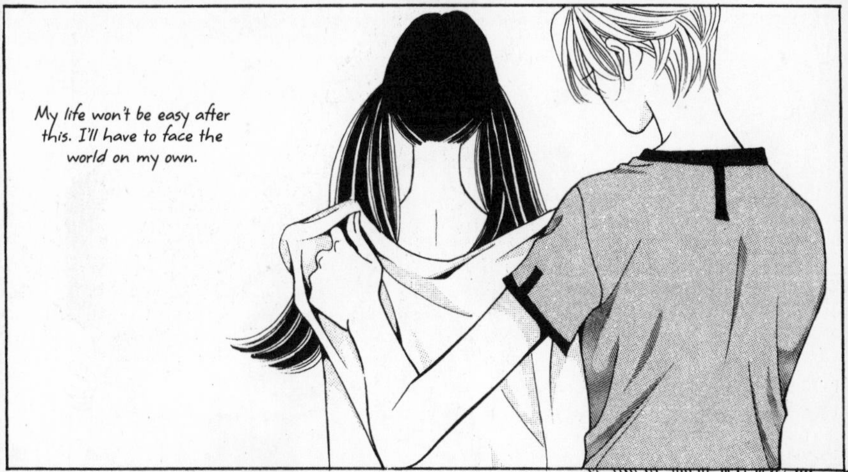
My life won't be easy after this. I'll have to face the world on my own.

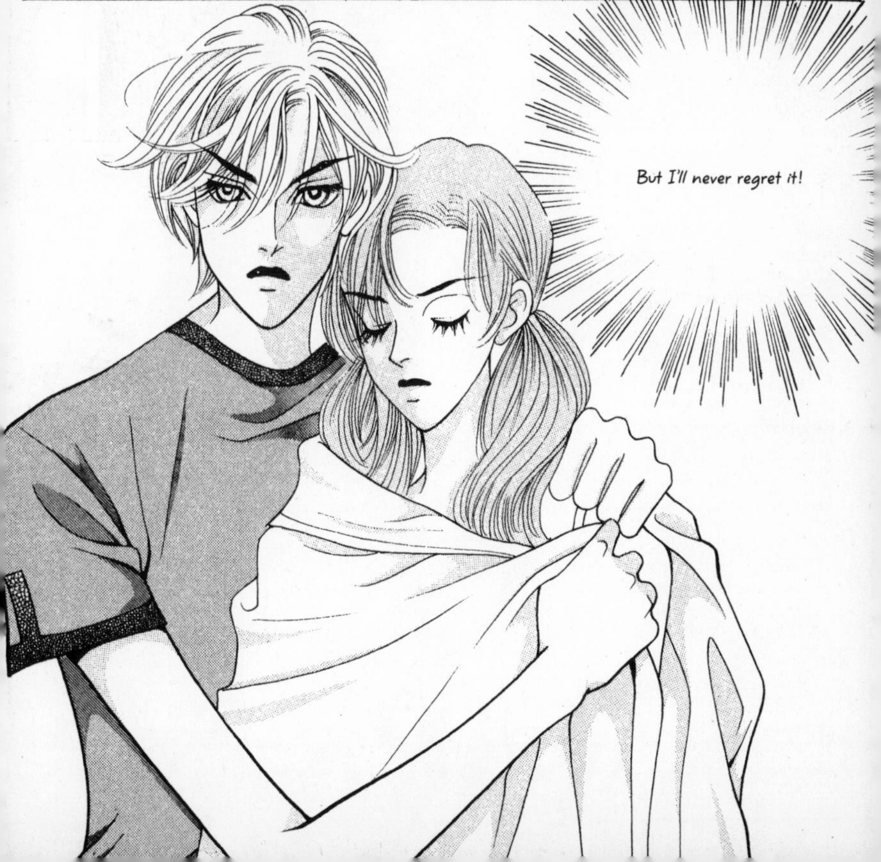
But I'll never regret it!

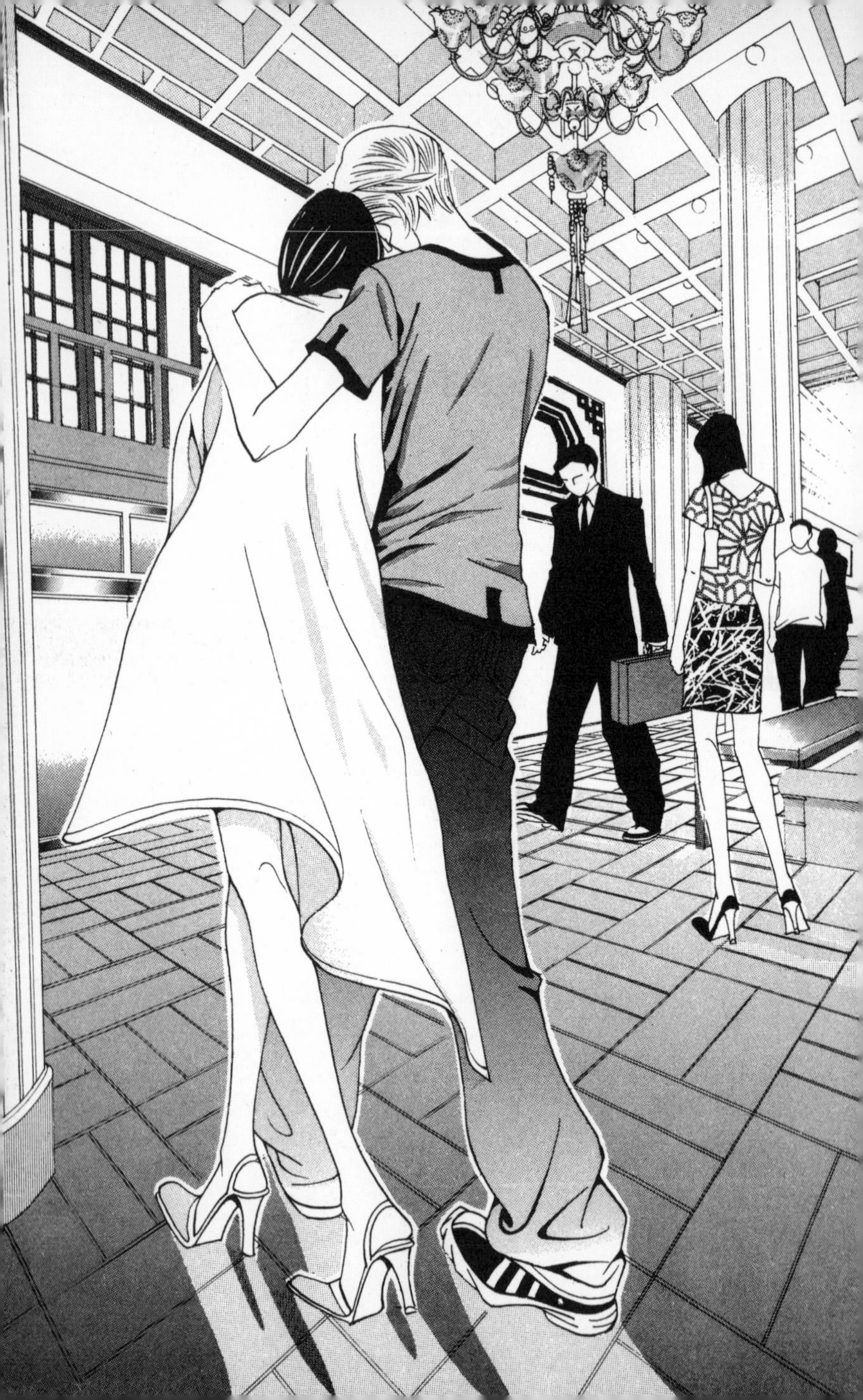

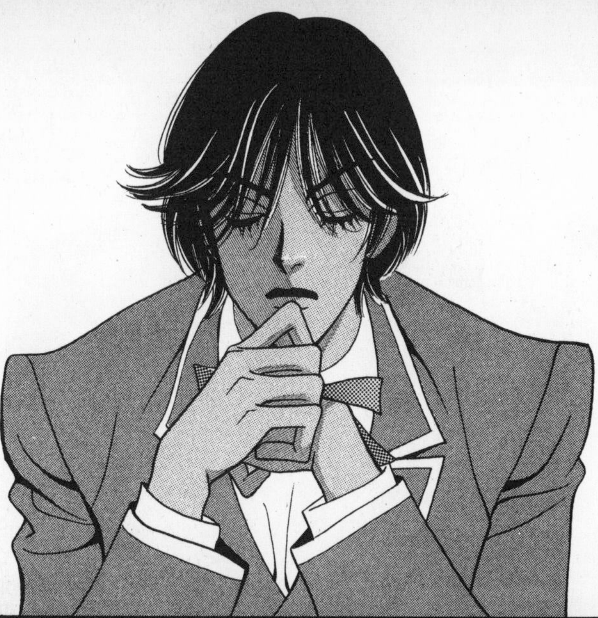

Part 24: Glass Castles

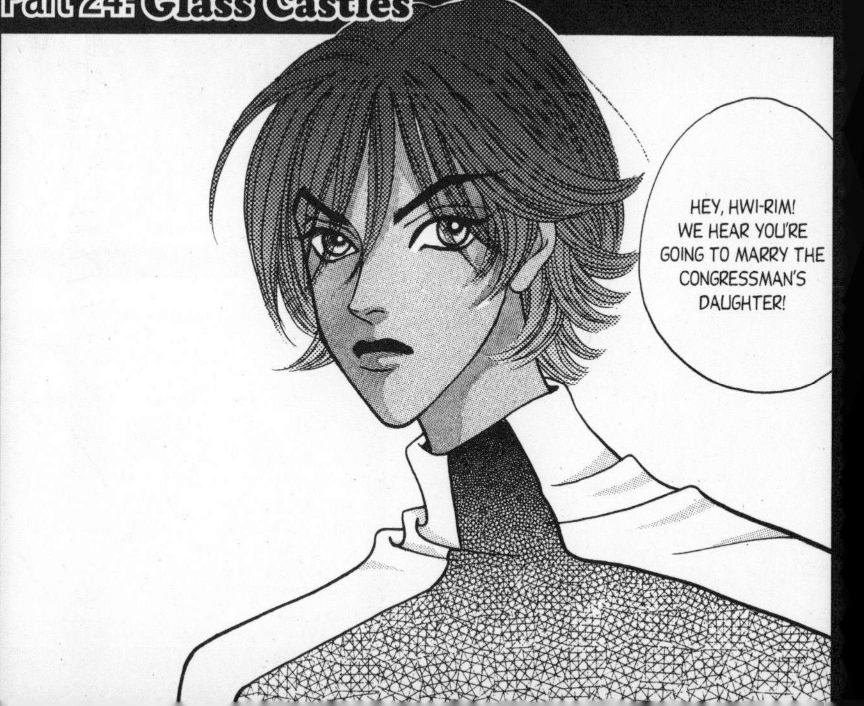
HEY, HWI-RIM! WE HEAR YOU'RE GOING TO MARRY THE CONGRESSMAN'S DAUGHTER!

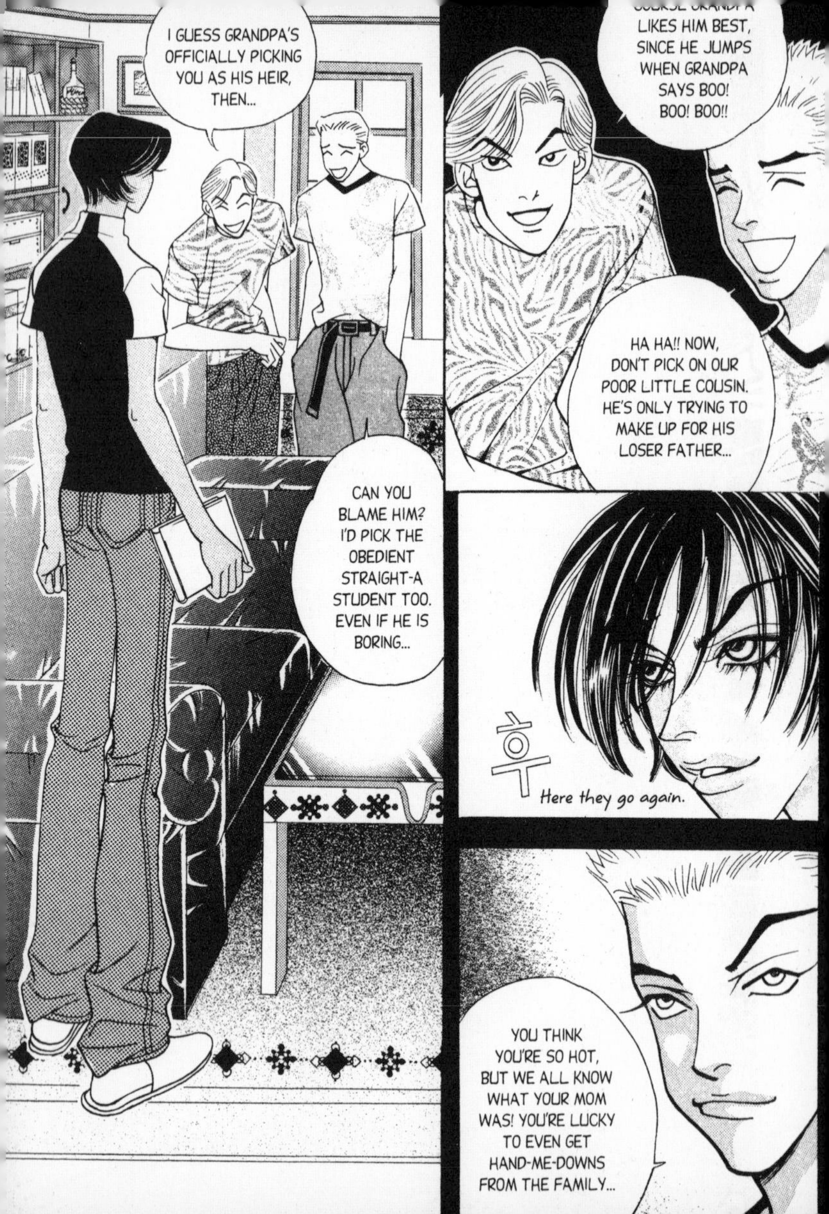
I GUESS GRANDPA'S OFFICIALLY PICKING YOU AS HIS HEIR, THEN...
CAN YOU BLAME HIM? I'D PICK THE OBEDIENT STRAIGHT-A STUDENT TOO. EVEN IF HE IS BORING...
LIKES HIM BEST, SINCE HE JUMPS WHEN GRANDPA SAYS BOO! BOO! BOO!!
HA HA!! NOW, DON'T PICK ON OUR POOR LITTLE COUSIN. HE'S ONLY TRYING TO MAKE UP FOR HIS LOSER FATHER...
후
Here they go again.
YOU THINK YOU'RE SO HOT, BUT WE ALL KNOW WHAT YOUR MOM WAS! YOU'RE LUCKY TO EVEN GET HAND-ME-DOWNS FROM THE FAMILY...

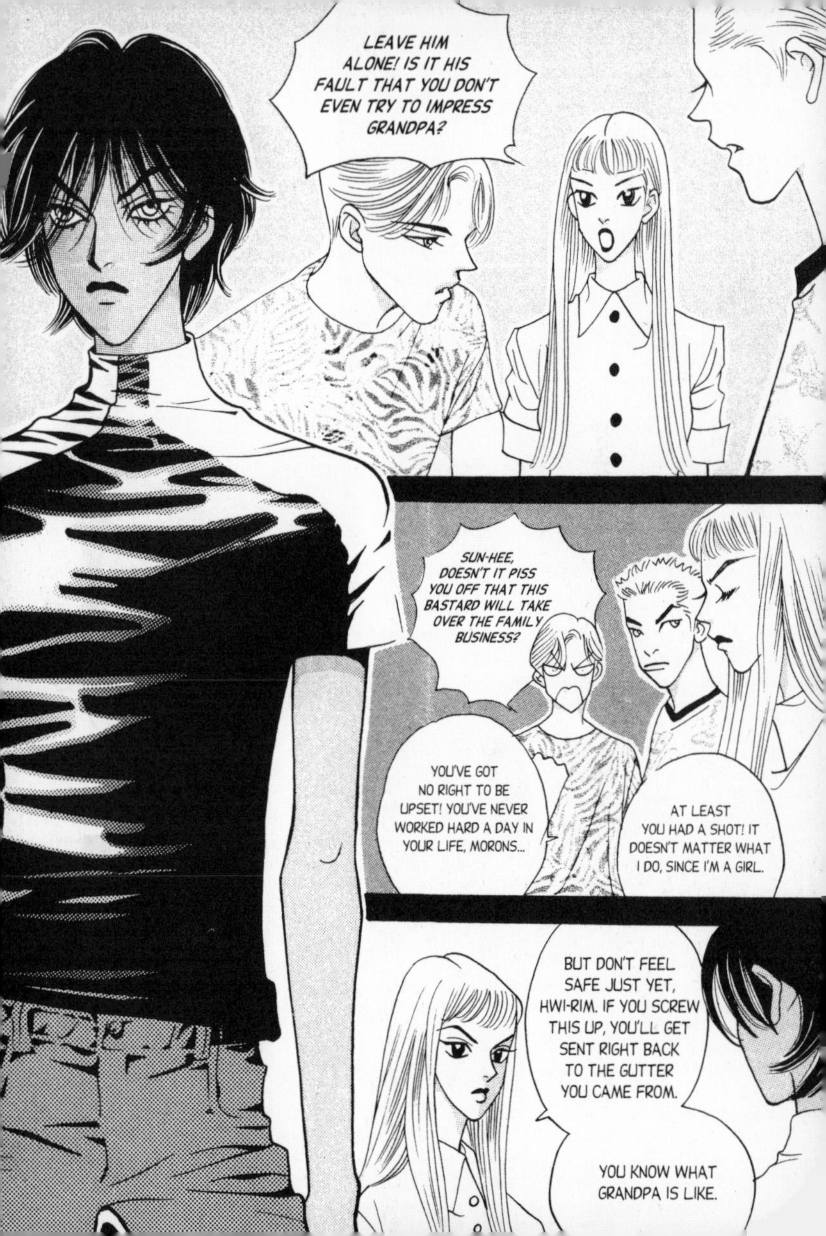
LEAVE HIM ALONE! IS IT HIS FAULT THAT YOU DON'T EVEN TRY TO IMPRESS GRANDPA?
SUN-HEE, DOESN'T IT PISS YOU OFF THAT THIS BASTARD WILL TAKE OVER THE FAMILY BUSINESS?
YOU'VE GOT NO RIGHT TO BE UPSET! YOU'VE NEVER WORKED HARD A DAY IN YOUR LIFE, MORONS...
AT LEAST YOU HAD A SHOT! IT DOESN'T MATTER WHAT I DO, SINCE I'M A GIRL.
BUT DON'T FEEL SAFE JUST YET, HWI-RIM. IF YOU SCREW THIS UP, YOU'LL GET SENT RIGHT BACK TO THE GUTTER YOU CAME FROM.
YOU KNOW WHAT GRANDPA IS LIKE.

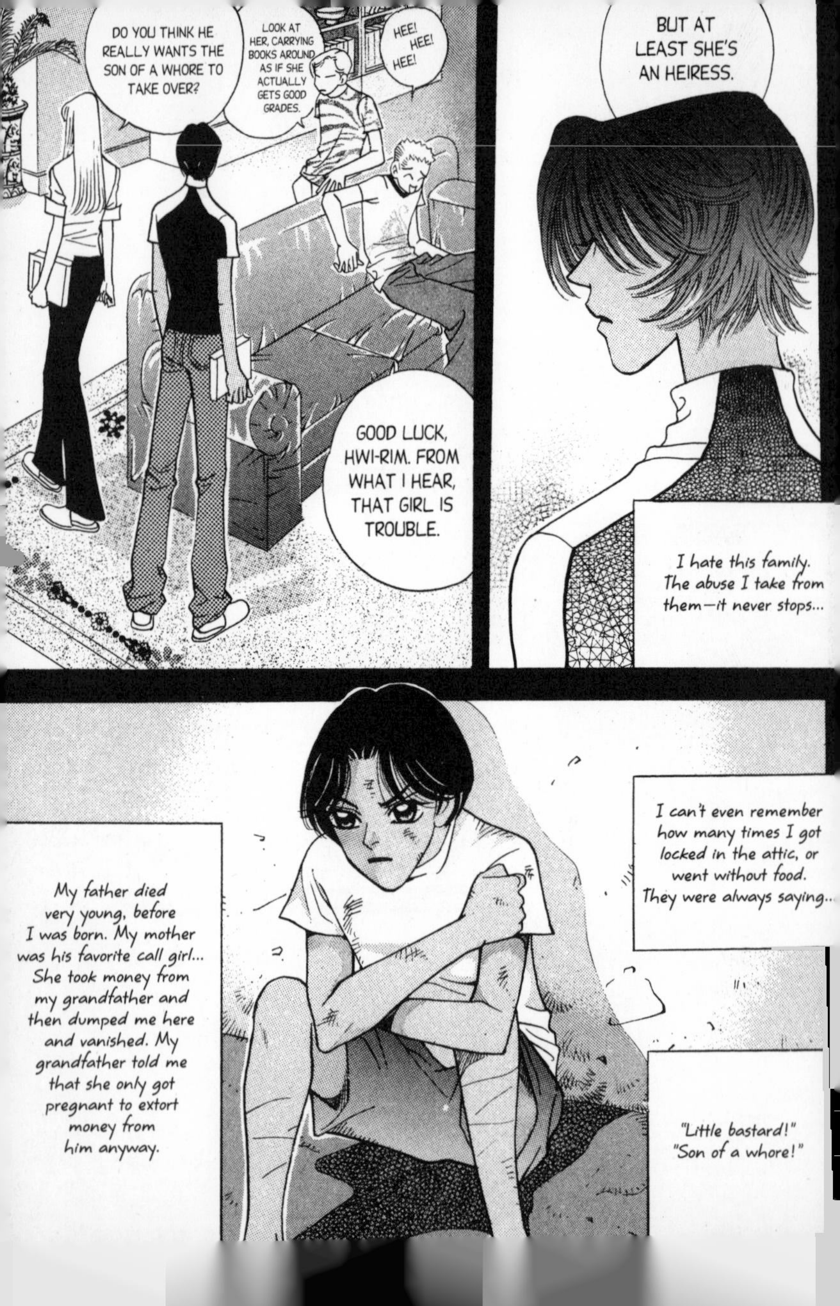
DO YOU THINK HE REALLY WANTS THE SON OF A WHORE TO TAKE OVER?
LOOK AT HER, CARRYING BOOKS AROUND AS IF SHE ACTUALLY GETS GOOD GRADES.
HEE! HEE! HEE!
GOOD LUCK, HWI-RIM. FROM WHAT I HEAR, THAT GIRL IS TROUBLE.
BUT AT LEAST SHE'S AN HEIRESS.
I hate this family. The abuse I take from them—it never stops...
My father died very young, before I was born. My mother was his favorite call girl... She took money from my grandfather and then dumped me here and vanished. My grandfather told me that she only got pregnant to extort money from him anyway.
I can't even remember how many times I got locked in the attic, or went without food. They were always saying...
"Little bastard!" "Son of a whore!"

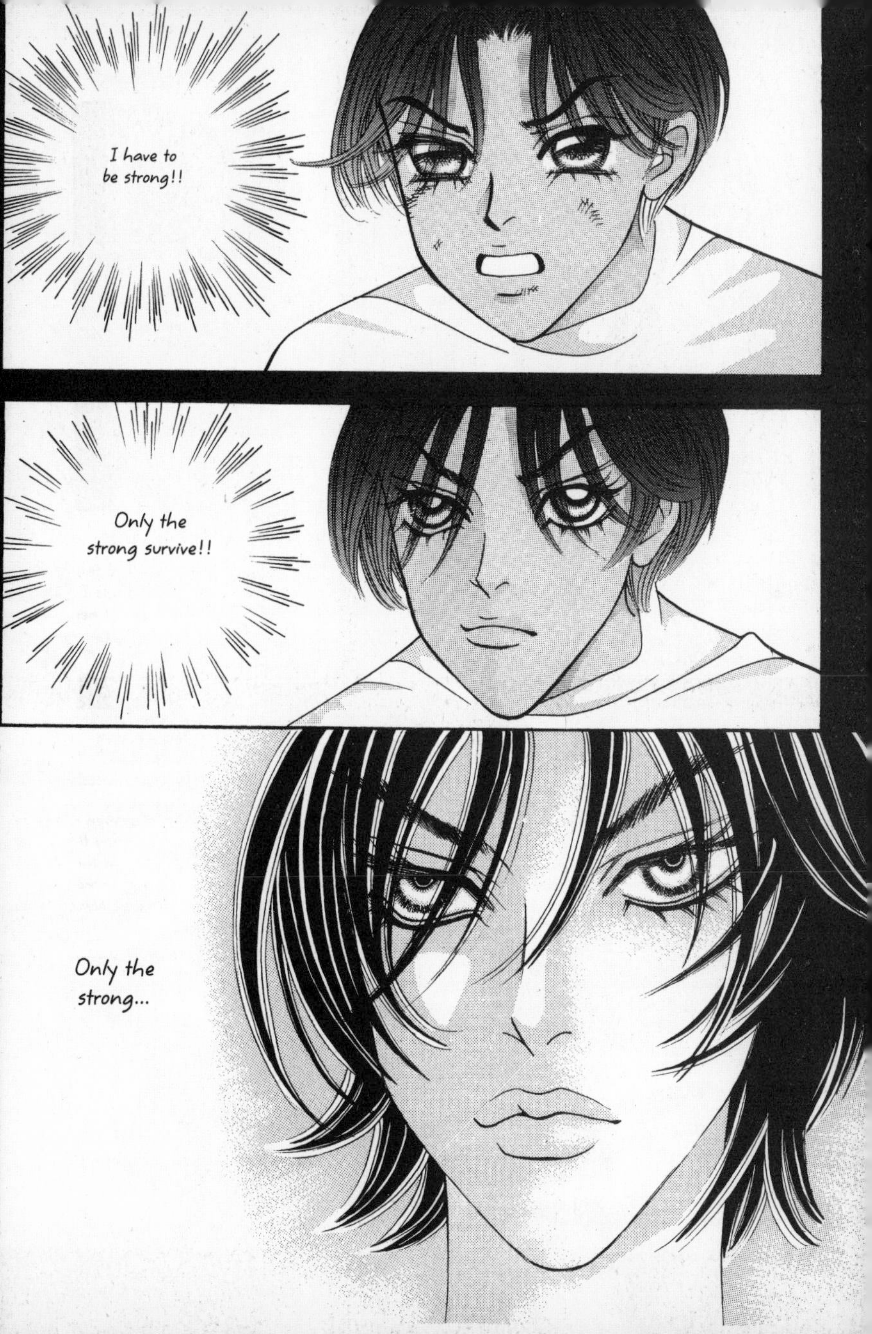
I have to be strong!!
Only the strong survive!!
Only the strong...

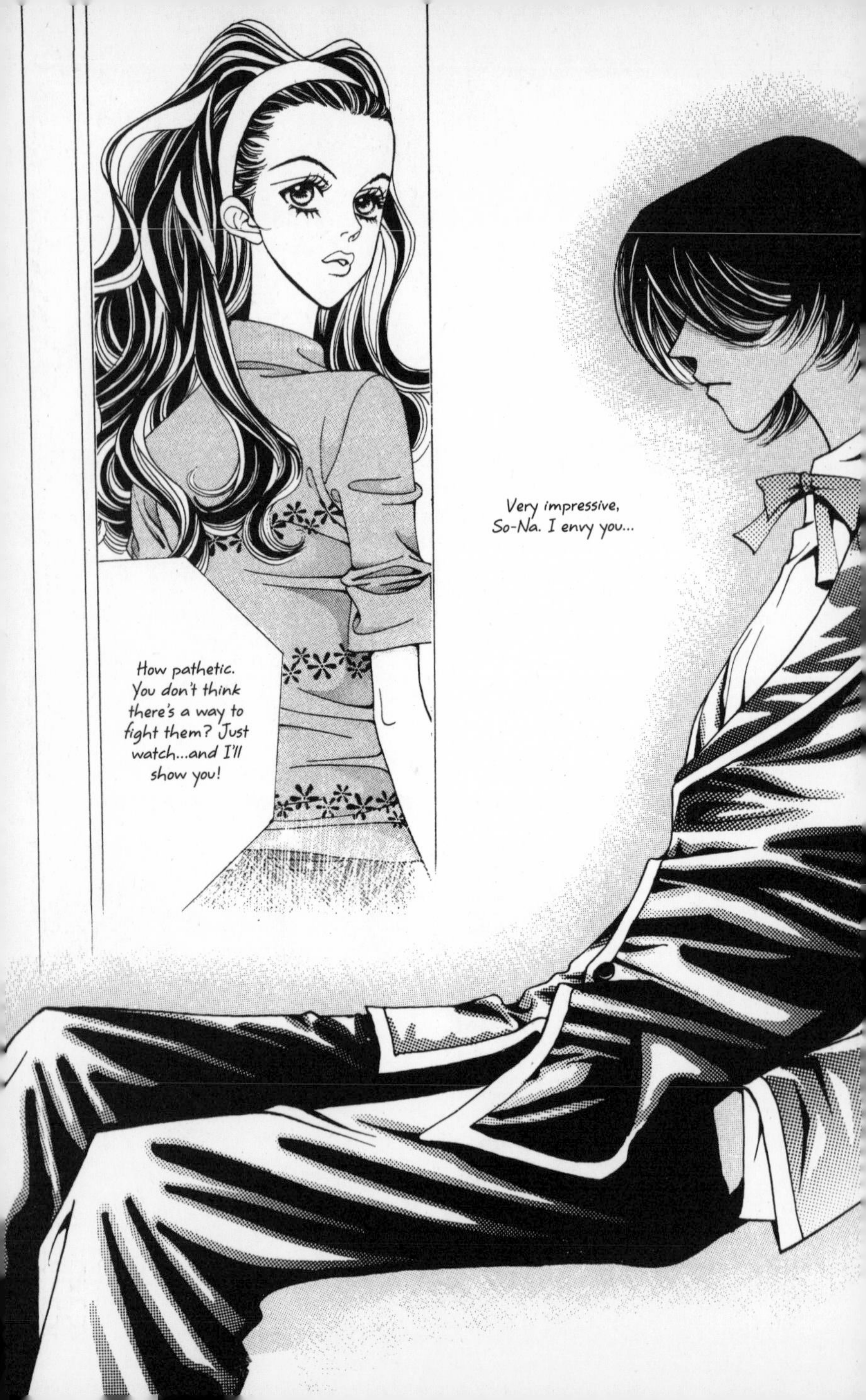
Very impressive, So-Na. I envy you...
How pathetic. You don't think there's a way to fight them? Just watch...and I'll show you!

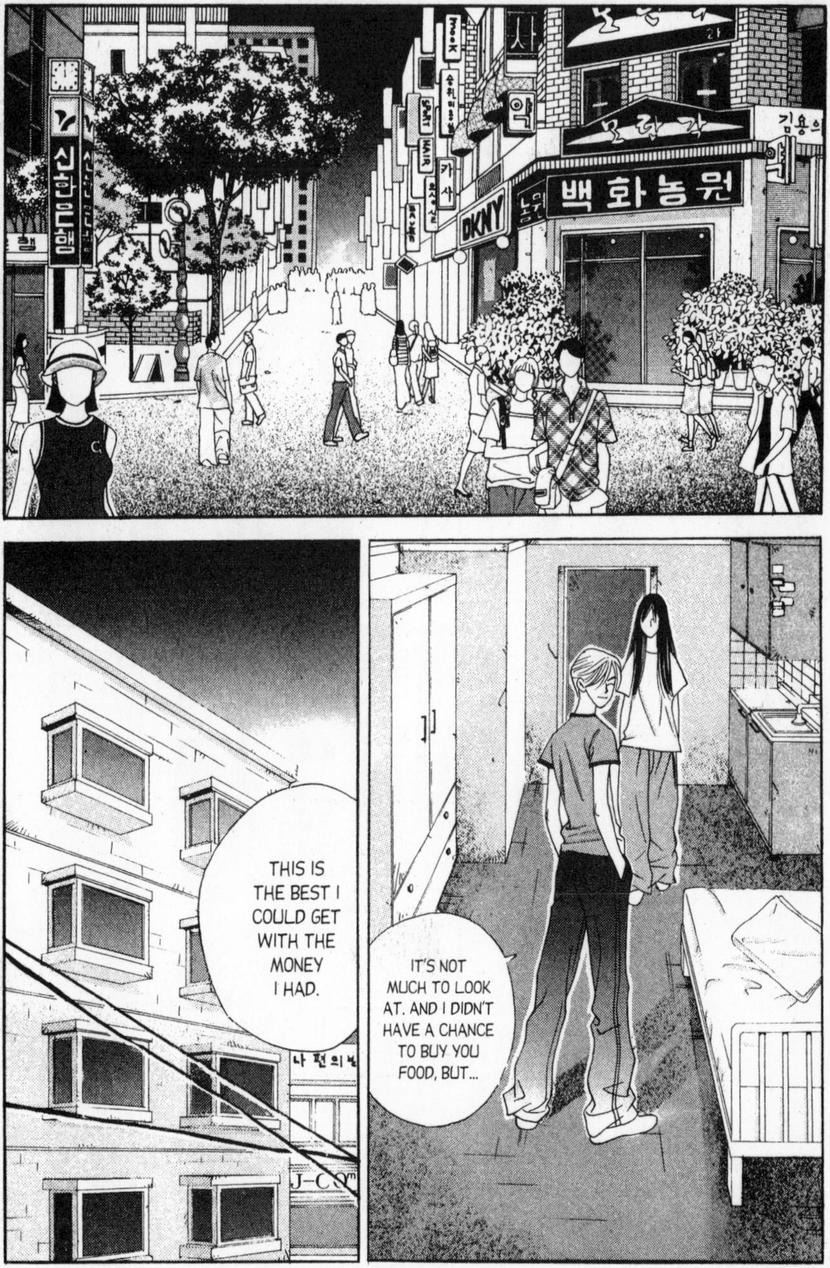
신한은행
DKNY
모란각
백화농원
THIS IS THE BEST I COULD GET WITH THE MONEY I HAD.
IT'S NOT MUCH TO LOOK AT. AND I DIDN'T HAVE A CHANCE TO BUY YOU FOOD, BUT...

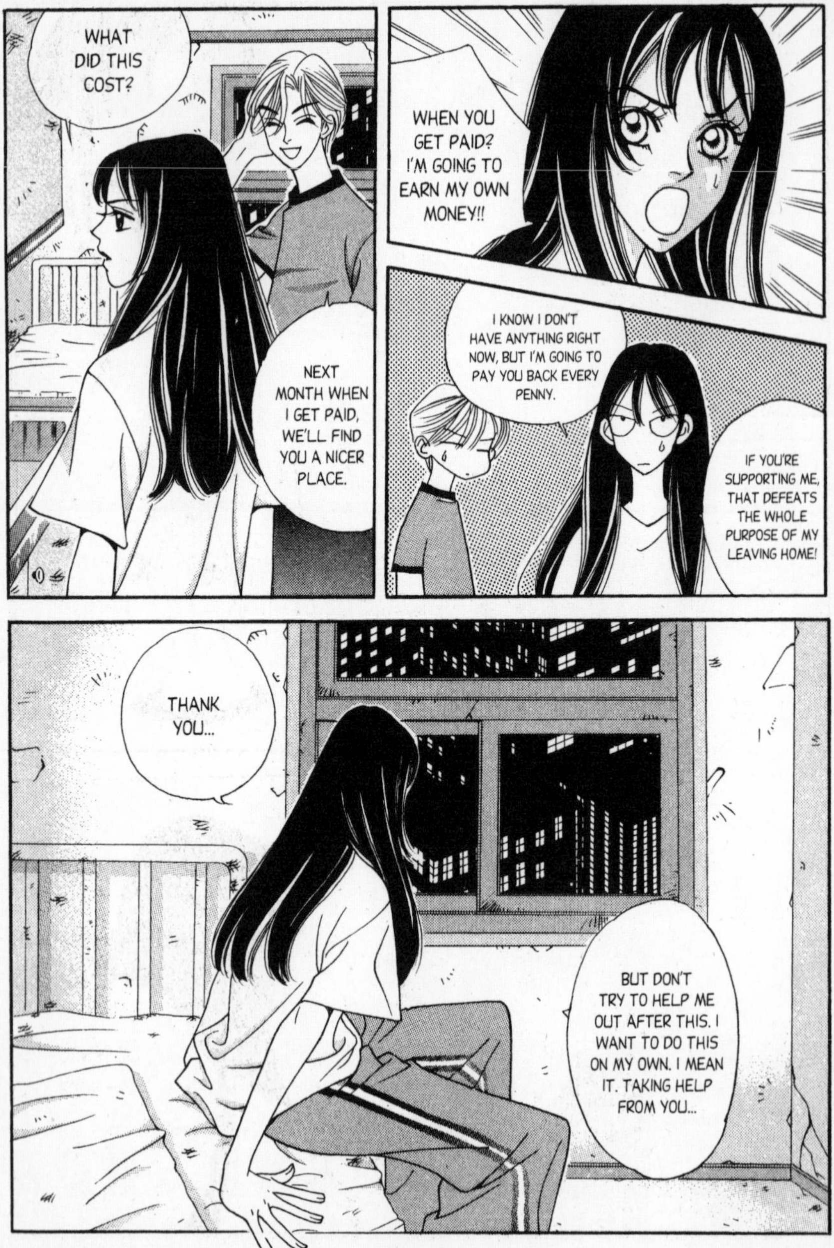
WHAT DID THIS COST?
NEXT MONTH WHEN I GET PAID, WE'LL FIND YOU A NICER PLACE.
WHEN YOU GET PAID? I'M GOING TO EARN MY OWN MONEY!!
I KNOW I DON'T HAVE ANYTHING RIGHT NOW, BUT I'M GOING TO PAY YOU BACK EVERY PENNY.
IF YOU'RE SUPPORTING ME, THAT DEFEATS THE WHOLE PURPOSE OF MY LEAVING HOME!
THANK YOU...
BUT DON'T TRY TO HELP ME OUT AFTER THIS. I WANT TO DO THIS ON MY OWN. I MEAN IT. TAKING HELP FROM YOU...

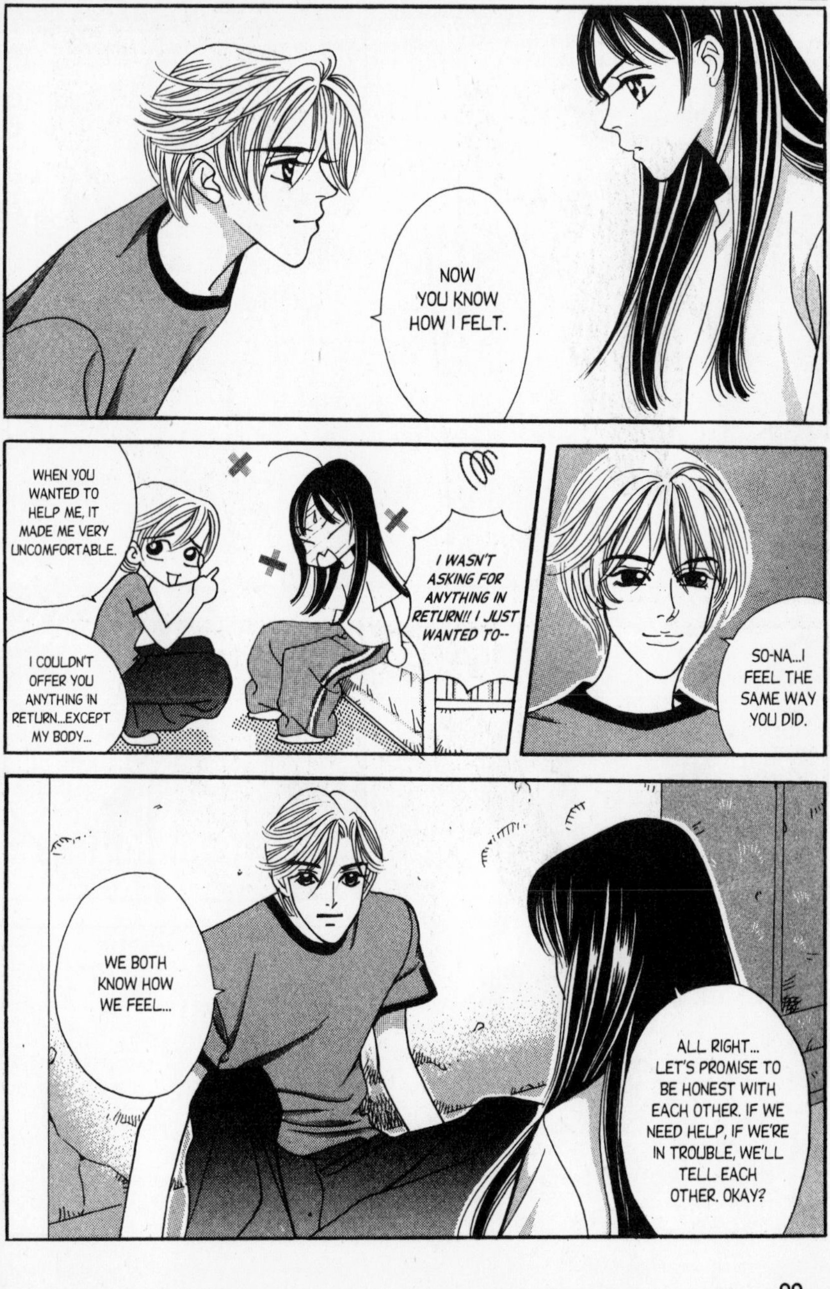
NOW YOU KNOW HOW I FELT.
SO-NA...I FEEL THE SAME WAY YOU DID.
WHEN YOU WANTED TO HELP ME, IT MADE ME VERY UNCOMFORTABLE.
I COULDN'T OFFER YOU ANYTHING IN RETURN...EXCEPT MY BODY...
I WASN'T ASKING FOR ANYTHING IN RETURN!! I JUST WANTED TO--
WE BOTH KNOW HOW WE FEEL...
ALL RIGHT... LET'S PROMISE TO BE HONEST WITH EACH OTHER. IF WE NEED HELP, IF WE'RE IN TROUBLE, WE'LL TELL EACH OTHER. OKAY?

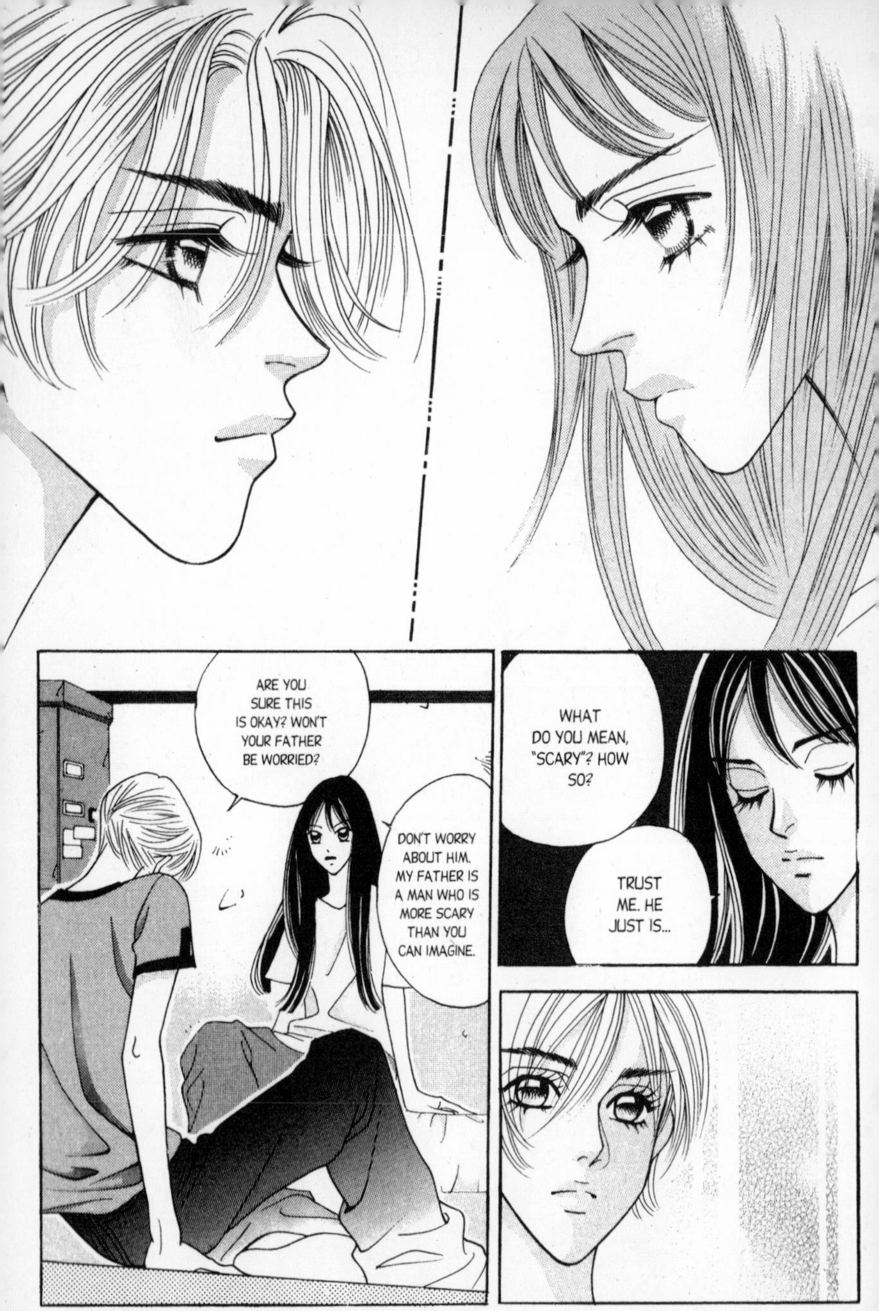
ARE YOU SURE THIS IS OKAY? WON'T YOUR FATHER BE WORRIED?
DON'T WORRY ABOUT HIM. MY FATHER IS A MAN WHO IS MORE SCARY THAN YOU CAN IMAGINE.
WHAT DO YOU MEAN, "SCARY"? HOW SO?
TRUST ME. HE JUST IS...

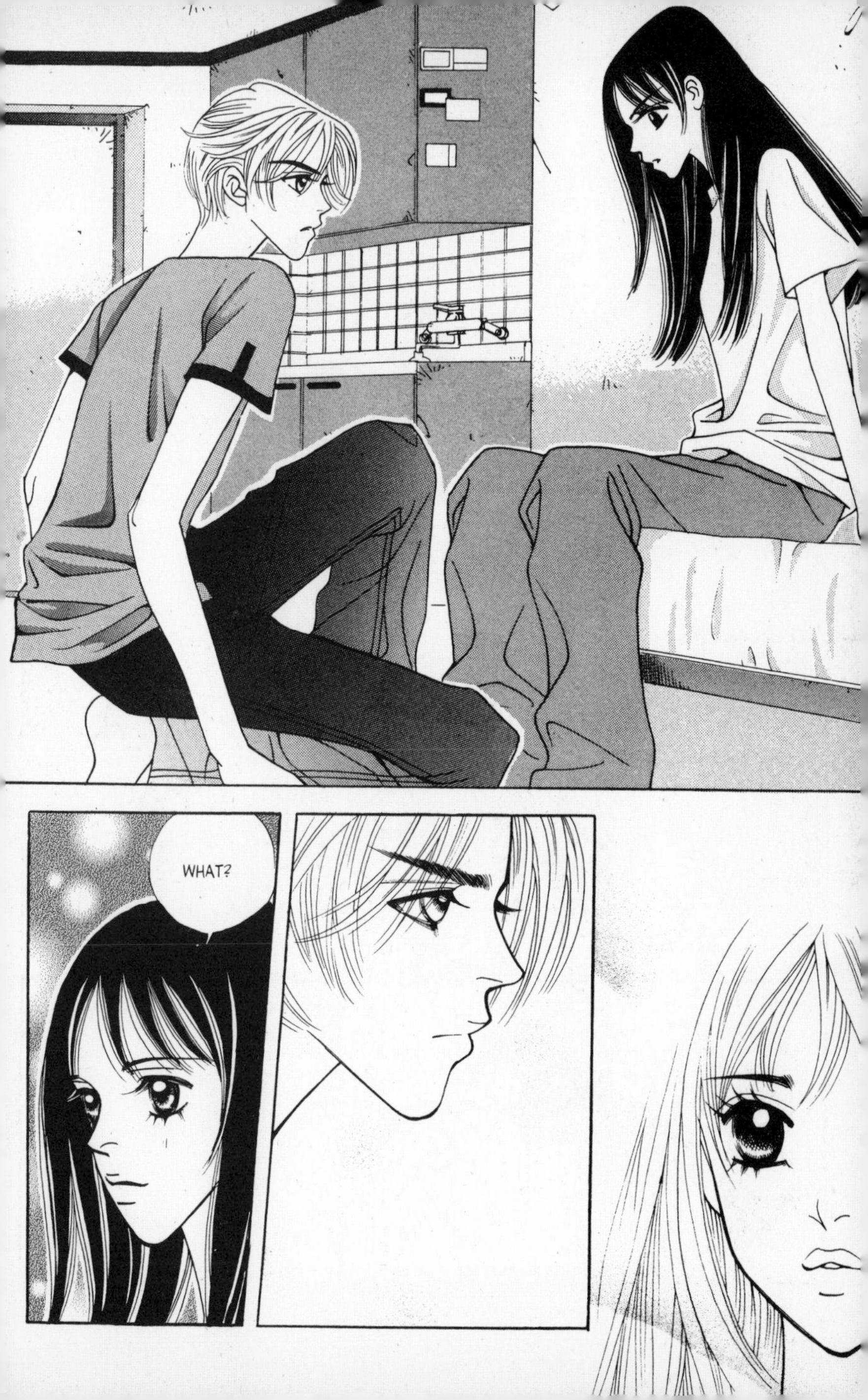
WHAT?

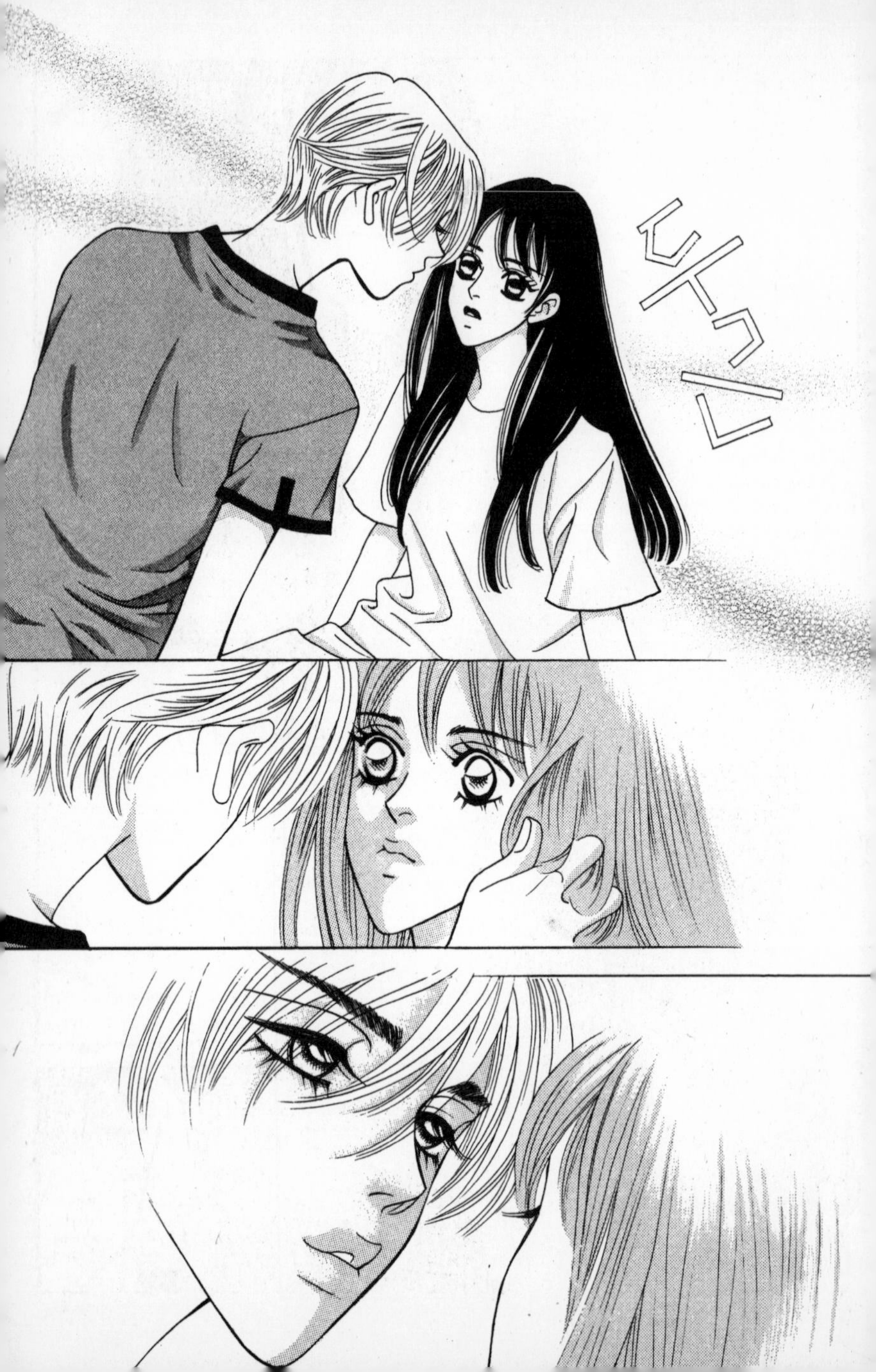

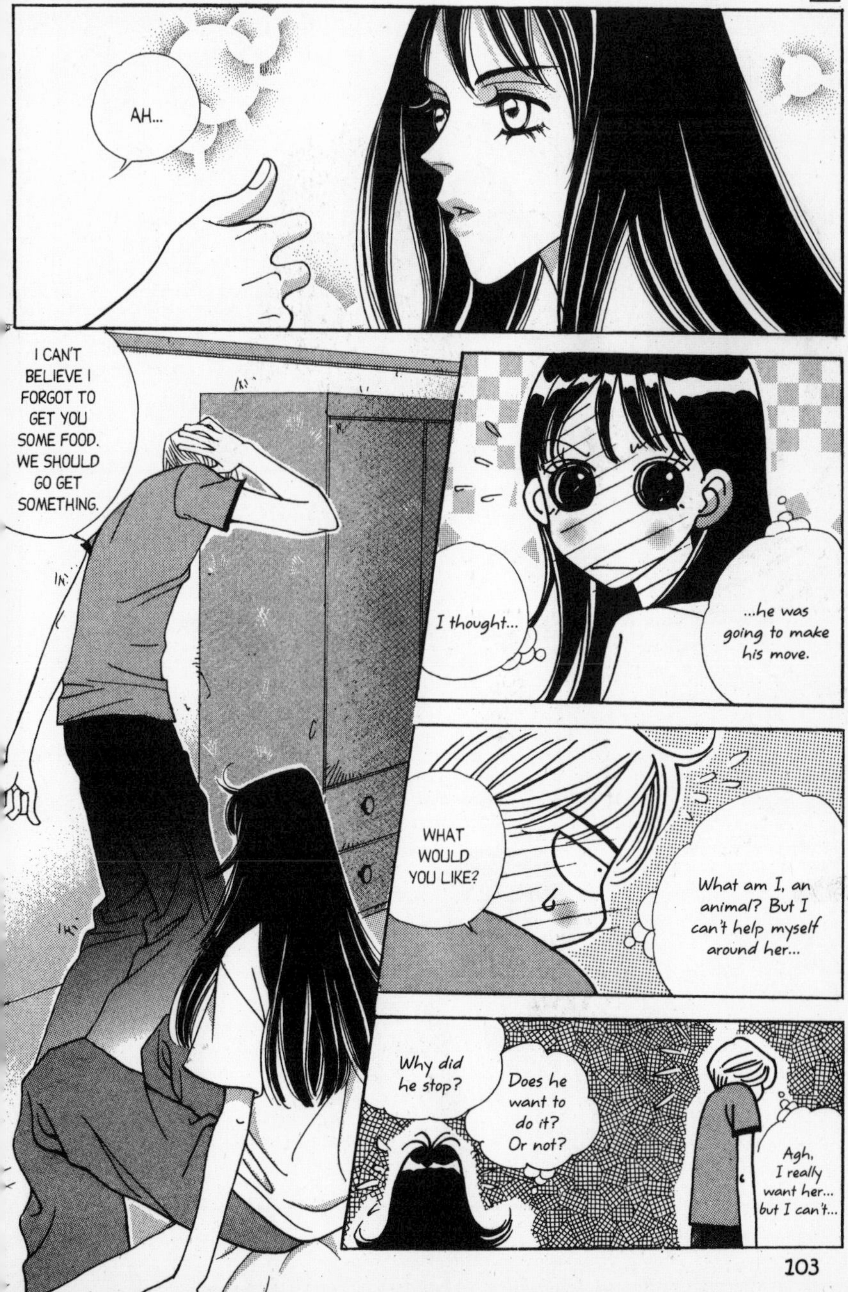
AH...
I thought...
...he was going to make his move.
WHAT WOULD YOU LIKE?
What am I, an animal? But I can't help myself around her...
I CAN'T BELIEVE I FORGOT TO GET YOU SOME FOOD. WE SHOULD GO GET SOMETHING.
Agh, I really want her... but I can't...
Does he want to do it? Or not?
Why did he stop?

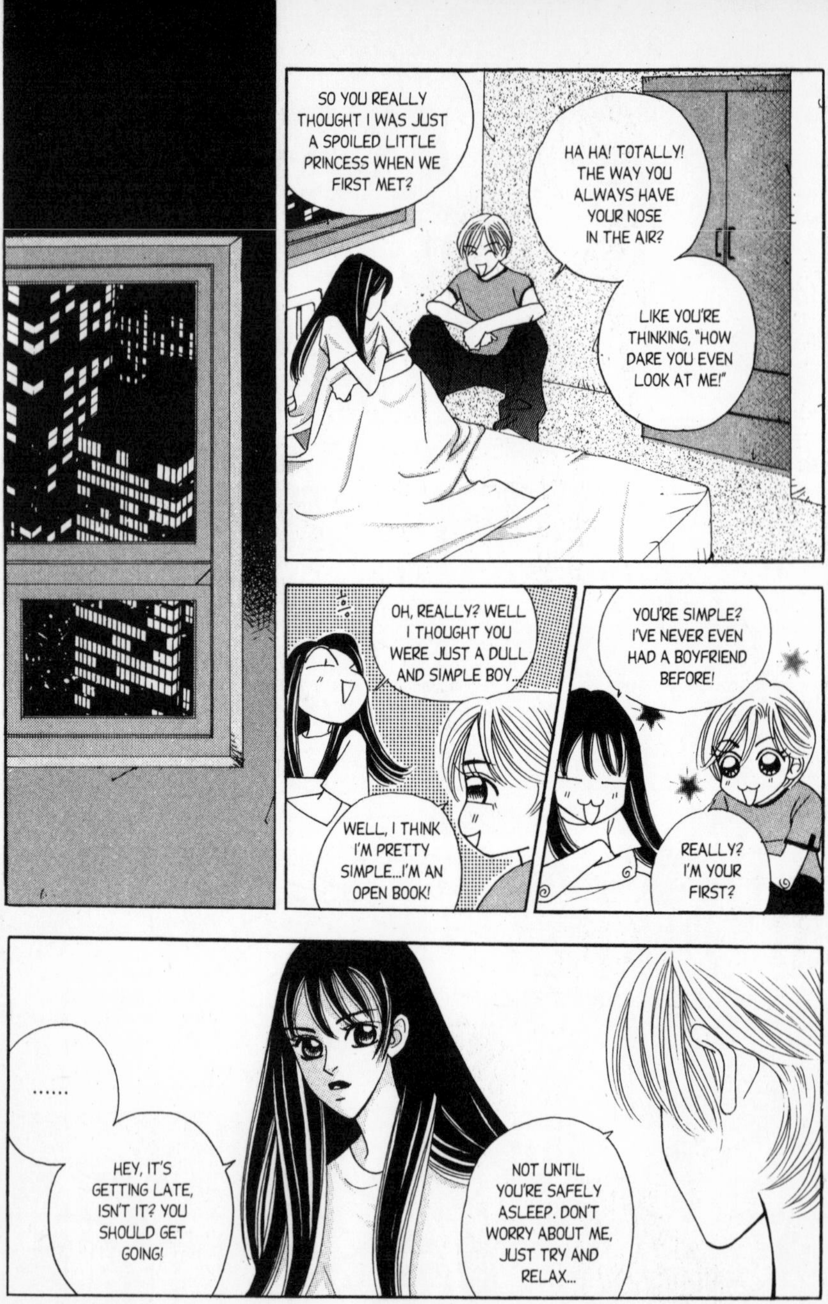
SO YOU REALLY THOUGHT I WAS JUST A SPOILED LITTLE PRINCESS WHEN WE FIRST MET?
HA HA! TOTALLY! THE WAY YOU ALWAYS HAVE YOUR NOSE IN THE AIR?
LIKE YOU'RE THINKING, "HOW DARE YOU EVEN LOOK AT ME!"
OH, REALLY? WELL I THOUGHT YOU WERE JUST A DULL AND SIMPLE BOY...
WELL, I THINK I'M PRETTY SIMPLE...I'M AN OPEN BOOK!
YOU'RE SIMPLE? I'VE NEVER EVEN HAD A BOYFRIEND BEFORE!
REALLY? I'M YOUR FIRST?
......
HEY, IT'S GETTING LATE, ISN'T IT? YOU SHOULD GET GOING!
NOT UNTIL YOU'RE SAFELY ASLEEP. DON'T WORRY ABOUT ME, JUST TRY AND RELAX...

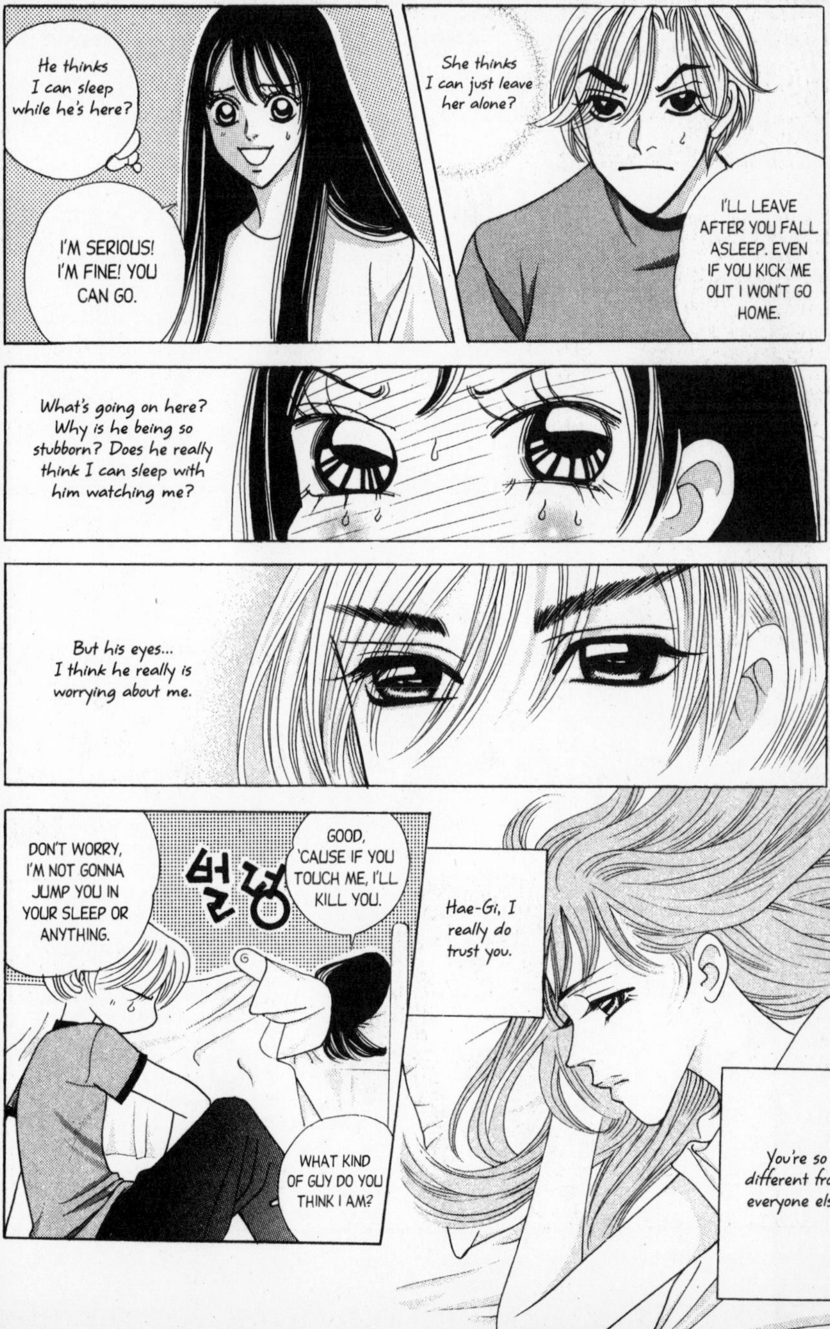
He thinks I can sleep while he's here?
I'M SERIOUS! I'M FINE! YOU CAN GO.
She thinks I can just leave her alone?
I'LL LEAVE AFTER YOU FALL ASLEEP. EVEN IF YOU KICK ME OUT I WON'T GO HOME.
What's going on here? Why is he being so stubborn? Does he really think I can sleep with him watching me?
But his eyes... I think he really is worrying about me.
DON'T WORRY, I'M NOT GONNA JUMP YOU IN YOUR SLEEP OR ANYTHING.
벌렁
GOOD, 'CAUSE IF YOU TOUCH ME, I'LL KILL YOU.
WHAT KIND OF GUY DO YOU THINK I AM?
Hae-Gi, I really do trust you.
You're so different from everyone else.

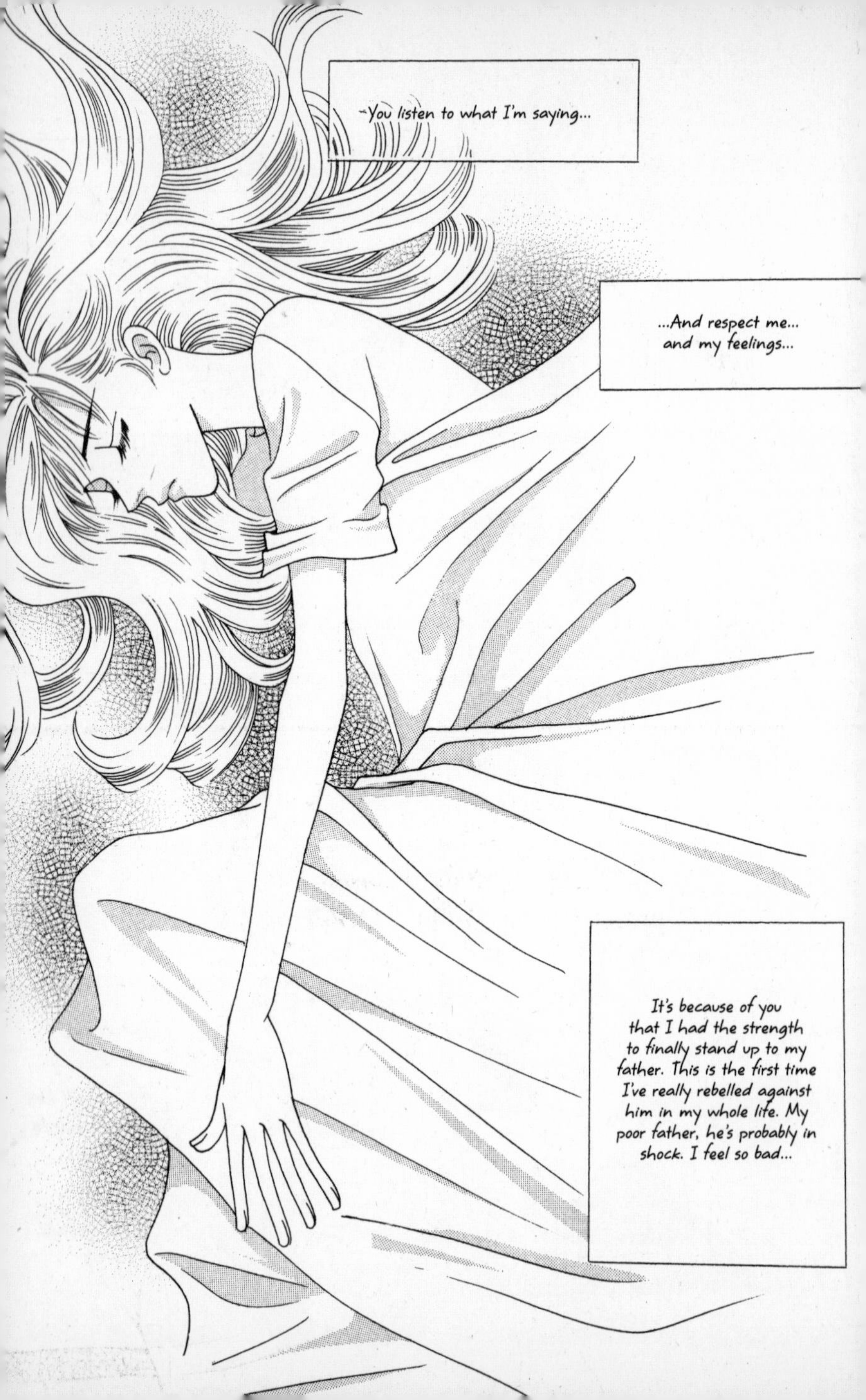
~You listen to what I'm saying...
...And respect me... and my feelings...
It's because of you that I had the strength to finally stand up to my father. This is the first time I've really rebelled against him in my whole life. My poor father, he's probably in shock. I feel so bad...

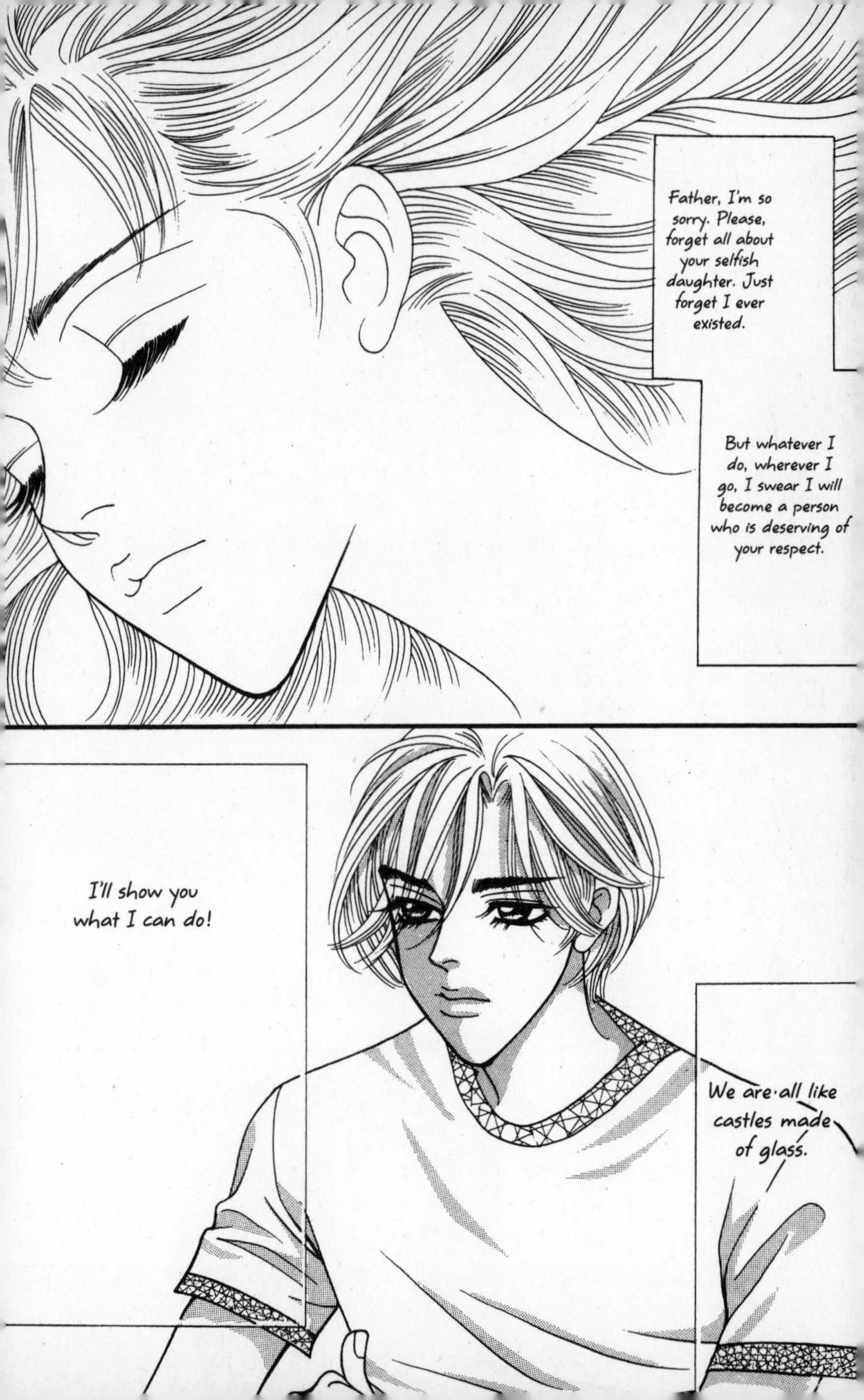
Father, I'm so sorry. Please, forget all about your selfish daughter. Just forget I ever existed.
But whatever I do, wherever I go, I swear I will become a person who is deserving of your respect.
I'll show you what I can do!
We are all like castles made of glass.

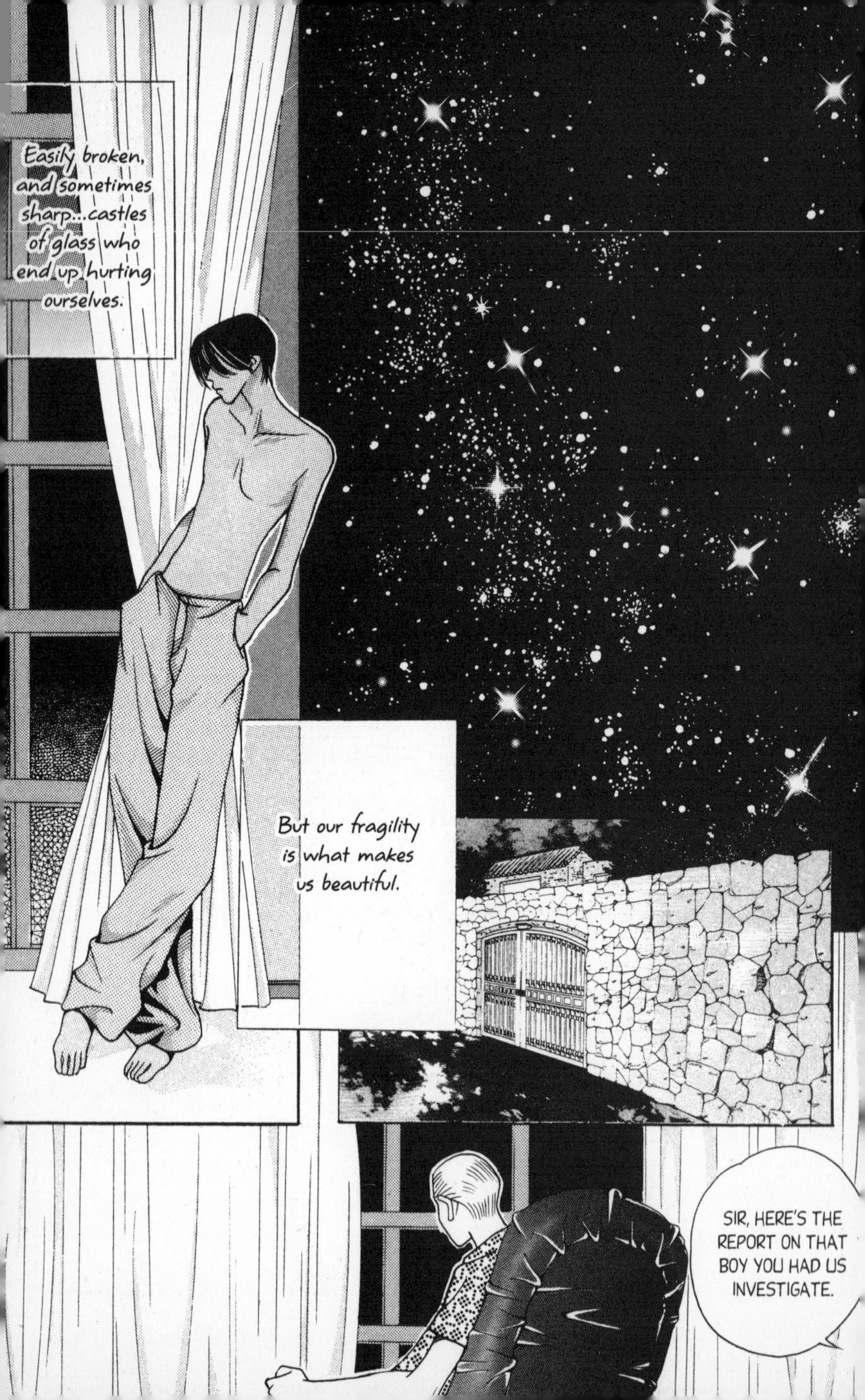
Easily broken, and sometimes sharp...castles of glass who end up hurting ourselves.
But our fragility is what makes us beautiful.
SIR, HERE'S THE REPORT ON THAT BOY YOU HAD US INVESTIGATE.

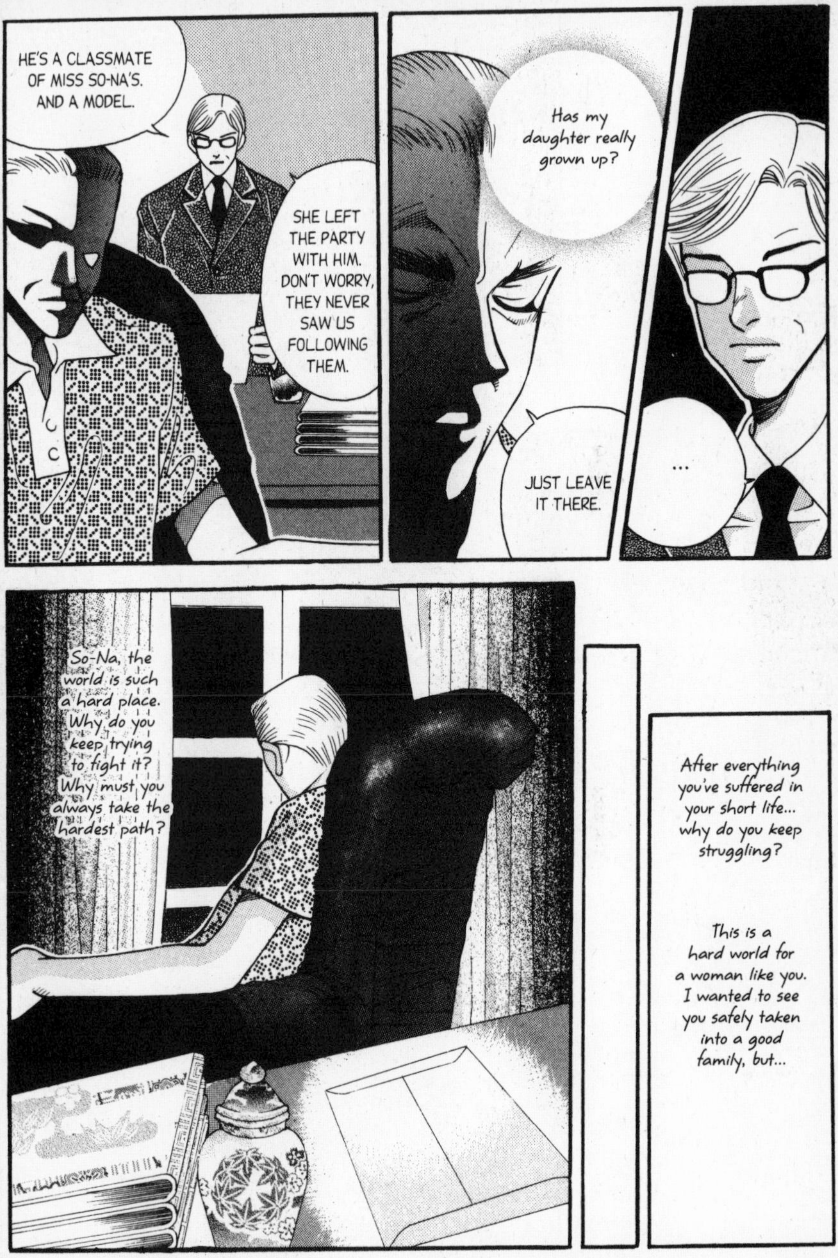
HE'S A CLASSMATE OF MISS SO-NA'S. AND A MODEL.
SHE LEFT THE PARTY WITH HIM. DON'T WORRY, THEY NEVER SAW US FOLLOWING THEM.
Has my daughter really grown up?
JUST LEAVE IT THERE.
...
So-Na, the world is such a hard place. Why do you keep trying to fight it? Why must you always take the hardest path?
After everything you've suffered in your short life... why do you keep struggling?
This is a hard world for a woman like you. I wanted to see you safely taken into a good family, but...

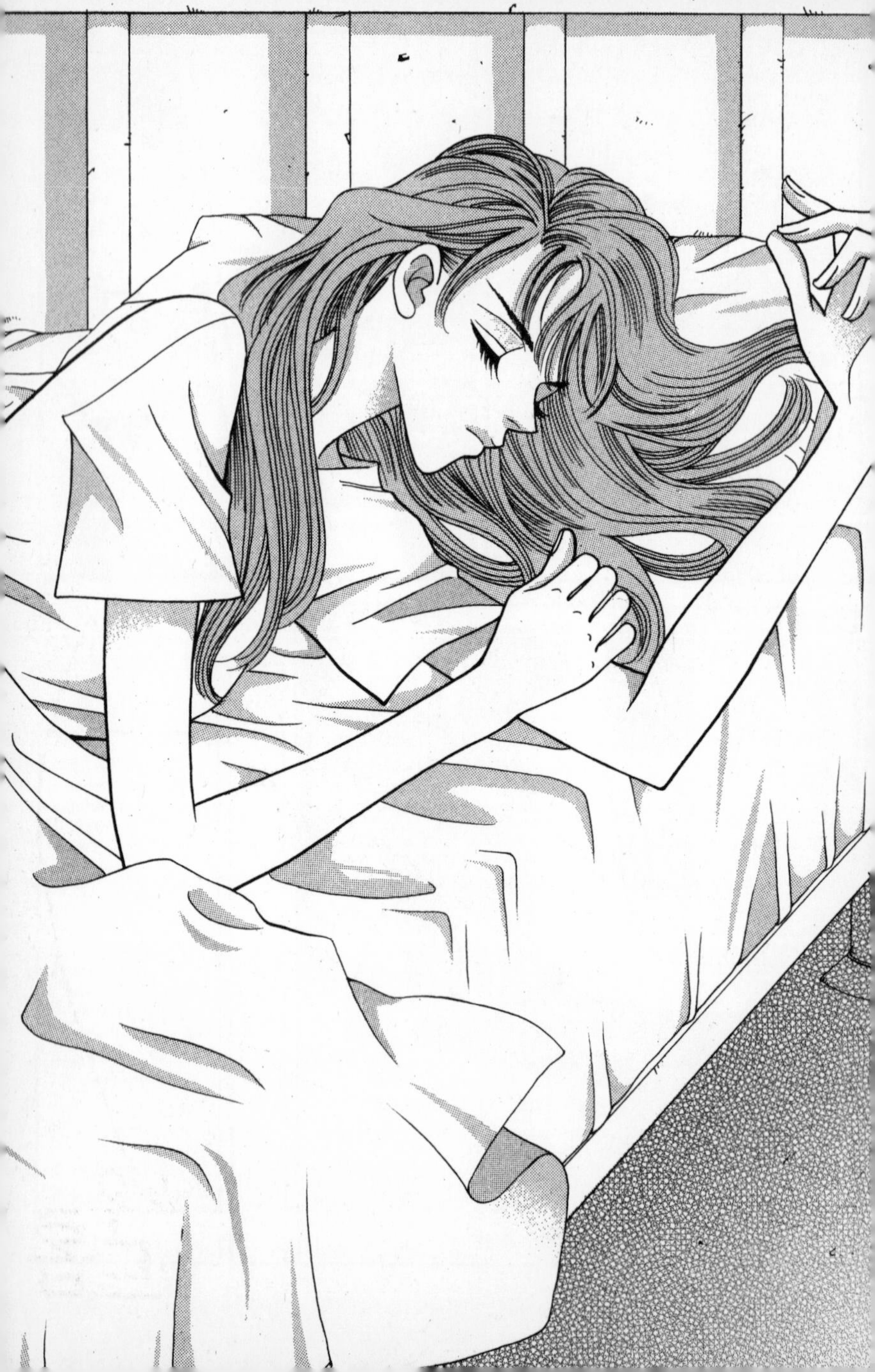

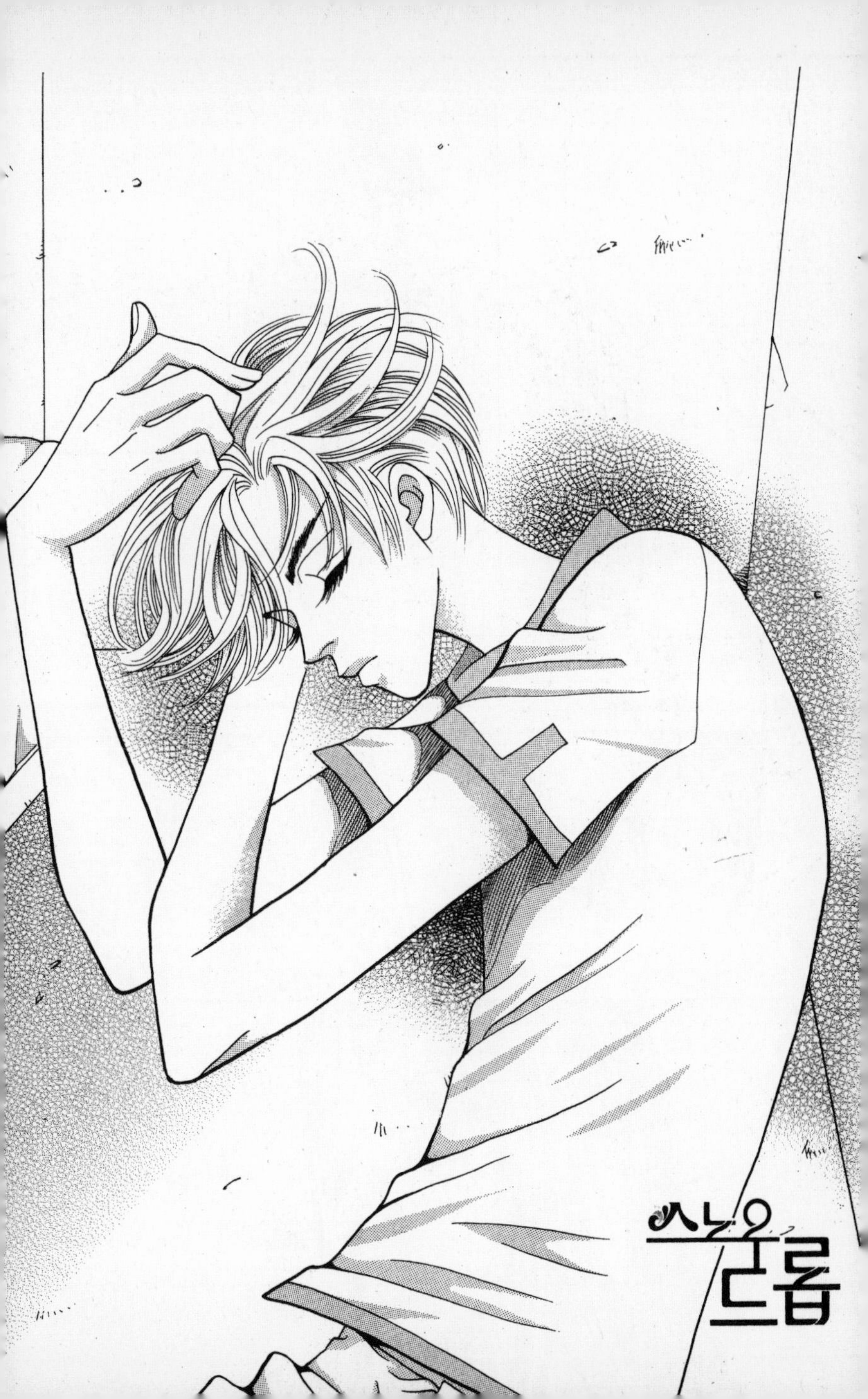
스노우 드롭

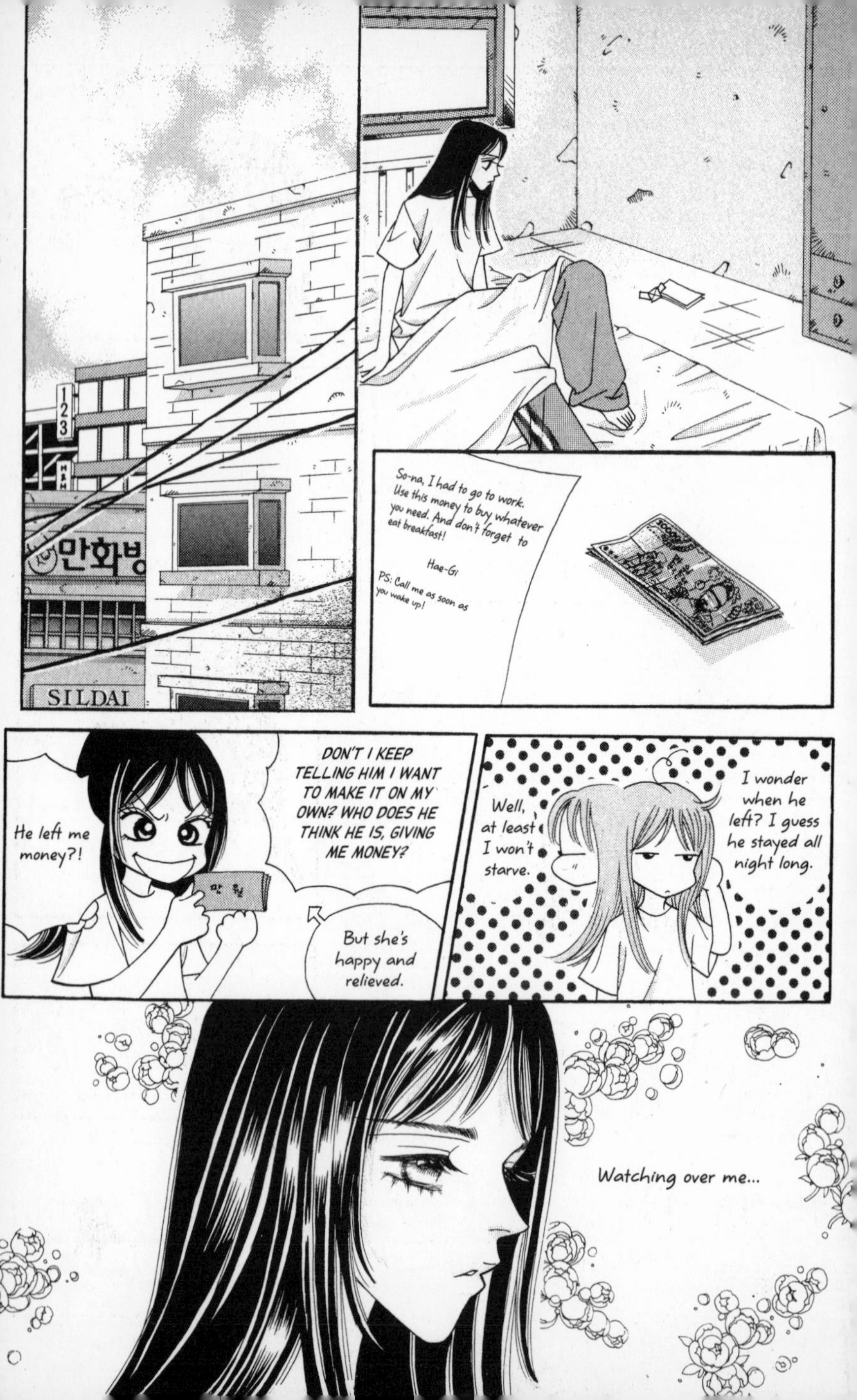
123
만화방
SILDAI
So-na, I had to go to work. Use this money to buy whatever you need. And don't forget to eat breakfast!
Hae-Gi
PS: Call me as soon as you wake up!
He left me money?!
DON'T I KEEP TELLING HIM I WANT TO MAKE IT ON MY OWN? WHO DOES HE THINK HE IS, GIVING ME MONEY?
But she's happy and relieved.
Well, at least I won't starve.
I wonder when he left? I guess he stayed all night long.
Watching over me...

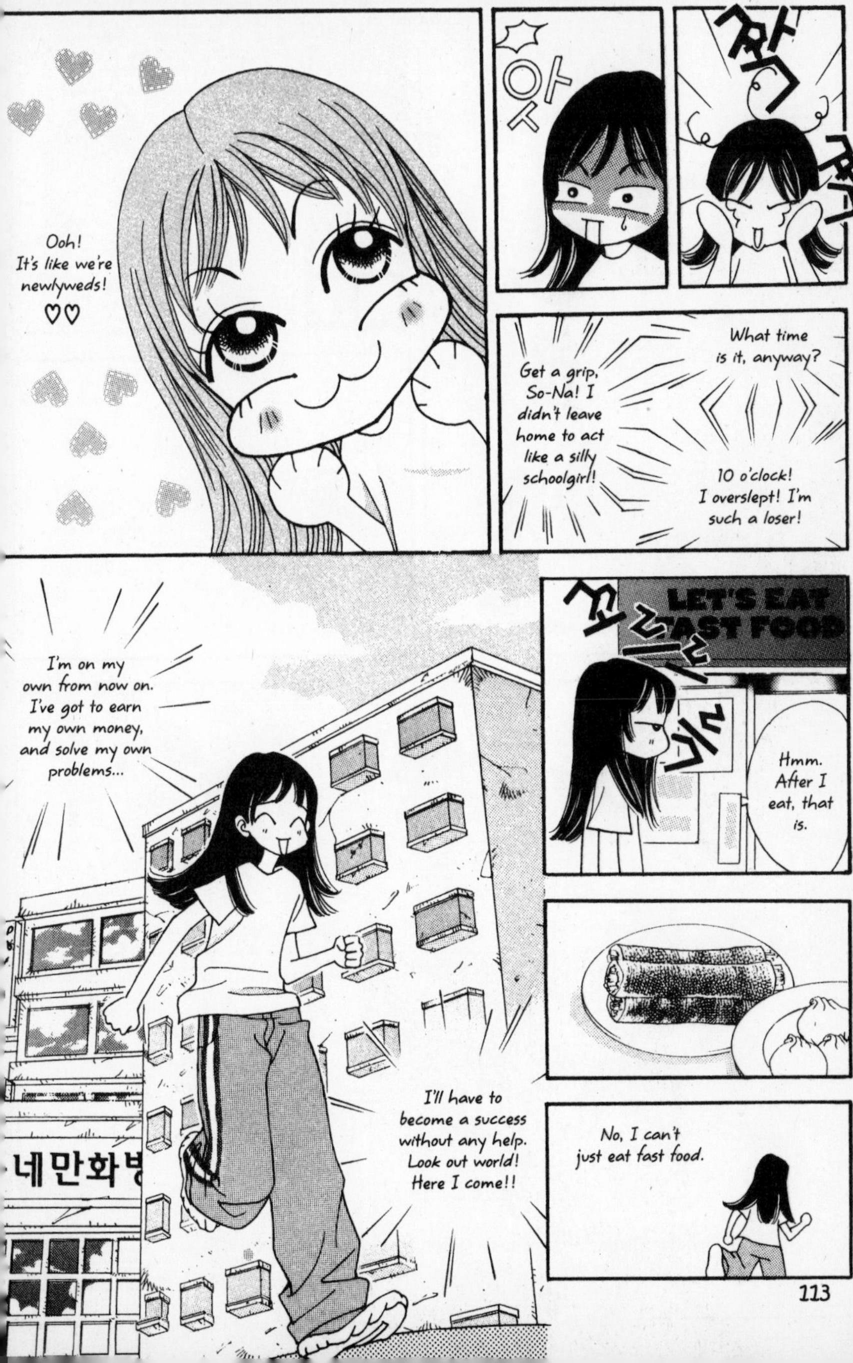

Ooh! It's like we're newlyweds! ♡♡
앗
짝 짝
Get a grip, So-Na! I didn't leave home to act like a silly schoolgirl!
What time is it, anyway?
10 o'clock! I overslept! I'm such a loser!
I'm on my own from now on. I've got to earn my own money, and solve my own problems...
I'll have to become a success without any help. Look out world! Here I come!!
네만화방
LET'S EAT FAST FOOD
꼬르르륵
Hmm. After I eat, that is.
No, I can't just eat fast food.

THANK YOU! COME AGAIN!

휘청

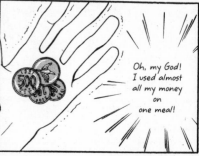

Oh, my God! I used almost all my money on one meal!

I'd better get a job right away!

But, how do I find a job?

And where?

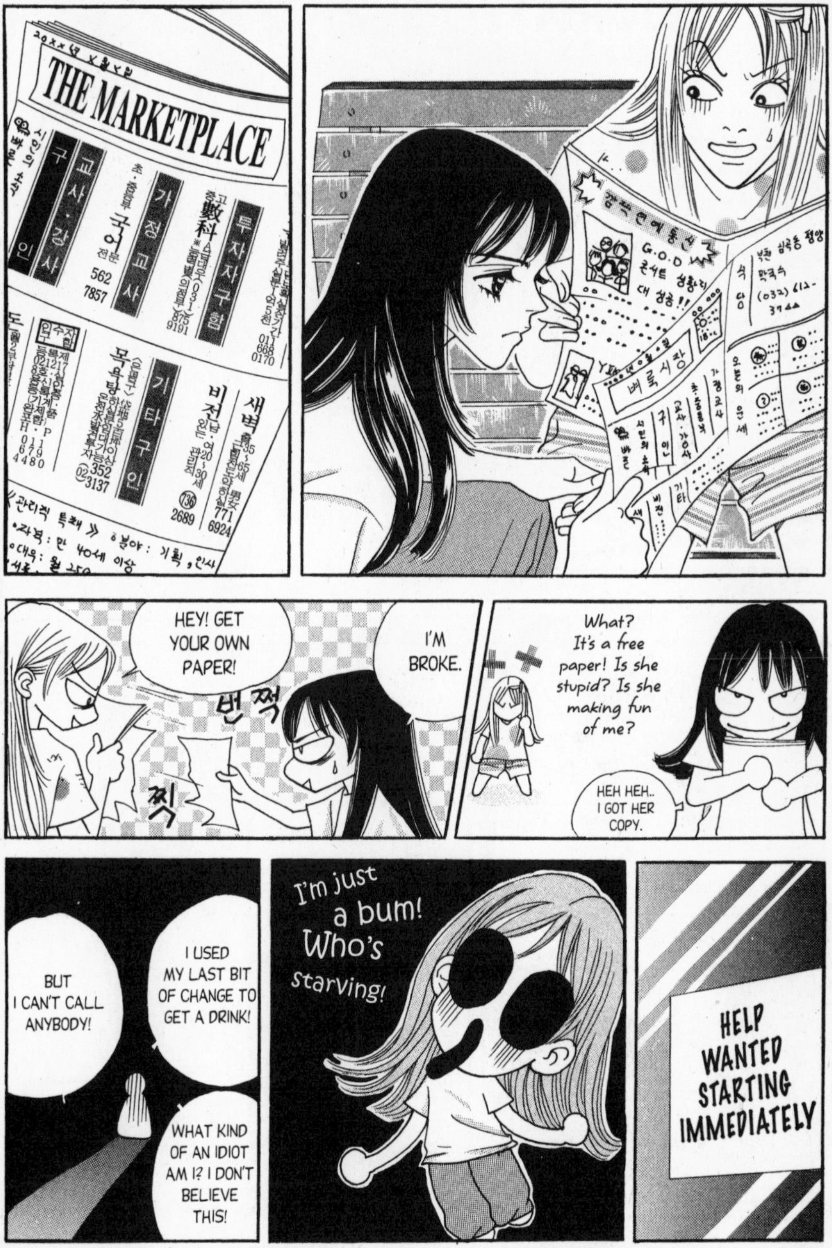
THE MARKETPLACE
투자자구함
가정교사
교사·강사
구인
기타구인
HEY! GET YOUR OWN PAPER!
I'M BROKE.
번쩍
찍
What? It's a free paper! Is she stupid? Is she making fun of me?
HEH HEH.. I GOT HER COPY.
BUT I CAN'T CALL ANYBODY!
I USED MY LAST BIT OF CHANGE TO GET A DRINK!
WHAT KIND OF AN IDIOT AM I? I DON'T BELIEVE THIS!
I'm just a bum! Who's starving!
HELP WANTED STARTING IMMEDIATELY

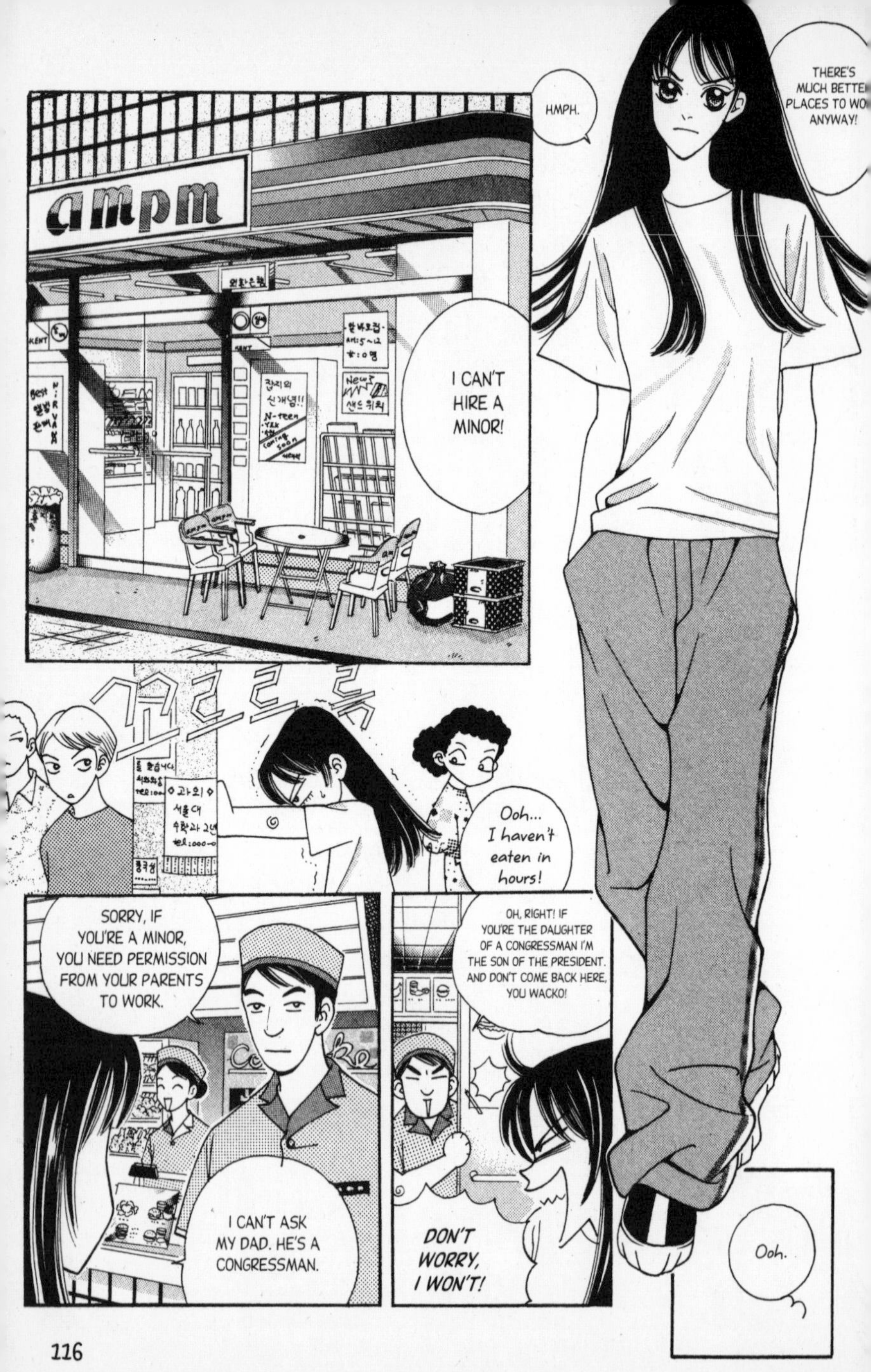
ampm
I CAN'T HIRE A MINOR!
HMPH.
THERE'S MUCH BETTE PLACES TO WO ANYWAY!
Ooh... I haven't eaten in hours!
SORRY, IF YOU'RE A MINOR, YOU NEED PERMISSION FROM YOUR PARENTS TO WORK.
I CAN'T ASK MY DAD. HE'S A CONGRESSMAN.
OH, RIGHT! IF YOU'RE THE DAUGHTER OF A CONGRESSMAN I'M THE SON OF THE PRESIDENT. AND DON'T COME BACK HERE, YOU WACKO!
DON'T WORRY, I WON'T!
Ooh.

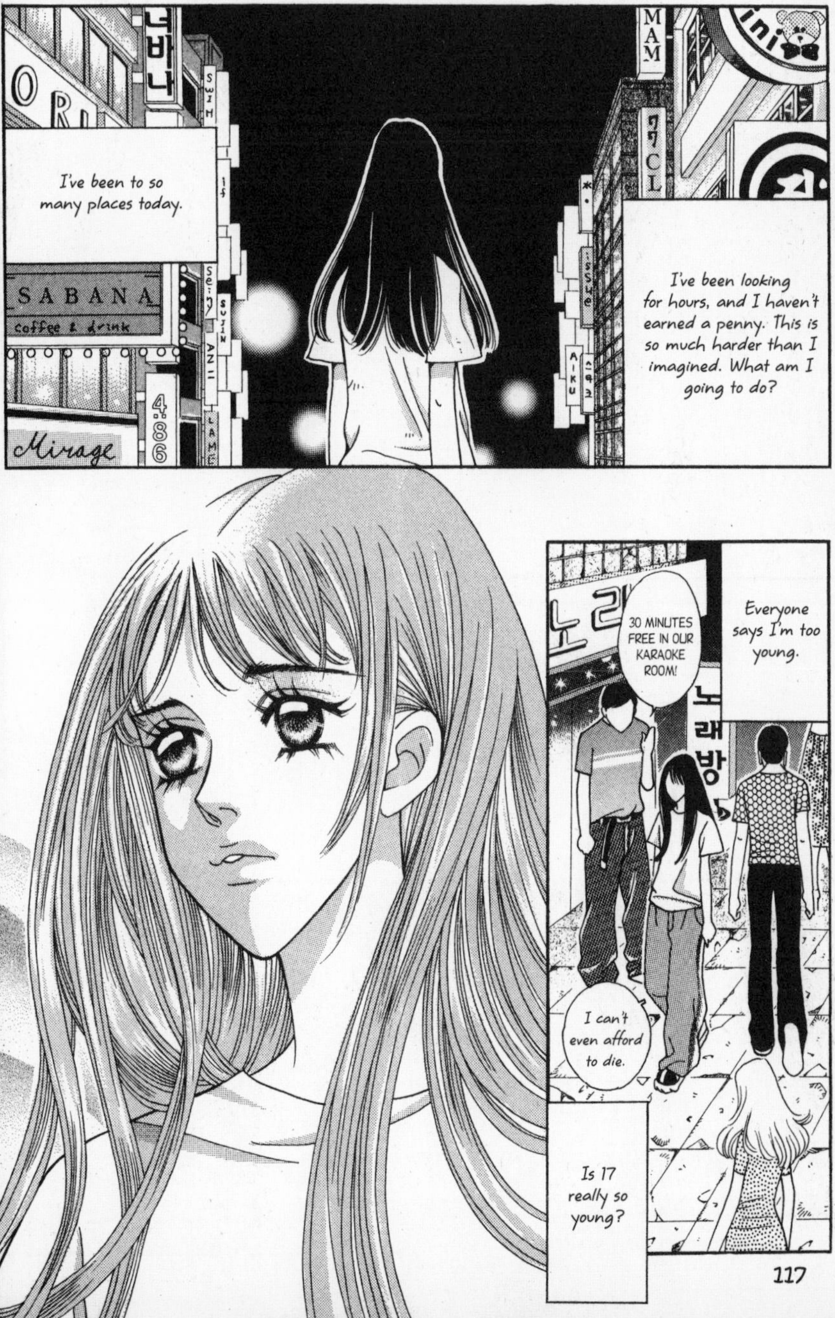
I've been to so many places today.
SABANA
coffee & drink
Mirage
I've been looking for hours, and I haven't earned a penny. This is so much harder than I imagined. What am I going to do?
30 MINUTES FREE IN OUR KARAOKE ROOM!
Everyone says I'm too young.
I can't even afford to die.
Is 17 really so young?

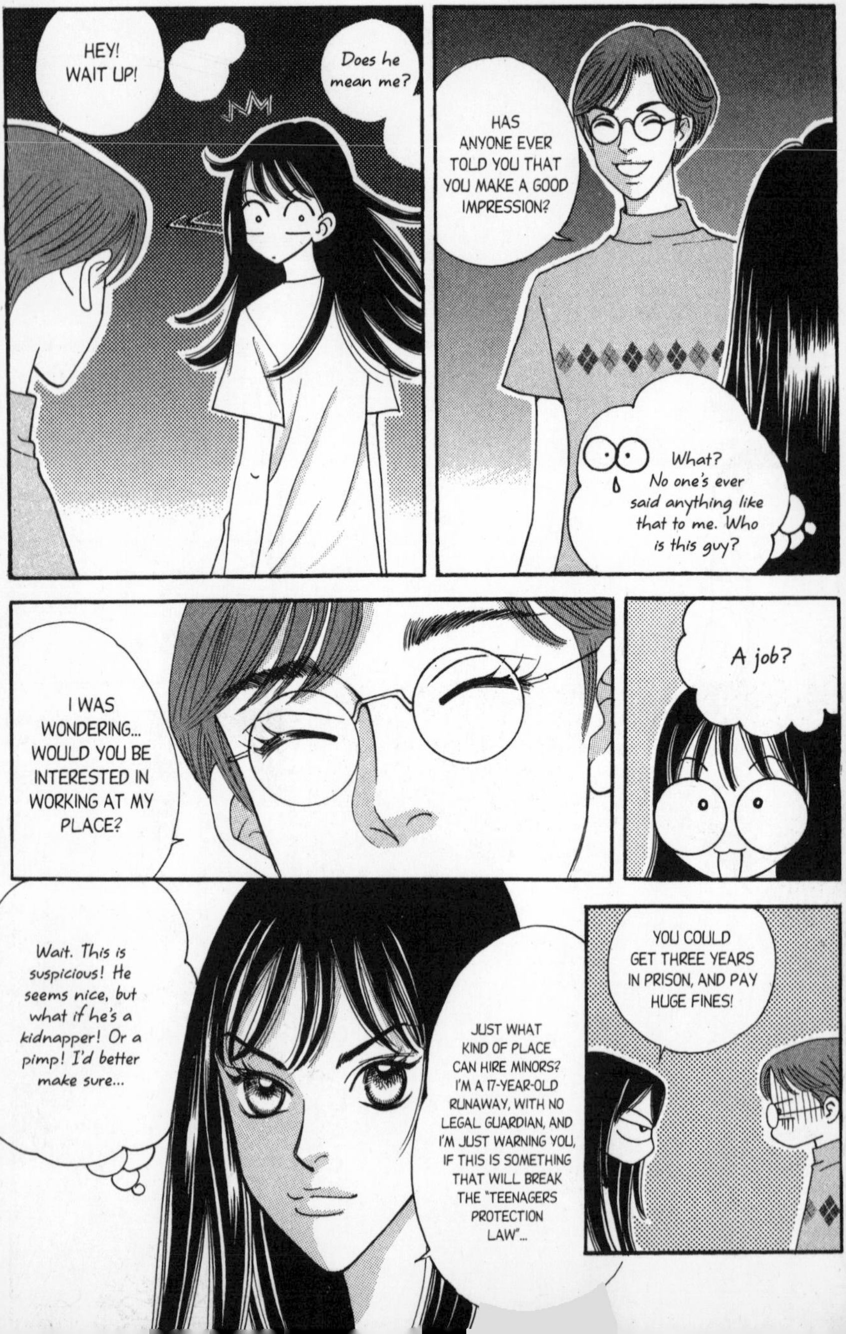
HEY! WAIT UP!
Does he mean me?
HAS ANYONE EVER TOLD YOU THAT YOU MAKE A GOOD IMPRESSION?
What? No one's ever said anything like that to me. Who is this guy?
I WAS WONDERING... WOULD YOU BE INTERESTED IN WORKING AT MY PLACE?
A job?
Wait. This is suspicious! He seems nice, but what if he's a kidnapper! Or a pimp! I'd better make sure...
JUST WHAT KIND OF PLACE CAN HIRE MINORS? I'M A 17-YEAR-OLD RUNAWAY, WITH NO LEGAL GUARDIAN, AND I'M JUST WARNING YOU, IF THIS IS SOMETHING THAT WILL BREAK THE "TEENAGERS PROTECTION LAW"...
YOU COULD GET THREE YEARS IN PRISON, AND PAY HUGE FINES!

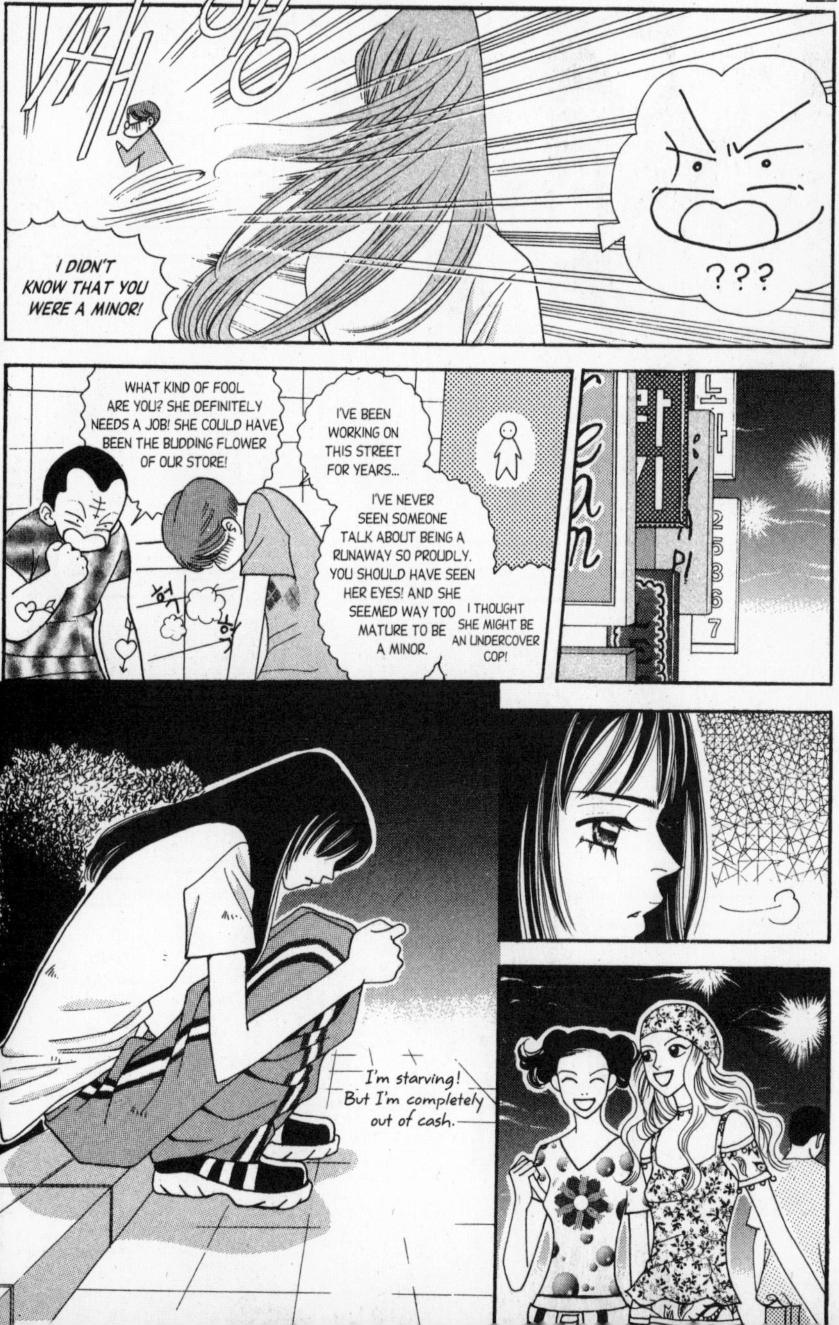
I DIDN'T KNOW THAT YOU WERE A MINOR!
???
WHAT KIND OF FOOL ARE YOU? SHE DEFINITELY NEEDS A JOB! SHE COULD HAVE BEEN THE BUDDING FLOWER OF OUR STORE!
I'VE BEEN WORKING ON THIS STREET FOR YEARS...
I'VE NEVER SEEN SOMEONE TALK ABOUT BEING A RUNAWAY SO PROUDLY. YOU SHOULD HAVE SEEN HER EYES! AND SHE SEEMED WAY TOO MATURE TO BE A MINOR.
I THOUGHT SHE MIGHT BE AN UNDERCOVER COP!
I'm starving! But I'm completely out of cash.

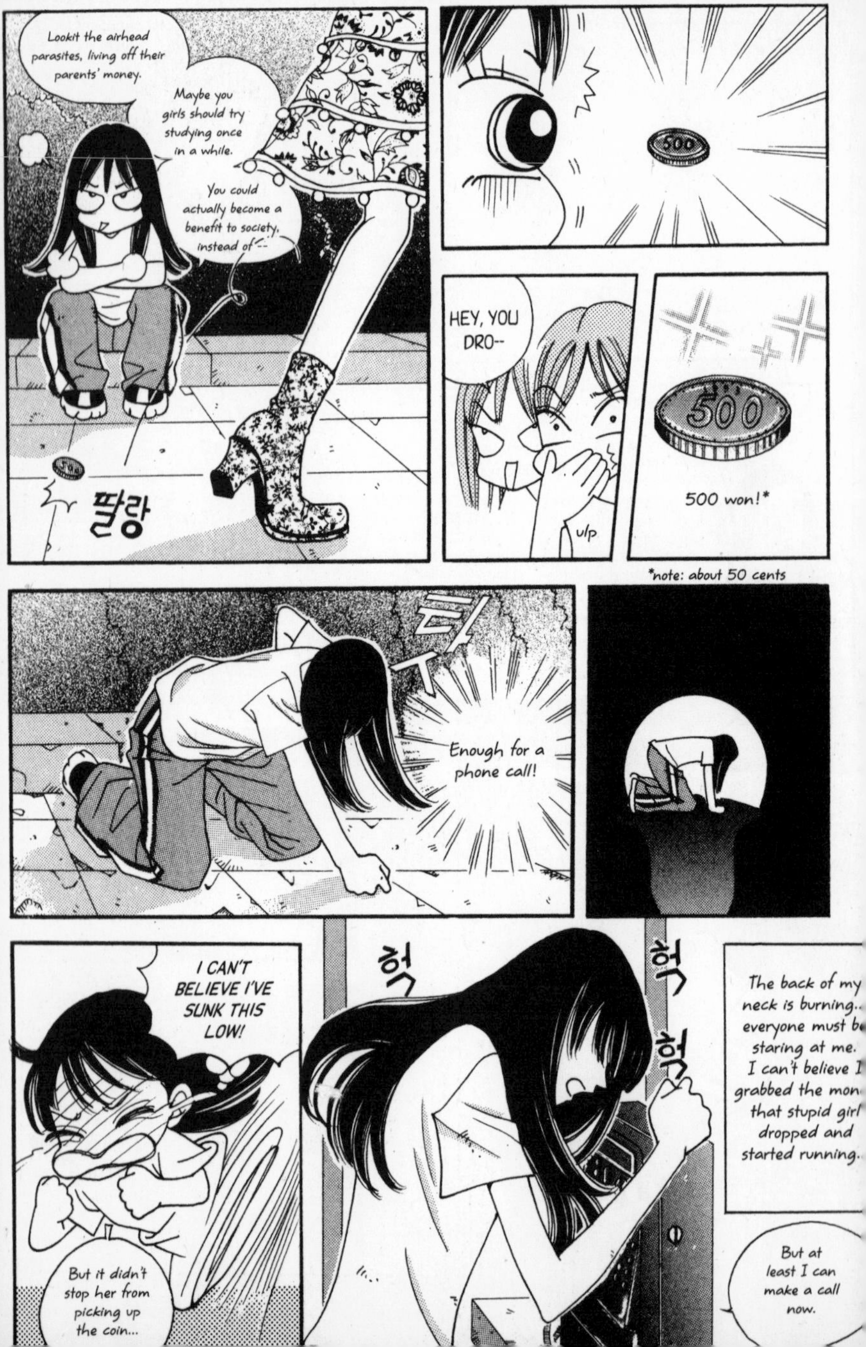
Lookit the airhead parasites, living off their parents' money.
Maybe you girls should try studying once in a while.
You could actually become a benefit to society, instead of--
딸랑
HEY, YOU DRO--
ulp
500 won!*
*note: about 50 cents
티
Enough for a phone call!
I CAN'T BELIEVE I'VE SUNK THIS LOW!
But it didn't stop her from picking up the coin...
헉
헉
헉
The back of my neck is burning.. everyone must b staring at me. I can't believe I grabbed the mon that stupid girl dropped and started running..
But at least I can make a call now.

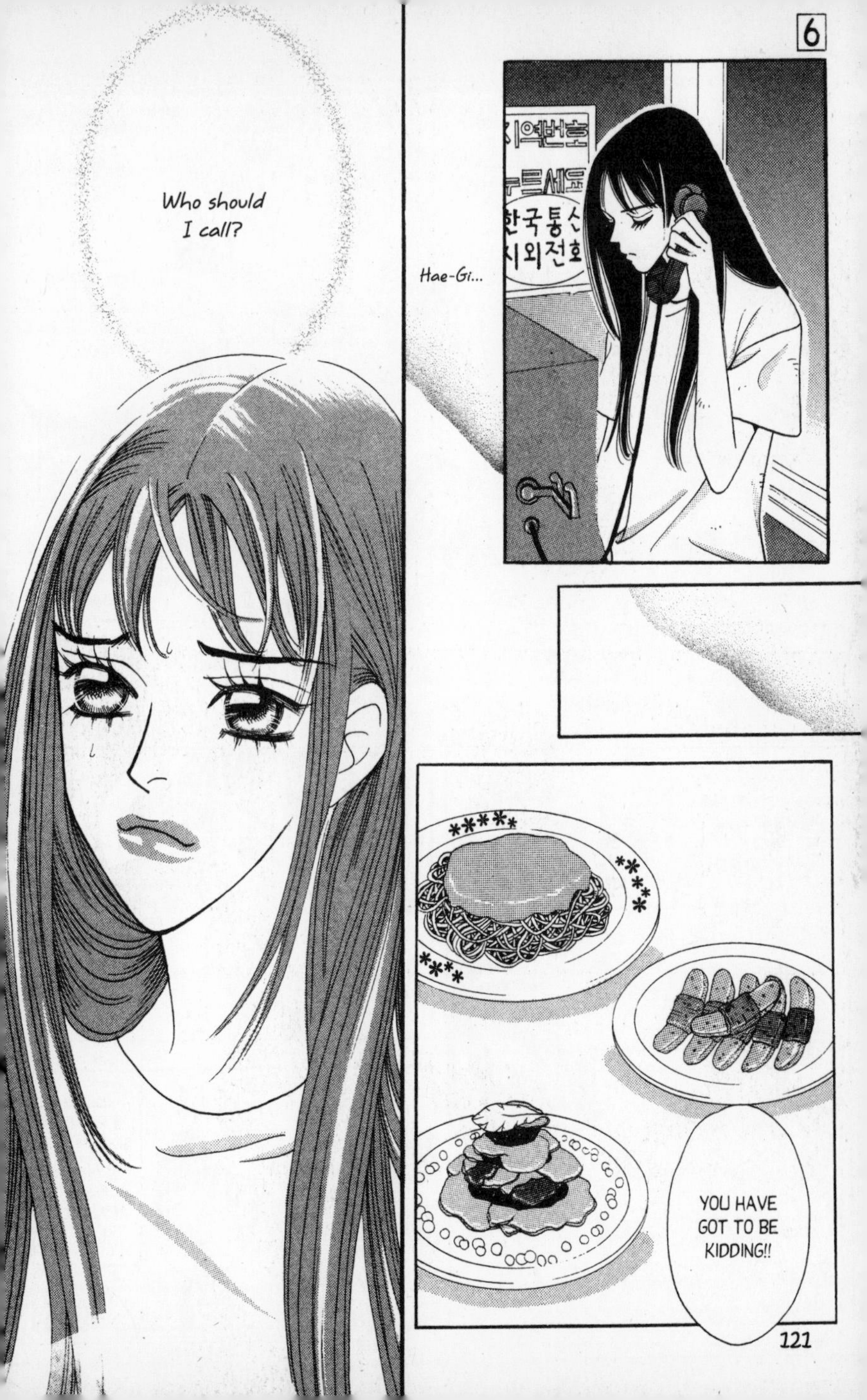
Who should I call?
한국통신
Hae-Gi...
YOU HAVE GOT TO BE KIDDING!!

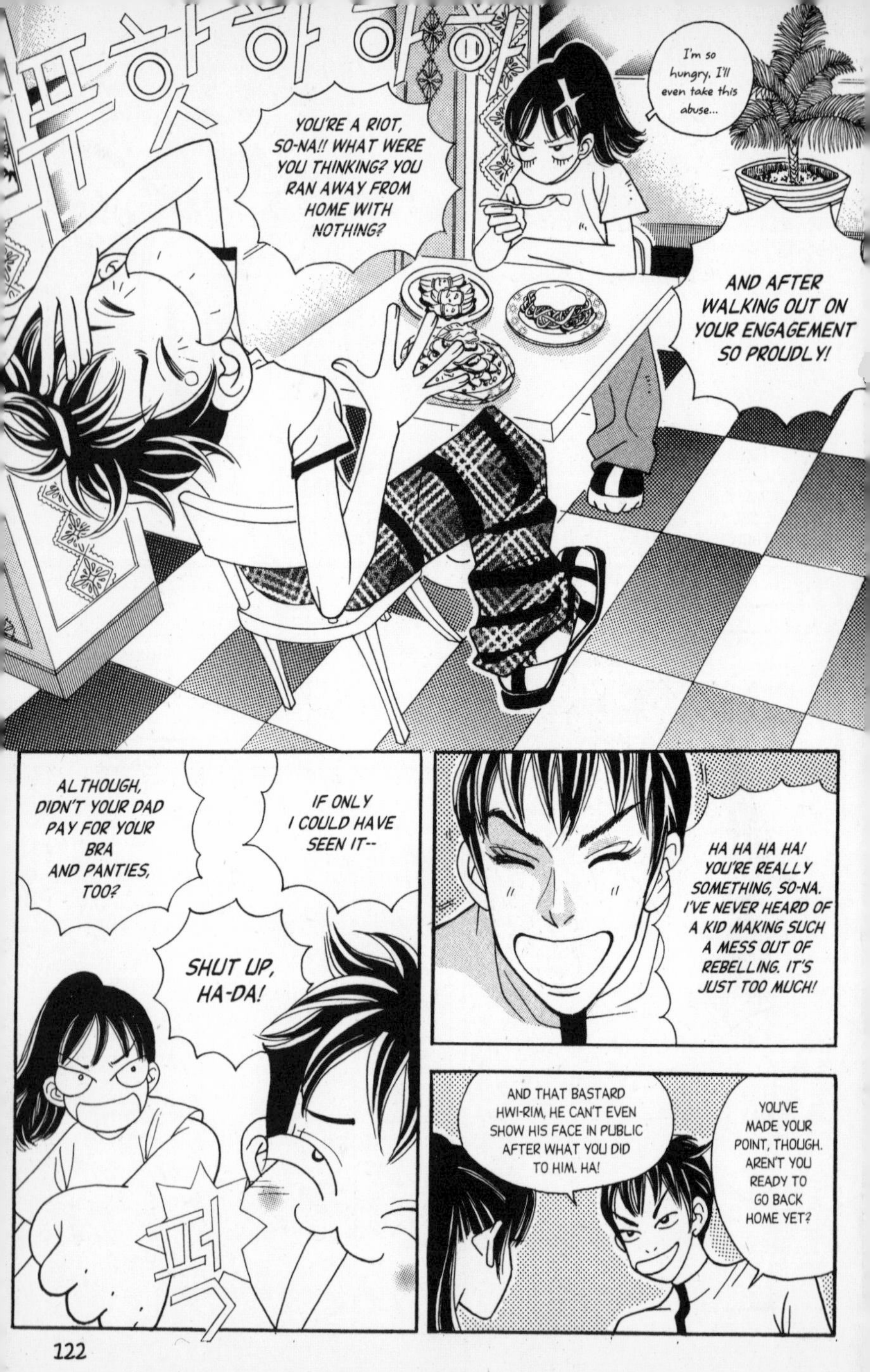
푸핫하하하
YOU'RE A RIOT, SO-NA!! WHAT WERE YOU THINKING? YOU RAN AWAY FROM HOME WITH NOTHING?
I'm so hungry, I'll even take this abuse...
AND AFTER WALKING OUT ON YOUR ENGAGEMENT SO PROUDLY!
ALTHOUGH, DIDN'T YOUR DAD PAY FOR YOUR BRA AND PANTIES, TOO?
IF ONLY I COULD HAVE SEEN IT--
SHUT UP, HA-DA!
퍽
HA HA HA HA! YOU'RE REALLY SOMETHING, SO-NA. I'VE NEVER HEARD OF A KID MAKING SUCH A MESS OUT OF REBELLING. IT'S JUST TOO MUCH!
AND THAT BASTARD HWI-RIM, HE CAN'T EVEN SHOW HIS FACE IN PUBLIC AFTER WHAT YOU DID TO HIM. HA!
YOU'VE MADE YOUR POINT, THOUGH. AREN'T YOU READY TO GO BACK HOME YET?

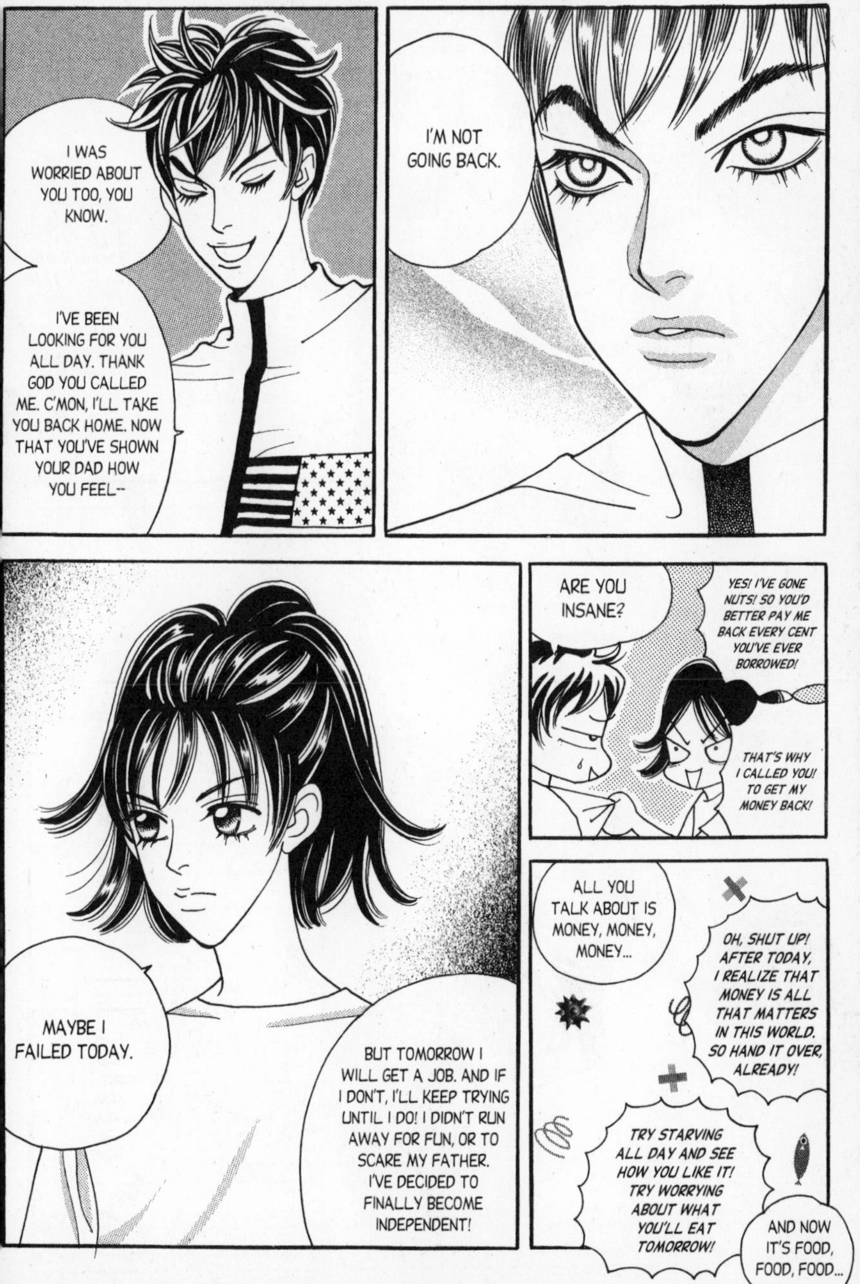
I WAS WORRIED ABOUT YOU TOO, YOU KNOW.
I'VE BEEN LOOKING FOR YOU ALL DAY. THANK GOD YOU CALLED ME. C'MON, I'LL TAKE YOU BACK HOME. NOW THAT YOU'VE SHOWN YOUR DAD HOW YOU FEEL--
I'M NOT GOING BACK.
MAYBE I FAILED TODAY.
BUT TOMORROW I WILL GET A JOB. AND IF I DON'T, I'LL KEEP TRYING UNTIL I DO! I DIDN'T RUN AWAY FOR FUN, OR TO SCARE MY FATHER. I'VE DECIDED TO FINALLY BECOME INDEPENDENT!
ARE YOU INSANE?
YES! I'VE GONE NUTS! SO YOU'D BETTER PAY ME BACK EVERY CENT YOU'VE EVER BORROWED!
THAT'S WHY I CALLED YOU! TO GET MY MONEY BACK!
ALL YOU TALK ABOUT IS MONEY, MONEY, MONEY...
OH, SHUT UP! AFTER TODAY, I REALIZE THAT MONEY IS ALL THAT MATTERS IN THIS WORLD. SO HAND IT OVER, ALREADY!
TRY STARVING ALL DAY AND SEE HOW YOU LIKE IT! TRY WORRYING ABOUT WHAT YOU'LL EAT TOMORROW!
AND NOW IT'S FOOD, FOOD, FOOD...

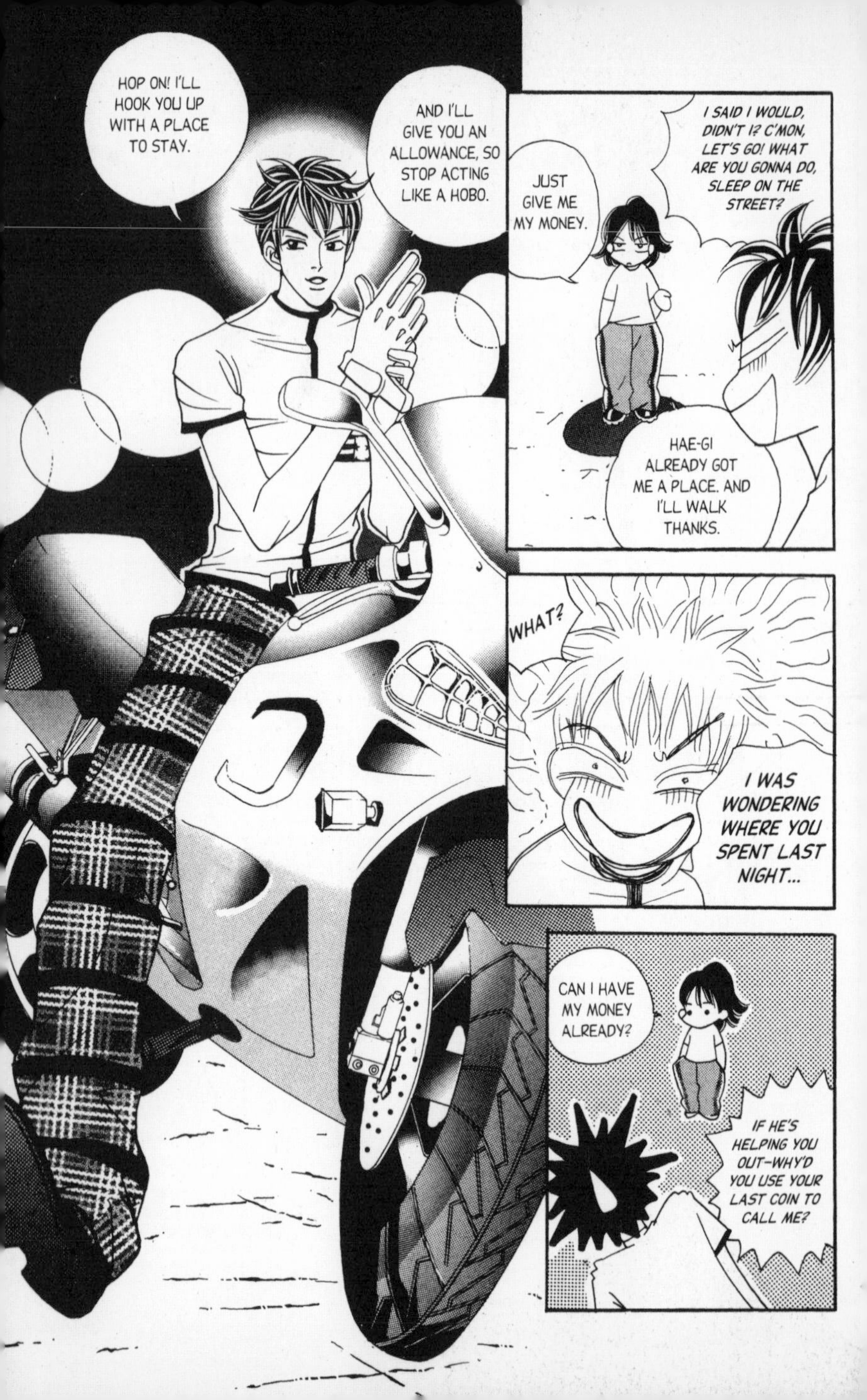
HOP ON! I'LL HOOK YOU UP WITH A PLACE TO STAY.
AND I'LL GIVE YOU AN ALLOWANCE, SO STOP ACTING LIKE A HOBO.
JUST GIVE ME MY MONEY.
I SAID I WOULD, DIDN'T I? C'MON, LET'S GO! WHAT ARE YOU GONNA DO, SLEEP ON THE STREET?
HAE-GI ALREADY GOT ME A PLACE. AND I'LL WALK THANKS.
WHAT?
I WAS WONDERING WHERE YOU SPENT LAST NIGHT...
CAN I HAVE MY MONEY ALREADY?
IF HE'S HELPING YOU OUT-WHY'D YOU USE YOUR LAST COIN TO CALL ME?

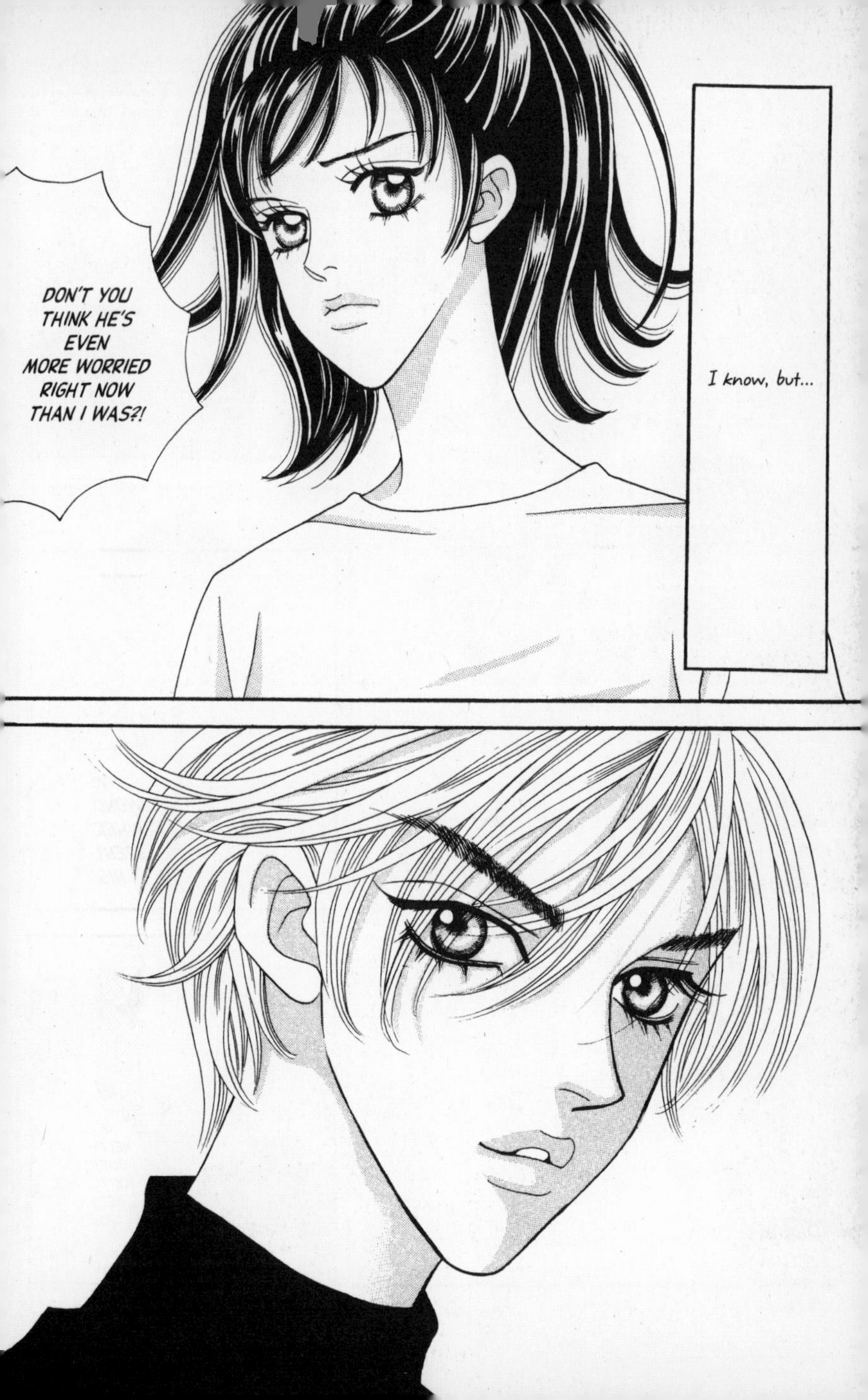
DON'T YOU THINK HE'S EVEN MORE WORRIED RIGHT NOW THAN I WAS?!
I know, but...

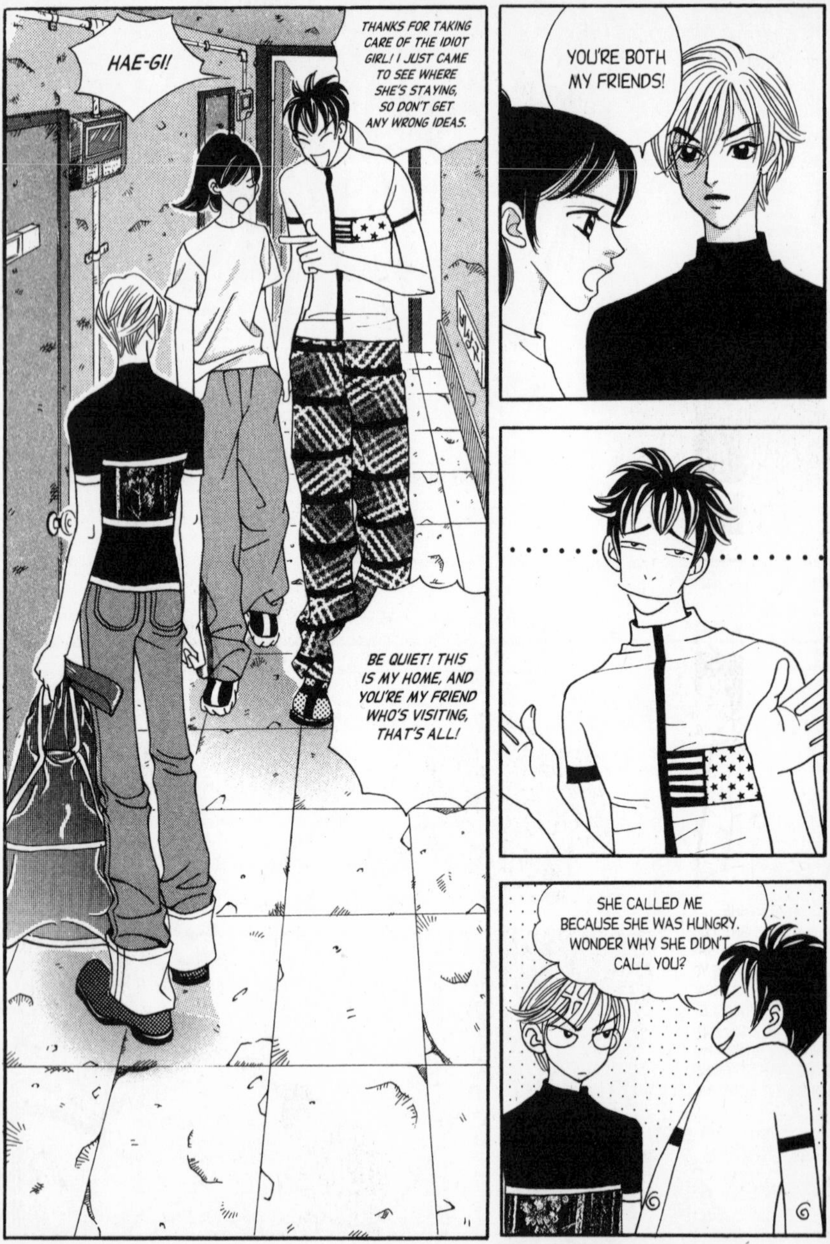
HAE-GI!
THANKS FOR TAKING CARE OF THE IDIOT GIRL! I JUST CAME TO SEE WHERE SHE'S STAYING, SO DON'T GET ANY WRONG IDEAS.
BE QUIET! THIS IS MY HOME, AND YOU'RE MY FRIEND WHO'S VISITING, THAT'S ALL!
YOU'RE BOTH MY FRIENDS!
.....
SHE CALLED ME BECAUSE SHE WAS HUNGRY. WONDER WHY SHE DIDN'T CALL YOU?

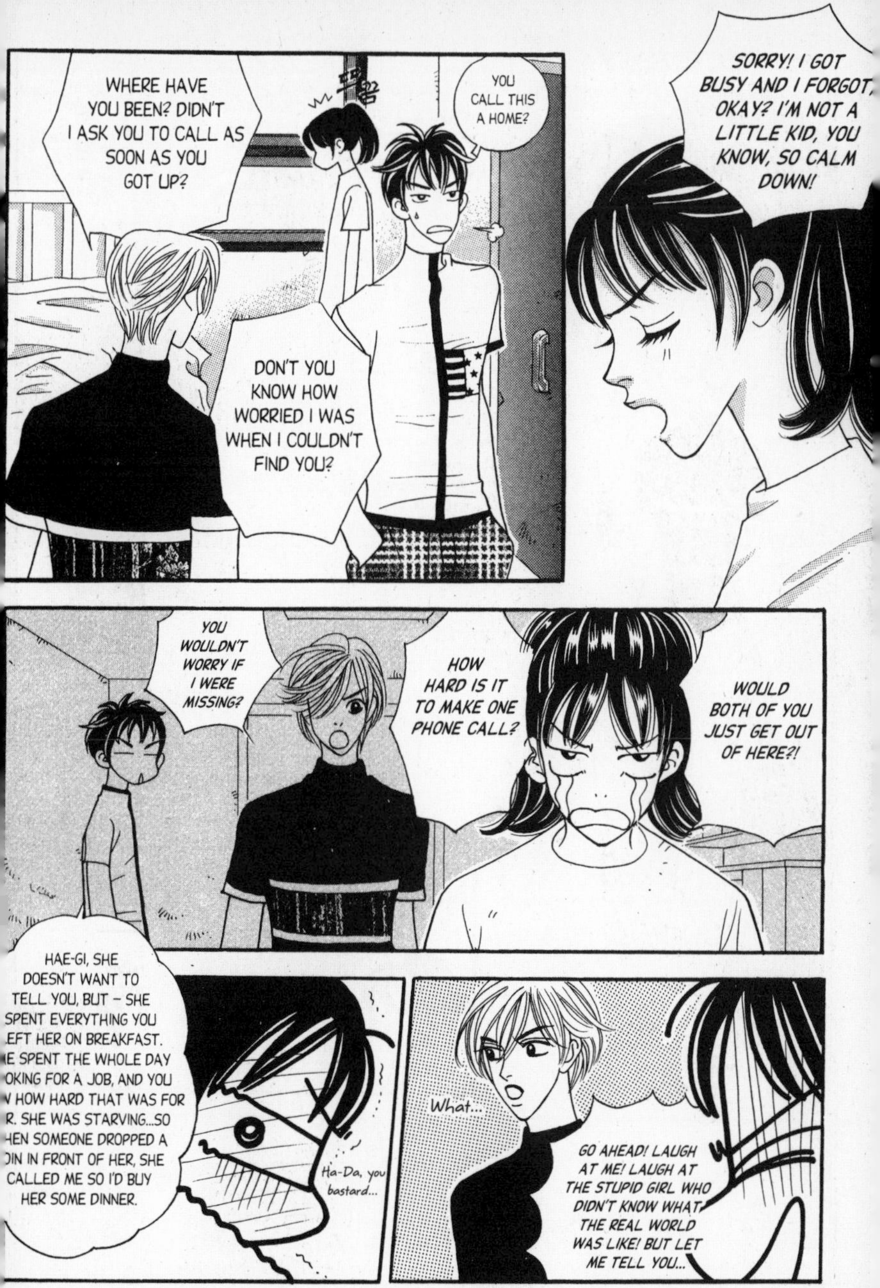
WHERE HAVE YOU BEEN? DIDN'T I ASK YOU TO CALL AS SOON AS YOU GOT UP?
YOU CALL THIS A HOME?
DON'T YOU KNOW HOW WORRIED I WAS WHEN I COULDN'T FIND YOU?
SORRY! I GOT BUSY AND I FORGOT, OKAY? I'M NOT A LITTLE KID, YOU KNOW, SO CALM DOWN!
YOU WOULDN'T WORRY IF I WERE MISSING?
HOW HARD IS IT TO MAKE ONE PHONE CALL?
WOULD BOTH OF YOU JUST GET OUT OF HERE?!
HAE-GI, SHE DOESN'T WANT TO TELL YOU, BUT -- SHE SPENT EVERYTHING YOU LEFT HER ON BREAKFAST. E SPENT THE WHOLE DAY OKING FOR A JOB, AND YOU V HOW HARD THAT WAS FOR R. SHE WAS STARVING...SO HEN SOMEONE DROPPED A OIN IN FRONT OF HER, SHE CALLED ME SO I'D BUY HER SOME DINNER.
Ha-Da, you bastard...
What...
GO AHEAD! LAUGH AT ME! LAUGH AT THE STUPID GIRL WHO DIDN'T KNOW WHAT THE REAL WORLD WAS LIKE! BUT LET ME TELL YOU...

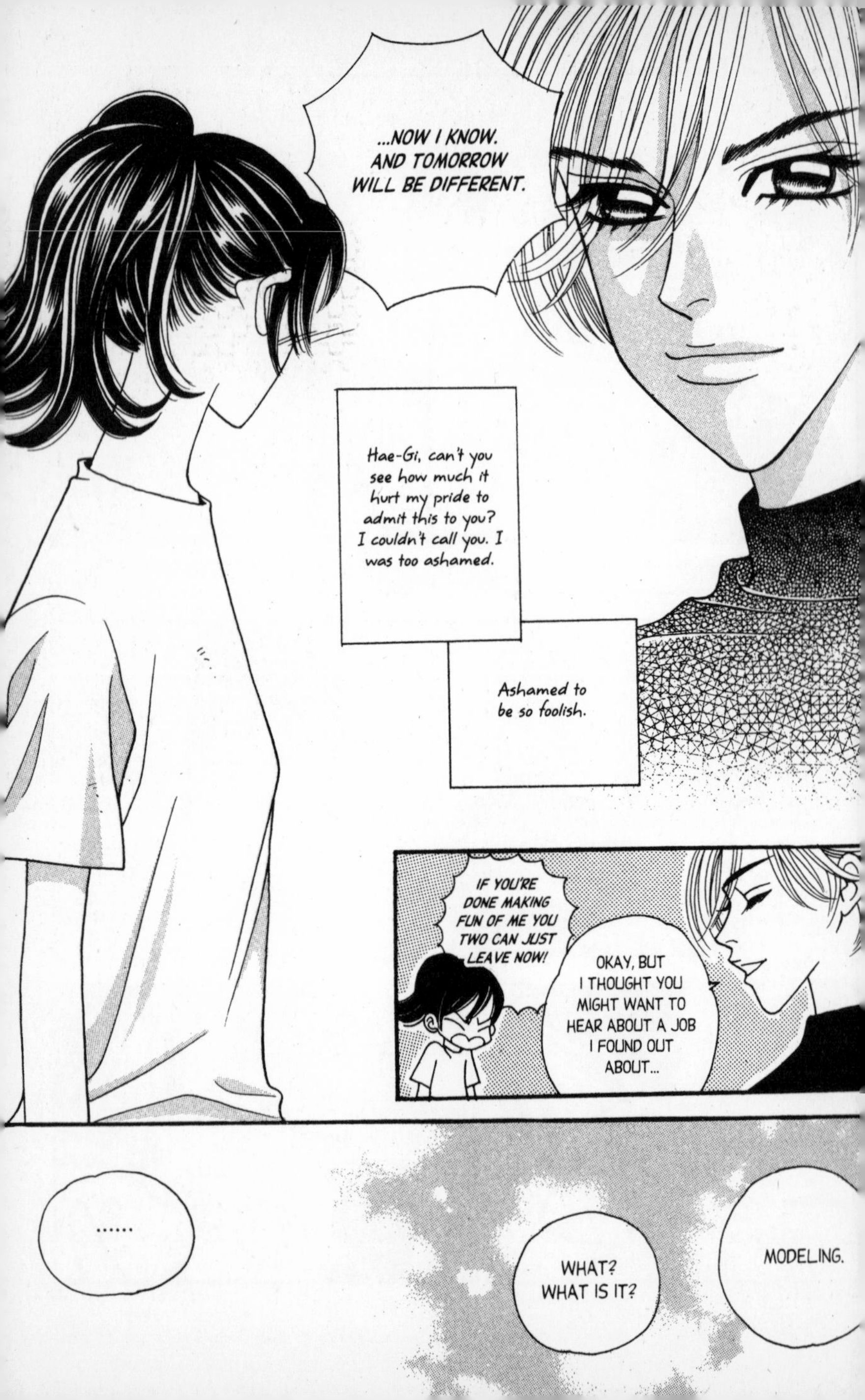
...NOW I KNOW. AND TOMORROW WILL BE DIFFERENT.
Hae-Gi, can't you see how much it hurt my pride to admit this to you? I couldn't call you. I was too ashamed.
Ashamed to be so foolish.
IF YOU'RE DONE MAKING FUN OF ME YOU TWO CAN JUST LEAVE NOW!
OKAY, BUT I THOUGHT YOU MIGHT WANT TO HEAR ABOUT A JOB I FOUND OUT ABOUT...
......
WHAT? WHAT IS IT?
MODELING.

HER? AN ATHLETE'S-FOOT MODEL, MAYBE...
THERE'S A SHOW COMING UP AND THEY WANT A BRAND-NEW MODEL FOR IT. OF COURSE, YOU'LL HAVE TO AUDITION, BUT...
...IF YOU MODEL, YOU CAN STILL GO TO SCHOOL, AND THE PAY'S GOOD ENOUGH THAT YOU DON'T HAVE TO WORRY ABOUT PAYING YOUR BILLS.
BUT I WANT TO MAKE IT WITHOUT YOUR HELP!
DON'T BE STUPID!! MODELING IS 100 PERCENT ABOUT YOUR ABILITY. I CAN'T DO ANYTHING TO HELP YOU GET THE JOB.
HEY, SO-NA, IF IT'S A JOB HAE-GI CAN MANAGE, YOU COULD DO IT, EASY! AND YOU'VE BEEN APPROACHED BY TALENT SCOUTS A BUNCH OF TIMES, REMEMBER?
YOU'RE TALL, PRETTY, AND YOUR LEGS ARE AWESOME. OF COURSE, YOUR CHEST IS AS FLAT AS A BOARD BUT...

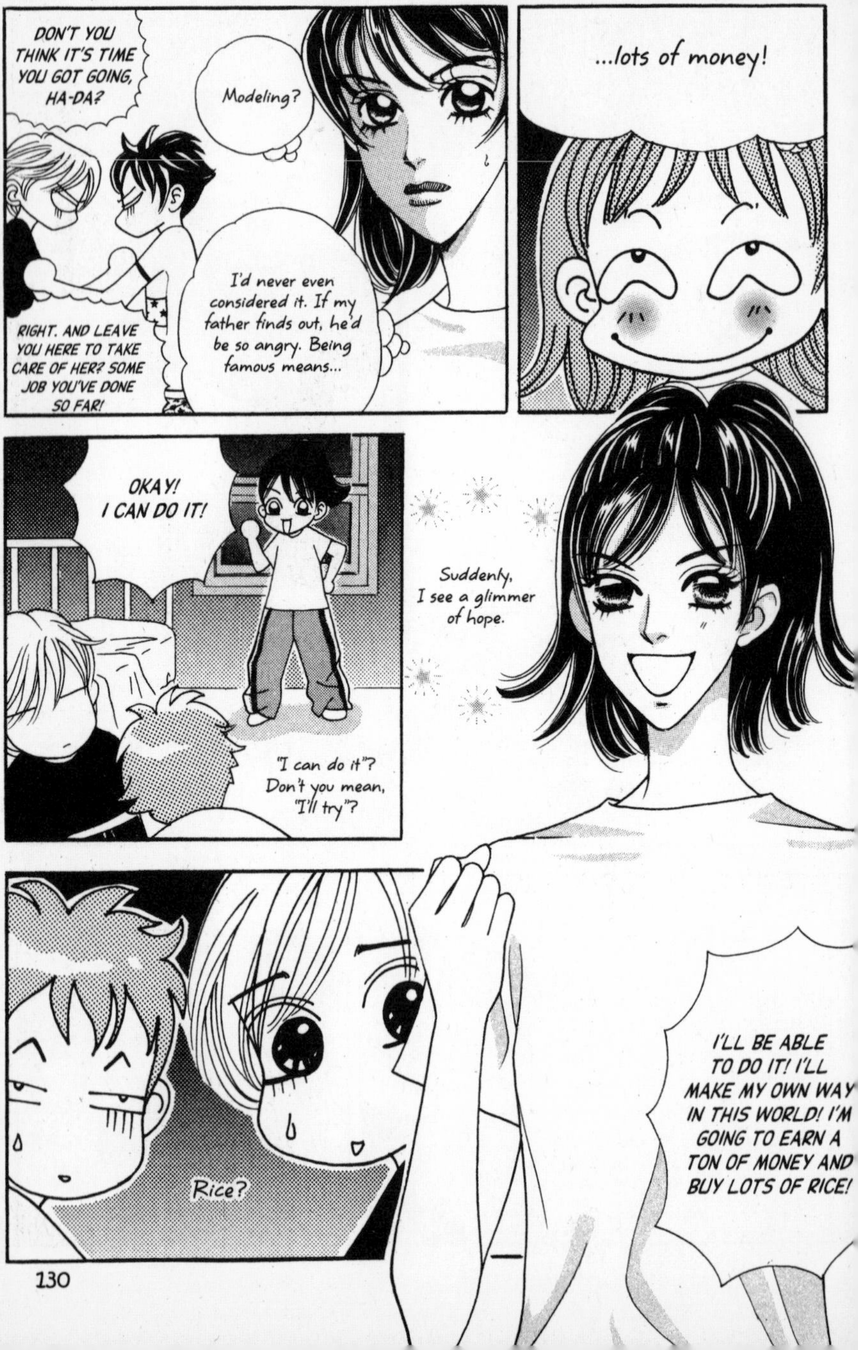
DON'T YOU THINK IT'S TIME YOU GOT GOING, HA-DA?
Modeling?
I'd never even considered it. If my father finds out, he'd be so angry. Being famous means...
RIGHT. AND LEAVE YOU HERE TO TAKE CARE OF HER? SOME JOB YOU'VE DONE SO FAR!
...lots of money!
OKAY! I CAN DO IT!
"I can do it"? Don't you mean, "I'll try"?
Suddenly, I see a glimmer of hope.
I'LL BE ABLE TO DO IT! I'LL MAKE MY OWN WAY IN THIS WORLD! I'M GOING TO EARN A TON OF MONEY AND BUY LOTS OF RICE!
Rice?

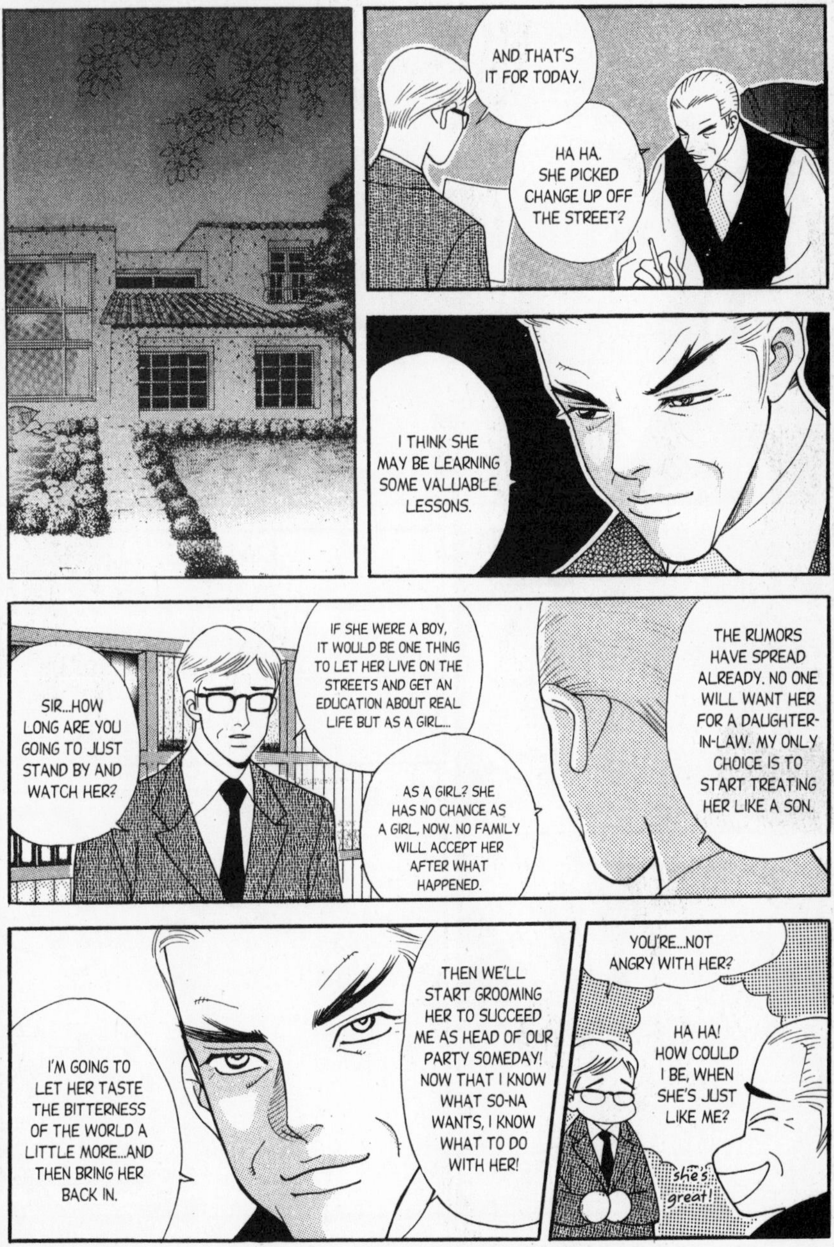
AND THAT'S IT FOR TODAY.
HA HA. SHE PICKED CHANGE UP OFF THE STREET?
I THINK SHE MAY BE LEARNING SOME VALUABLE LESSONS.
SIR...HOW LONG ARE YOU GOING TO JUST STAND BY AND WATCH HER?
IF SHE WERE A BOY, IT WOULD BE ONE THING TO LET HER LIVE ON THE STREETS AND GET AN EDUCATION ABOUT REAL LIFE BUT AS A GIRL...
AS A GIRL? SHE HAS NO CHANCE AS A GIRL, NOW. NO FAMILY WILL ACCEPT HER AFTER WHAT HAPPENED.
THE RUMORS HAVE SPREAD ALREADY. NO ONE WILL WANT HER FOR A DAUGHTER-IN-LAW. MY ONLY CHOICE IS TO START TREATING HER LIKE A SON.
I'M GOING TO LET HER TASTE THE BITTERNESS OF THE WORLD A LITTLE MORE...AND THEN BRING HER BACK IN.
THEN WE'LL START GROOMING HER TO SUCCEED ME AS HEAD OF OUR PARTY SOMEDAY! NOW THAT I KNOW WHAT SO-NA WANTS, I KNOW WHAT TO DO WITH HER!
YOU'RE...NOT ANGRY WITH HER?
HA HA! HOW COULD I BE, WHEN SHE'S JUST LIKE ME?
she's great!

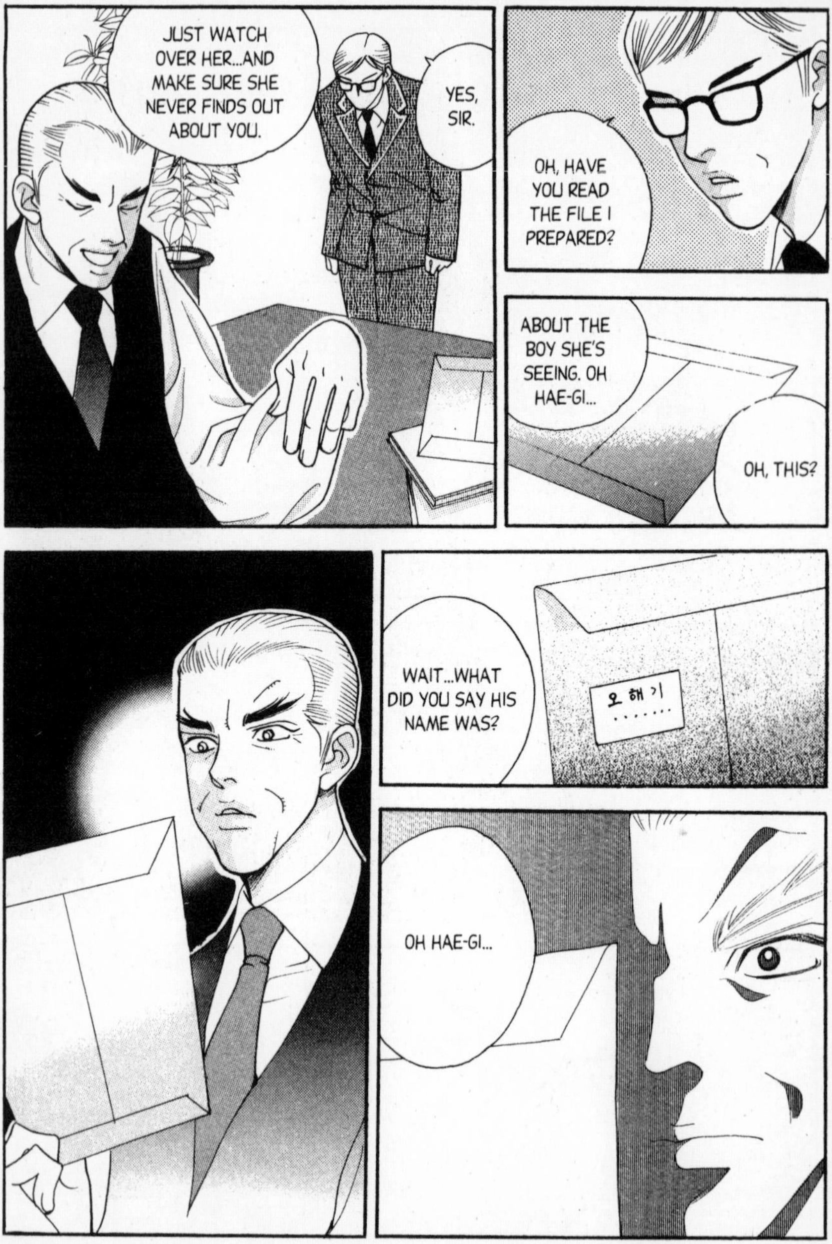
JUST WATCH OVER HER...AND MAKE SURE SHE NEVER FINDS OUT ABOUT YOU.
YES, SIR.
OH, HAVE YOU READ THE FILE I PREPARED?
ABOUT THE BOY SHE'S SEEING. OH HAE-GI...
OH, THIS?
WAIT...WHAT DID YOU SAY HIS NAME WAS?
오 해 기
OH HAE-GI...

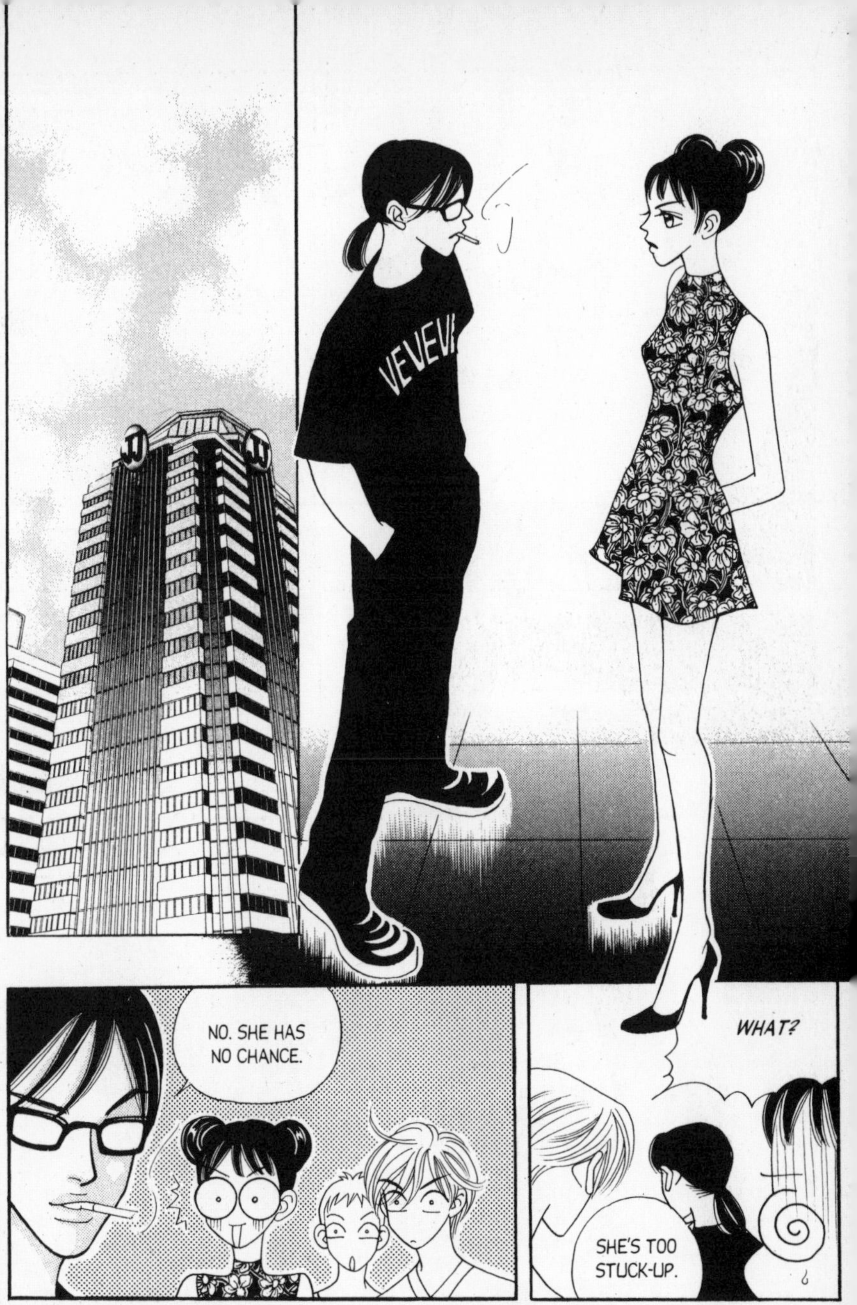
VEVEVI
WHAT?
SHE'S TOO STUCK-UP.
NO. SHE HAS NO CHANCE.

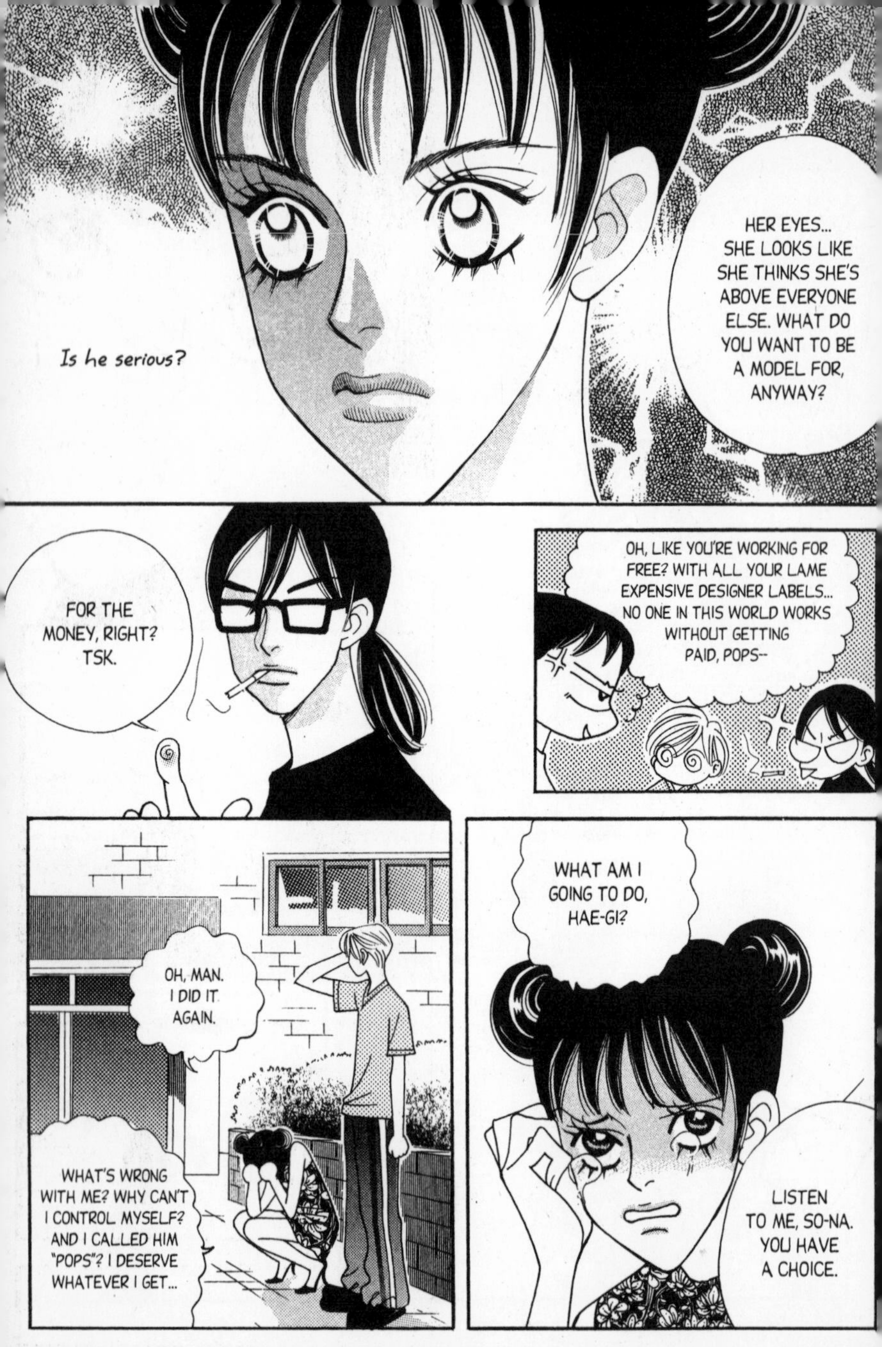
HER EYES... SHE LOOKS LIKE SHE THINKS SHE'S ABOVE EVERYONE ELSE. WHAT DO YOU WANT TO BE A MODEL FOR, ANYWAY?
Is he serious?
FOR THE MONEY, RIGHT? TSK.
OH, LIKE YOU'RE WORKING FOR FREE? WITH ALL YOUR LAME EXPENSIVE DESIGNER LABELS... NO ONE IN THIS WORLD WORKS WITHOUT GETTING PAID, POPS--
OH, MAN. I DID IT AGAIN.
WHAT'S WRONG WITH ME? WHY CAN'T I CONTROL MYSELF? AND I CALLED HIM "POPS"? I DESERVE WHATEVER I GET...
WHAT AM I GOING TO DO, HAE-GI?
LISTEN TO ME, SO-NA. YOU HAVE A CHOICE.

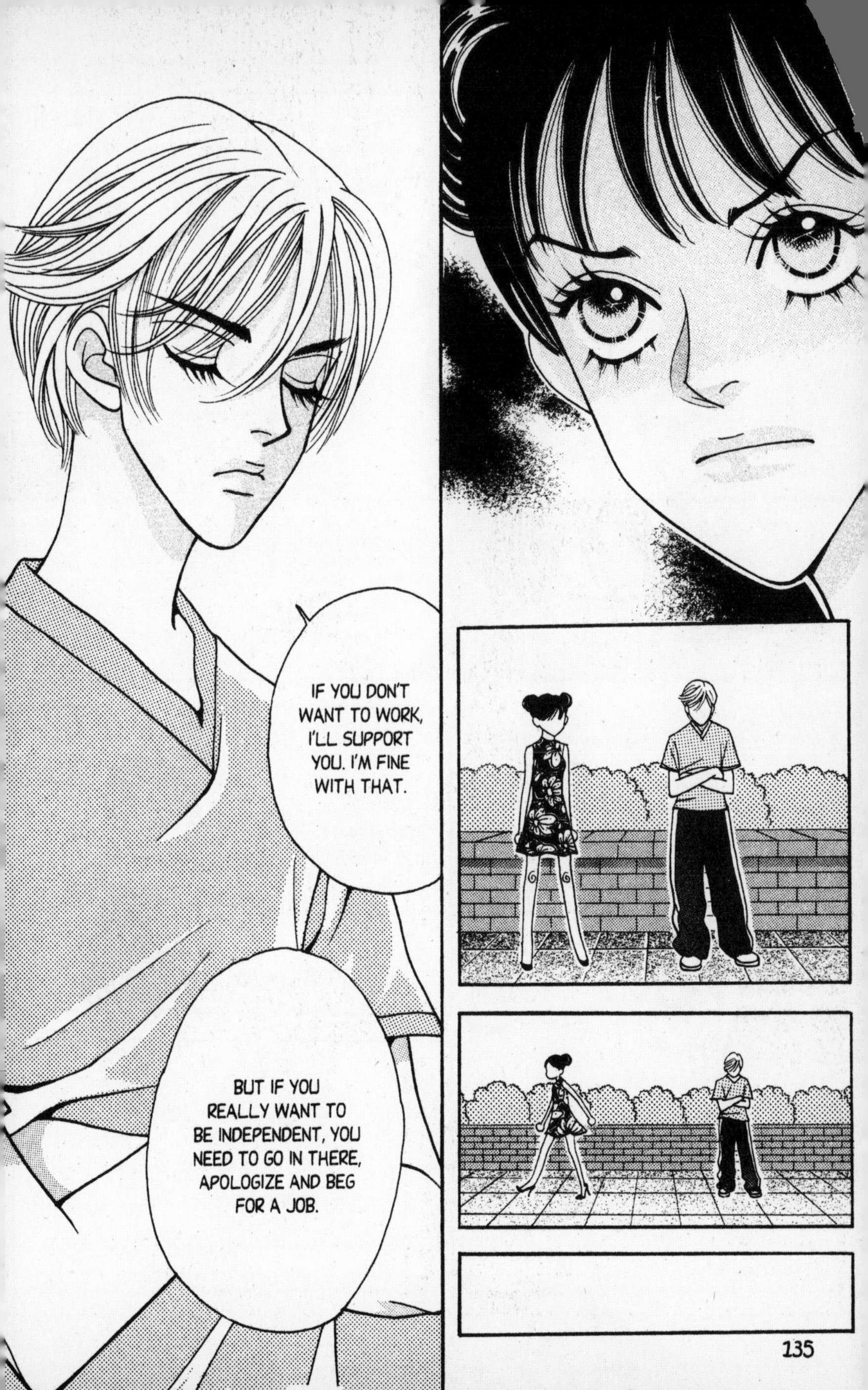
IF YOU DON'T WANT TO WORK, I'LL SUPPORT YOU. I'M FINE WITH THAT.
BUT IF YOU REALLY WANT TO BE INDEPENDENT, YOU NEED TO GO IN THERE, APOLOGIZE AND BEG FOR A JOB.

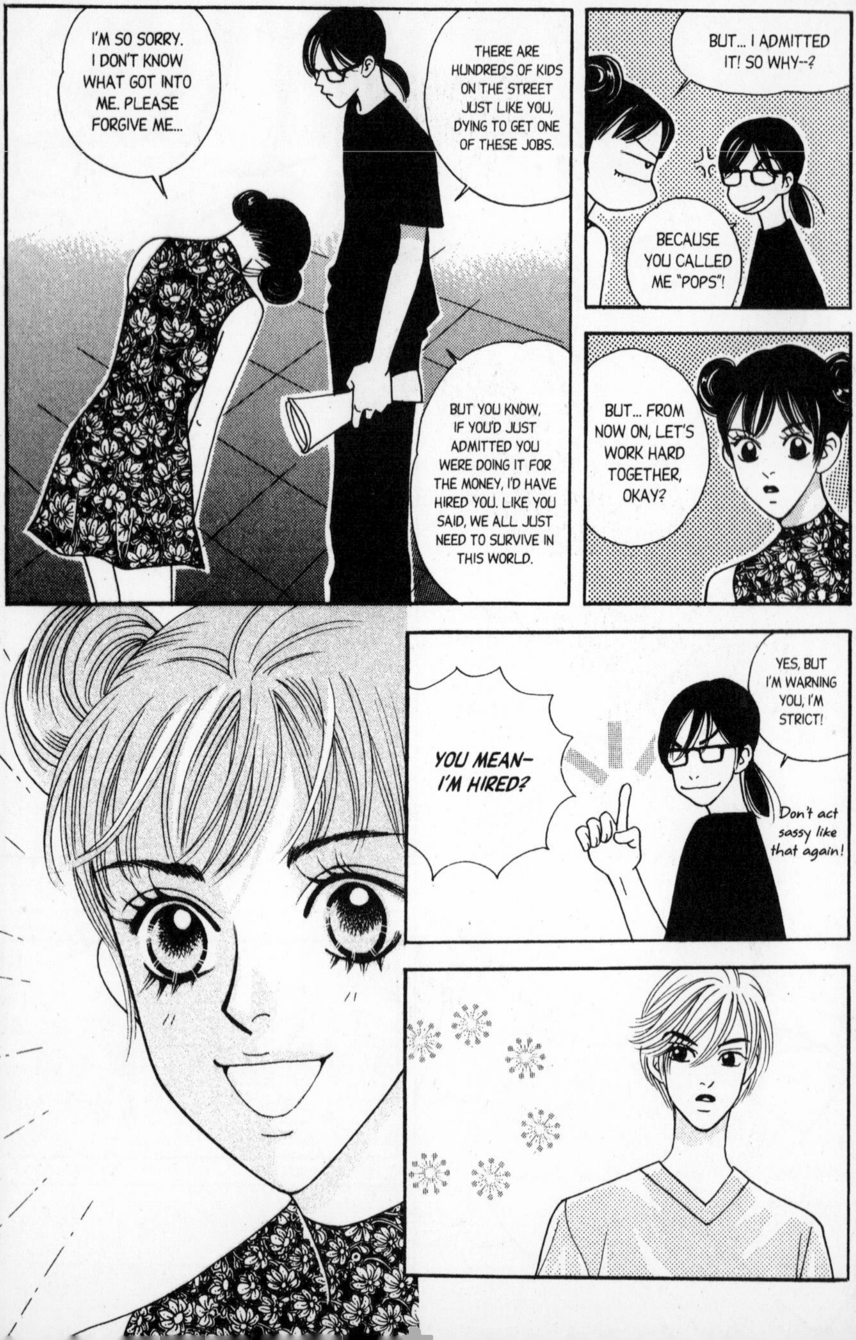
I'M SO SORRY. I DON'T KNOW WHAT GOT INTO ME. PLEASE FORGIVE ME...
THERE ARE HUNDREDS OF KIDS ON THE STREET JUST LIKE YOU, DYING TO GET ONE OF THESE JOBS.
BUT YOU KNOW, IF YOU'D JUST ADMITTED YOU WERE DOING IT FOR THE MONEY, I'D HAVE HIRED YOU. LIKE YOU SAID, WE ALL JUST NEED TO SURVIVE IN THIS WORLD.
BUT... I ADMITTED IT! SO WHY--?
BECAUSE YOU CALLED ME "POPS"!
BUT... FROM NOW ON, LET'S WORK HARD TOGETHER, OKAY?
YOU MEAN- I'M HIRED?
YES, BUT I'M WARNING YOU, I'M STRICT!
Don't act sassy like that again!

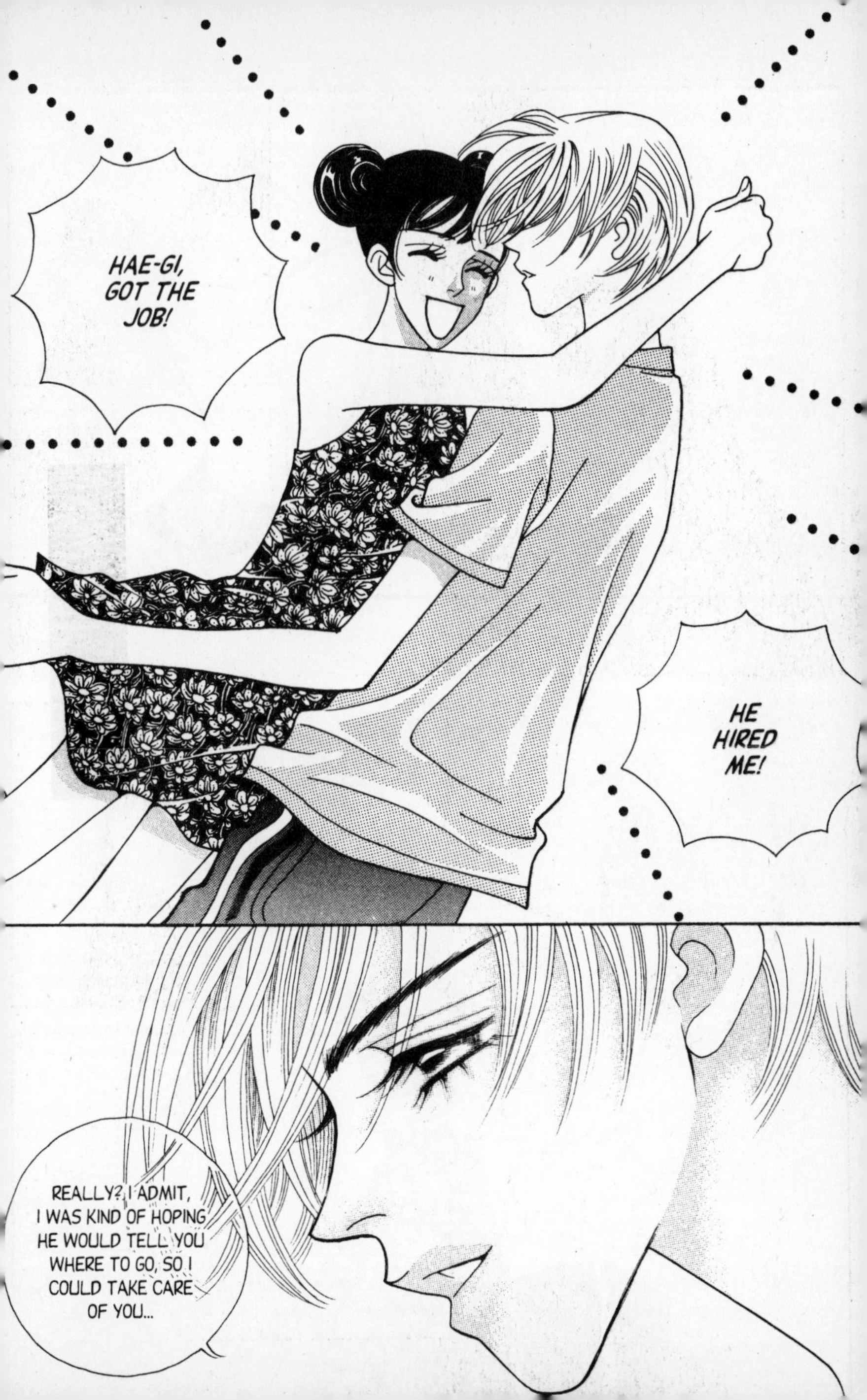
HE HIRED ME!
HAE-GI, GOT THE JOB!
REALLY? I ADMIT, I WAS KIND OF HOPING HE WOULD TELL YOU WHERE TO GO, SO I COULD TAKE CARE OF YOU...

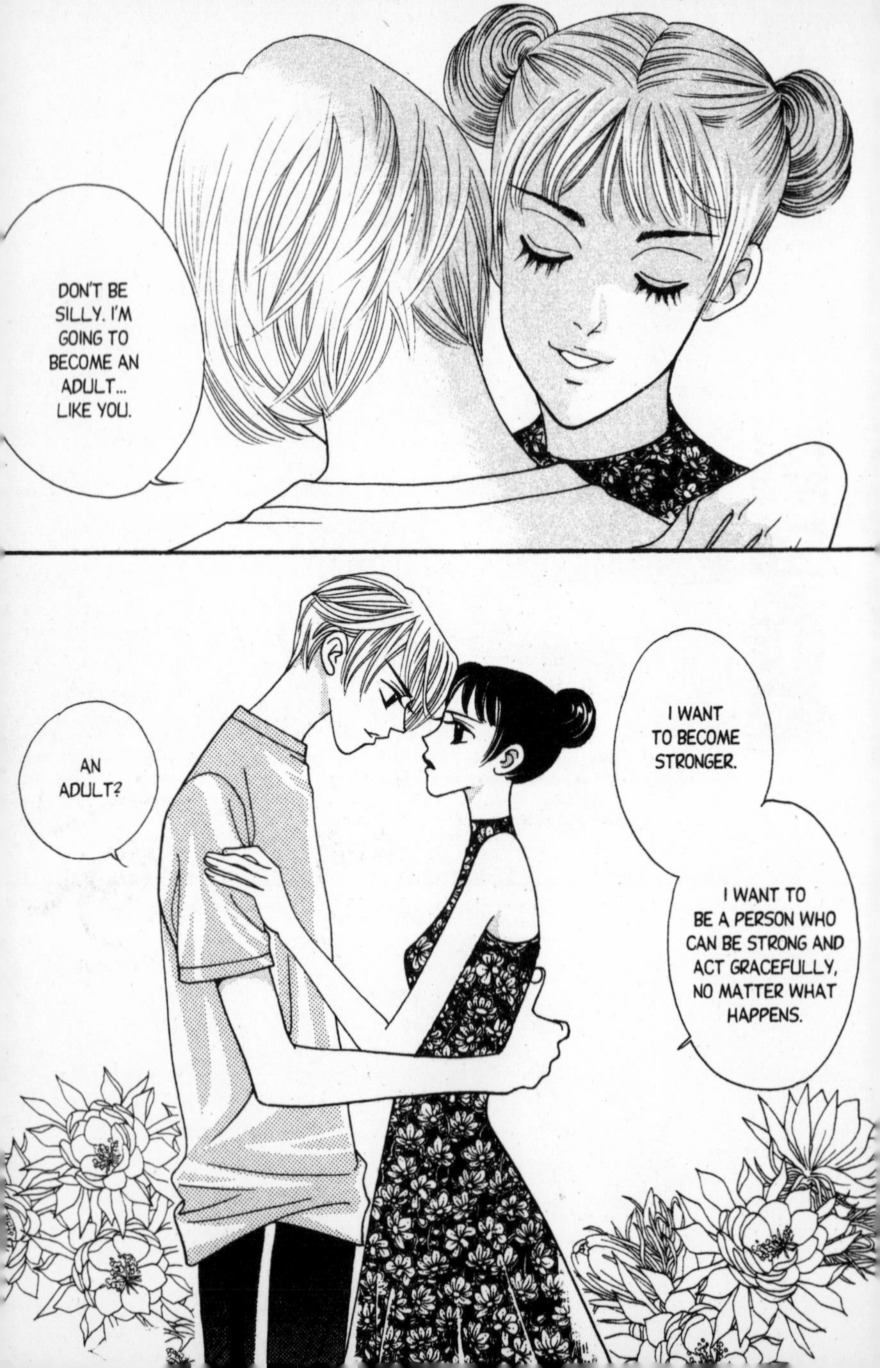
DON'T BE SILLY. I'M GOING TO BECOME AN ADULT... LIKE YOU.
AN ADULT?
I WANT TO BECOME STRONGER.
I WANT TO BE A PERSON WHO CAN BE STRONG AND ACT GRACEFULLY, NO MATTER WHAT HAPPENS.

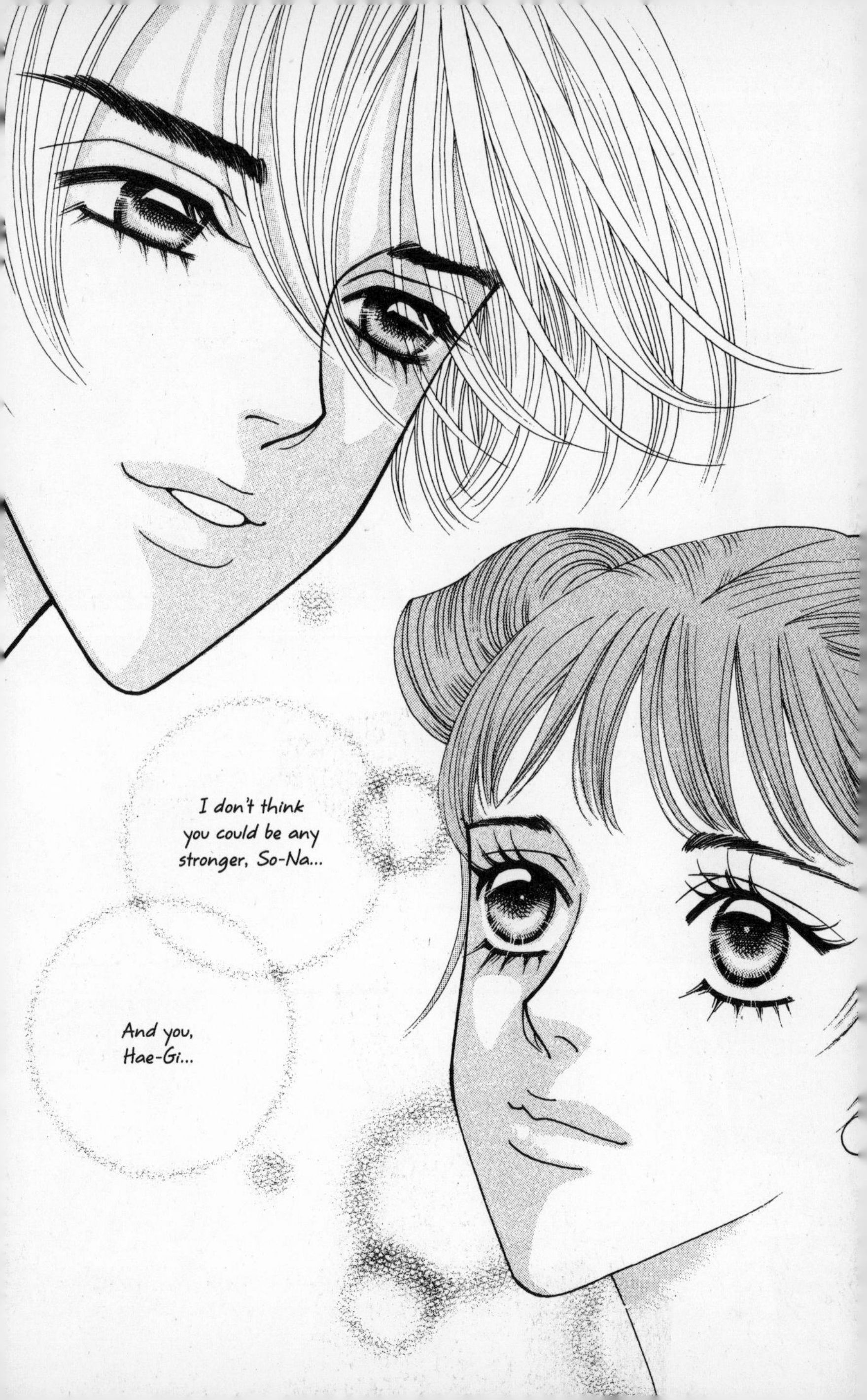
I don't think you could be any stronger, So-Na...
And you, Hae-Gi...

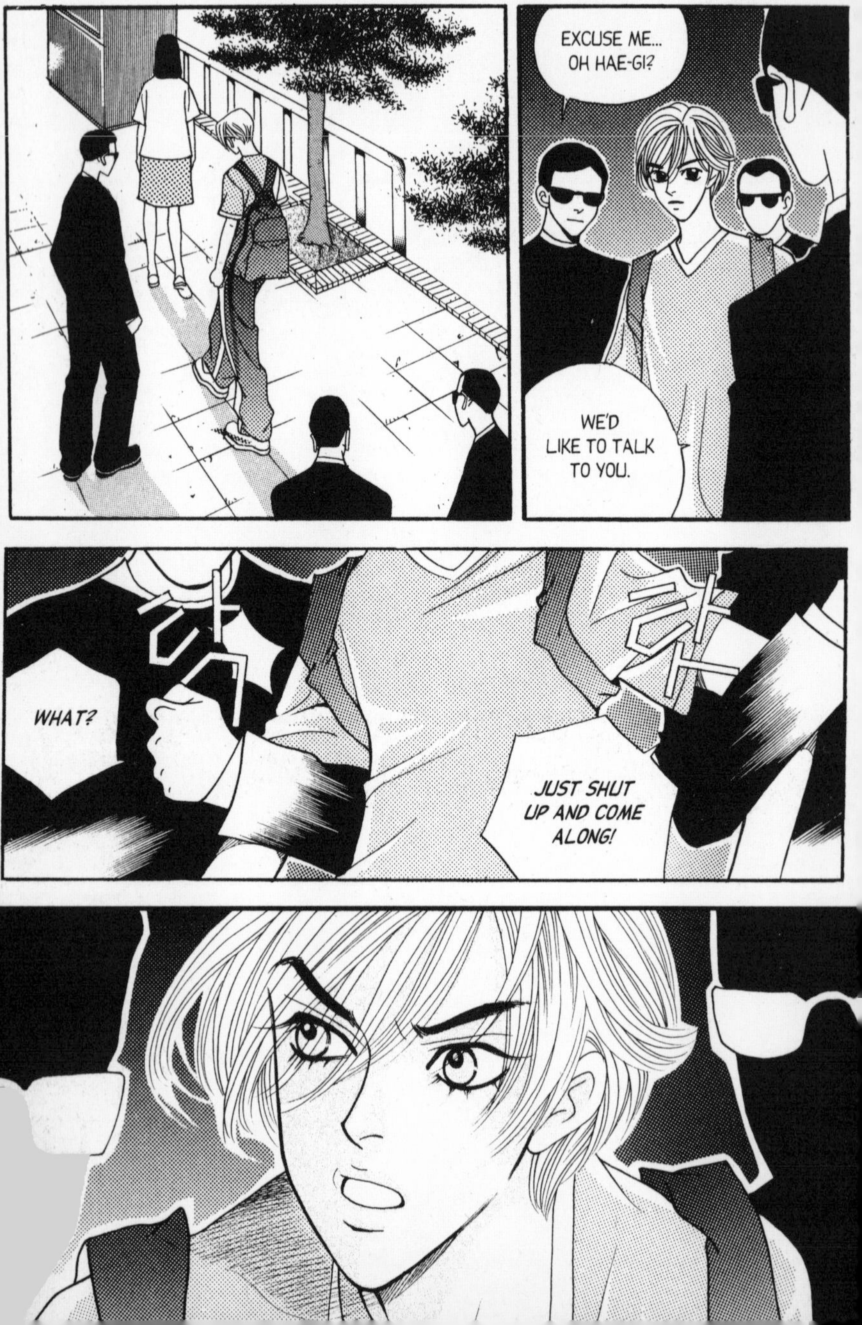
EXCUSE ME... OH HAE-GI?
WE'D LIKE TO TALK TO YOU.
WHAT?
JUST SHUT UP AND COME ALONG!

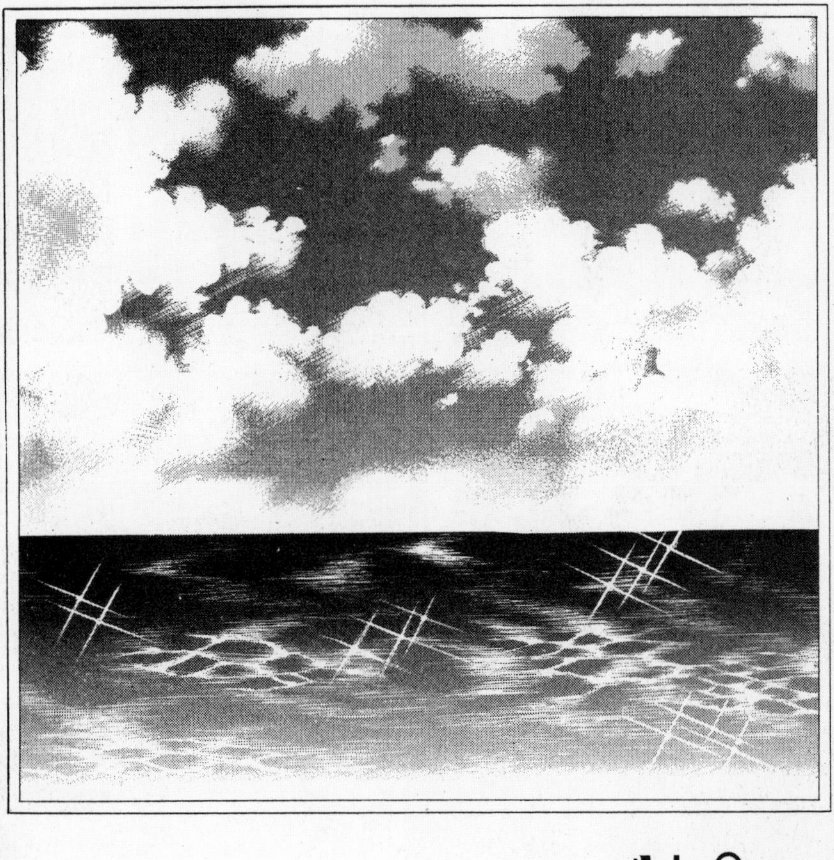

스노우
드롭

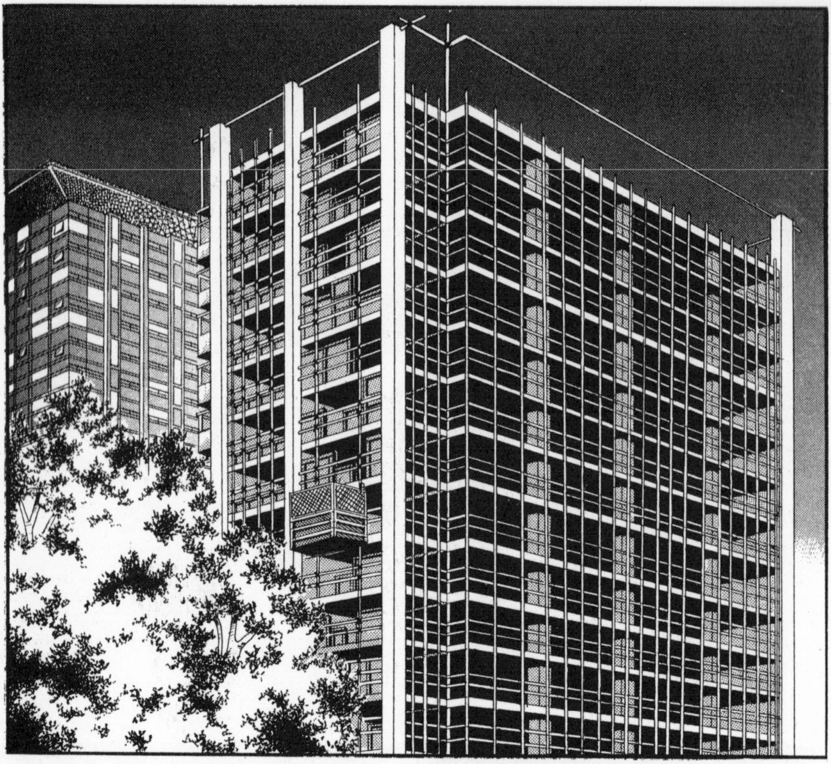

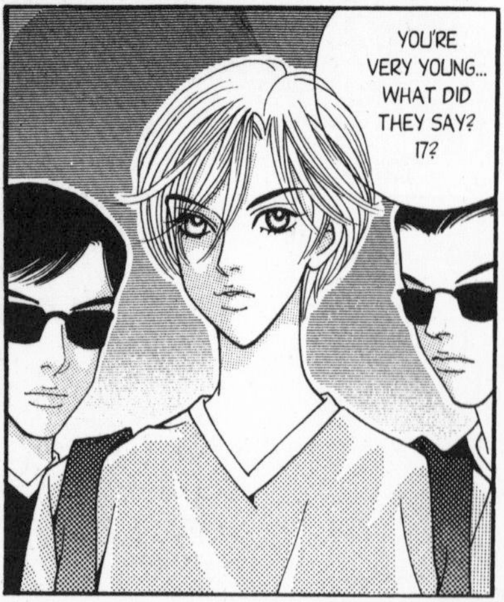
YOU'RE VERY YOUNG... WHAT DID THEY SAY? 17?

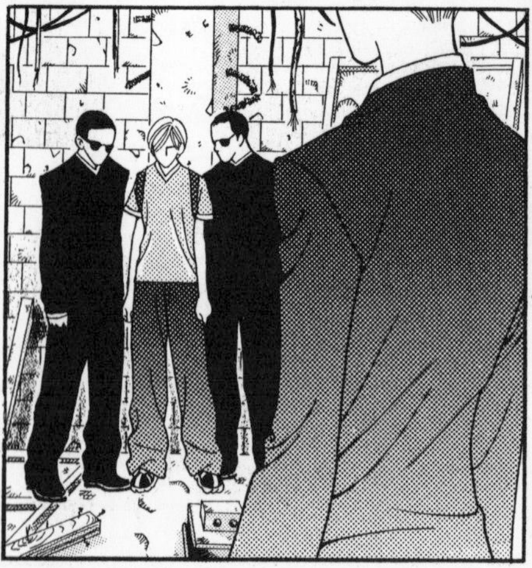

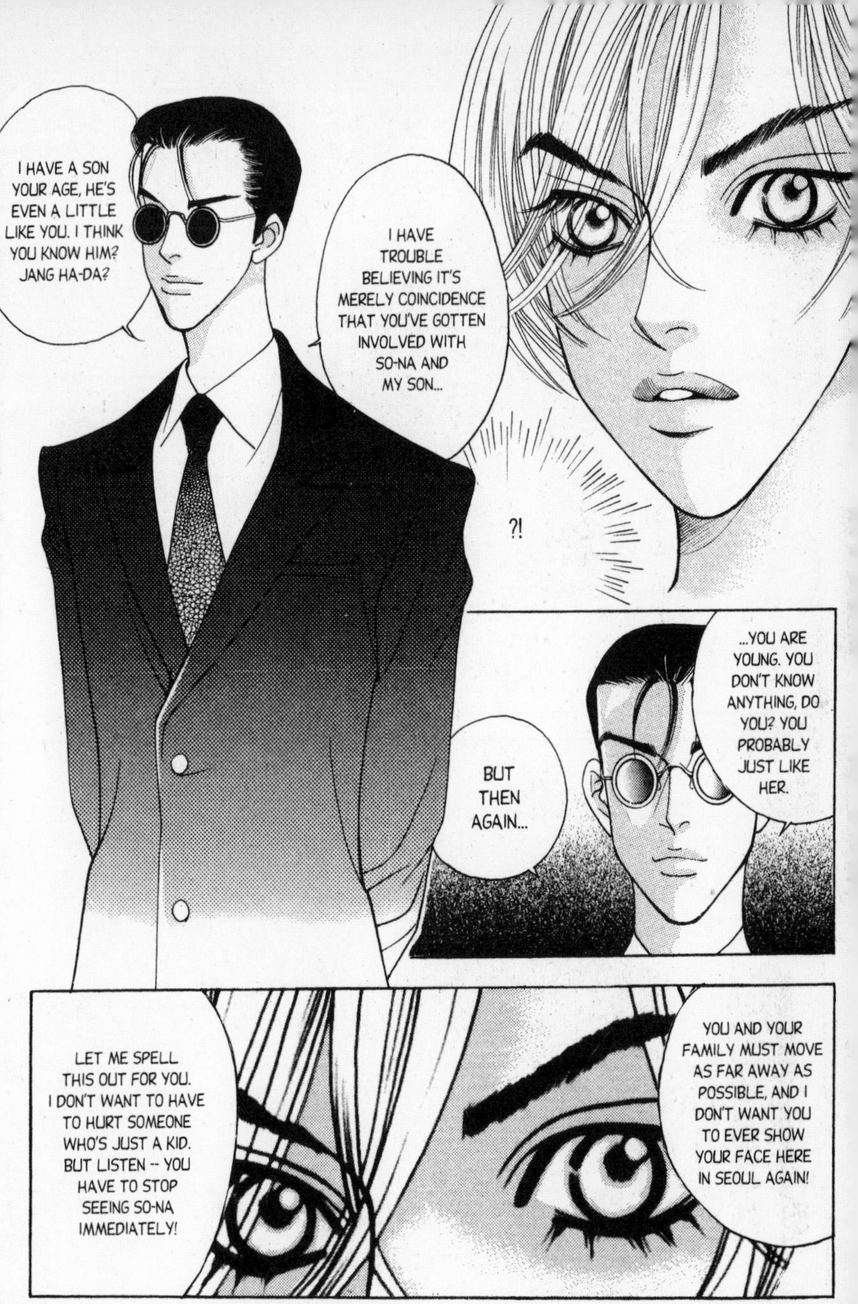
I HAVE A SON YOUR AGE, HE'S EVEN A LITTLE LIKE YOU. I THINK YOU KNOW HIM? JANG HA-DA?
I HAVE TROUBLE BELIEVING IT'S MERELY COINCIDENCE THAT YOU'VE GOTTEN INVOLVED WITH SO-NA AND MY SON...
?!
BUT THEN AGAIN...
...YOU ARE YOUNG. YOU DON'T KNOW ANYTHING, DO YOU? YOU PROBABLY JUST LIKE HER.
LET ME SPELL THIS OUT FOR YOU. I DON'T WANT TO HAVE TO HURT SOMEONE WHO'S JUST A KID. BUT LISTEN -- YOU HAVE TO STOP SEEING SO-NA IMMEDIATELY!
YOU AND YOUR FAMILY MUST MOVE AS FAR AWAY AS POSSIBLE, AND I DON'T WANT YOU TO EVER SHOW YOUR FACE HERE IN SEOUL AGAIN!

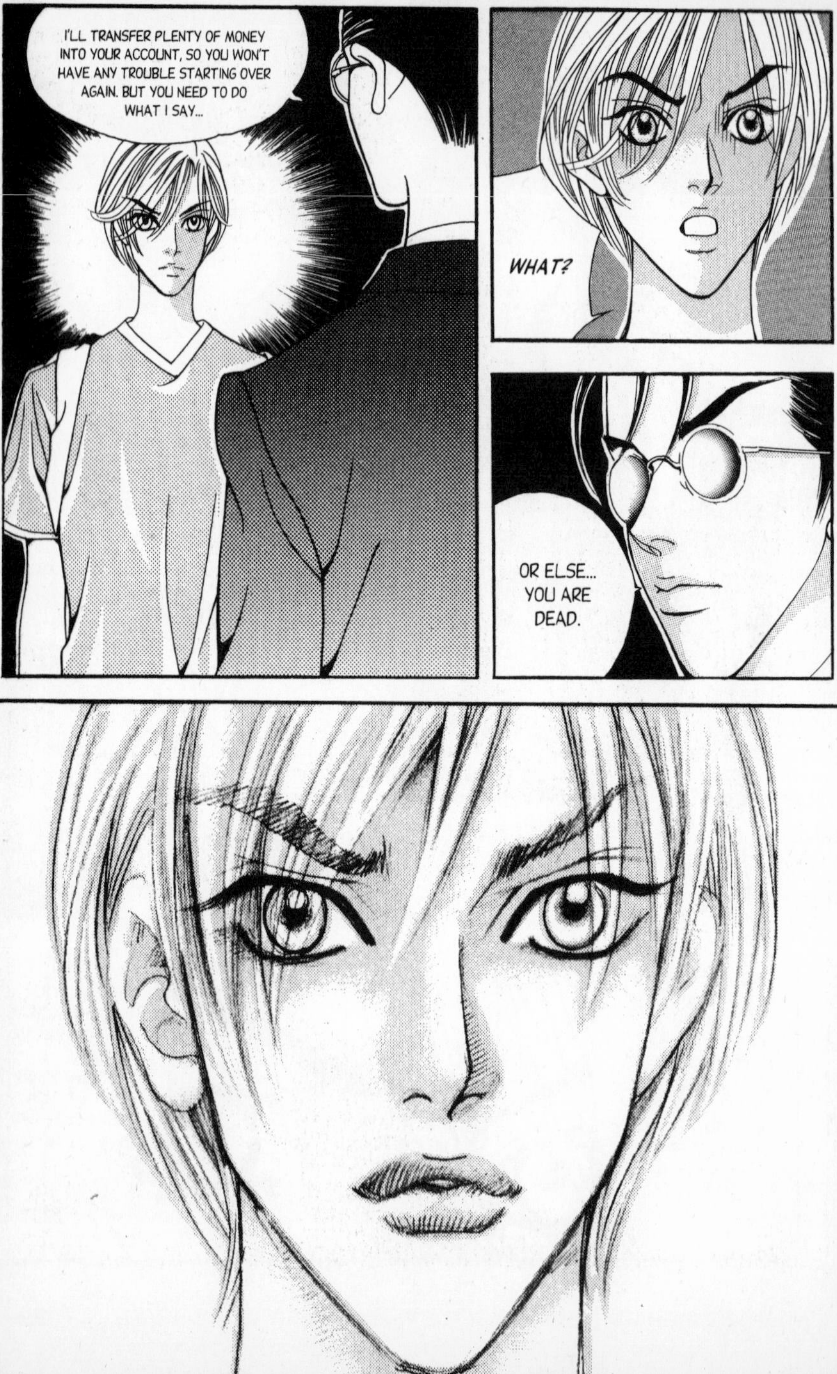
I'LL TRANSFER PLENTY OF MONEY INTO YOUR ACCOUNT, SO YOU WON'T HAVE ANY TROUBLE STARTING OVER AGAIN. BUT YOU NEED TO DO WHAT I SAY...
WHAT?
OR ELSE... YOU ARE DEAD.

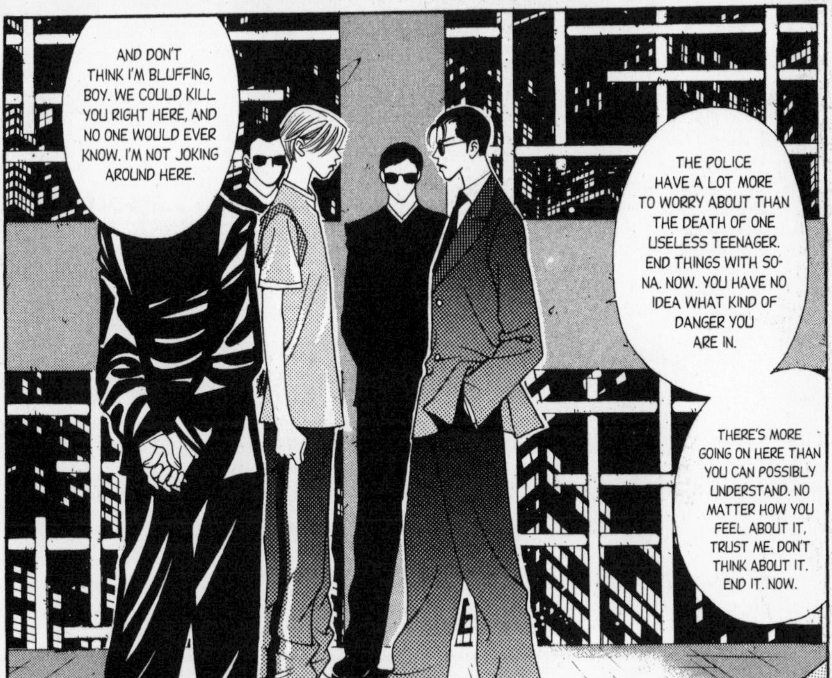
AND DON'T THINK I'M BLUFFING, BOY. WE COULD KILL YOU RIGHT HERE, AND NO ONE WOULD EVER KNOW. I'M NOT JOKING AROUND HERE.
THE POLICE HAVE A LOT MORE TO WORRY ABOUT THAN THE DEATH OF ONE USELESS TEENAGER. END THINGS WITH SO-NA. NOW. YOU HAVE NO IDEA WHAT KIND OF DANGER YOU ARE IN.
THERE'S MORE GOING ON HERE THAN YOU CAN POSSIBLY UNDERSTAND. NO MATTER HOW YOU FEEL ABOUT IT, TRUST ME. DON'T THINK ABOUT IT. END IT. NOW.

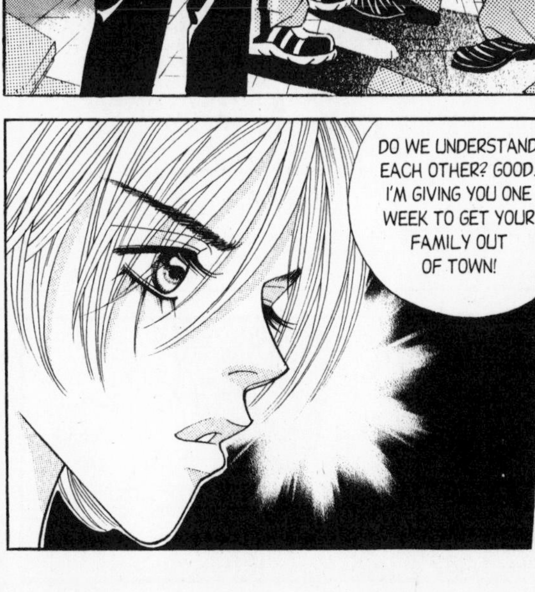
DO WE UNDERSTAND EACH OTHER? GOOD. I'M GIVING YOU ONE WEEK TO GET YOUR FAMILY OUT OF TOWN!

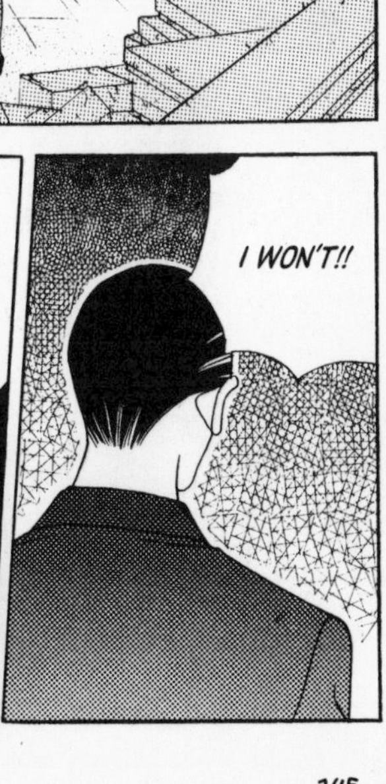
I WON'T!!

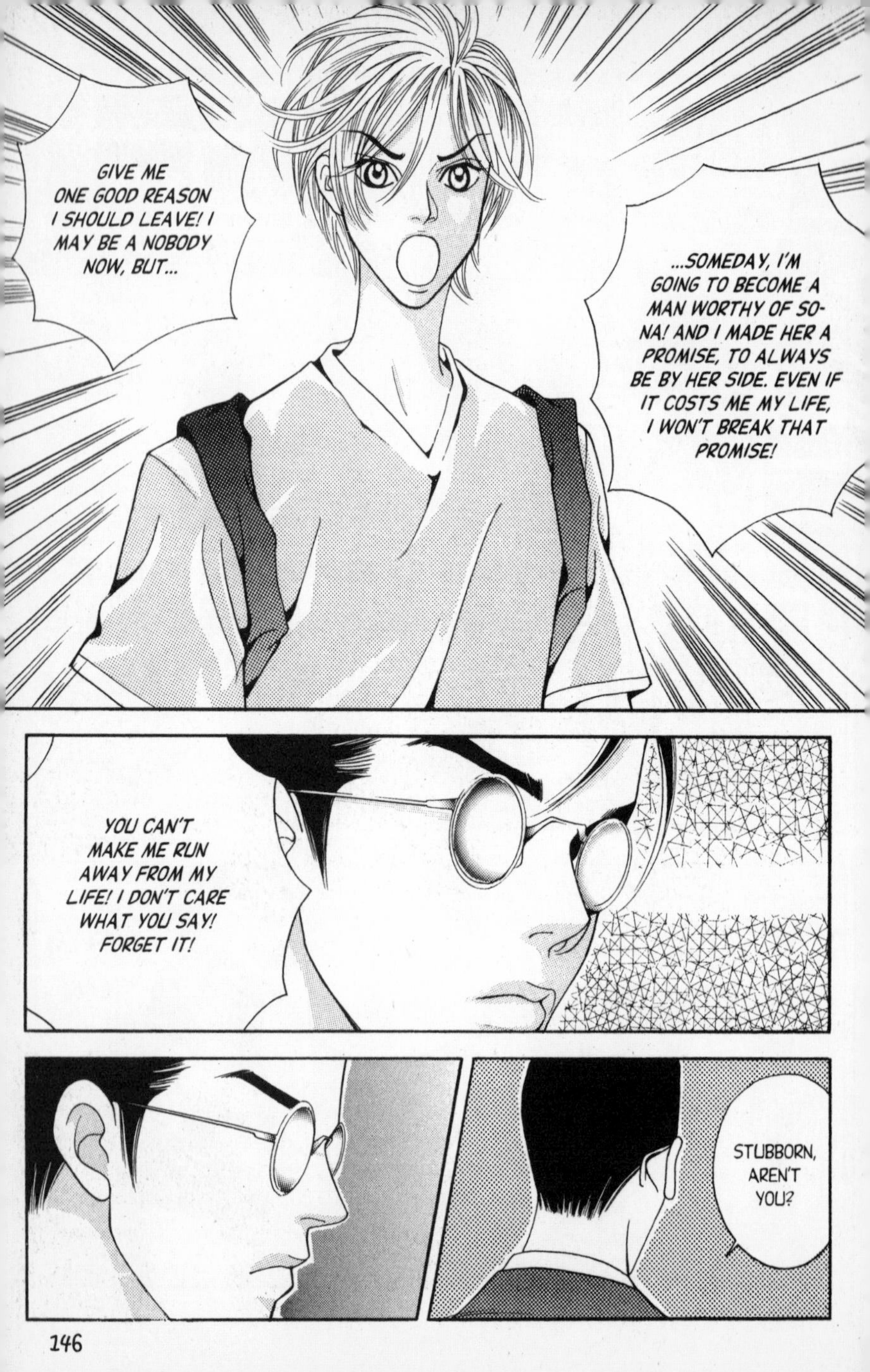
GIVE ME ONE GOOD REASON I SHOULD LEAVE! I MAY BE A NOBODY NOW, BUT...
...SOMEDAY, I'M GOING TO BECOME A MAN WORTHY OF SO-NA! AND I MADE HER A PROMISE, TO ALWAYS BE BY HER SIDE. EVEN IF IT COSTS ME MY LIFE, I WON'T BREAK THAT PROMISE!
YOU CAN'T MAKE ME RUN AWAY FROM MY LIFE! I DON'T CARE WHAT YOU SAY! FORGET IT!
STUBBORN, AREN'T YOU?

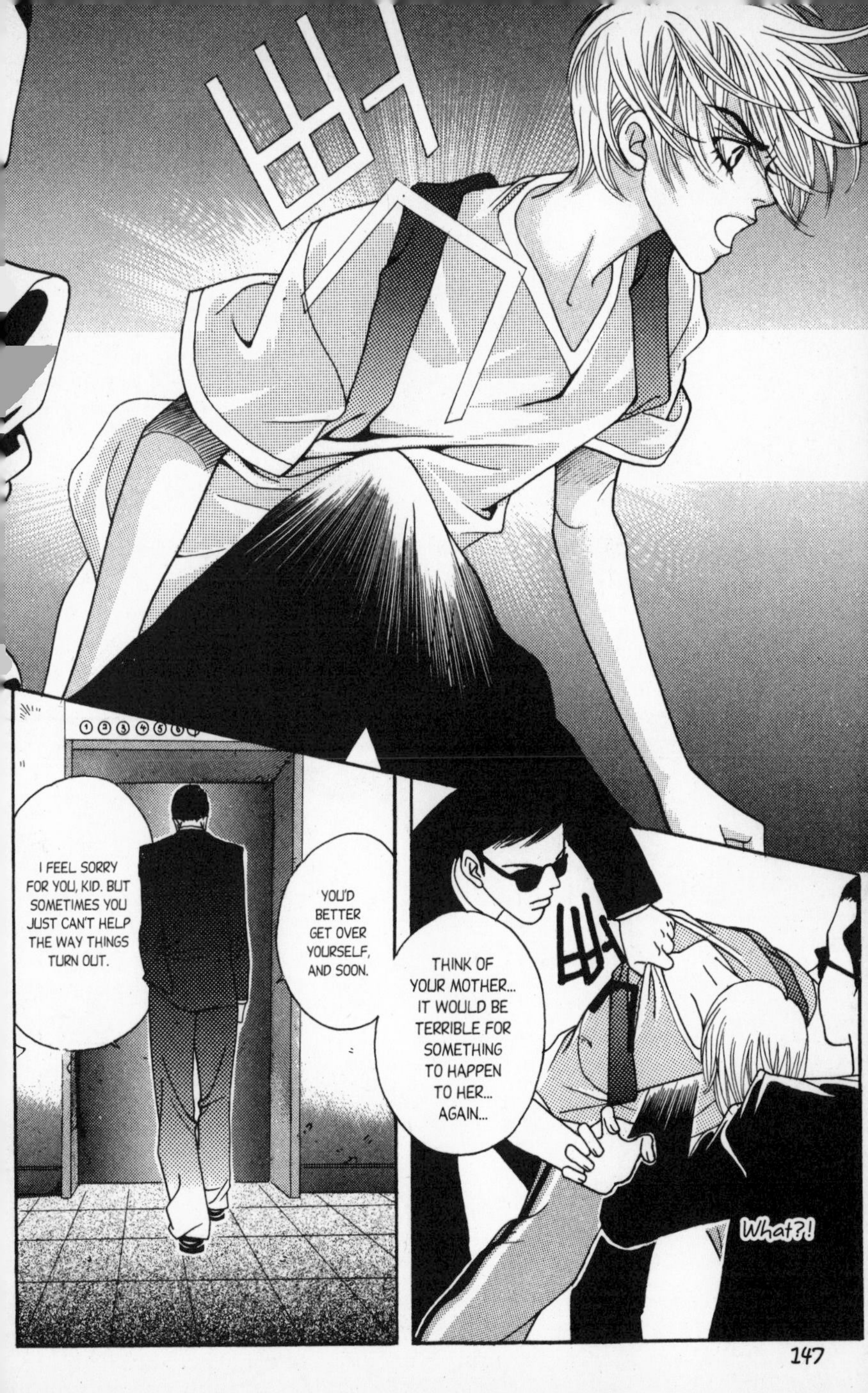
YOU'D BETTER GET OVER YOURSELF, AND SOON.
THINK OF YOUR MOTHER... IT WOULD BE TERRIBLE FOR SOMETHING TO HAPPEN TO HER... AGAIN...
What?!
I FEEL SORRY FOR YOU, KID. BUT SOMETIMES YOU JUST CAN'T HELP THE WAY THINGS TURN OUT.

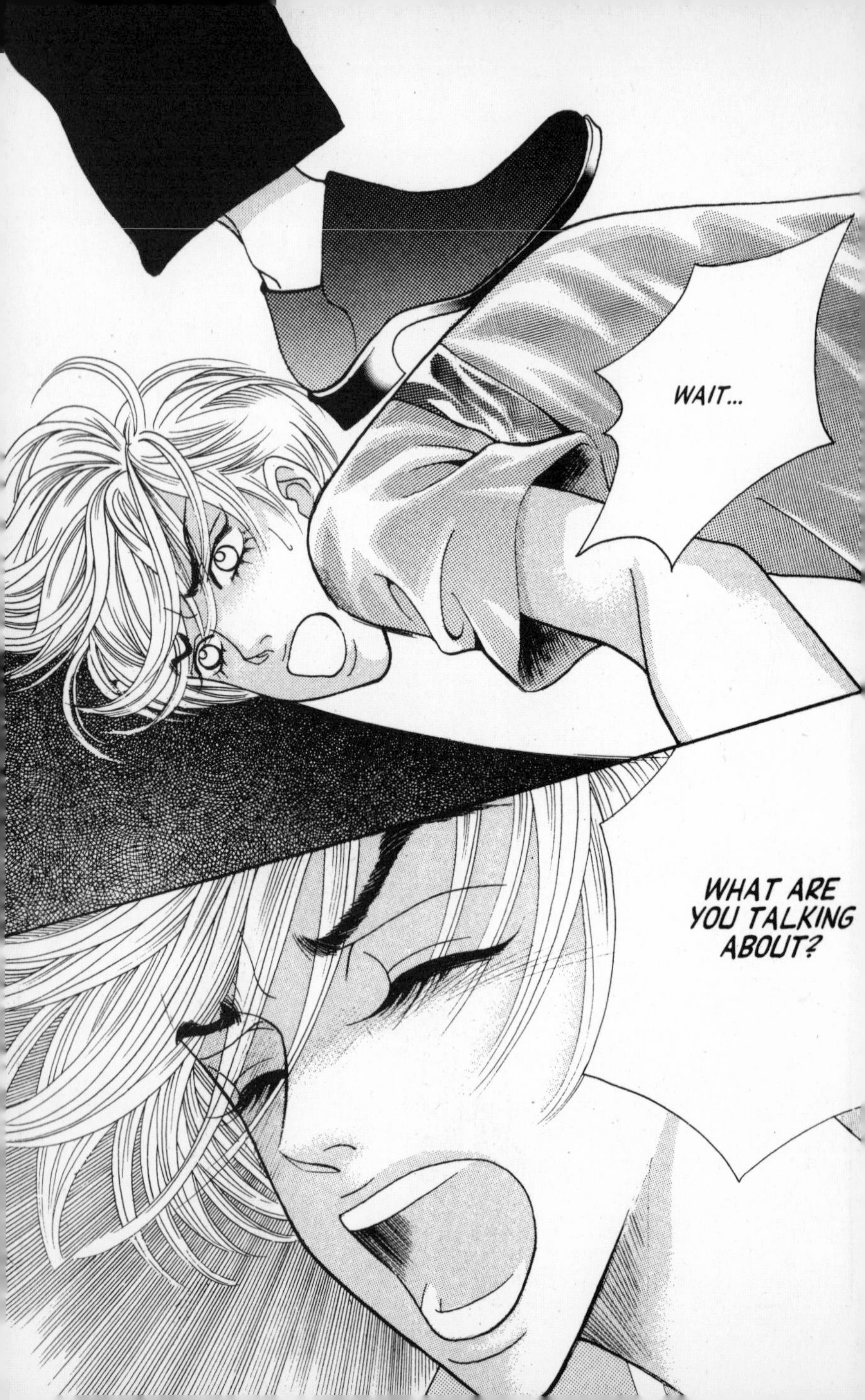
WAIT...
WHAT ARE YOU TALKING ABOUT?

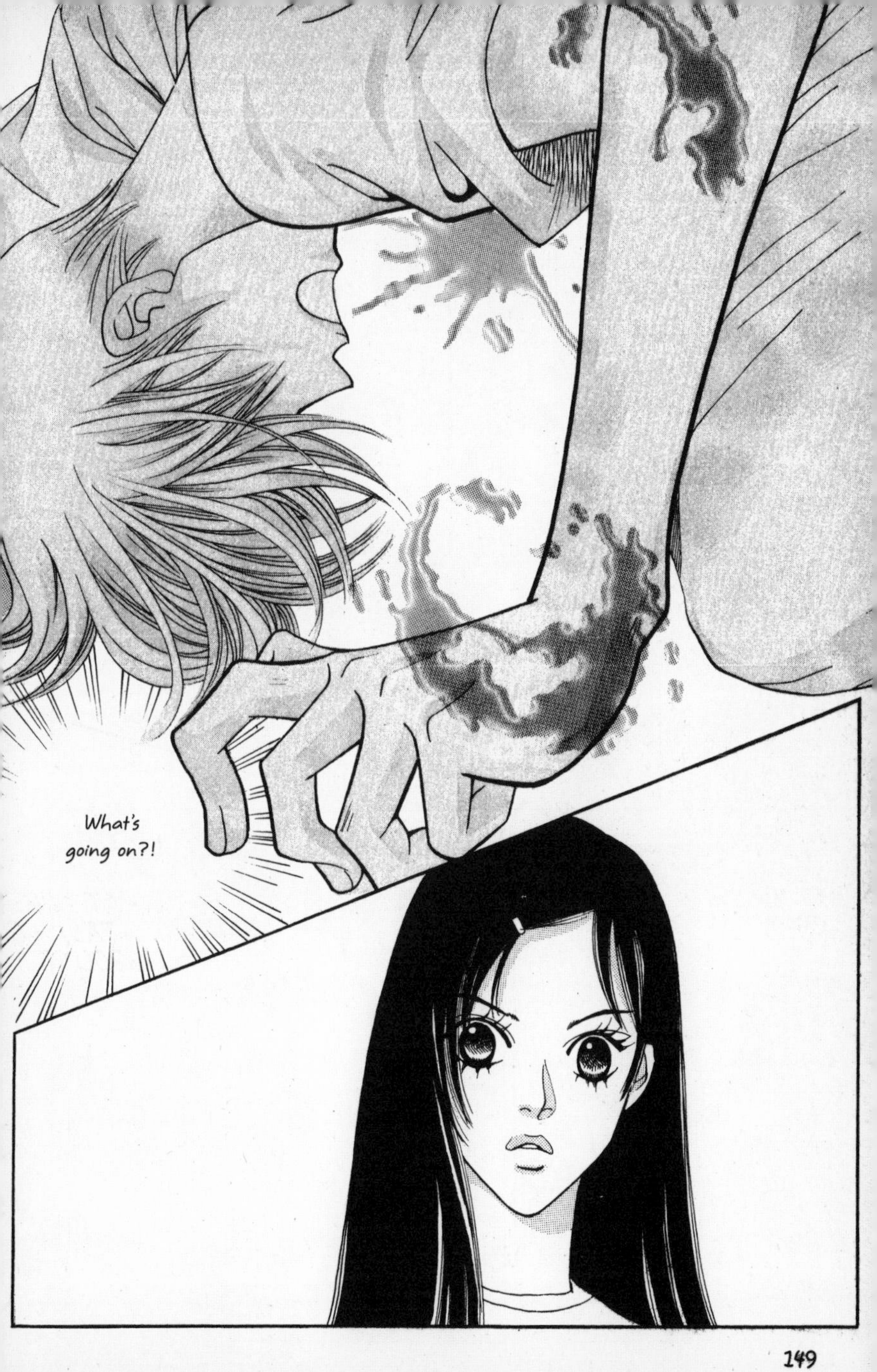
What's going on?!

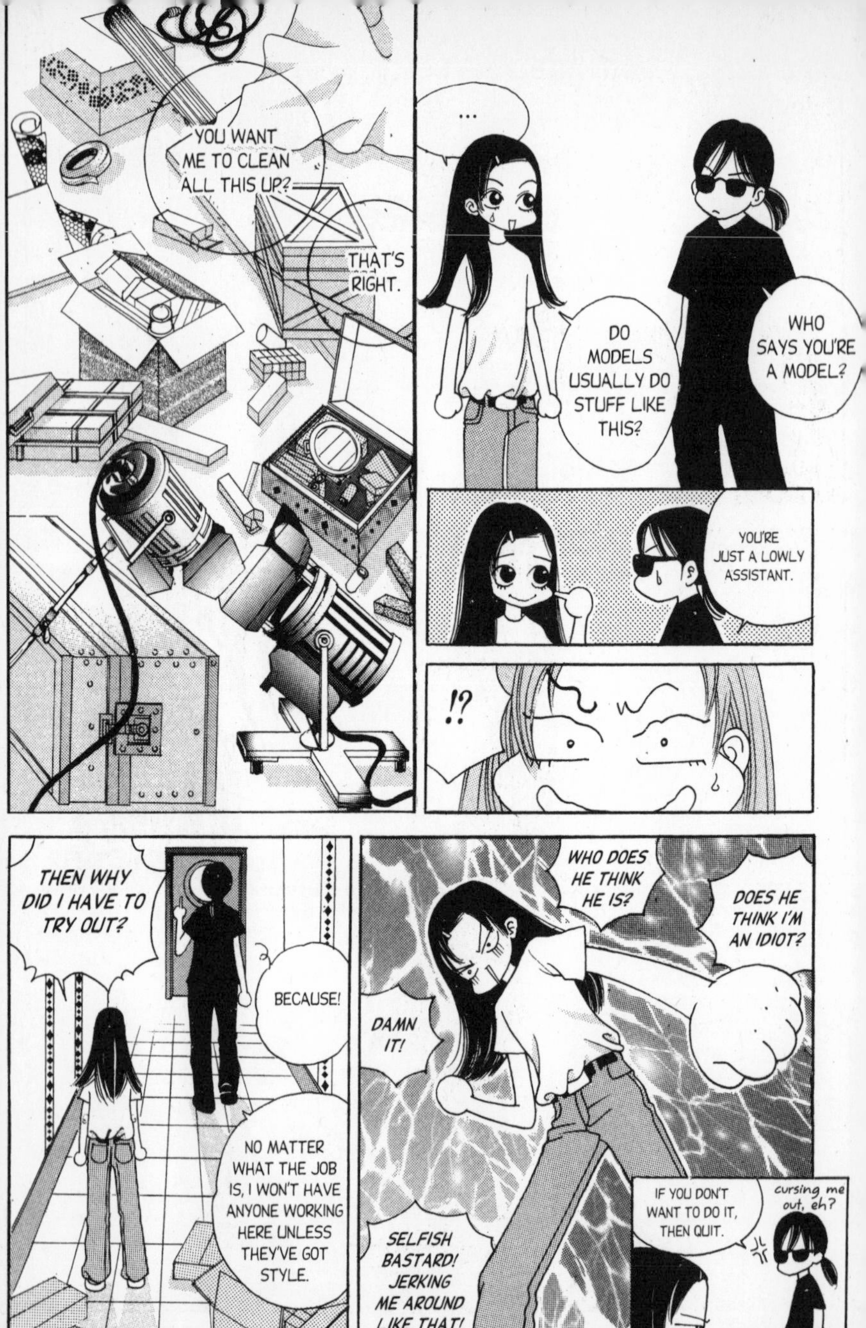
YOU WANT ME TO CLEAN ALL THIS UP?
THAT'S RIGHT.
...
DO MODELS USUALLY DO STUFF LIKE THIS?
WHO SAYS YOU'RE A MODEL?
YOU'RE JUST A LOWLY ASSISTANT.
!?
THEN WHY DID I HAVE TO TRY OUT?
BECAUSE!
NO MATTER WHAT THE JOB IS, I WON'T HAVE ANYONE WORKING HERE UNLESS THEY'VE GOT STYLE.
WHO DOES HE THINK HE IS?
DOES HE THINK I'M AN IDIOT?
DAMN IT!
SELFISH BASTARD! JERKING ME AROUND LIKE THAT!
IF YOU DON'T WANT TO DO IT, THEN QUIT.
cursing me out, eh?

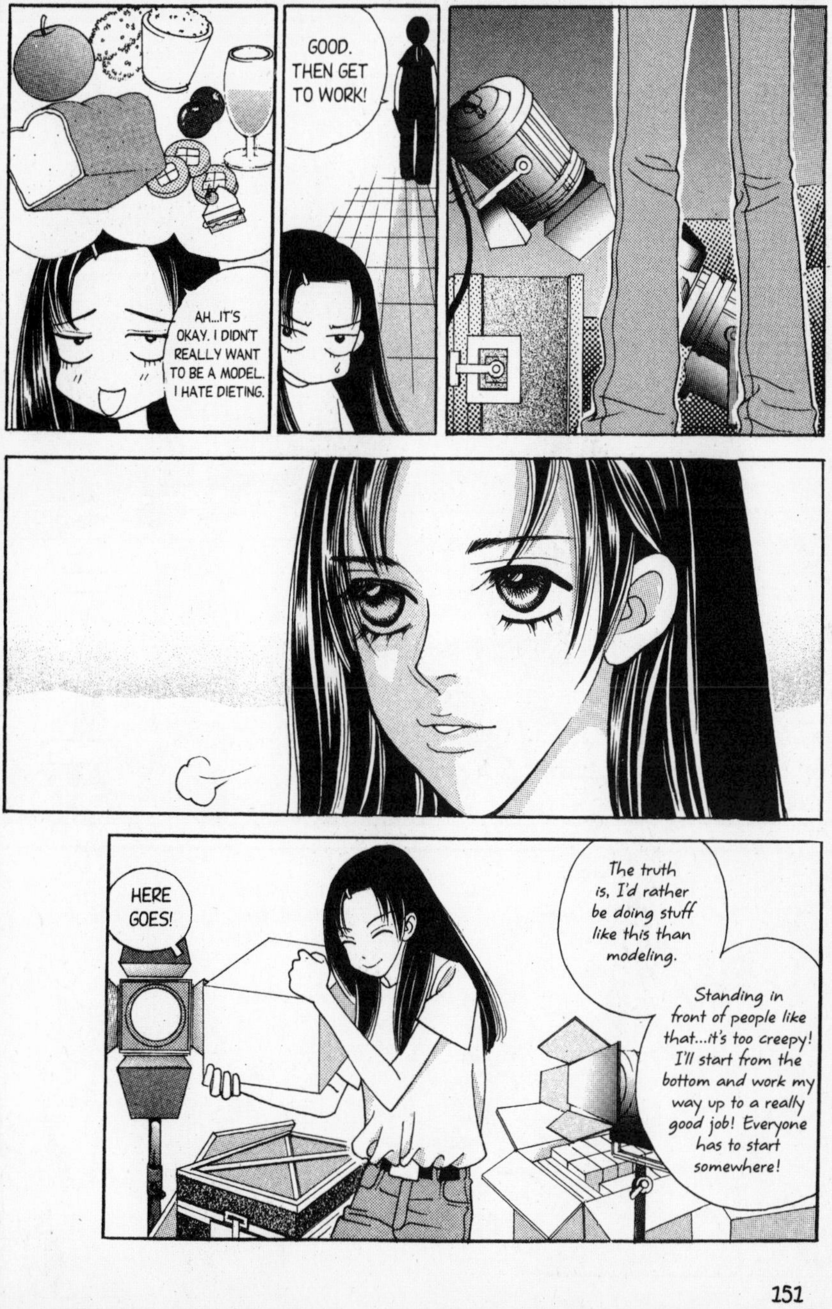
AH...IT'S OKAY. I DIDN'T REALLY WANT TO BE A MODEL. I HATE DIETING.
GOOD. THEN GET TO WORK!
HERE GOES!
The truth is, I'd rather be doing stuff like this than modeling.
Standing in front of people like that...it's too creepy! I'll start from the bottom and work my way up to a really good job! Everyone has to start somewhere!

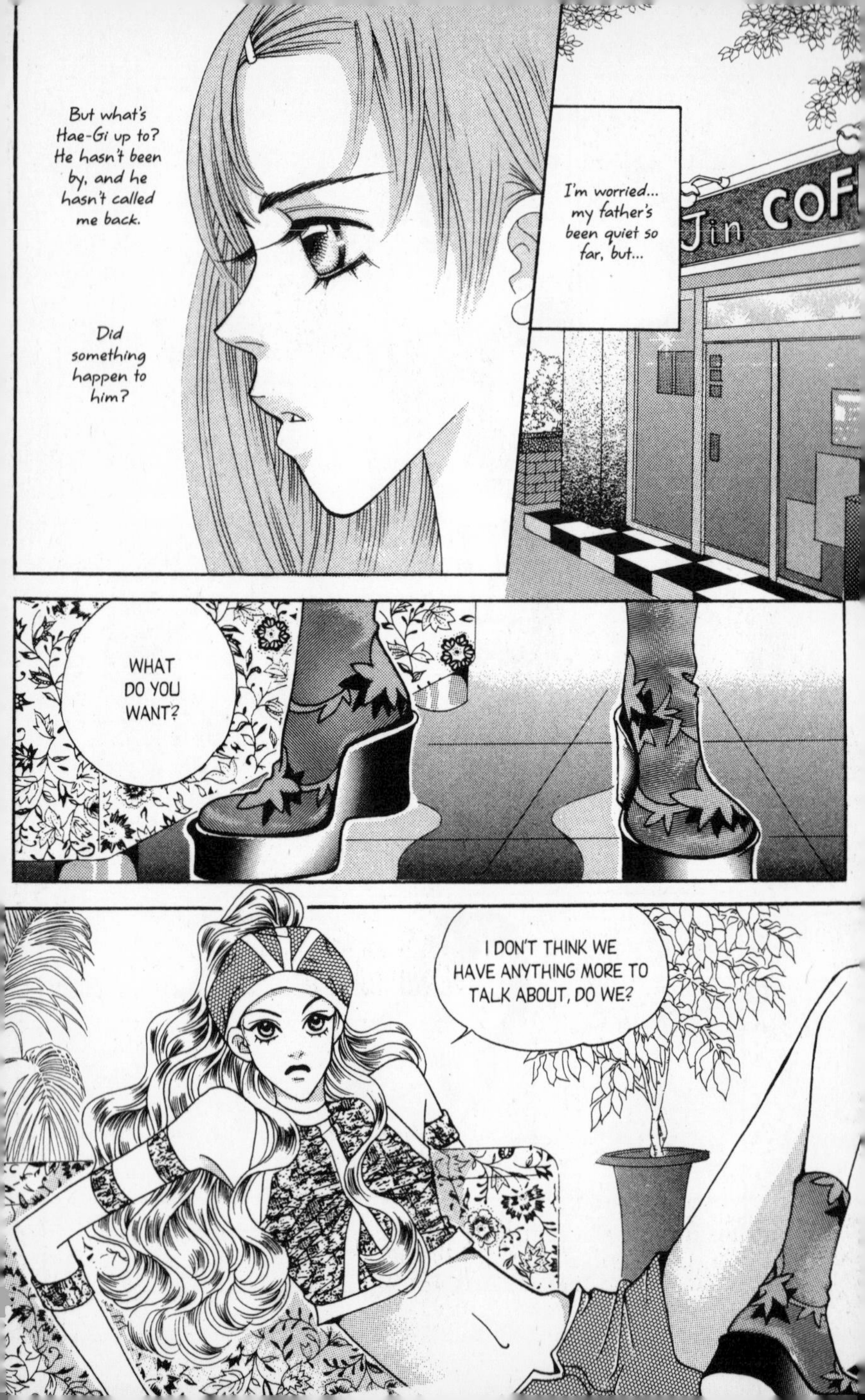
But what's Hae-Gi up to? He hasn't been by, and he hasn't called me back.
Did something happen to him?
I'm worried... my father's been quiet so far, but...
Jin COF
WHAT DO YOU WANT?
I DON'T THINK WE HAVE ANYTHING MORE TO TALK ABOUT, DO WE?

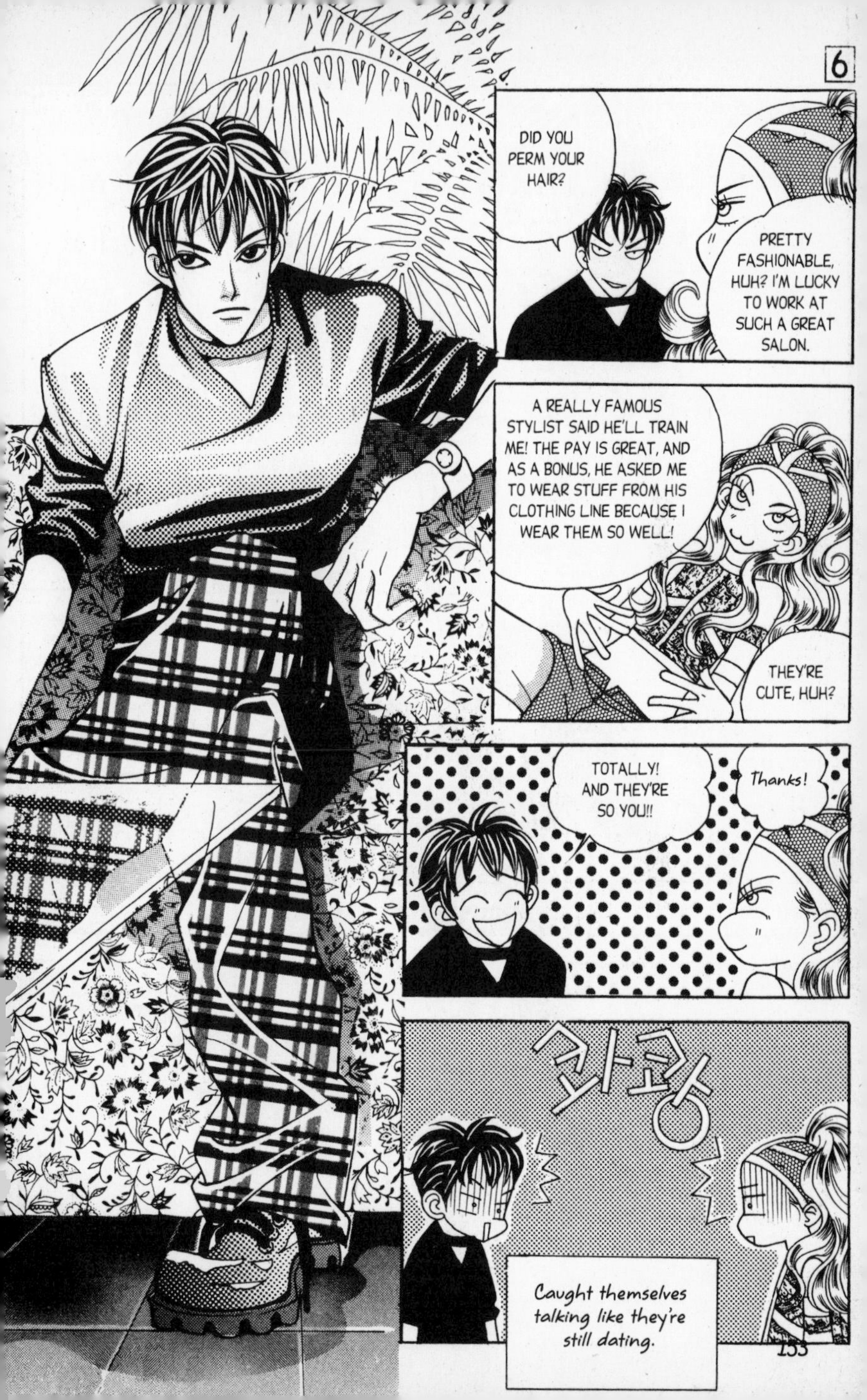
6
DID YOU PERM YOUR HAIR?
PRETTY FASHIONABLE, HUH? I'M LUCKY TO WORK AT SUCH A GREAT SALON.
A REALLY FAMOUS STYLIST SAID HE'LL TRAIN ME! THE PAY IS GREAT, AND AS A BONUS, HE ASKED ME TO WEAR STUFF FROM HIS CLOTHING LINE BECAUSE I WEAR THEM SO WELL!
THEY'RE CUTE, HUH?
Thanks!
TOTALLY! AND THEY'RE SO YOU!!
Caught themselves talking like they're still dating.

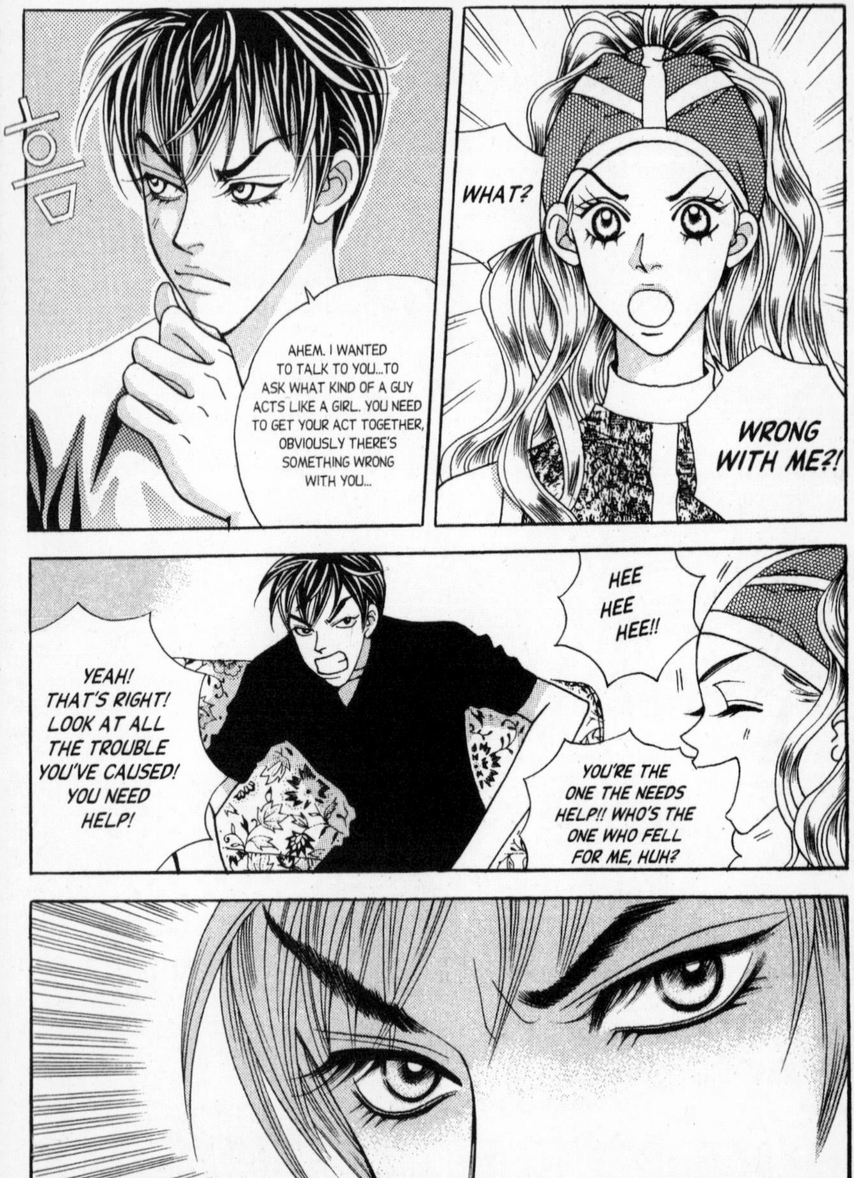
AHEM. I WANTED TO TALK TO YOU...TO ASK WHAT KIND OF A GUY ACTS LIKE A GIRL. YOU NEED TO GET YOUR ACT TOGETHER, OBVIOUSLY THERE'S SOMETHING WRONG WITH YOU...
WHAT?
WRONG WITH ME?!
YEAH! THAT'S RIGHT! LOOK AT ALL THE TROUBLE YOU'VE CAUSED! YOU NEED HELP!
HEE HEE HEE!!
YOU'RE THE ONE THE NEEDS HELP!! WHO'S THE ONE WHO FELL FOR ME, HUH?

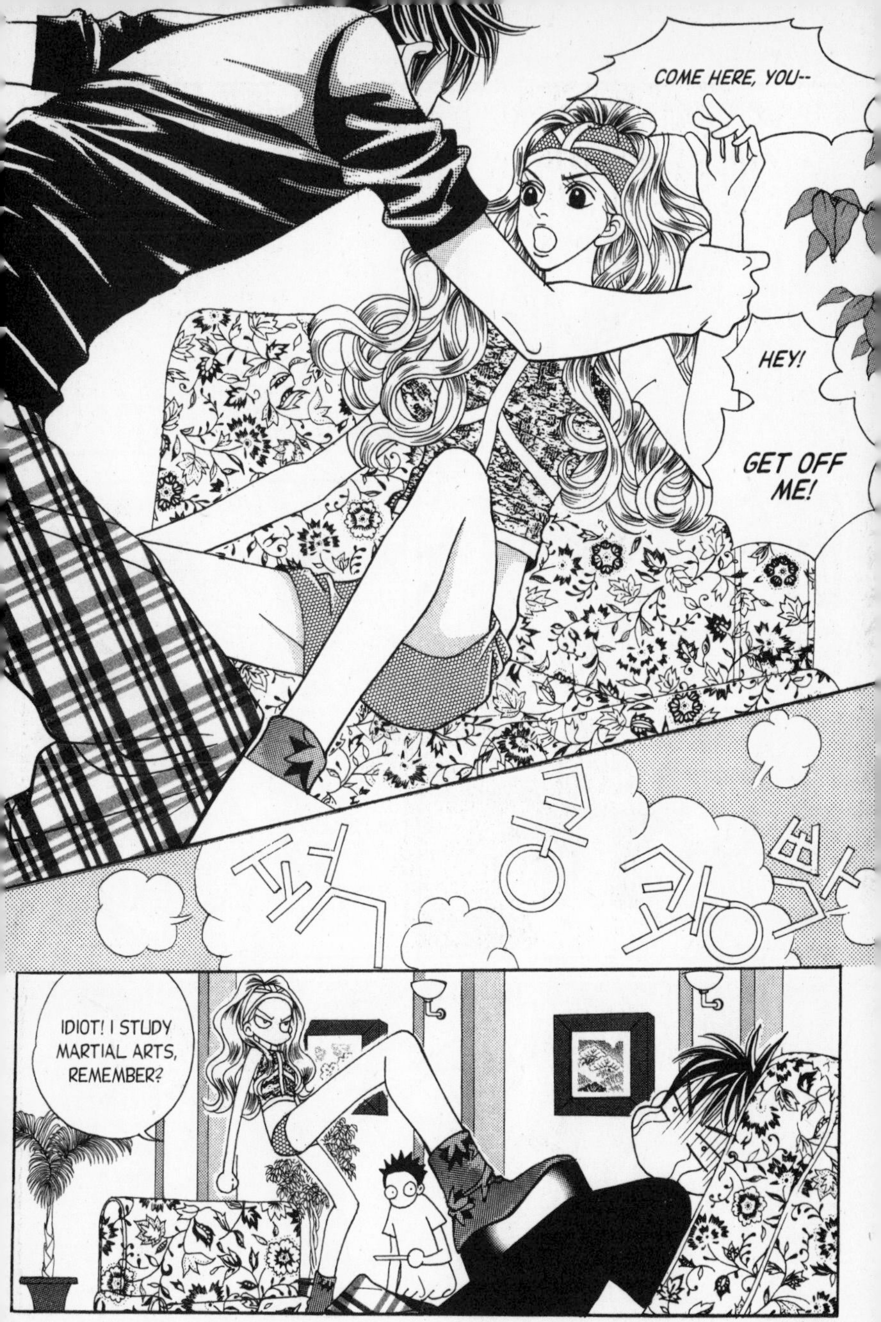
COME HERE, YOU--
HEY!
GET OFF ME!
IDIOT! I STUDY MARTIAL ARTS, REMEMBER?

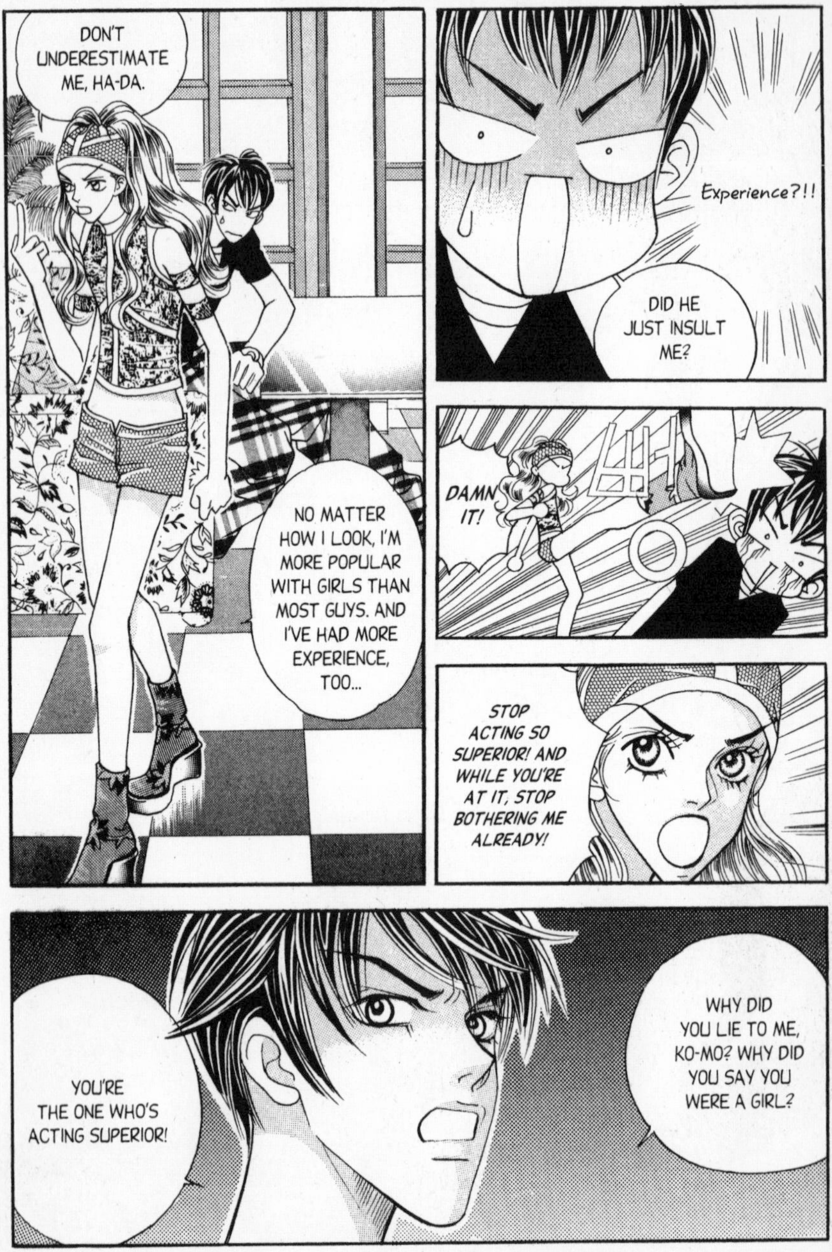
DON'T UNDERESTIMATE ME, HA-DA.
NO MATTER HOW I LOOK, I'M MORE POPULAR WITH GIRLS THAN MOST GUYS. AND I'VE HAD MORE EXPERIENCE, TOO...
Experience?!!
DID HE JUST INSULT ME?
DAMN IT!
STOP ACTING SO SUPERIOR! AND WHILE YOU'RE AT IT, STOP BOTHERING ME ALREADY!
YOU'RE THE ONE WHO'S ACTING SUPERIOR!
WHY DID YOU LIE TO ME, KO-MO? WHY DID YOU SAY YOU WERE A GIRL?

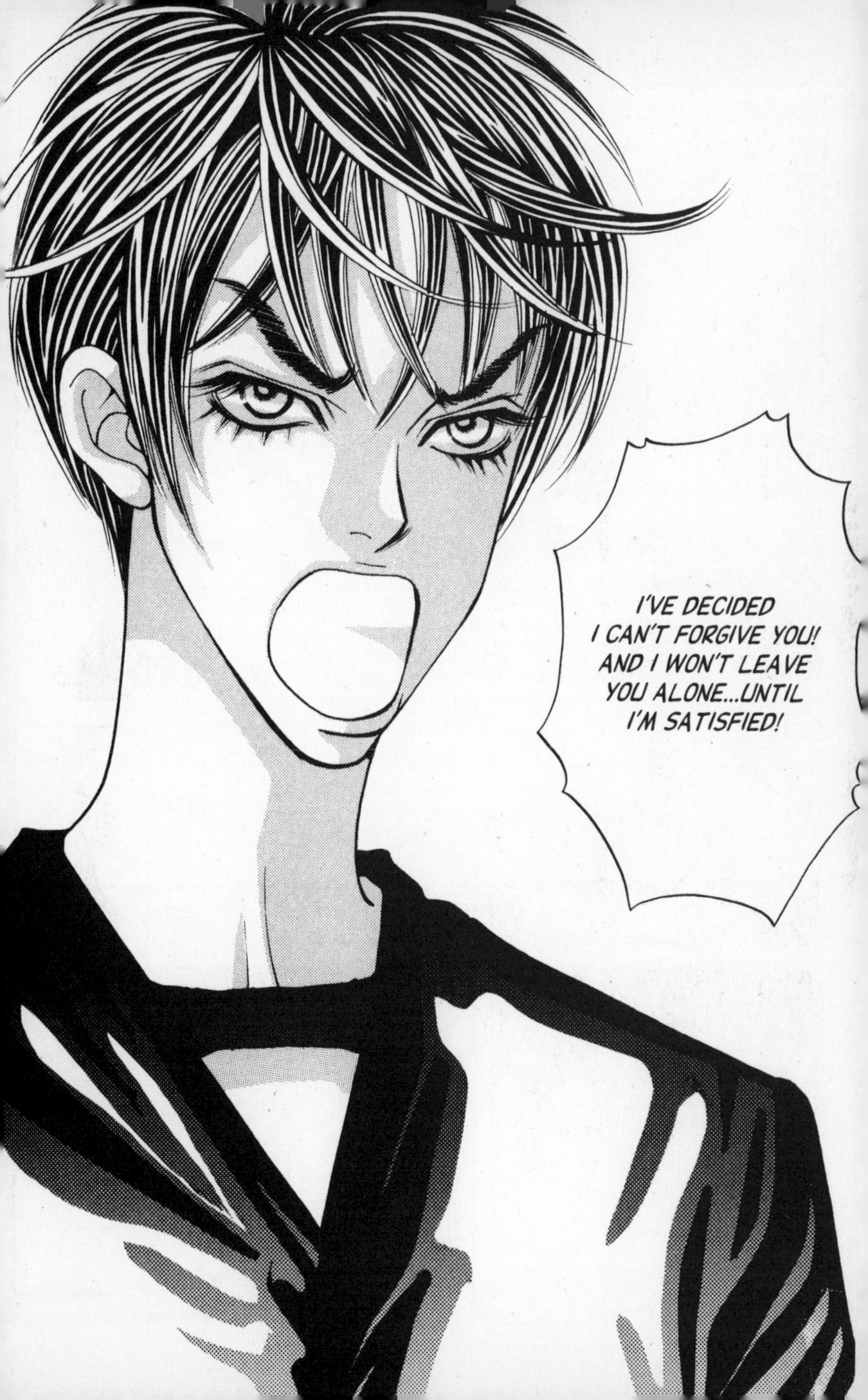
I'VE DECIDED I CAN'T FORGIVE YOU! AND I WON'T LEAVE YOU ALONE...UNTIL I'M SATISFIED!

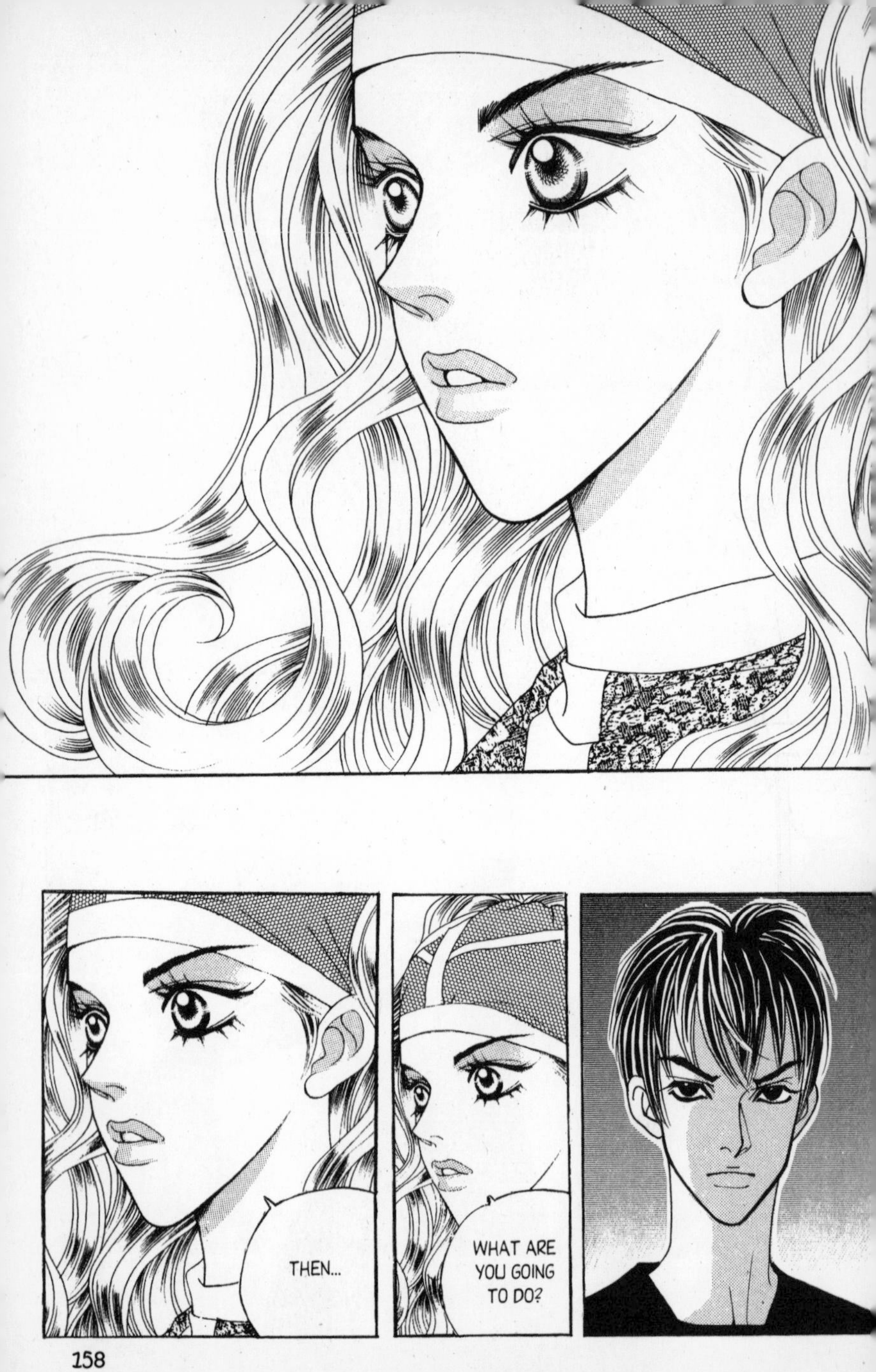
THEN...
WHAT ARE YOU GOING TO DO?

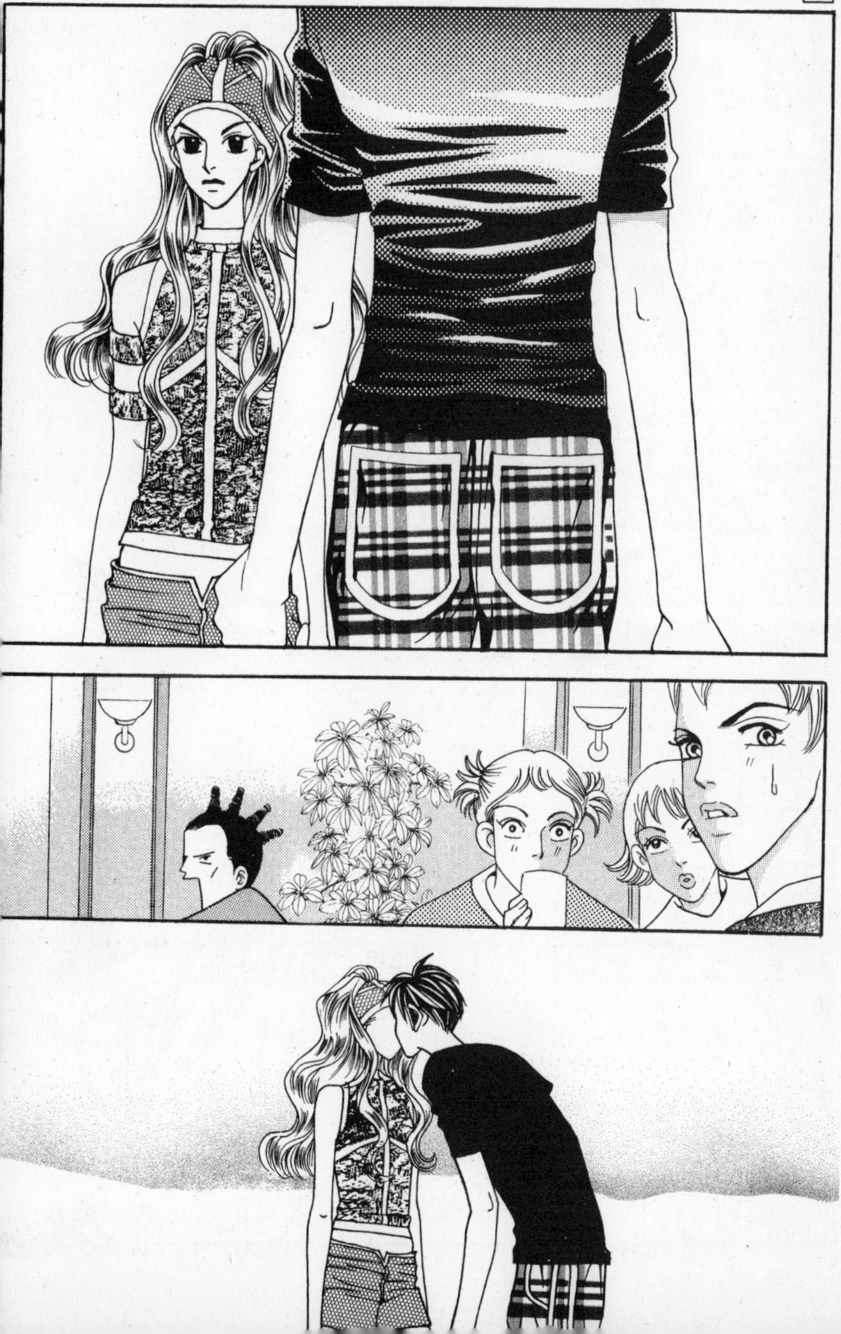

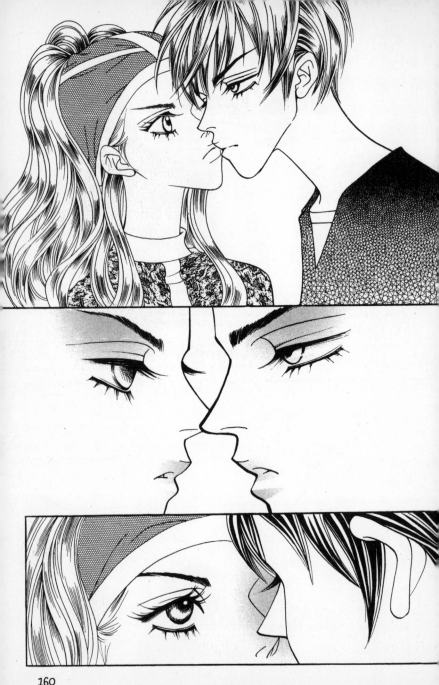

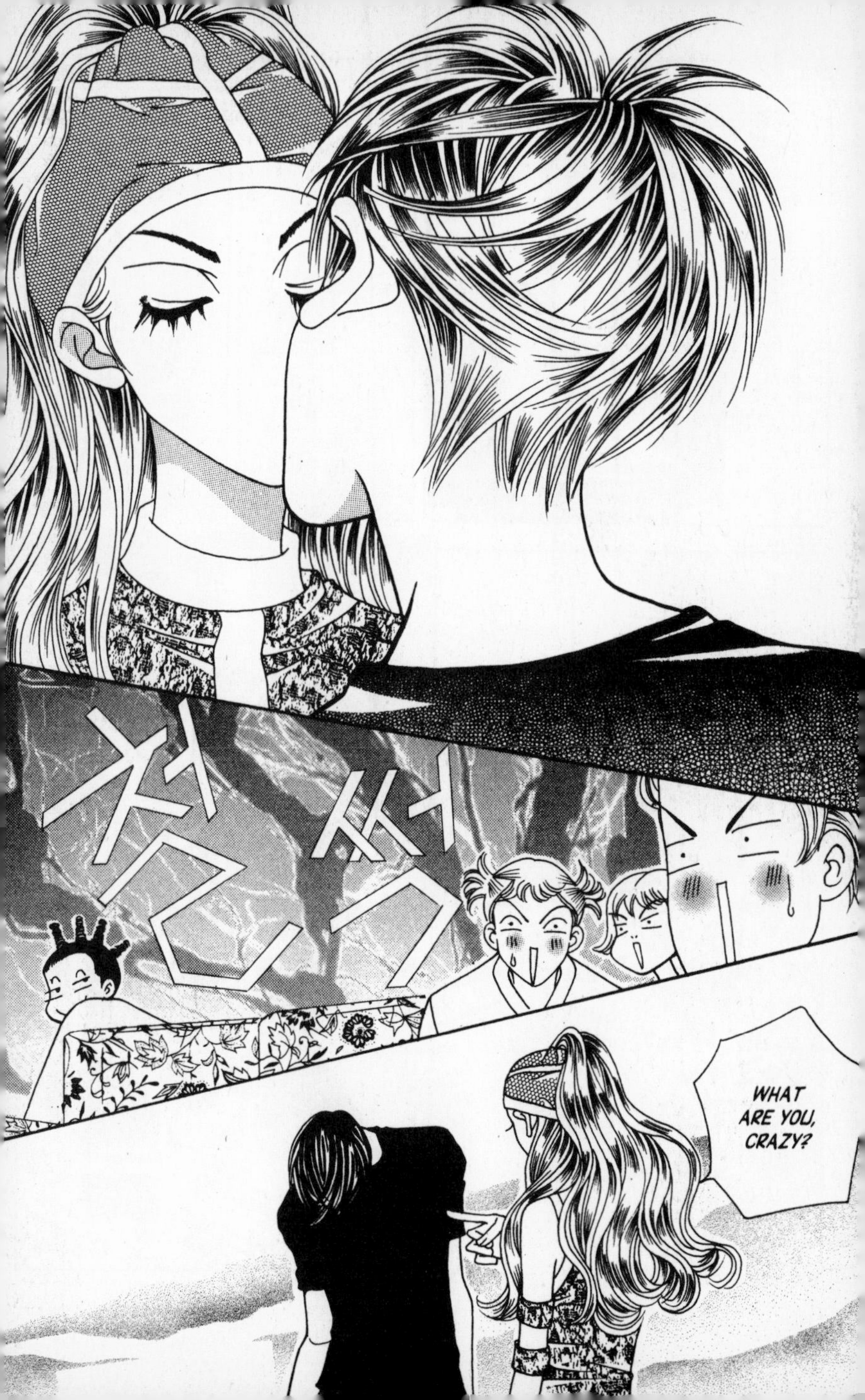
WHAT ARE YOU, CRAZY?

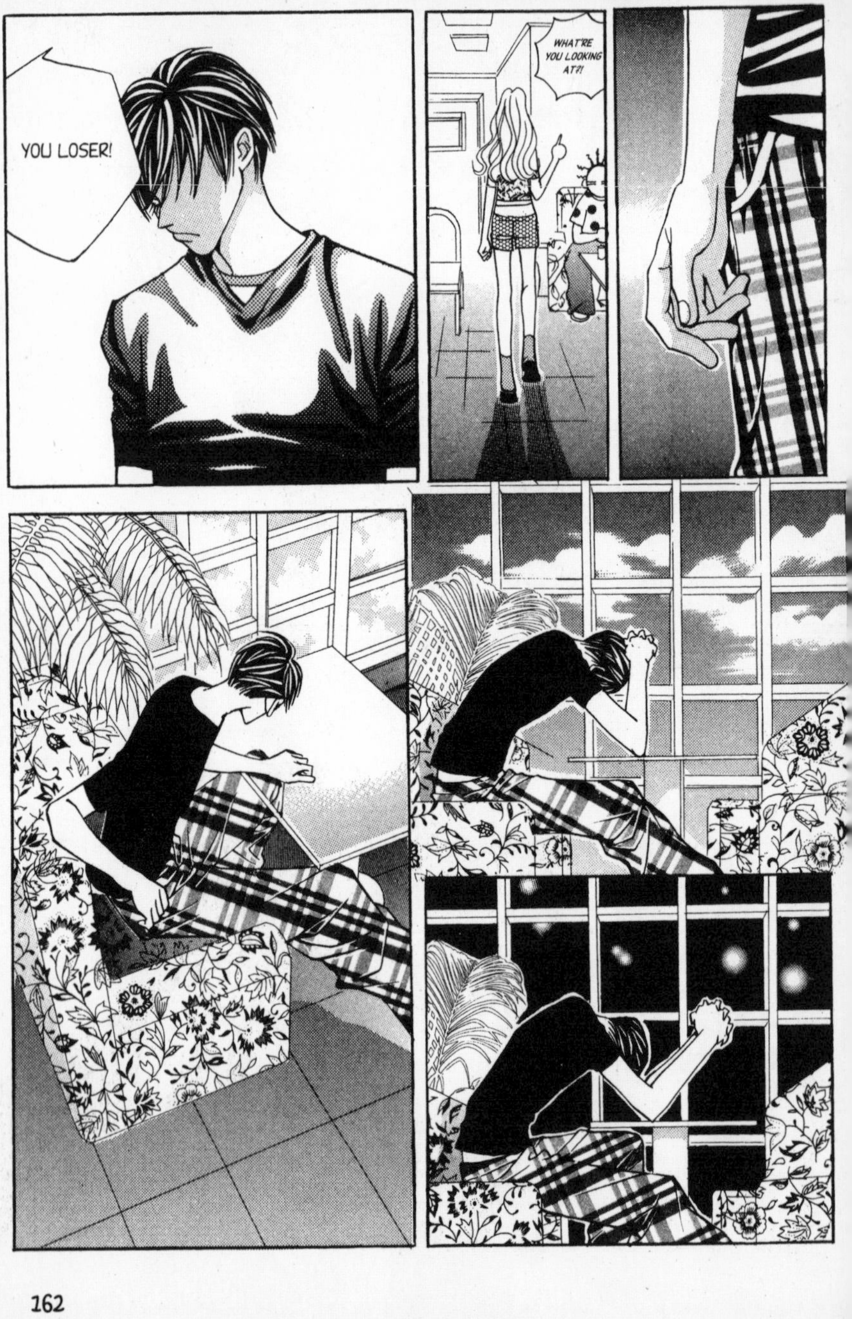
WHAT'RE YOU LOOKING AT?!
YOU LOSER!

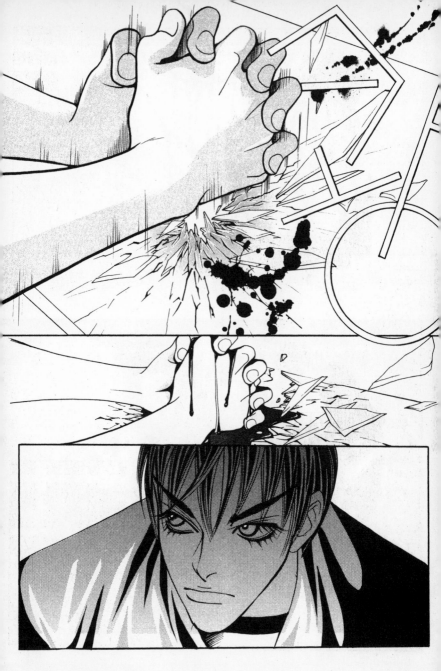

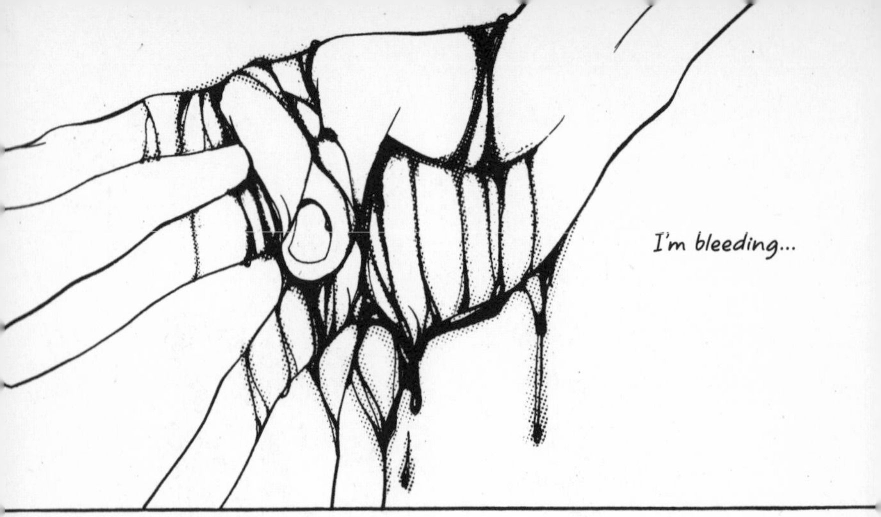
I'm bleeding...

Damn him.

Who cares?

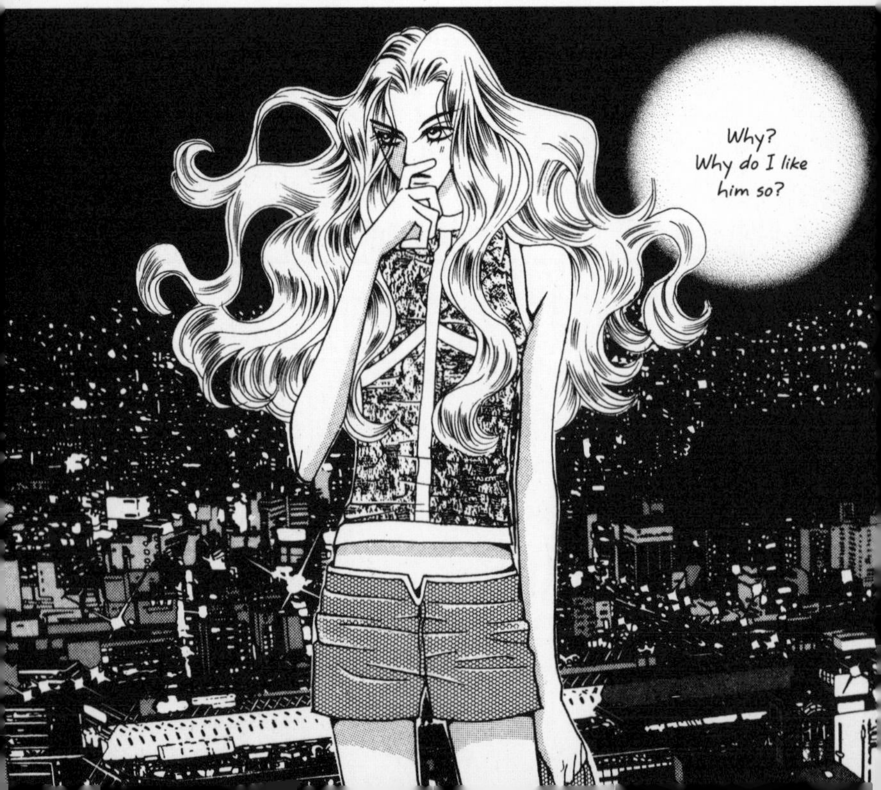
Why?
Why do I like
him so?

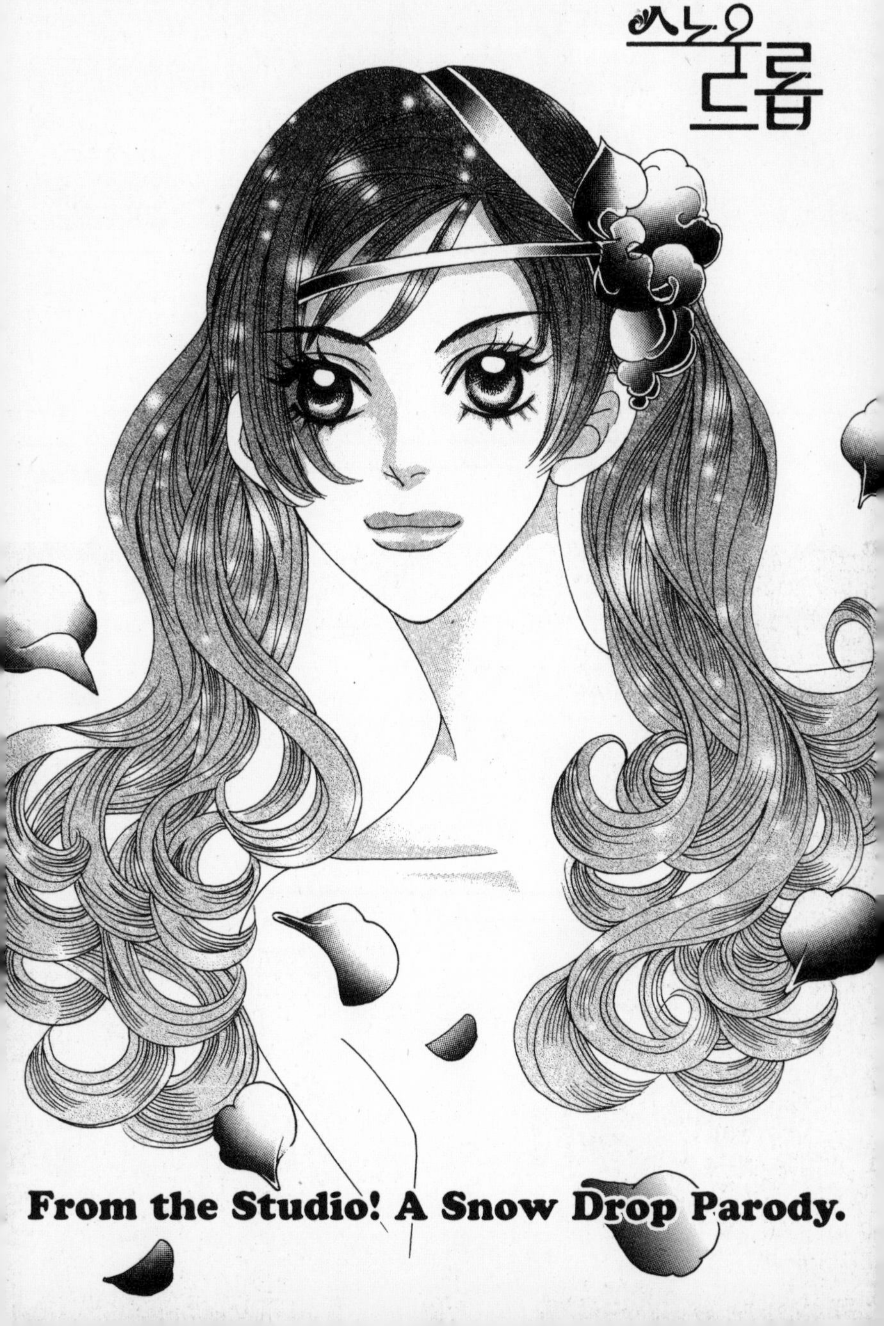
스노우 드롭
From the Studio! A Snow Drop Parody.

S.O... Snow Drop - Special Edition

CHOI HERE!! I'VE COME THIS FAR BECAUSE OF ALL YOUR LOVE AND SUPPORT...

AND NOW, TO REPAY YOU, I BRING YOU THIS SPECIAL VERSION OF SNOW DROP! JUST RELAX, SUSPEND DISBELIEF AND GO ALONG FOR THE RIDE...

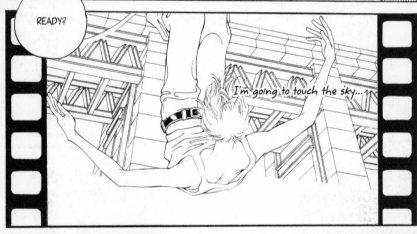

READY?

I'm going to touch the sky...

That stream was really just 20" deep!!

KLONK!!

OWW...IT'S SO PAINFUL WORKING TO SUPPORT YOUR FAMILY.

IT HURTS ME MORE THAN YOU!!

And now... Jang Ha-Da, on the prowl!!

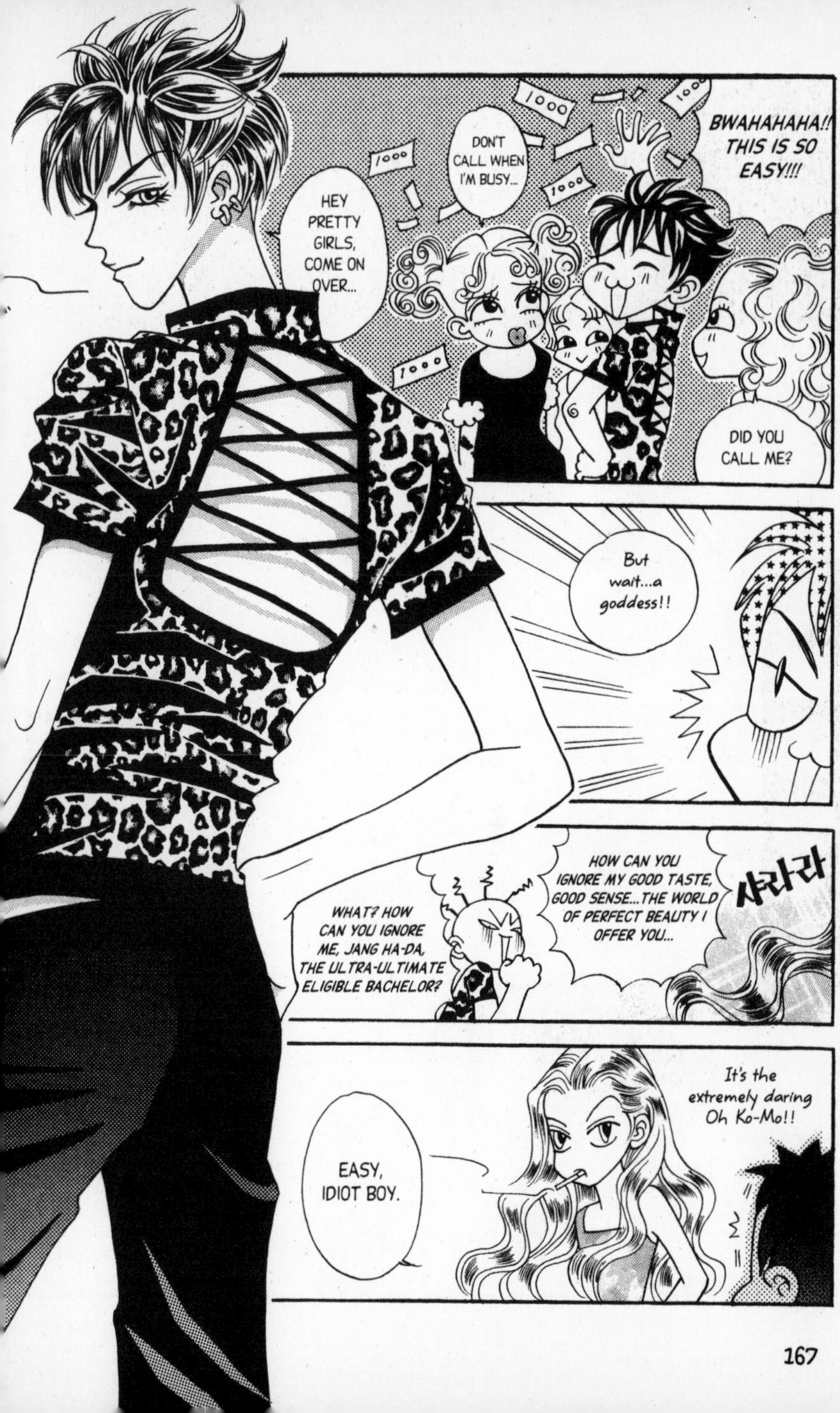
HEY PRETTY GIRLS, COME ON OVER...
DON'T CALL WHEN I'M BUSY...
BWAHAHAHA!! THIS IS SO EASY!!!
DID YOU CALL ME?
But wait...a goddess!!
WHAT? HOW CAN YOU IGNORE ME, JANG HA-DA, THE ULTRA-ULTIMATE ELIGIBLE BACHELOR?
HOW CAN YOU IGNORE MY GOOD TASTE, GOOD SENSE...THE WORLD OF PERFECT BEAUTY I OFFER YOU...
사라라
EASY, IDIOT BOY.
It's the extremely daring Oh Ko-Mo!!

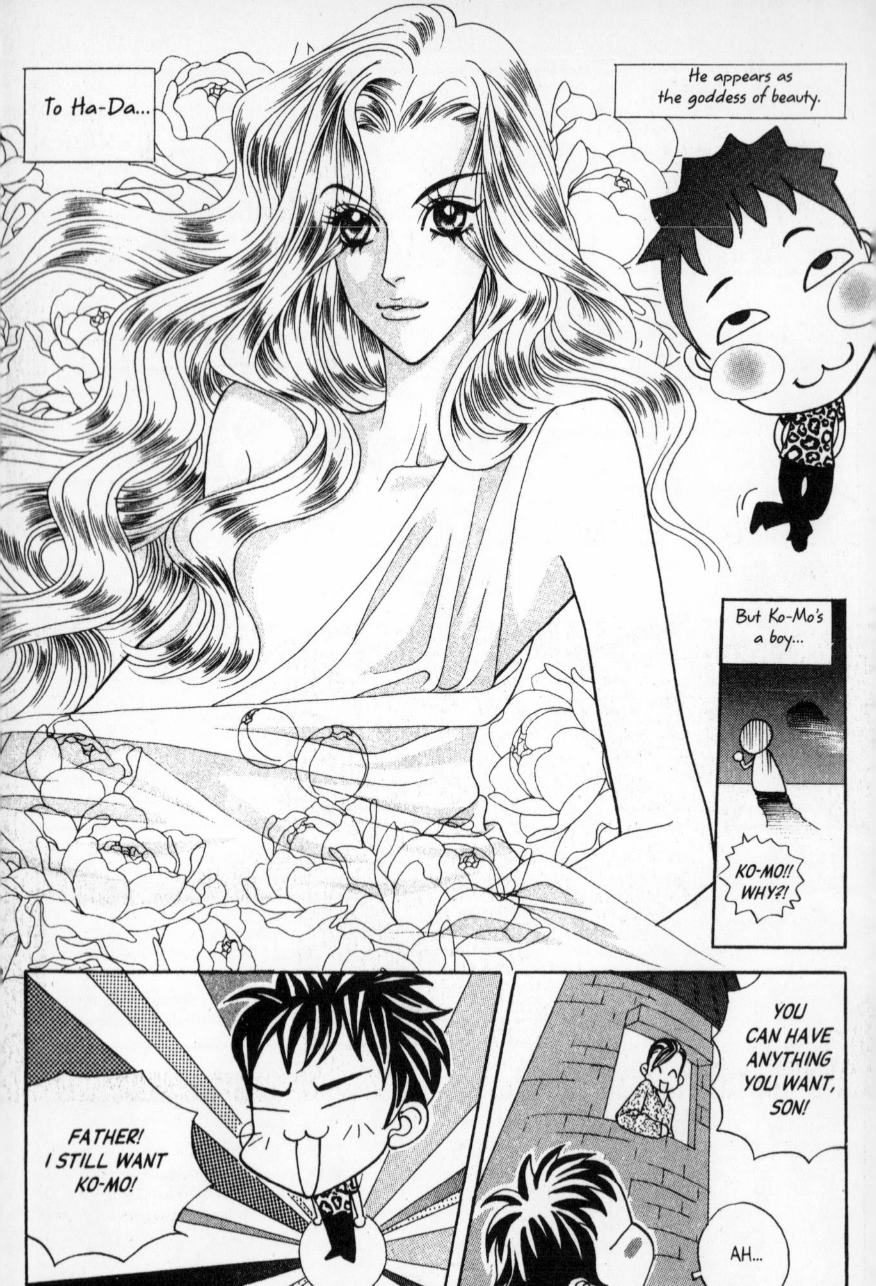
To Ha-Da...
He appears as the goddess of beauty.
But Ko-Mo's a boy...
KO-MO!! WHY?!
YOU CAN HAVE ANYTHING YOU WANT, SON!
AH...
FATHER! I STILL WANT KO-MO!

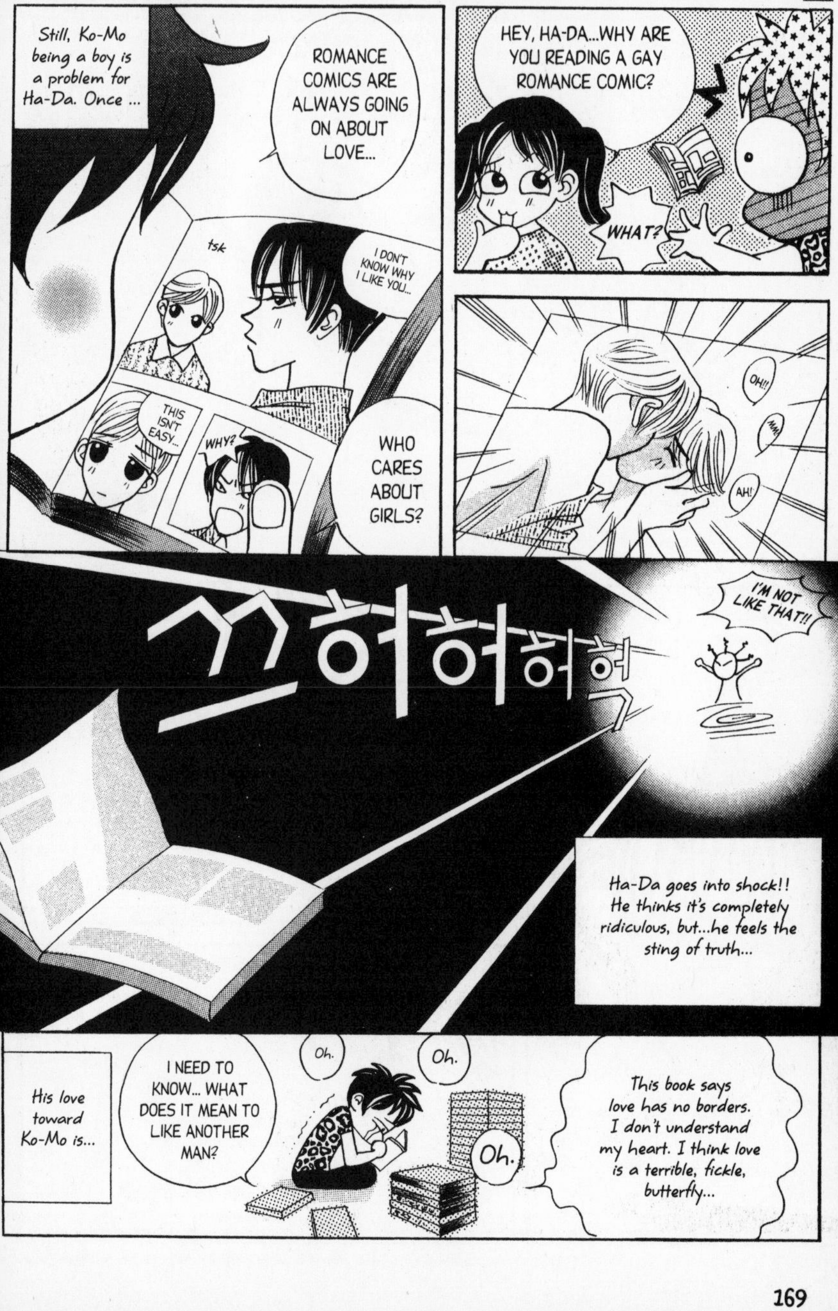
HEY, HA-DA...WHY ARE YOU READING A GAY ROMANCE COMIC?
WHAT?
OH!!
MM
AH!
Still, Ko-Mo being a boy is a problem for Ha-Da. Once ...
ROMANCE COMICS ARE ALWAYS GOING ON ABOUT LOVE...
tsk
I DON'T KNOW WHY I LIKE YOU...
THIS ISN'T EASY...
WHY?
WHO CARES ABOUT GIRLS?
I'M NOT LIKE THAT!!
Ha-Da goes into shock!! He thinks it's completely ridiculous, but...he feels the sting of truth...
This book says love has no borders. I don't understand my heart. I think love is a terrible, fickle, butterfly...
Oh.
Oh.
Oh.
I NEED TO KNOW... WHAT DOES IT MEAN TO LIKE ANOTHER MAN?
His love toward Ko-Mo is...

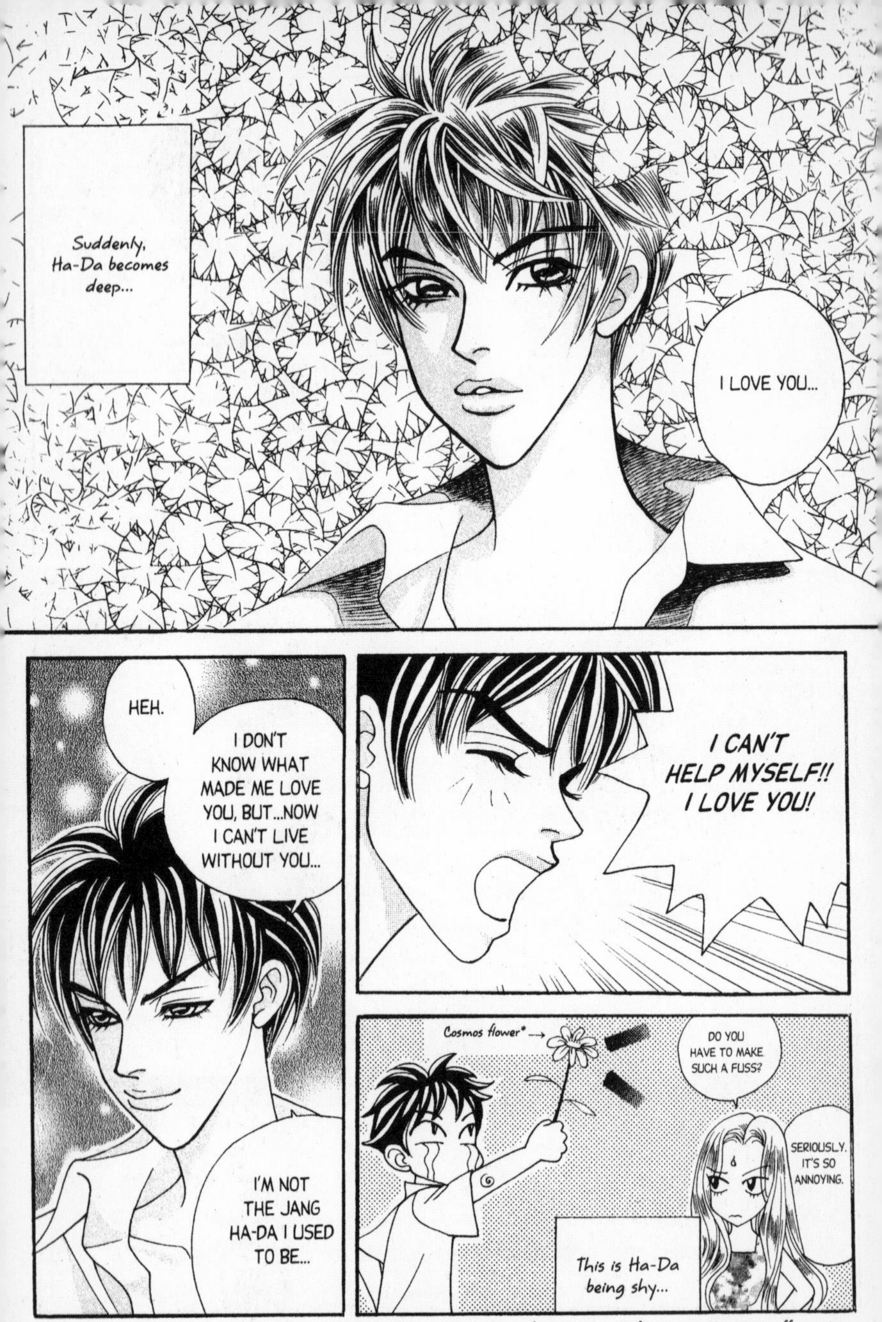
Suddenly, Ha-Da becomes deep...
I LOVE YOU...
I CAN'T HELP MYSELF!! I LOVE YOU!
Cosmos flower*
DO YOU HAVE TO MAKE SUCH A FUSS?
SERIOUSLY. IT'S SO ANNOYING.
This is Ha-Da being shy...
HEH.
I DON'T KNOW WHAT MADE ME LOVE YOU, BUT...NOW I CAN'T LIVE WITHOUT YOU...
I'M NOT THE JANG HA-DA I USED TO BE...

*Note: Ko-Mo was named after the Cosmos flower that Ha-Da is offering him.

6

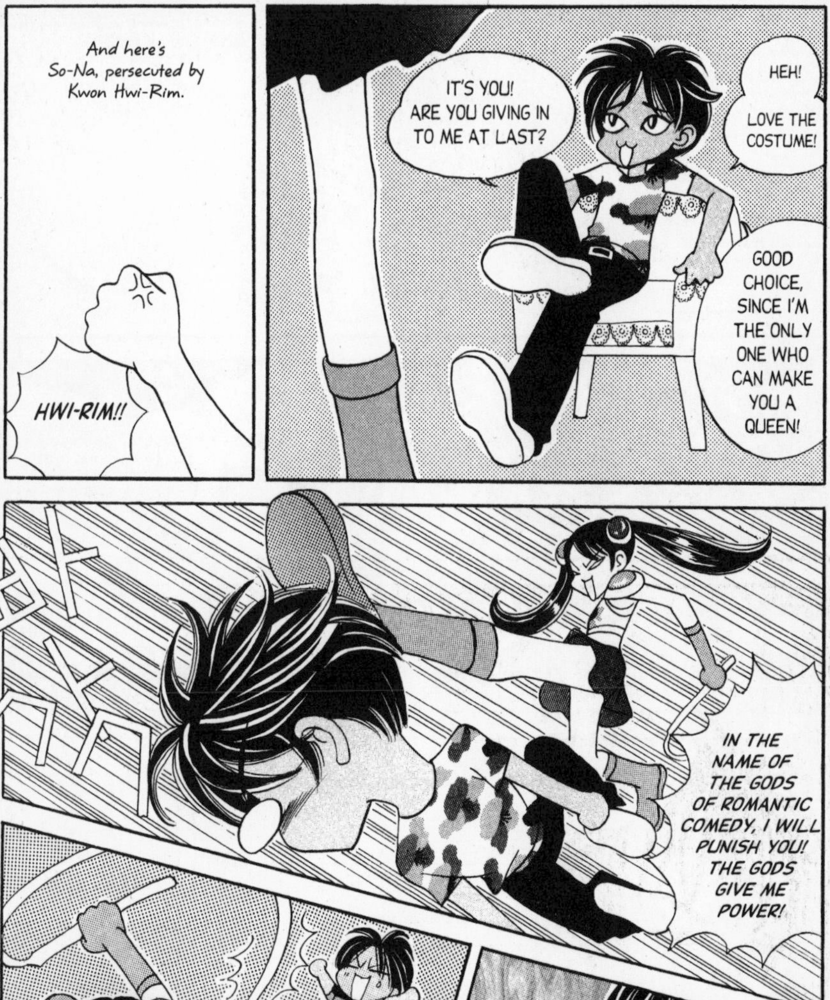

HEH! LOVE THE COSTUME!
IT'S YOU! ARE YOU GIVING IN TO ME AT LAST?
GOOD CHOICE, SINCE I'M THE ONLY ONE WHO CAN MAKE YOU A QUEEN!
And here's So-Na, persecuted by Kwon Hwi-Rim.
HWI-RIM!!
IN THE NAME OF THE GODS OF ROMANTIC COMEDY, I WILL PUNISH YOU! THE GODS GIVE ME POWER!
Uh oh! The evil king Hwi-Rim transforms into a villain!
KEEP GOING! I LOVE IT!
HOW DARE YOU DISRESPECT ME!! DIE, YOU FOOL!

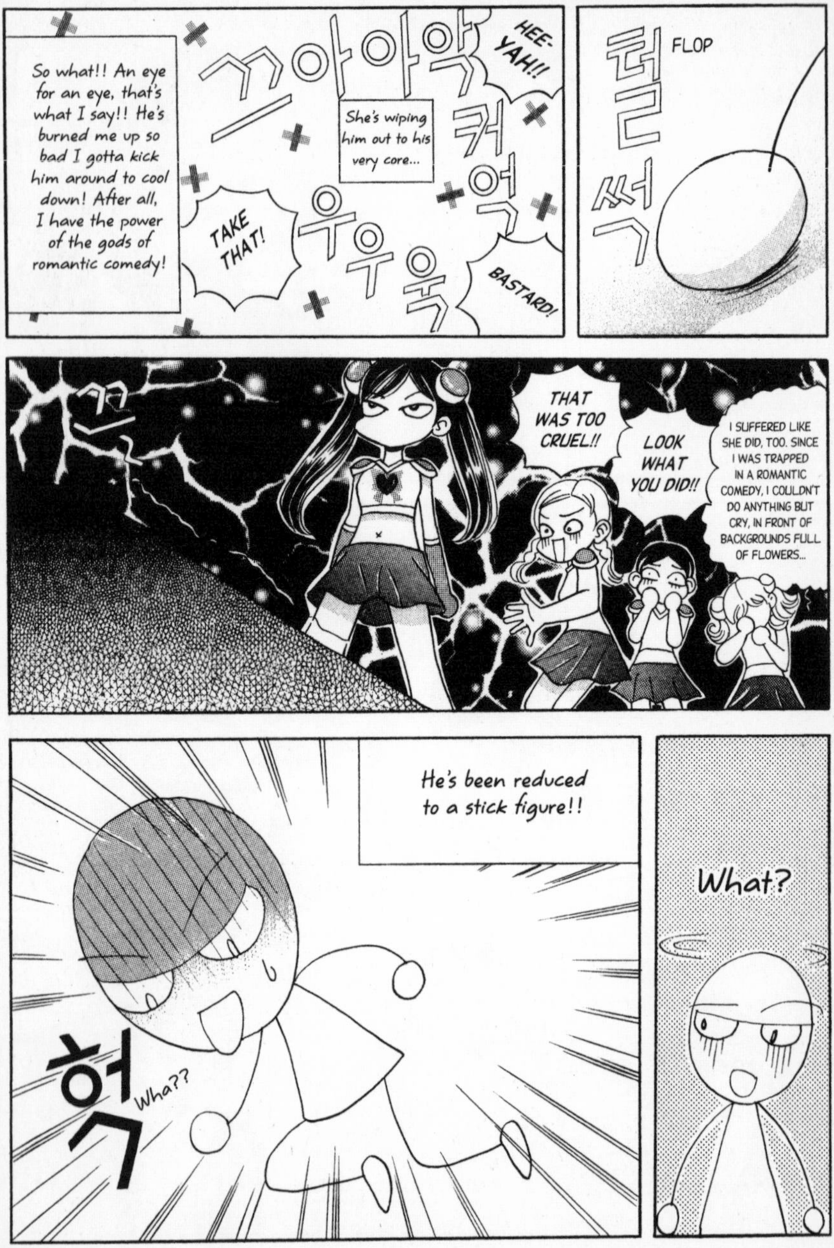
So what!! An eye for an eye, that's what I say!! He's burned me up so bad I gotta kick him around to cool down! After all, I have the power of the gods of romantic comedy!
끄아아악
HEE-YAH!!
She's wiping him out to his very core...
커억
TAKE THAT!
우우욱
BASTARD!
털썩
FLOP
THAT WAS TOO CRUEL!!
LOOK WHAT YOU DID!!
I SUFFERED LIKE SHE DID, TOO. SINCE I WAS TRAPPED IN A ROMANTIC COMEDY, I COULDN'T DO ANYTHING BUT CRY, IN FRONT OF BACKGROUNDS FULL OF FLOWERS...
He's been reduced to a stick figure!!
헉
Wha??
What?

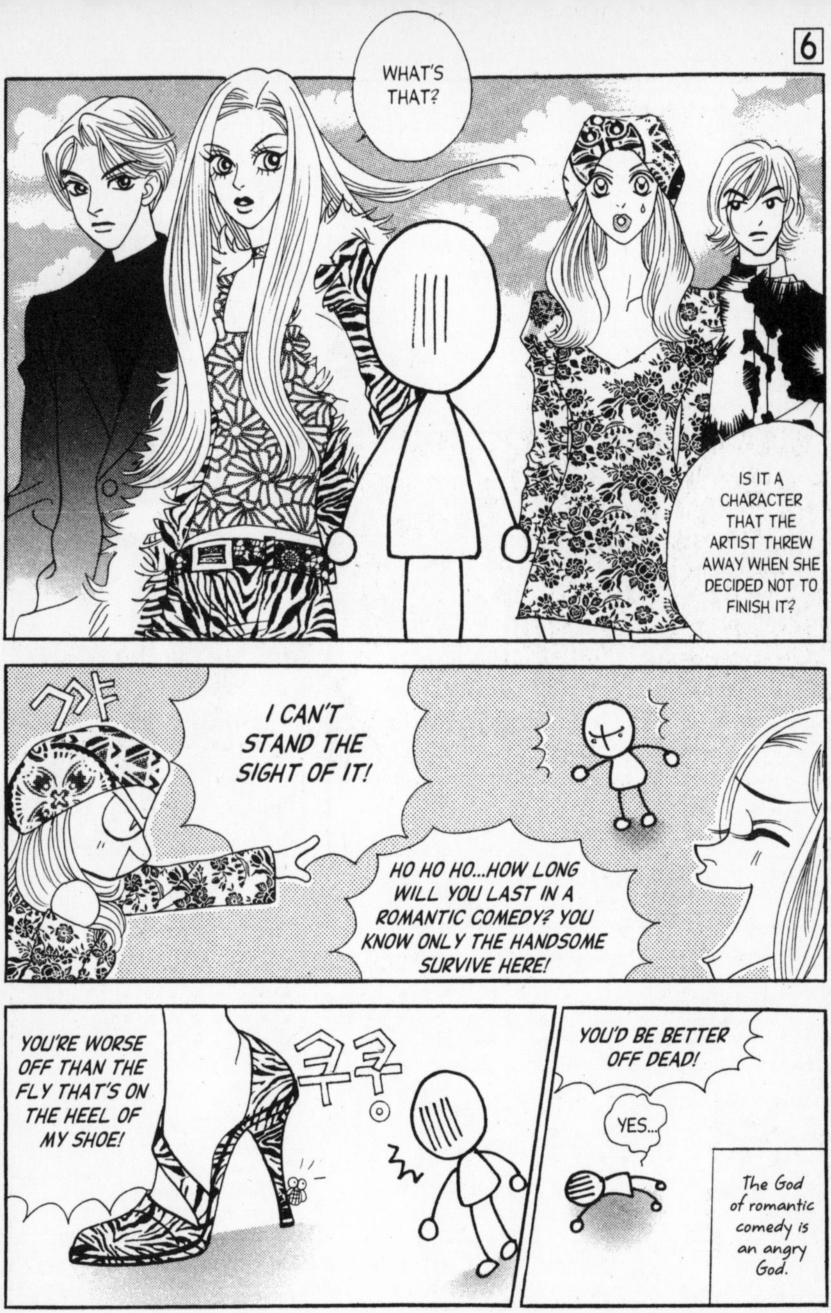
WHAT'S THAT?
IS IT A CHARACTER THAT THE ARTIST THREW AWAY WHEN SHE DECIDED NOT TO FINISH IT?
I CAN'T STAND THE SIGHT OF IT!
HO HO HO...HOW LONG WILL YOU LAST IN A ROMANTIC COMEDY? YOU KNOW ONLY THE HANDSOME SURVIVE HERE!
YOU'RE WORSE OFF THAN THE FLY THAT'S ON THE HEEL OF MY SHOE!
쿠쿠
YOU'D BE BETTER OFF DEAD!
YES...
The God of romantic comedy is an angry God.

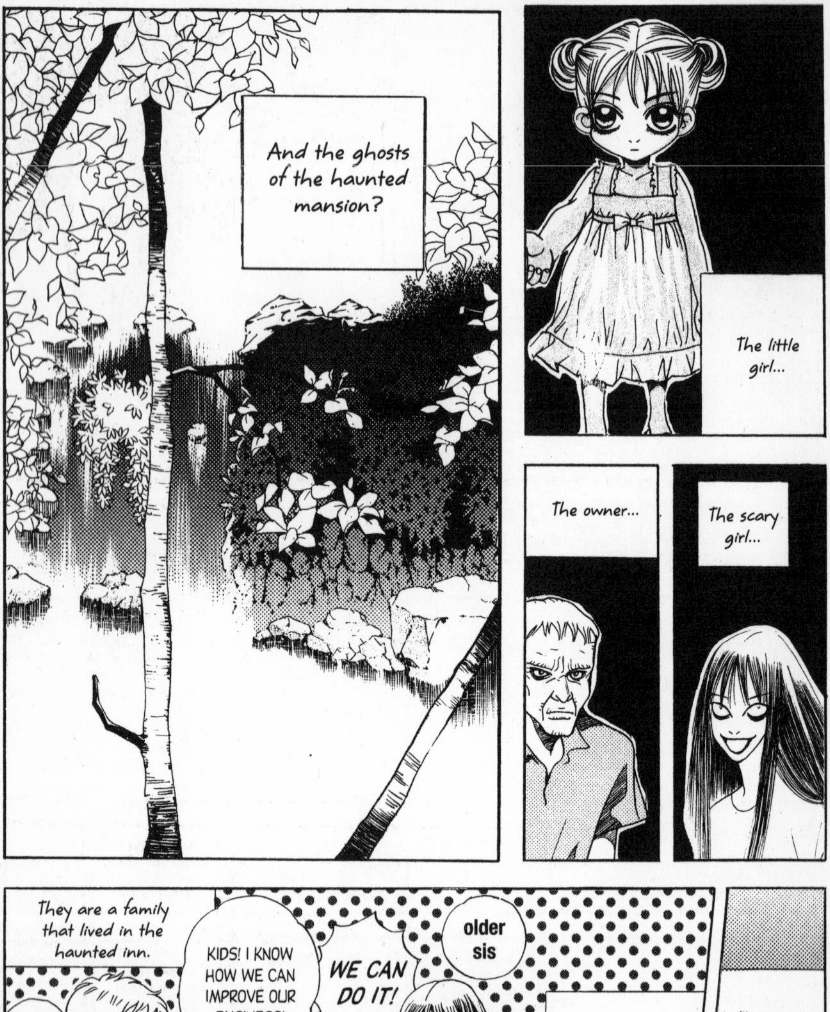
And the ghosts of the haunted mansion?
The little girl...
The owner...
The scary girl...
They are a family that lived in the haunted inn.
Dad
KIDS! I KNOW HOW WE CAN IMPROVE OUR BUSINESS!
WE CAN DO IT!
little sis
YAY!!
older sis
They decided to turn their bizarre looks to their advantage and act like ghosts.
They even installed the latest in SFX technology.

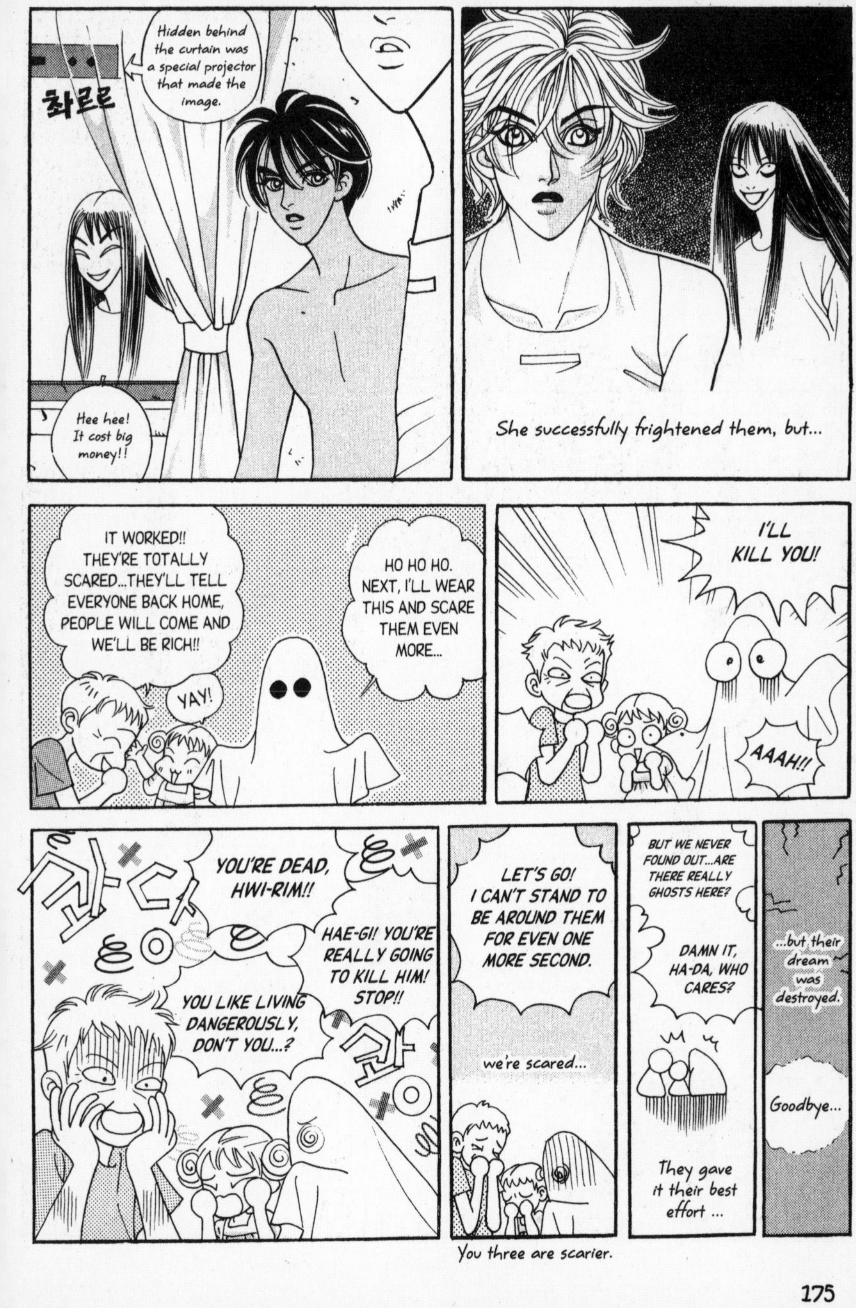
Hidden behind the curtain was a special projector that made the image.
촤르르
Hee hee! It cost big money!!
She successfully frightened them, but...
IT WORKED!! THEY'RE TOTALLY SCARED...THEY'LL TELL EVERYONE BACK HOME, PEOPLE WILL COME AND WE'LL BE RICH!!
YAY!
HO HO HO. NEXT, I'LL WEAR THIS AND SCARE THEM EVEN MORE...
I'LL KILL YOU!
AAAH!!
YOU'RE DEAD, HWI-RIM!!
HAE-GI! YOU'RE REALLY GOING TO KILL HIM! STOP!!
YOU LIKE LIVING DANGEROUSLY, DON'T YOU...?
LET'S GO! I CAN'T STAND TO BE AROUND THEM FOR EVEN ONE MORE SECOND.
we're scared...
You three are scarier.
BUT WE NEVER FOUND OUT...ARE THERE REALLY GHOSTS HERE?
DAMN IT, HA-DA, WHO CARES?
They gave it their best effort ...
...but their dream was destroyed.
Goodbye...

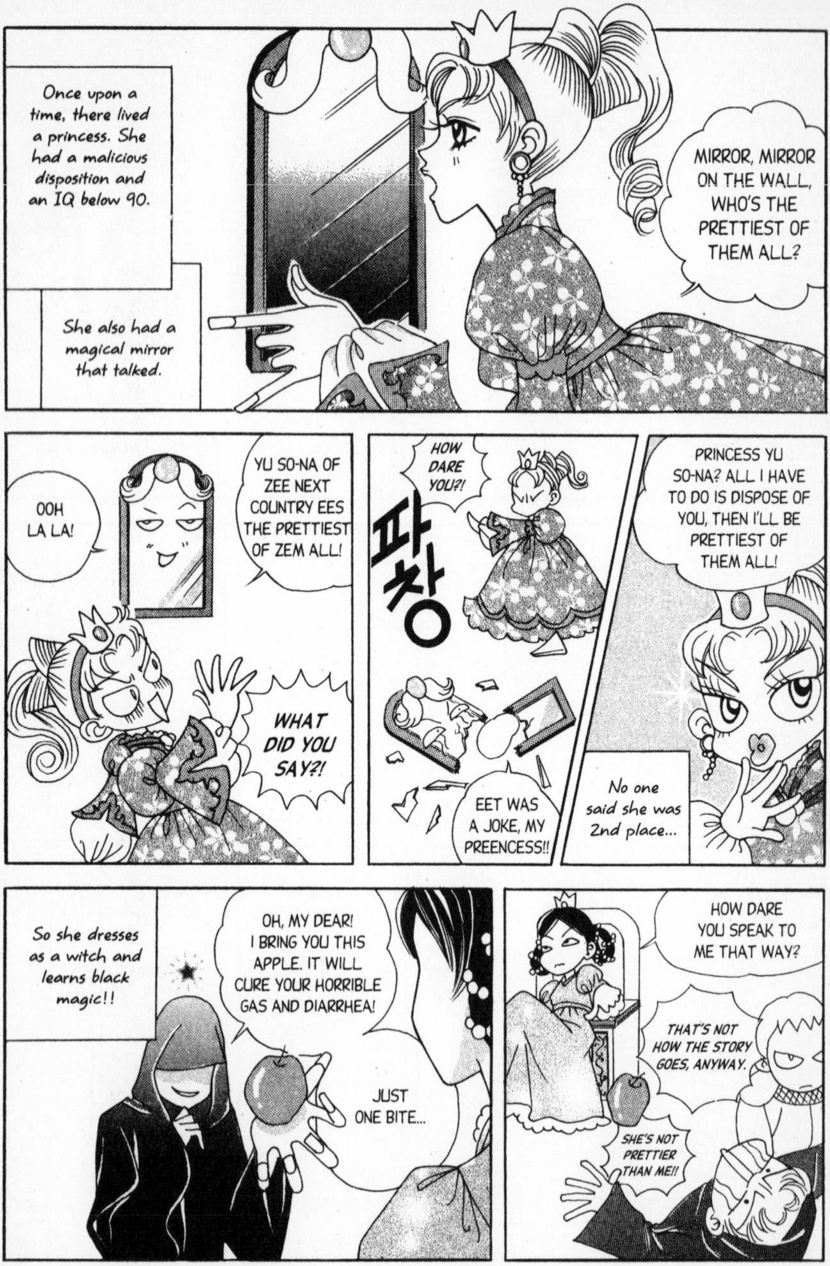
Once upon a time, there lived a princess. She had a malicious disposition and an IQ below 90.
She also had a magical mirror that talked.
MIRROR, MIRROR ON THE WALL, WHO'S THE PRETTIEST OF THEM ALL?
OOH LA LA!
YU SO-NA OF ZEE NEXT COUNTRY EES THE PRETTIEST OF ZEM ALL!
WHAT DID YOU SAY?!
HOW DARE YOU?!
파창
EET WAS A JOKE, MY PREENCESS!!
PRINCESS YU SO-NA? ALL I HAVE TO DO IS DISPOSE OF YOU, THEN I'LL BE PRETTIEST OF THEM ALL!
No one said she was 2nd place...
So she dresses as a witch and learns black magic!!
OH, MY DEAR! I BRING YOU THIS APPLE. IT WILL CURE YOUR HORRIBLE GAS AND DIARRHEA!
JUST ONE BITE...
HOW DARE YOU SPEAK TO ME THAT WAY?
THAT'S NOT HOW THE STORY GOES, ANYWAY.
SHE'S NOT PRETTIER THAN ME!!

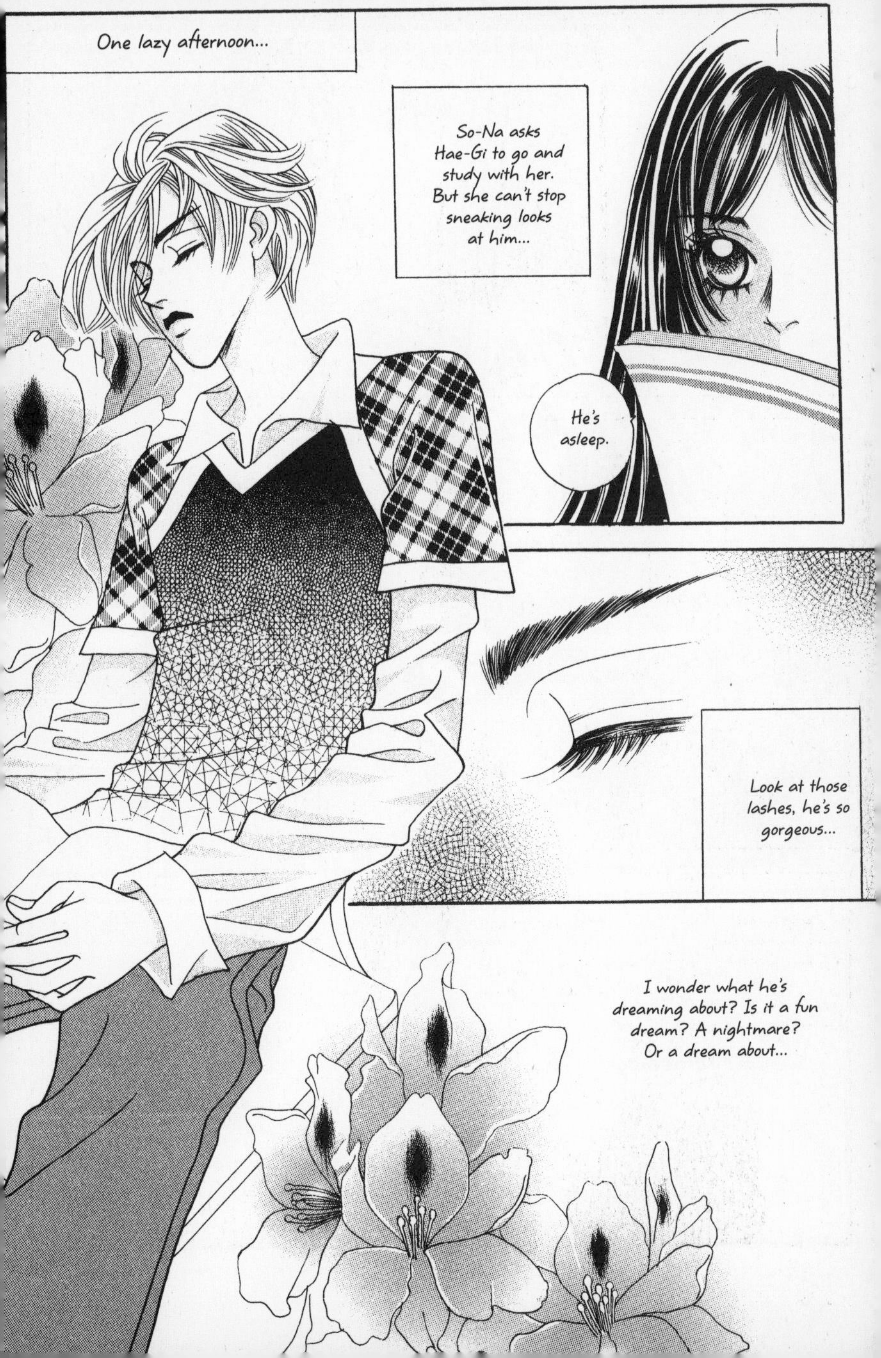
One lazy afternoon...
So-Na asks Hae-Gi to go and study with her. But she can't stop sneaking looks at him...
He's asleep.
Look at those lashes, he's so gorgeous...
I wonder what he's dreaming about? Is it a fun dream? A nightmare? Or a dream about...

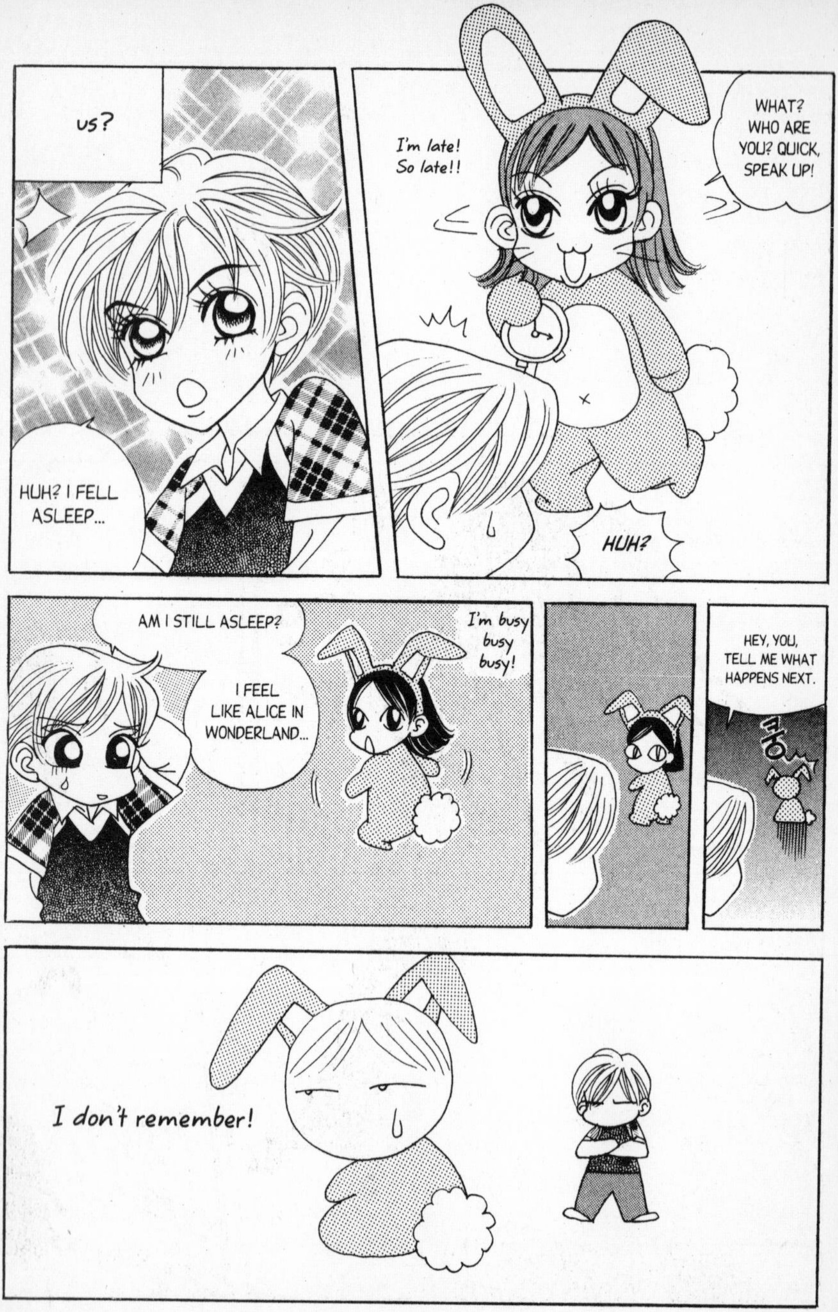
us?
HUH? I FELL ASLEEP...
I'm late! So late!!
WHAT? WHO ARE YOU? QUICK, SPEAK UP!
HUH?
AM I STILL ASLEEP?
I FEEL LIKE ALICE IN WONDERLAND...
I'm busy busy busy!
HEY, YOU, TELL ME WHAT HAPPENS NEXT.
쿵
I don't remember!

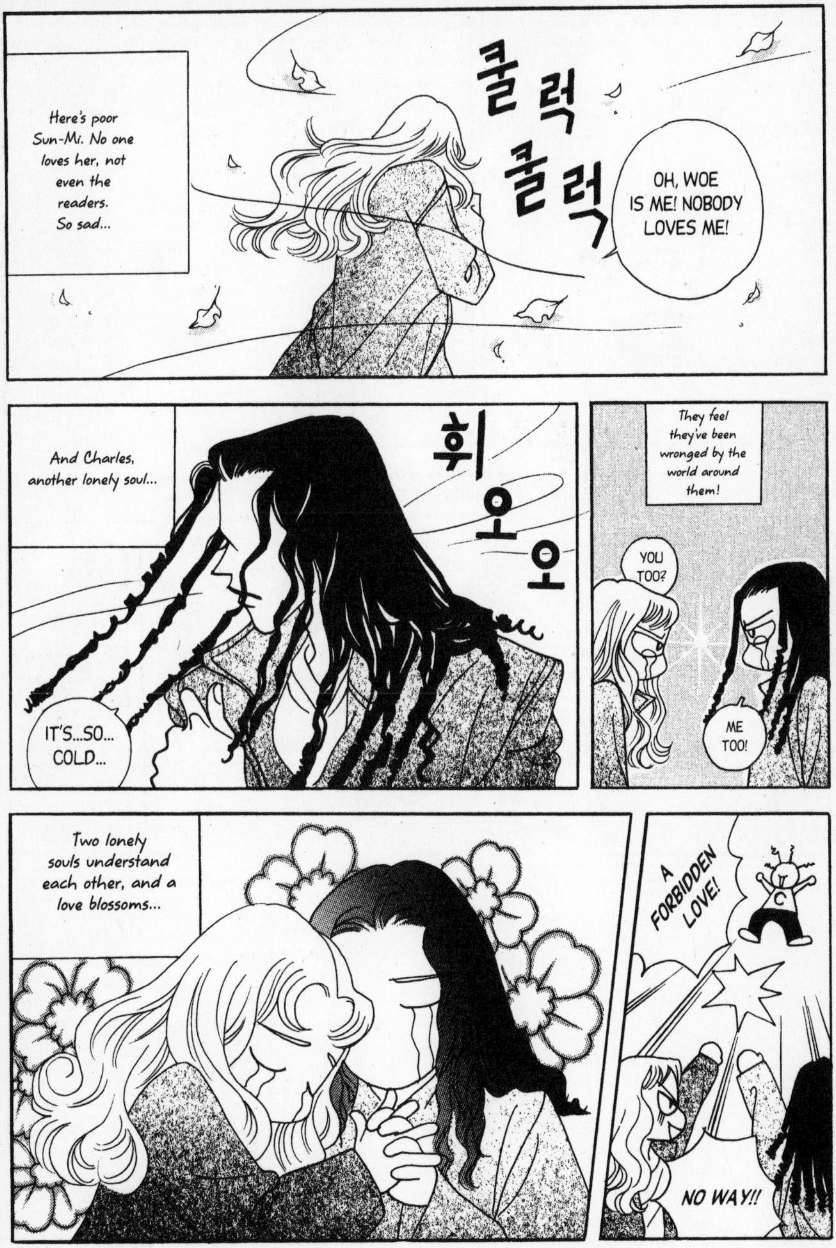
Here's poor Sun-Mi. No one loves her, not even the readers. So sad...
쿨럭 쿨럭
OH, WOE IS ME! NOBODY LOVES ME!
And Charles, another lonely soul...
휘오오
IT'S...SO... COLD...
They feel they've been wronged by the world around them!
YOU TOO?
ME TOO!
Two lonely souls understand each other, and a love blossoms...
A FORBIDDEN LOVE!
NO WAY!!

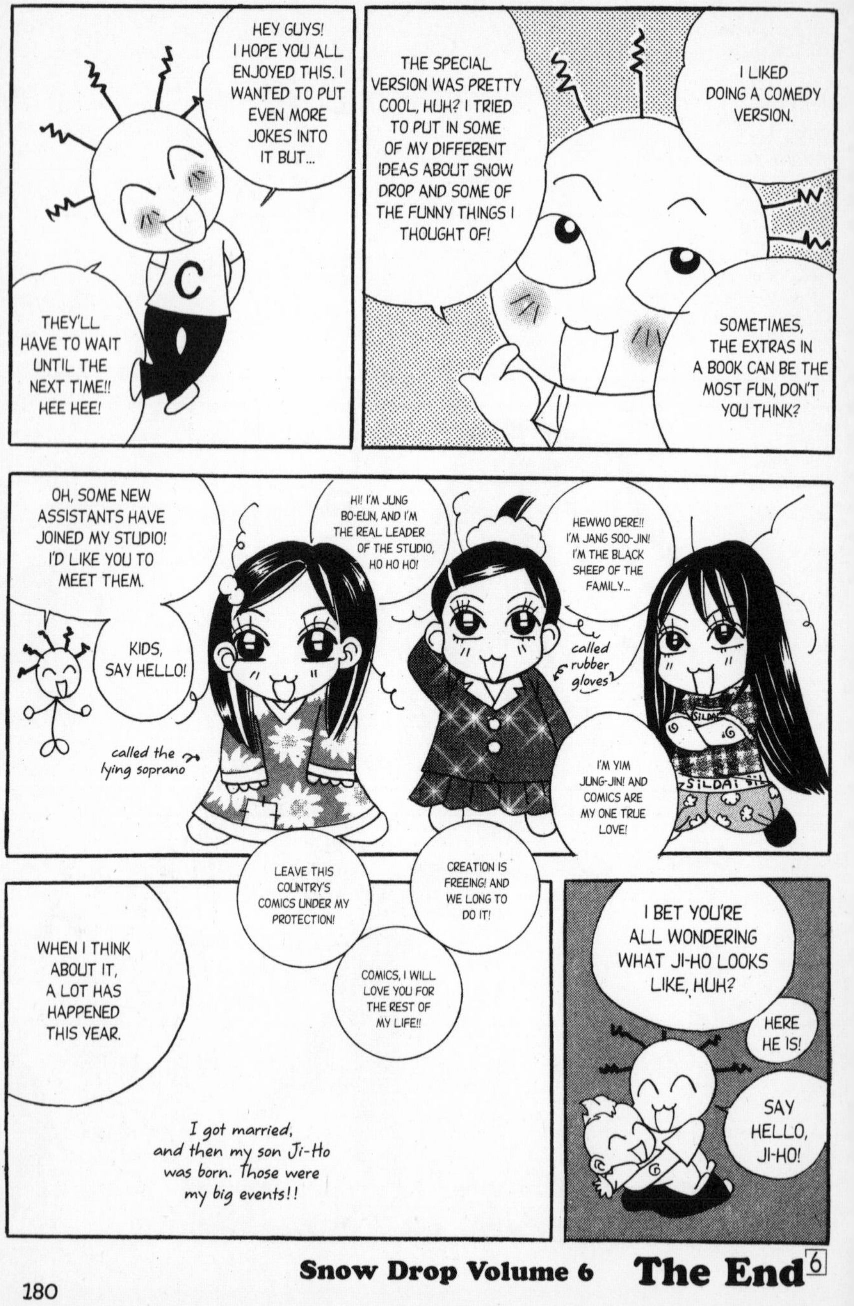
HEY GUYS! I HOPE YOU ALL ENJOYED THIS. I WANTED TO PUT EVEN MORE JOKES INTO IT BUT...
THEY'LL HAVE TO WAIT UNTIL THE NEXT TIME!! HEE HEE!
THE SPECIAL VERSION WAS PRETTY COOL, HUH? I TRIED TO PUT IN SOME OF MY DIFFERENT IDEAS ABOUT SNOW DROP AND SOME OF THE FUNNY THINGS I THOUGHT OF!
I LIKED DOING A COMEDY VERSION.
SOMETIMES, THE EXTRAS IN A BOOK CAN BE THE MOST FUN, DON'T YOU THINK?
OH, SOME NEW ASSISTANTS HAVE JOINED MY STUDIO! I'D LIKE YOU TO MEET THEM.
KIDS, SAY HELLO!
HI! I'M JUNG BO-EUN, AND I'M THE REAL LEADER OF THE STUDIO, HO HO HO!
called the lying soprano
HEWWO DERE!! I'M JANG SOO-JIN! I'M THE BLACK SHEEP OF THE FAMILY...
called rubber gloves
SILDAI
I'M YIM JUNG-JIN! AND COMICS ARE MY ONE TRUE LOVE!
LEAVE THIS COUNTRY'S COMICS UNDER MY PROTECTION!
CREATION IS FREEING! AND WE LONG TO DO IT!
COMICS, I WILL LOVE YOU FOR THE REST OF MY LIFE!!
WHEN I THINK ABOUT IT, A LOT HAS HAPPENED THIS YEAR.
I got married, and then my son Ji-Ho was born. Those were my big events!!
I BET YOU'RE ALL WONDERING WHAT JI-HO LOOKS LIKE, HUH?
HERE HE IS!
SAY HELLO, JI-HO!

Snow Drop Volume 6 **The End** 6

Coming in January

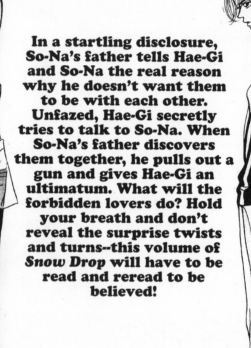

Snow Drop

Volume Seven

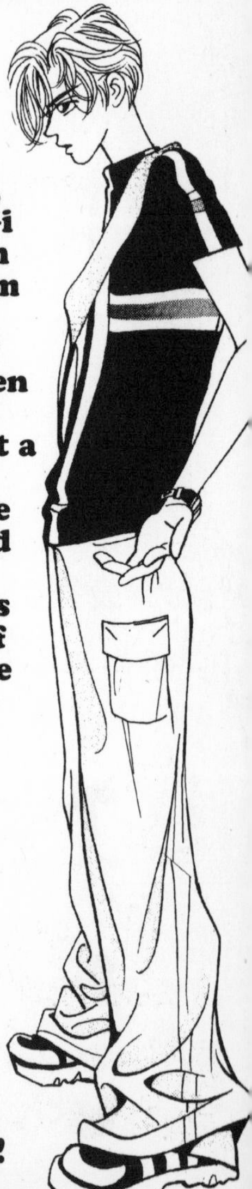

In a startling disclosure, So-Na's father tells Hae-Gi and So-Na the real reason why he doesn't want them to be with each other. Unfazed, Hae-Gi secretly tries to talk to So-Na. When So-Na's father discovers them together, he pulls out a gun and gives Hae-Gi an ultimatum. What will the forbidden lovers do? Hold your breath and don't reveal the surprise twists and turns--this volume of *Snow Drop* will have to be read and reread to be believed!

**Drop in for
SNOW DROP Volume 7!**

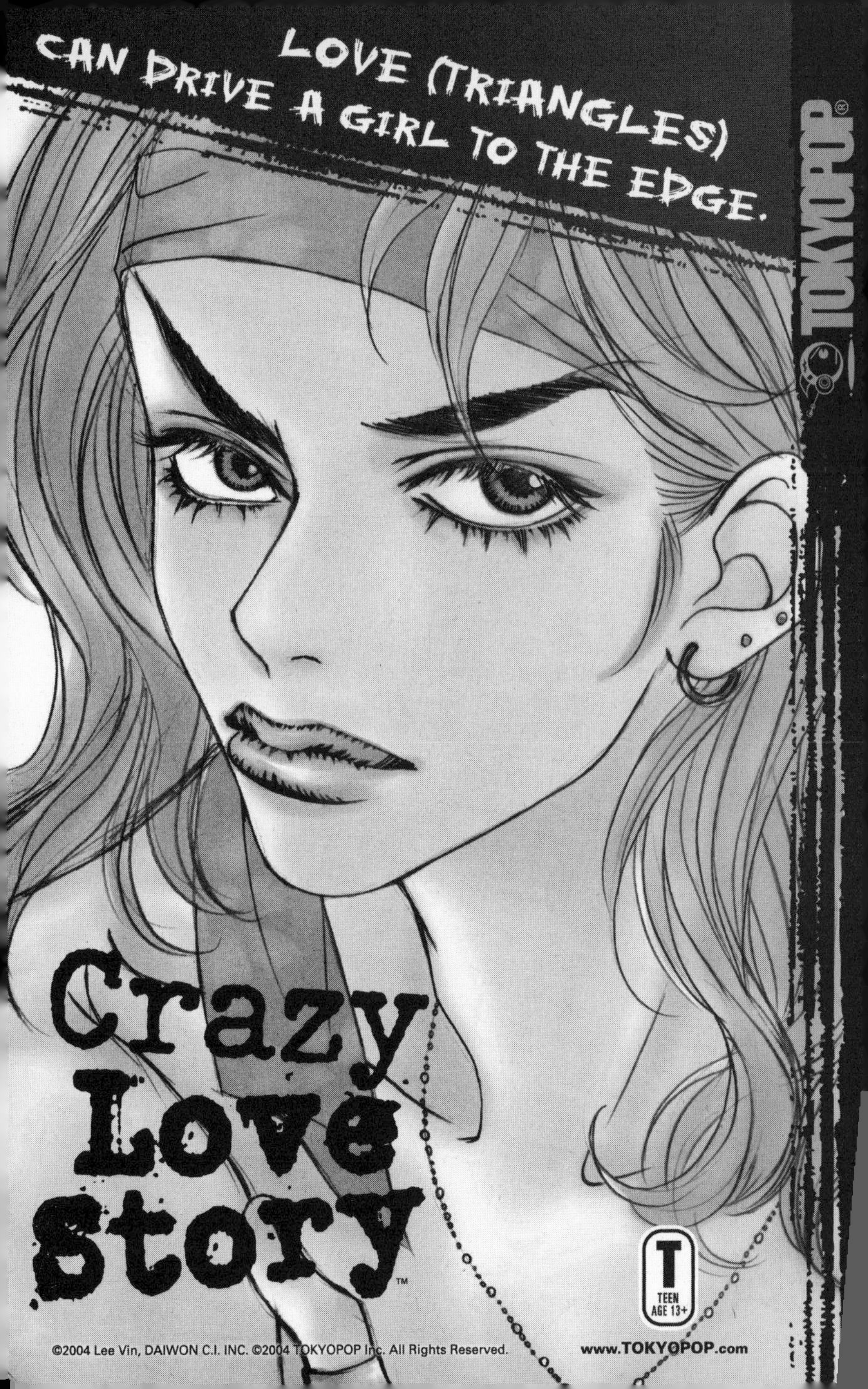

LOVE (TRIANGLES)
CAN DRIVE A GIRL TO THE EDGE.
TOKYOPOP
Crazy Love Story™
T
TEEN
AGE 13+
©2004 Lee Vin, DAIWON C.I. INC. ©2004 TOKYOPOP Inc. All Rights Reserved.
www.TOKYOPOP.com

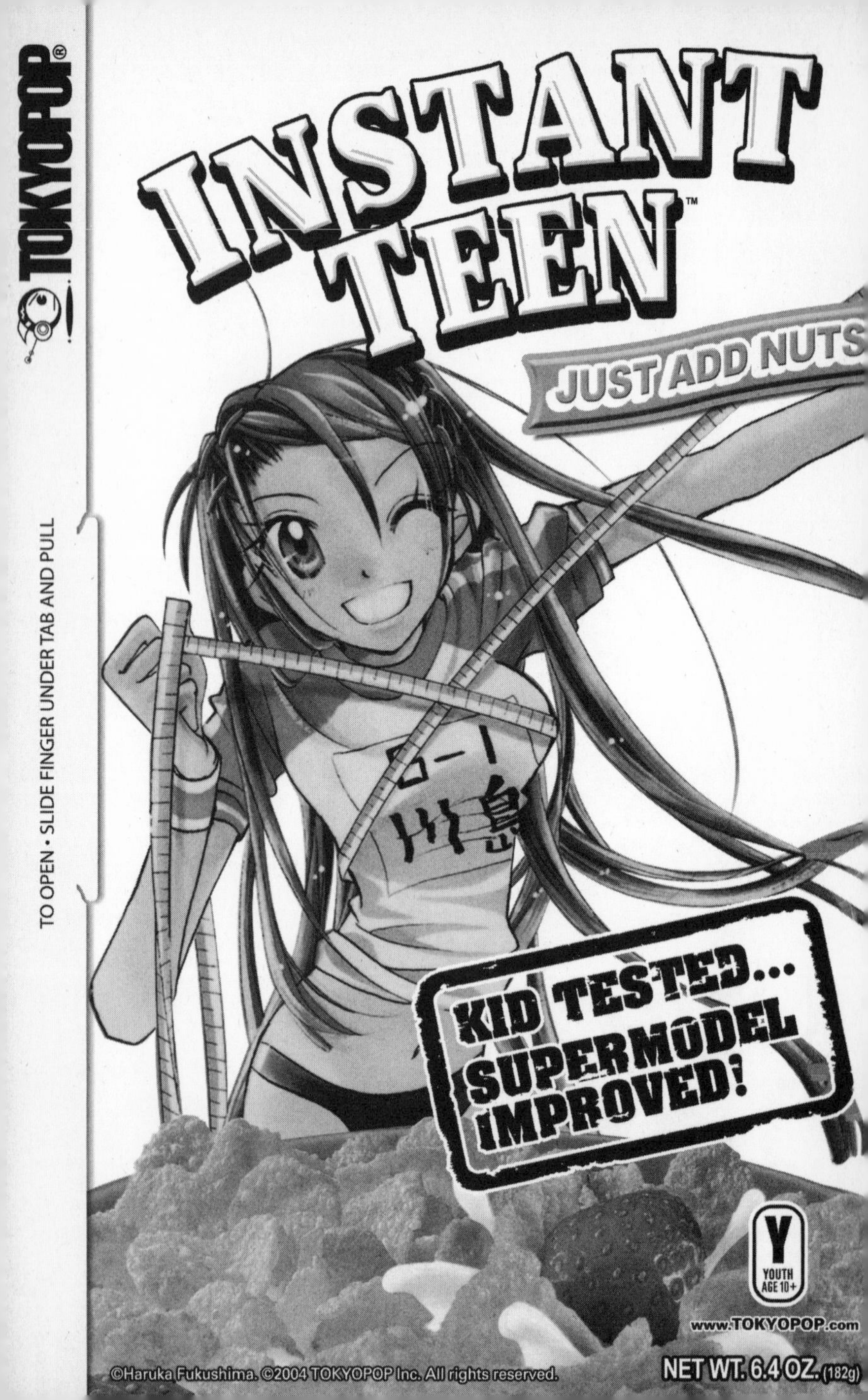
TOKYOPOP®
TO OPEN • SLIDE FINGER UNDER TAB AND PULL
INSTANT TEEN™
JUST ADD NUTS
KID TESTED...
SUPERMODEL IMPROVED!
Y
YOUTH AGE 10+
www.TOKYOPOP.com
©Haruka Fukushima. ©2004 TOKYOPOP Inc. All rights reserved.
NET WT. 6.4 OZ. (182g)

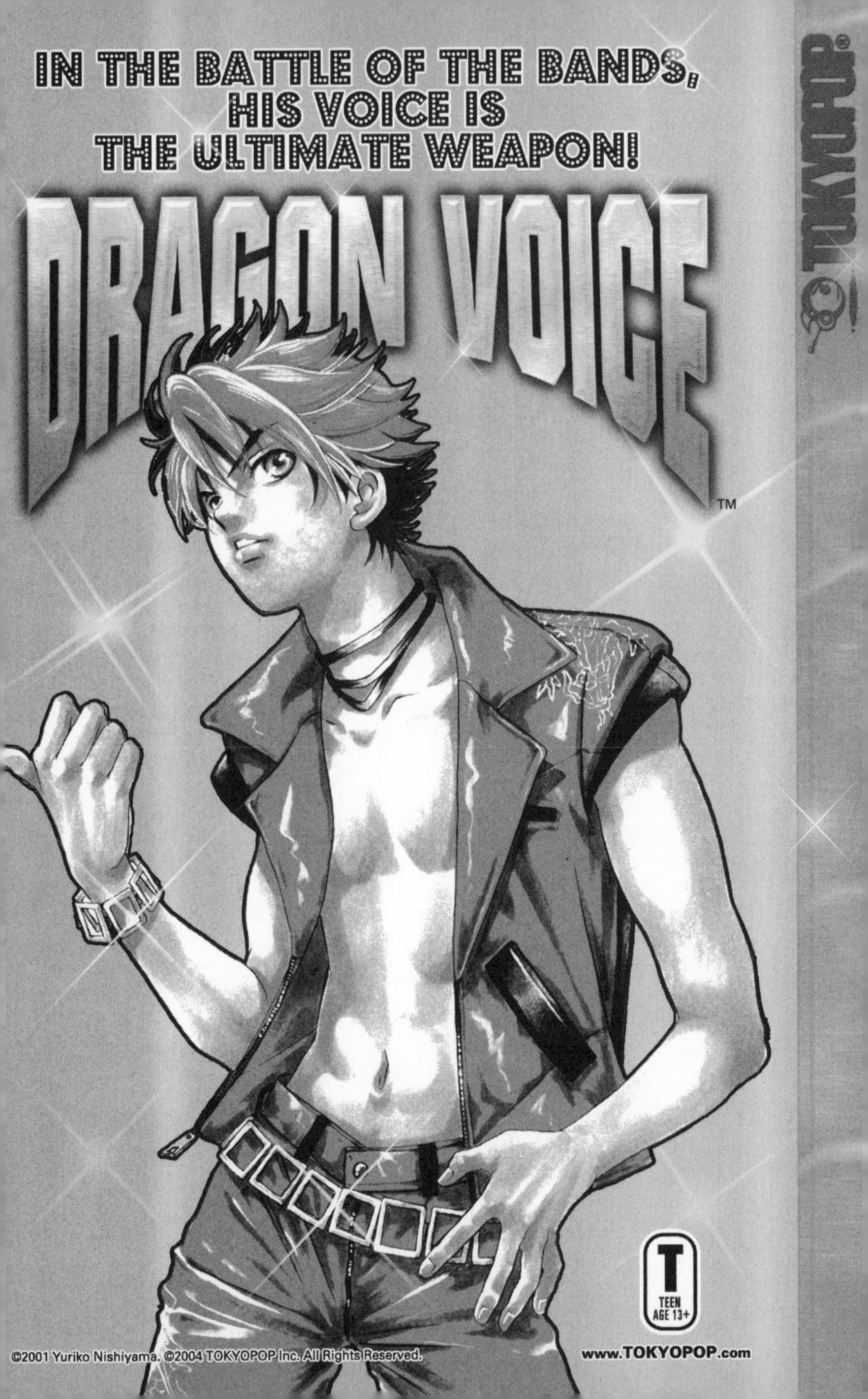
IN THE BATTLE OF THE BANDS, HIS VOICE IS THE ULTIMATE WEAPON!
DRAGON VOICE™
TOKYOPOP®
T TEEN AGE 13+
©2001 Yuriko Nishiyama. ©2004 TOKYOPOP Inc. All Rights Reserved.
www.TOKYOPOP.com

TOKYOPOP
A touching story about a regular guy with an irregular gift.
HANDS OFF!
TM
T TEEN AGE 13+
©1998 Kasane Katsumoto. ©2004 TOKYOPOP Inc. All Rights Reserved.
www.TOKYOPOP.com

One
rocks to live.
One
lives to rock.
They've got nothing in common...except each other.
TOKYOPOP
One™
T
TEEN
AGE 13+
©2003 Lee Vin / DAIWON C.I. Inc. ©2004 TOKYOPOP Inc. All rights reserved.
www.TOKYOPOP.com

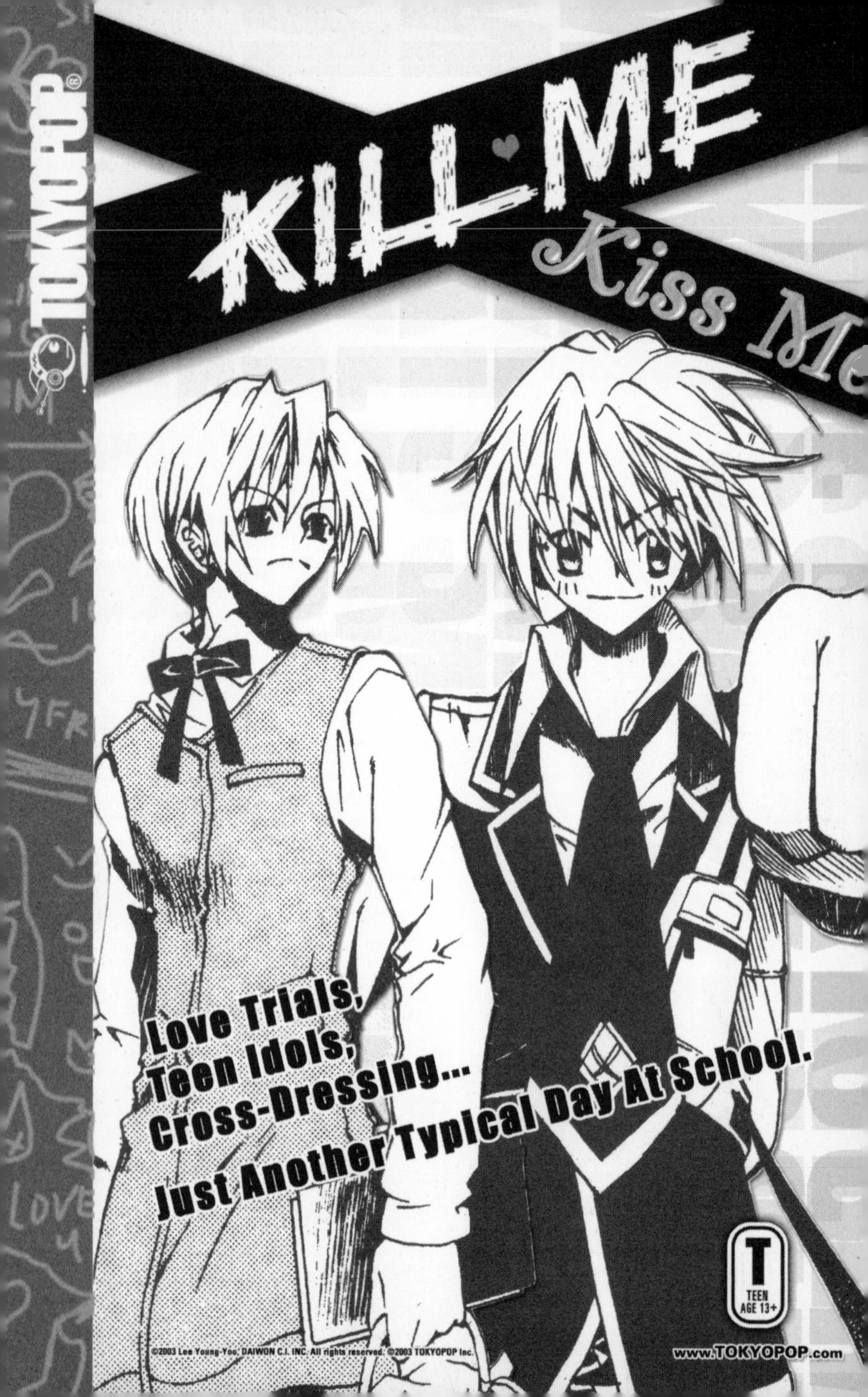

TOKYOPOP
KILL ME
Kiss Me
Love Trials,
Teen Idols,
Cross-Dressing...
Just Another Typical Day At School.
T
TEEN
AGE 13+
©2003 Lee Young-Yoo, DAIWON C.I. INC. All rights reserved. ©2003 TOKYOPOP Inc.
www.TOKYOPOP.com

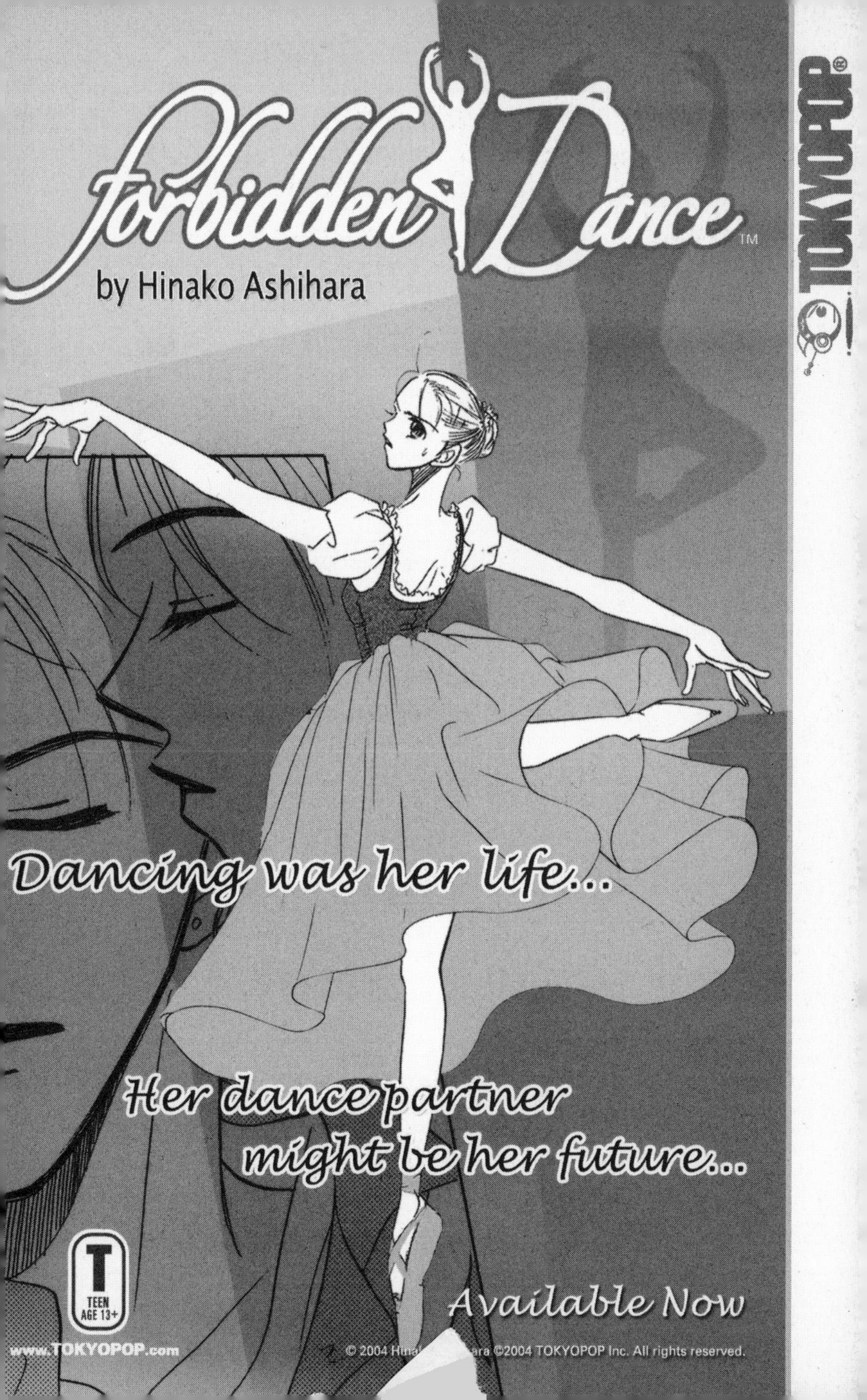
TOKYOPOP
Forbidden Dance™
by Hinako Ashihara
Dancing was her life...
Her dance partner
might be her future...
T
TEEN
AGE 13+
Available Now
www.TOKYOPOP.com
©2004 TOKYOPOP Inc. All rights reserved.

ALSO AVAILABLE FROM TOKYOPOP.

MANGA

.HACK//LEGEND OF THE TWILIGHT
@LARGE
ABENOBASHI: MAGICAL SHOPPING ARCADE
A.I. LOVE YOU
AI YORI AOSHI
ANGELIC LAYER
ARM OF KANNON
BABY BIRTH
BATTLE ROYALE
BATTLE VIXENS
BOYS BE...
BRAIN POWERED
BRIGADOON
B'TX
CANDIDATE FOR GODDESS, THE
CARDCAPTOR SAKURA
CARDCAPTOR SAKURA - MASTER OF THE CLOW
CHOBITS
CHRONICLES OF THE CURSED SWORD
CLAMP SCHOOL DETECTIVES
CLOVER
COMIC PARTY
CONFIDENTIAL CONFESSIONS
CORRECTOR YUI
COWBOY BEBOP
COWBOY BEBOP: SHOOTING STAR
CRAZY LOVE STORY
CRESCENT MOON
CROSS
CULDCEPT
CYBORG 009
D•N•ANGEL
DEMON DIARY
DEMON ORORON, THE
DEUS VITAE
DIABOLO
DIGIMON
DIGIMON TAMERS
DIGIMON ZERO TWO
DOLL
DRAGON HUNTER
DRAGON KNIGHTS
DRAGON VOICE
DREAM SAGA
DUKLYON: CLAMP SCHOOL DEFENDERS
EERIE QUEERIE!
ERICA SAKURAZAWA: COLLECTED WORKS
ET CETERA
ETERNITY
EVIL'S RETURN
FAERIES' LANDING
FAKE
FLCL
FLOWER OF THE DEEP SLEEP, THE
FORBIDDEN DANCE
FRUITS BASKET

G GUNDAM
GATEKEEPERS
GETBACKERS
GIRL GOT GAME
GRAVITATION
GTO
GUNDAM SEED ASTRAY
GUNDAM WING
GUNDAM WING: BATTLEFIELD OF PACIFISTS
GUNDAM WING: ENDLESS WALTZ
GUNDAM WING: THE LAST OUTPOST (G-UNIT)
HANDS OFF!
HAPPY MANIA
HARLEM BEAT
HYPER RUNE
I.N.V.U.
IMMORTAL RAIN
INITIAL D
INSTANT TEEN: JUST ADD NUTS
ISLAND
JING: KING OF BANDITS
JING: KING OF BANDITS - TWILIGHT TALES
JULINE
KARE KANO
KILL ME, KISS ME
KINDAICHI CASE FILES, THE
KING OF HELL
KODOCHA: SANA'S STAGE
LAMENT OF THE LAMB
LEGAL DRUG
LEGEND OF CHUN HYANG, THE
LES BIJOUX
LOVE HINA
LOVE OR MONEY
LUPIN III
LUPIN III: WORLD'S MOST WANTED
MAGIC KNIGHT RAYEARTH I
MAGIC KNIGHT RAYEARTH II
MAHOROMATIC: AUTOMATIC MAIDEN
MAN OF MANY FACES
MARMALADE BOY
MARS
MARS: HORSE WITH NO NAME
MINK
MIRACLE GIRLS
MIYUKI-CHAN IN WONDERLAND
MODEL
MOURYOU KIDEN: LEGEND OF THE NYMPHS
NECK AND NECK
ONE
ONE I LOVE, THE
PARADISE KISS
PARASYTE
PASSION FRUIT
PEACH GIRL
PEACH GIRL: CHANGE OF HEART
PET SHOP OF HORRORS
PITA-TEN

07.15.04T

ALSO AVAILABLE FROM TOKYOPOP

PLANET LADDER
PLANETES
PRESIDENT DAD
PRIEST
PRINCESS AI
PSYCHIC ACADEMY
QUEEN'S KNIGHT, THE
RAGNAROK
RAVE MASTER
REALITY CHECK
REBIRTH
REBOUND
REMOTE
RISING STARS OF MANGA
SABER MARIONETTE J
SAILOR MOON
SAINT TAIL
SAIYUKI
SAMURAI DEEPER KYO
SAMURAI GIRL REAL BOUT HIGH SCHOOL
SCRYED
SEIKAI TRILOGY, THE
SGT. FROG
SHAOLIN SISTERS
SHIRAHIME-SYO: SNOW GODDESS TALES
SHUTTERBOX
SKULL MAN, THE
SNOW DROP
SORCERER HUNTERS
STONE
SUIKODEN III
SUKI
THREADS OF TIME
TOKYO BABYLON
TOKYO MEW MEW
TOKYO TRIBES
TRAMPS LIKE US
UNDER THE GLASS MOON
VAMPIRE GAME
VISION OF ESCAFLOWNE, THE
WARRIORS OF TAO
WILD ACT
WISH
WORLD OF HARTZ
X-DAY
ZODIAC P.I.

NOVELS

CLAMP SCHOOL PARANORMAL INVESTIGATORS
SAILOR MOON
SLAYERS

ART BOOKS

ART OF CARDCAPTOR SAKURA
ART OF MAGIC KNIGHT RAYEARTH, THE
PEACH: MIWA UEDA ILLUSTRATIONS

ANIME GUIDES

COWBOY BEBOP
GUNDAM TECHNICAL MANUALS
SAILOR MOON SCOUT GUIDES

TOKYOPOP KIDS

STRAY SHEEP

CINE-MANGA™

ALADDIN
CARDCAPTORS
DUEL MASTERS
FAIRLY ODDPARENTS, THE
FAMILY GUY
FINDING NEMO
G.I. JOE SPY TROOPS
GREATEST STARS OF THE NBA: SHAQUILLE O'NEAL
GREATEST STARS OF THE NBA: TIM DUNCAN
JACKIE CHAN ADVENTURES
JIMMY NEUTRON: BOY GENIUS, THE ADVENTURES OF
KIM POSSIBLE
LILO & STITCH: THE SERIES
LIZZIE MCGUIRE
LIZZIE MCGUIRE MOVIE, THE
MALCOLM IN THE MIDDLE
POWER RANGERS: DINO THUNDER
POWER RANGERS: NINJA STORM
PRINCESS DIARIES 2
RAVE MASTER
SHREK 2
SIMPLE LIFE, THE
SPONGEBOB SQUAREPANTS
SPY KIDS 2
SPY KIDS 3-D: GAME OVER
TEENAGE MUTANT NINJA TURTLES
THAT'S SO RAVEN
TOTALLY SPIES
TRANSFORMERS: ARMADA
TRANSFORMERS: ENERGON

You want it? We got it!
A full range of TOKYOPOP
products are available now at:
www.TOKYOPOP.com/shop

07.15.04T